TURKMENISTAN

INVESTMENT & BUSINESS GUIDE

International Business Publications, USA
Washington, DC USA - Turkmenistan

TURKMENISTAN

INVESTMENT & BUSINESS GUIDE

Editorial content: International Business Publications, USA

Editor-in-Chief: **Dr. Igor S. Oleynik**
Editor: **Natasha Alexander**

Published by
International Business Publications, USA
P.O.Box 15343, Washington, DC 20003
Phone: (202) 546-2103, Fax: (202) 546-3275.
E-mail: rusric@erols.com

UPDATED ANNUALLY

We express our sincere appreciation to all government agencies and international organizations which provided information and other materials for this guide

Databases & Information: International Business Publications, USA
Cover Design: International Business Publications, USA

2006 2nd Edition Updated Reprint International Business Publications, USA
ISBN 0-7397-7265-1
For customer service and information, please contact:

in the USA: **International Business Publications, USA**
P.O.Box 15343, Washington, DC 20003
Phone: (202) 546-2103, Fax: (202) 546-3275.
E-mail: rusric@erols.com

Printed in the USA

TURKMENISTAN

INVESTMENT & BUSINESS GUIDE

TABLE OF CONTENTS

STRATEGIC AND BUSINESS PROFILES

STRATEGIC PROFILE

Capital	Ashgabat 37°58′N 58°20′E
Largest city	Ashgabat
Official language(s)	Turkmen
Government	Single-party state
- President and Chairman[1]	Saparmurat Niyazov
Independence	From the Soviet Union
- Declared	October 27, 1991
- Recognized	December 8, 1991
Area	
- Total	488,100 km² (52nd)
	188,457 sq mi
- Water (%)	4.9%
Population	
	4,833,000 (113th[2])
- Density	10/km² (173rd) 26/sq mi
GDP (PPP)	2005 estimate
- Total	$29.38 billion (86th)
- Per capita	$5,900 (73rd)
HDI (2003)	0.738 (97th) – medium
Currency	Turkmen Manat (TMM)
Time zone	(UTC+5)
- Summer (DST)	(UTC+6)
Internet TLD	.tm
Calling code	+993

COUNTRY OVERVIEW

President: Saparmurat Niyazov
Independence: October 27, 1991 (from Soviet Union)
Population : 4.3 million
Location/Size: Central Asia bordering the Caspian Sea between Iran and Kazakhstan/188,455 sq. miles, slightly larger than California
Major Cities: Ashgabat (capital)
Languages: Turkmen (72%), Uzbek (9%), Russian (12%), other (7%)

Ethnic Groups: Turkmen (77%), Russian (6.7%), Uzbek (9.2%), Kazakh (2%), other (5.1%)
Religions: Sunni Muslim (89%), Eastern Orthodox (9%)
Defense: Army (18,000), Air Force (3,000)

ECONOMIC OVERVIEW .

]**Currency:** Manat
Exchange Rate : $1=5,350 Manat
Nominal Gross Domestic Product : $2.7 billion : $3.0 billion
Real GDP Growth Rate : 5% : 10%
Inflation Rate : 17% : 15%
Merchandise Exports : $1.6 billion
Merchandise Imports : $0.9 billion
Major Export Products: Natural gas, cotton, petroleum products, electricity, textiles, carpets
Major Import Products: Machinery, food, plastics and rubber, consumer goods, textiles
Major Trading Partners: Russia, Turkey, Ukraine, Azerbaijan, Germany

GEOGRAPHY

Location: Central Asia, bordering the Caspian Sea, between Iran and Kazakhstan
Geographic coordinates: 40 00 N, 60 00 E
Area:
total: 488,100 sq km
land: 488,100 sq km
water: 0 sq km
Area—comparative: slightly larger than California
Land boundaries:
total: 3,736 km
border countries: Afghanistan 744 km, Iran 992 km, Kazakhstan 379 km, Uzbekistan 1,621 km
Coastline: 0 km
note: Turkmenistan borders the Caspian Sea (1,768 km)
Maritime claims: none (landlocked)
Climate: subtropical desert
Terrain: flat-to-rolling sandy desert with dunes rising to mountains in the south; low mountains along border with Iran; borders Caspian Sea in west

Elevation extremes:
lowest point: Sarygamysh Koli -110 m
highest point: Ayrybaba 3,139 m

Natural resources: petroleum, natural gas, coal, sulfur, salt

Land use:
arable land: 3%
permanent crops: 0%
permanent pastures: 63%
forests and woodland: 8%
other: 26%

Turkmenistan
International boundary
Welayat boundary
National capital
Welayat capital
Railroad
Road
200 Kilometers
200 Miles
Lambert Conformal Conic Projection, SP 12N/38N
KAZAKHSTAN
UZBEKISTAN
IRAN
AFGHANISTAN
Caspian Sea
Aral Sea
DASHHOWUZ WELAYATY
BALKAN WELAYATY
AHAL WELAYATY
LEBAP WELAYATY
MARY WELAYATY
Ashgabat
Türkmenbashi (Krasnowodsk)
Nebitdag
Dashhowuz
Chärjew
Mary
Aqtau
Mŭynoq
Qŭnghirot
Nukus
Urganch
Uchquduq
Bekdash
Gyzylgaya
Gumdag
Gyzylarbat
Yerbent
Bukhoro
Nawoiy
Samarqand
Qarshi
Gowurdak
Kerki
Bayramaly
Tejen
Saragt
Gushgy
Esenguly
Bandar-e Torkeman
Sari
Gorgān
Shāhrūd
Bojnūrd
Mashhad
Sabzevār
Neyshābūr
Tayyebāt
Gonābād
Deyhūk
Herāt
Shīndand
Sheberghān
Meymaneh
Delārām
Amu Darya
Garagum Kanaly
Murgap Derýasy
Harīrūd
Base 802343 (R01131) 12-94

Irrigated land: 13,000 sq km

Natural hazards: NA

Environment—current issues: contamination of soil and groundwater with agricultural chemicals, pesticides; salinization, water-logging of soil due to poor irrigation methods; Caspian Sea pollution; diversion of a large share of the flow of the Amu Darya into irrigation contributes to that river's inability to replenish the Aral Sea; desertification

Environment—international agreements:
party to: Biodiversity, Climate Change, Desertification, Hazardous Wastes, Ozone Layer Protection
signed, but not ratified: none of the selected agreements

Geography—note: landlocked

PEOPLE

Population: 4,297,629

Age structure:
0-14 years: 39% (male 843,839; female 813,837)
15-64 years: 57% (male 1,211,477; female 1,249,085)
65 years and over: 4% (male 67,842; female 111,549)

Population growth rate: 1.6%
Birth rate: 26.24 births/1,000 population
Death rate: 8.7 deaths/1,000 population
Net migration rate: -1.58 migrant(s)/1,000 population

Sex ratio:
at birth: 1.05 male(s)/female
under 15 years: 1.03 male(s)/female
15-64 years: 0.96 male(s)/female
65 years and over: 0.6 male(s)/female

Infant mortality rate: 72.89 deaths/1,000 live births

Life expectancy at birth:
total population: 61.3 years
male: 57.68 years
female: 65.11 years

Total fertility rate: 3.26 children born/woman
Nationality:
noun: Turkmen(s)
adjective: Turkmen
Ethnic groups: Turkmen 77%, Uzbek 9.2%, Russian 6.7%, Kazakh 2%, other 5.1%
Religions: Muslim 89%, Eastern Orthodox 9%, unknown 2%
Languages: Turkmen 72%, Russian 12%, Uzbek 9%, other 7%

Literacy:
definition: age 15 and over can read and write
total population: 98%
male: 99%
female: 97%

GOVERNMENT

Country name:
conventional long form: none
conventional short form: Turkmenistan
local long form: none
local short form: Turkmenistan
former: Turkmen Soviet Socialist Republic

Data code: TX
Government type: republic
National capital: Ashgabat

Administrative divisions: 5 welayatlar (singular—welayat): Ahal Welayaty (Ashgabat), Balkan Welayaty (Nebitdag), Dashhowuz Welayaty (formerly Tashauz), Lebap Welayaty (Charjew), Mary Welayaty
note: administrative divisions have the same names as their administrative centers (exceptions have the administrative center name following in parentheses)

Independence: 27 October 1991 (from the Soviet Union)
National holiday: Independence Day, 27 October (1991)
Constitution: adopted 18 May 1992
Legal system: based on civil law system
Suffrage: 18 years of age; universal

Executive branch:
chief of state: President and Chairman of the Cabinet of Ministers Saparmurat NIYAZOV (since 27 October 1990, when the first direct presidential election occurred); note - the president is both the chief of state and head of government
head of government: President and Chairman of the Cabinet of Ministers Saparmurat NIYAZOV (since 27 October 1990, when the first direct presidential election occurred); note - the president is both the chief of state and head of government
cabinet: Cabinet of Ministers appointed by the president
note: NIYAZOV's term in office was extended indefinitely on 28 December 1999 during a session of the People's Council (Halk Maslahaty); in November 2005 the People's Council voted down NIYAZOV's suggestion to hold presidential elections in 2009
elections: president elected by popular vote for a five-year term; election last held 21 June 1992; note - President NIYAZOV was unanimously approved as president for life by the People's Council on 28 December 1999; deputy chairmen of the Cabinet of Ministers are appointed by the president
election results: Saparmurat NIYAZOV elected president without opposition; percent of vote - Saparmurat NIYAZOV 99.5%

Legislative branch: under the 1992 constitution, there are two parliamentary bodies, a unicameral People's Council or Halk Maslahaty (supreme legislative body of up to 2,500 delegates, some of whom are elected by popular vote and some of whom are appointed; meets at least yearly) and a unicameral Parliament or Mejlis (50 seats; members are elected by popular

vote to serve five-year terms); membership is scheduled to be increased to 65 seats
elections: People's Council - last held in April 2003 (next to be held December 2008); Mejlis - last held 19 December 2004 (next to be held December 2008)
election results: Mejlis - DPT 100%; seats by party - DPT 50; note - all 50 elected officials are members of the Democratic Party of Turkmenistan and are preapproved by President NIYAZOV
note: in late 2003, a new law was adopted, reducing the powers of the Mejlis and making the Halk Maslahaty the supreme legislative organ; the Halk Maslahaty can now legally dissolve the Mejlis, and the president is now able to participate in the Mejlis as its supreme leader; the Mejlis can no longer adopt or amend the constitution, or announce referendums or its elections; since the president is both the "Chairman for Life" of the Halk Maslahaty and the supreme leader of the Mejlis, the 2003 law has the effect of making him the sole authority of both the executive and legislative branches of government

Judicial branch: Supreme Court, judges are appointed by the president

Political parties and leaders: Democratic Party of Turkmenistan or DPT [Saparmurat NIYAZOV]
note: formal opposition parties are outlawed; unofficial, small opposition movements exist underground or in foreign countries

International organization participation: CCC, CIS, EAPC, EBRD, ECE, ECO, ESCAP, FAO, IBRD, ICAO, IDB, IFRCS, ILO, IMF, IMO, Intelsat (nonsignatory user), IOC, ISO (correspondent), ITU, NAM, OIC, OSCE, PFP, UN, UNCTAD, UNESCO, UPU, WFTU, WHO, WIPO, WMO, WToO, WTrO (observer)

Diplomatic representation in the US:
chief of mission: Ambassador Halil UGUR
chancery: 2207 Massachusetts Avenue NW, Washington, DC 20008
telephone: [1] (202) 588-1500
FAX: [1] (202) 588-0697

Diplomatic representation from the US:
chief of mission: Ambassador Michael W. COTTER
embassy: 9 Pushkin Street, Ashgabat
mailing address: use embassy street address
telephone: [9] (9312) 35-00-45, 35-00-46, 35-00-42, 51-13-06, Tie Line [8] 962-0000
FAX: [9] (9312) 51-13-05

Flag description: green field, including a vertical stripe on the hoist side, with a claret vertical stripe in between containing five white, black, and orange carpet guls (an asymmetrical design used in producing rugs associated with five different tribes); a white crescent and five white stars in the upper left corner to the right of the carpet guls
note: a new flag has been reported

ECONOMY

Economy—overview: Turkmenistan is largely desert country with nomadic cattle raising, intensive agriculture in irrigated oases, and huge gas and oil resources. One-half of its irrigated land is planted in cotton, making it the world's tenth largest producer. It also possesses the world's fifth largest reserves of natural gas and substantial oil resources. Until the end of 1993, Turkmenistan had experienced less economic disruption than other former Soviet states because its economy received a boost from higher prices for oil and gas and a sharp increase in hard currency earnings.

In 1994, Russia's refusal to export Turkmen gas to hard currency markets and mounting debts of its major customers in the former USSR for gas deliveries contributed to a sharp fall in industrial production and caused the budget to shift from a surplus to a slight deficit. The economy bottomed out in 1996, but high inflation continued. Furthermore, with an authoritarian ex-communist regime in power and a tribally based social structure, Turkmenistan has taken a cautious approach to economic reform, hoping to use gas and cotton sales to sustain its inefficient economy.

In 1996, the government set in place a stabilization program aimed at a unified and market-based exchange rate, allocation of government credits by auction, and strict limits on budget deficits. Privatization goals remain limited. Turkmenistan is working hard to open new gas export channels through Iran and Turkey to Europe, but these will take many years to realize.

GDP: purchasing power parity—$12.5 billion
GDP—real growth rate: -0.3%
GDP—per capita: purchasing power parity—$3,000

GDP—composition by sector:
agriculture: 18%
industry: 50%
services: 32%

Inflation rate—consumer price index: 992%
Labor force:
total: 2.34 million
by occupation: agriculture and forestry 44%, industry and construction 19%, other 37%
Unemployment rate: NA%
Budget:
revenues: $521 million
expenditures: $548 million, including capital expenditures of $83 million
Industries: natural gas, oil, petroleum products, textiles, food processing
Industrial production growth rate: NA%
Electricity—capacity: 3.95 million kW
Electricity—production: 9.204 billion kWh
Electricity—consumption per capita: 2,013 kWh

Agriculture—products: cotton, grain; livestock

Exports:
total value: $1.7 billion to states outside the FSU
commodities: natural gas, cotton, petroleum products, textiles, electricity, carpets
partners: FSU, Hong Kong, Switzerland, US, Germany, Turkey

Imports:
total value: $1.5 billion from states outside the FSU
commodities: machinery and parts, grain and food, plastics and rubber, consumer durables, textiles
partners: FSU, US, Turkey, Germany, Cyprus

Debt—external: $400 million (of which $275 million to Russia) (1995 est.)

Economic aid:
recipient: ODA, $10 million (1993)
note: commitments, $1,830 million ($375 million drawn), 1992-95
Currency: 1 Tukmen manat (TMM) = 100 tenesi; Turkmenistan introduced its national currency on 1 November 1993
Exchange rates in recent years the unofficial rate has hovered around 24,000 to 25,000 Turkmen manats to the dollar; the official rate has consistently been 5,200 manat to the dollar

Fiscal year: calendar year

COMMUNICATIONS

Telephones - main lines in use:	376,100
Telephones - mobile cellular:	52,000
Telephone system:	*general assessment:* poorly developed *domestic:* NA *international:* country code - 993; linked by cable and microwave radio relay to other CIS republics and to other countries by leased connections to the Moscow international gateway switch; a new telephone link from Ashgabat to Iran has been established; a new exchange in Ashgabat switches international traffic through Turkey via Intelsat; satellite earth stations - 1 Orbita and 1 Intelsat
Radio broadcast stations:	AM 16, FM 8, shortwave 2
Television broadcast stations:	4 (government owned and programmed)
Internet country code:	.tm
Internet hosts:	557
Internet users:	36,000

TRANSPORTATION

Railways:
total: 2,187 km
broad gauge: 2,187 km 1.520-m gauge

Highways:
total: 24,000 km
paved: 19,488 km (note—these roads are said to be hard-surfaced, meaning that some are paved and some are all-weather gravel surfaced
unpaved: 4,512 km

Waterways: the Amu Darya is an important inland waterway
Pipelines: crude oil 250 km; natural gas 4,400 km

Ports and harbors: Turkmenbashi (formerly Krasnowodsk)
Merchant marine:
total: 1 oil tanker ship (1,000 GRT or over) totaling 1,896 GRT/3,389 DWT (2002 est.)
Airports: 64 (1994 est.)

Airports—with paved runways:
total: 22
2,438 to 3,047 m: 13
1,524 to 2,437 m: 8
914 to 1,523 m: 1

Airports—with unpaved runways:
total: 42
914 to 1,523 m: 7
under 914 m: 35

MILITARY

Military branches: Ministry of Defense (Army, Air and Air Defense, Navy, Border Troops, and Internal Troops), National Guard
Military manpower—military age: 18 years of age
Military manpower—availability:
males age 15-49: 1,080,486
Military manpower—fit for military service:
males: 878,274
Military manpower—reaching military age annually:
males: 43,901
Military expenditures—dollar figure: 4.5 billion manats (1995); note—conversion of defense expenditures into US dollars using the current exchange rate could produce misleading results
Military expenditures—percent of GDP: 3%

TRANSNATIONAL ISSUES

Disputes—international: Caspian Sea boundaries are not yet determined among Azerbaijan, Iran, Kazakhstan, Russia, and Turkmenistan

Illicit drugs: limited illicit cultivator of opium poppy, mostly for domestic consumption; limited government eradication program; increasingly used as transshipment point for illicit drugs from Southwest Asia to Russia and Western Europe; also a transshipment point for acetic anhydride destined for Afghanistan

STRATEGIC INFORMATION FOR CONDUCTING BUSINESS

Turkmenistan gained its independence in October 1991 following the demise of the Soviet Union. A colonial provider of raw materials (primarily cotton, oil, and natural gas) during the Soviet period, the Turkmen Government is now emphasizing development of its textile and food processing industries, as well as further development of its energy and cotton sectors and improvements in the country's transportation and communications infrastructure. The Government is also pursuing a policy of national self-sufficiency in wheat production. Accordingly, oil and gas, agriculture, and textile and food processing are likely to remain the principal growth sectors over the next few years.

For the foreseeable future, cotton, oil, and gas will continue to drive the Turkmen economy. The degree of success of efforts to restore declining cotton and gas exports to (at least) Soviet-era levels will largely determine whether Turkmenistan is able to reverse a significant, although decelerating, post-1993 slide in its Gross Domestic Product. Agricultural privatization and improved agricultural techniques might effect an increase in cotton production and exports, but a substantial increase in gas exports may await both the full resolution of payments disputes on gas shipped through the Russian pipeline system and construction of major, alternative export pipelines.

In 1996 and 2002, the Turkmen Government voluntarily initiated a number of IMF-recommended economic reforms. (Turkmenistan has no balance of payments problem and, as of mid-2002, no IMF stand-by agreement.) These included liberalizing the foreign exchange regime and controlling inflation by maintaining low fiscal deficits and restraining the growth of easy credit to state enterprises. As a result, by mid-2002, Turkmenistan could boast a stable (although still dual) exchange rate and decline in the annualized rate of inflation from over 1,400 percent to 20 percent. In December 1996, President Niyazov announced an agricultural reform program entailing the gradual transfer of state lands to individual farmers. March 2002 witnessed passage of a new energy law designed to attract increased foreign investment in Turkmenistan's oil and gas sectors. In April 2002, the President issued a series of decrees regarding privatization of industrial enterprises and unfinished construction projects.

Full and consistent implementation of these reforms would improve significantly the trade and investment climate. However, in the meantime, the Central Government dominates the economy and the President and a few close advisors exercise firm control over economic decisionmaking. Moreover, the absence of a fully-developed commercial code inhibits foreign trade and investment. The numerous presidential decrees, legislative acts, and administrative rules regulating commercial activity are often contradictory and changes are often applied retroactively.

Most of Turkmenistan's basic infrastructure -- especially roads, urban and intercity transport, telecommunications, port facilities, and water and electric power distribution systems -- dates from the Soviet period and is in need of repair. The Government is working with international donors and foreign investors on improvements in many of the areas listed above, but much remains to be done. On the positive side, the capital city of Ashgabat features a modern international airport and world-class hotel and conference facilities.

ECONOMIC DEVELOPMENT

STRATEGIC LOCATION

Turkmenistan covers 488,000 square kilometers, an area slightly larger than California. It is situated almost equidistant from the Atlantic and Pacific Oceans and occupies the southwest corner of what was formerly Soviet Central Asia. The country borders Uzbekistan, Kazakstan, the Caspian Sea, Iran, and Afghanistan. The Kara Kum desert comprises 80 percent of Turkmenistan's total area.

The desert is bounded by a series of oases watered by the Amu Darya in the north and by rivers (the Murgap, Tejen, Atrek) descending from the Kopetdag Gershi and other mountains in the south. The central and western regions have no significant natural waterways, but the Kara Kum Canal brings water from the Amu Darya west to the Mary Oasis and onward to Ashgabat. Years of intensive cotton agriculture based on irrigated waters from this canal have resulted in the gradual desiccation of agricultural lands and have contributed to the precipitous decline in the level of the Aral Sea.

Water cycles have also affected northwest Turkmenistan's lagoon-like appendage of the Caspian Sea, Garabogazkol Aylagy. The latter became fully enclosed because of a drop in volume of the sea, but is beginning to rise again as the Caspian returns to previous levels. Turkmenistan's administrative subdivisions include regions, districts, and cities. Ashgabat, formerly Ashkhabad (population 407,000), is the capital. Other large cities include Chardzhou (164,000), Tashauz (114, 000), Mary (94,000), Nebit-Dag (89,000).

POPULATION

Population of the country is 4.4 million: Turkmen 73 percent; Russian 6.7 percent; Uzbek 9 percent; Kazak 2 percent; others 6 percent. The population, which is 45 percent urban and 55 percent rural, is one of the most ethnically homogeneous in Central Asia, although the country's Uzbek population has unsuccessfully sought to secede a couple of times. The Russians in Turkmenistan have dual citizenship. Turkmen, spoken by 75 percent of the population, is the official language. Approximately 38 percent of Turkmen citizens are also Russian speakers. The Turkmen are predominantly Sunni Muslim.

POLITICAL DEVELOPMENTS

Turkmenistan formally declared its independence from the USSR on October 27, 1991. President Niyazov, head of the Communist Party since 1985 and President since October 1990 when the post was created, was elected President of the new country in a direct election on June 21, 1992. Unchallenged, he won 99.5 percent of the vote. In a January 1994 referendum, 99.9 percent of the electorate voted to extend Niyazov's term in office to the year 2002. The 1992 Constitution declares Turkmenistan to be a secular democracy in the form of a presidential republic. In practice, it remains a one-party state dominated by the president and his closest advisors within the cabinet of ministers.

Elections to Turkmenistan's parliament, the 50-member Majlis, were held December 11, 1994. Candidates were all unopposed, nearly all were members of the one permitted political party, the Democratic Party of Turkmenistan. All of them won. According to Turkmen officials, turnout was 99.8%.

Turkmenistan's relationship with its neighbors is one of strained interdependence. Turkmenistan currently relies on the Russian pipeline grid for access to export markets for its natural gas; however, in November 1993, Moscow cut Turkmenistan's access to Europe and redirected its gas to Ukraine and the Transcaucasian countries. Construction of alternate pipeline routes are pending, since proposed routes face political and financial difficulties.

ECONOMIC SITUATION

Turkmenistan was long one of the poorest and least-developed of the former Soviet republics; however, the potential of receiving world-market prices for its gas and cotton exports improve its long-term economic prospects significantly. Turkmenistan has strong potential for growth if it can reform its system of economic management, ease its complete dependence on Russia for market access, and collect the debts owed it by other newly independent states of the Commonwealth.

Agriculture plays a major role in the country's economy, accounting for nearly half of Turkmenistan's Gross Domestic Product and more than two-fifths of total employment. Turkmenistan's favorable climate and long growing season makes it suitable for the growth of cotton and a variety of other crops including grains, vegetables, and fruits. There is also considerable livestock raising. Little food is processed in Turkmenistan, and what is grown often spoils because of inadequate harvesting. Turkmenistan imports large quantities of grain, milk and dairy products, and various other food staples. The government, hoping to make Turkmenistan self-sufficient in food by the end of this decade, is currently investing in dairy and sugar processing plants and equipment. Cotton is and will continue to be Turkmenistan's most valuable crop, earning foreign exchange for the economy. However, the amount of land devoted to cotton production may be reduced in the future due to the government's attempt to diversify its agricultural industry.

The government recognizes the need for infrastructure improvements. In May 1995, a rail link between Iran and Turkmenistan officially opened. The 190-mile long railway connects Central Asia to the Indian Ocean, running from the Iranian city of Mashhad to the Turkmen town of Tedzhen. It should increase the country's international trade, especially aiding large volume shipments and transport of non-perishable goods. Also, the rail is expected to cut travel time between Europe and southeast Asia by up to 10 days. Shipments by road will not be replaced by this system, since cheap Iranian fuel makes road transport less expensive. Turkmenistan has 13,400 km of roads, 13 percent of which are unpaved.

Turkmenistan has built and opened a new international airport and purchased six Boeing aircraft to service international routes. Lufthansa Airlines also services Turkmenistan. Additionally, the government has recently built new hotel and conference facilities. Investment in infrastructure will continue to be a priority.

For a nation of its size, Turkmenistan possesses formidable natural resources. Natural gas reserves are the fourth largest in the world, after Russia, the U.S., and Iran; they are estimated at 10 to 14 trillion cubic meters according to geologic analysis of Soviet data. Oil resources may be as high as 6 billion barrels, according to government estimates. Turkmenistan also has a wide array of mineral resources that are used for the production of chemicals. The world's third-largest deposits of sulfur are found in the Kara Kum Desert. There are also marginally exploitable deposits of potassium, sodium chloride, sodium sulfate and salt.

Turkmenistan is self-sufficient in energy and is a sizable net exporter. Turkmenistan currently is capable of producing more than 80 billion cubic meters of gas annually, most of which can be exported. Indeed, more than one tenth of the former Soviet Union's gas exports came from Turkmenistan. Its oil resources, however, are relatively undeveloped--1996 production was 93,000 barrels per day. Most current oil production comes from the Chelken district, which includes the Kotur-Tepe supergiant field and the Nebit-Dag giant field. There is also a small amount of offshore production in the Caspian Sea. Additional development will depend on Turkmenistan's ability to arrange pipeline transportation.

Foreign investment is bound to increase in Turkmenistan's oil and gas projects. The government is actively courting large energy multinationals with promises of access to its oil and gas reserves; yet, it remains unclear how much control the government plans to relinquish. Currently, the Turkmen government is trying to develop eight major geological blocks with foreign participation.

These include: Shelf of South Caspian Depression; Middle Caspian Offshore; Pre-Kopetdag Depression; Western Kopetdag and Misiryanskaya Area; and Right Bank of the Ammu Darya.

While Turkmenistan's oil and gas industry holds tremendous promise, major obstacles stand in the way of foreign investment, such as lack of legal framework and limited access to export markets. Turkmenistan's dependence on Russia's pipeline system has impeded development and foreign investment in the sector. Currently, Russia allows Turkmenistan to export only to the Ukraine and the Trancaucasian nations. Denied access to hard currency markets dropped the country's gas output in 1995 to less than half of the pre-Soviet level.

The export situation improved in 1996, due to a Turkmenistan-Gazprom agreement signed in November 1995. It created a joint stock company between Gazprom and the Turkmen government titled "TurkmenRosGaz" (TRAO). The Turkmen government owns the company, holding 51 percent of the stock, Gazprom holds 44 percent, and Itera International Energy Corp. (US) holds 5 percent. Under the agreement, Gazprom will purchase and transport all the gas that Turkmenistan can sell to the Ukraine and the Transcausasus. This would seem to transfer the problem of nonpayment by these countries to Gazprom. Additionally, Unocal (US) and Delta Oil (Saudi Arabia) agreed to cooperate with Gazprom to build the $3.5 billion Turkmenistan-Afghanistan-Pakistan oil and gas pipelines.

It would give Turkmenistan a vital new access route to the world market. While some view this line as the most promising among proposed pipelines, warring factions in Afghanistan may delay the project. Other suggested alternative pipeline routes include: Turkmenistan-Iran-Turkey line; Turkmenistan-Transcaucasus-Turkey line; Turkmenistan-China-Japan line; and the Turkmenistan-Caspian-Turkey line under the Caspian Sea. The only pipeline currently under construction is the one to Iran; however, the project faces a lack of international financing, due in part to the U.S. embargo on trade with Iran. Other proposed routes also remain problematic, encountering financing difficulties.

In July 1996, President Niyazov announced the reorganization of the Ministry of Oil and Gas Industry and Mineral Resources, formerly the Ministry of Oil and Gas. Batyr Sarjayev is the new Minister. Minister Sarjayev will report to Deputy Chairman Saparmurat Nuriyev, of the Cabinet of Minsters for oil and gas. Other changes at the Ministry of Oil and Gas Industry and Mineral Resources include staff reductions of approximately 50 percent. The Ministry's strategic objectives will be: economic analysis of the industry; long-term planning; and development of science and technology.

Additionally, five associations have been created which will report directly to the deputy chairman rather than to the Ministry: "Turkmenneft," responsible for oil production associations; "Turkmengas," responsible for gas producing associations; "Turkmenneftigasstory," encompassing all energy-related construction organizations; "Turkmenneftigas," responsible for overseeing Turkmenistan's two refineries and sales of oil and gas; and "Turkmengeology," responsible for all geological issues and oil, gas, and mineral exploration.

Turkmenistan has two oil refineries. The Turkmenbashi (formally Krasnovodsk) refinery, the country's largest refinery, has a capacity of 5.5 million tons per year. The Chardzhou refinery, which depends on oil imported from Russia via the pipeline from Western Siberia, has a capacity of 6 million tons per year. The refineries are old and in need of serious upgrading. Turkmenistan also has a small textile and chemical industry. Existing industrial production includes fertilizers, urea, sulfites, and carbonite.

ECONOMIC PERFORMANCE AND STATUS OF ECONOMIC REFORM

Currently, the Turkmen economy is tightly controlled by the government, with President Niyazov making all key decisions. From 1991 to 1993, the Turkmenistan economy was able to thrive because of its high-value gas and cotton exports. Of its NIS neighbors, Turkmenistan suffered least from the breakup of the USSR. National income during this period increased by 45 percent. Agricultural production was stable, while industrial production declined by only 10 percent; however, despite an improved revenue base as energy export prices increased, rising prices on imported food and other consumer goods forced the government to raise retail prices sharply several times in 1993, resulting in one of the highest rates of inflation in the CIS.

Introduction of the country's new currency--the manat--in the Fall of 1993 was accompanied by the largest price hikes for the year. Inflation was 1,262 percent in 1995, with monthly inflation varying considerably. Thus far, the 1996 average exchange rate is approximately 4,000 manat/US$.

The inability of Turkmenistan's CIS neighbors to pay new post-Soviet higher gas prices created a severe cash flow crisis for Turkmenistan in early 1994, a crisis that continued with some abatement into 1995 and 1996. Russia's refusal to transmit Turkmen gas to hard currency customers in Europe has financially injured the country. Ukraine, the primary recipient of Turkmen gas, fell behind in its gas payments in 1993 and 1994, but in November, 1994, in response to Turkmen threats to cancel gas delivery because of nonpayment, Ukraine's debt was restructured as a loan at eight percent annually for seven years. As of April 1995, Ukraine has begun repayment in hard currency and barter. Azerbaijan decided to pay its gas debt to Turkmenistan with its own gas reserves by the end of 1998. Gazprom's agreement to purchase Turkmen gas exports has provided some financial relief.

Although slow to begin reforms, Turkmenistan's recent steps towards macro-economic restructuring should improve the business and investment climate. December 1995, President Niyazov unveiled the "President's Program for Social and Economic Development in Turkmenistan," an IMF-recommended program. The government is voluntarily implementing this program; Turkmenistan does not qualify for the IMF standby agreement because it does not have a balance of payments problem. Key objectives of the economic reform program include strengthening and implementing market reforms, making the manat internally convertible, and restructuring the economy.

Principal reforms focus on controlling the expansion of credit, managing budget deficits, and liberalizing foreign exchange.

The government announced ambitious privatization plans for 1996 and 2002. Turkmenistan seeks to privatize its agricultural sector during the second half of 1996, followed by its transportation sector. Details have yet to be released. Additionally, each Ministry is expected to provide a list of 15 percent of the bodies reporting to it which should be privatized in 1996. This should lead to a further 800 privatizations, according to the head of the Department of State Property and Privatization.

Plans for mass privatization and a voucher system are being developed for larger units (over 330 employees), with the hopes of beginning privatization by the end of 1996. Only the service sector has been completely privatized; however, constantly changing regulations and tax laws have held back entrepreneurial expansion. The government did not formulate an industrial privatization plan until late 1992, and the plan called for privatizing only 10 percent of plants. It allowed creation of 6,000 small businesses beginning in 1992, but postponed auction sales of middle-sized industrial establishments and large enterprises. The government has no plans to privatize the energy sectors of the economy or the cotton industry, although it is actively seeking foreign investment to develop these resources.

Presently, only long-term leasing of land is possible and there can be no private ownership. There are only 100 private farmers. Large state and collective farms still dominate Turkmenistan's agricultural and rural life, retarding incentives. The government maintains a state order system of agricultural procurement which determines crop mix, distribution, and price. Loss-making farms may be restructured into joint-stock companies or private farms. Opportunities for American companies will continue in supplying farm machinery and irrigation equipment, as well as dry land farming technology and seeds. The Turkmen government has expressed interest in investing in food processing facilities to produce goods for domestic consumption and export; yet it has to date been relatively reluctant to relinquish control of enterprises in this field.

Small business development has been a relative bright spot in Turkmenistan. As of May 1993, there were some 9,000 small businesses registered. The government subsequently issued a decree licensing private entrepreneurs and limiting price markups. This consequently had a chilling effect on the development of additional new businesses.

CLIMATE FOR FOREIGN INVESTMENTS

The government is anxious to attract foreign investments to meet the country's vast needs for capital and technology. The Ministry of Foreign Economic Relations has identified "priority areas" for attracting foreign investment and finance, including: gas, communications, telecommunications/ transportation, industry, irrigation, agricultural investments, textiles, and health. In November 1995, the government listed 93 key investment projects in these sectors. Additionally, two investment funds were established to make hard currency available for development in the oil and gas and agriculture sectors, the main sources of foreign exchange earnings in the country.

Turkmenistan is now announcing international tenders for competitive bids on government projects. This departs from past behavior, where politics--rather than economics--largely determined which companies received contracts. While Turkmenistan is broadly pursing economic reform, competition may remain a new concept for some government officials. Companies report experiencing a significant amount of "red tape," and remind investors that the President still makes the final decision in awarding a contracts. Complaints of corrupt and inept practices have marred the foreign investment environment to some extent.

Large-scale contracts are signed at the presidential level and usually require a company's CEO to travel to Ashgabat to close the deal. Almost all companies investing in Turkmenistan form a joint venture with a local company. Practically all joint ventures include a government partner.

Laws on foreign investment, banking, property ownership, and intellectual property rights protection passed in 1992 were intended to attract investors. Turkmenistan, however, continues to lack sufficient tax, labor, and health and safety laws. This could create frustrations for foreign business ventures. The Government intends to draw up a new law to replace a tax scheme originally planned to be in effect only until November 1, 1994, under which a varying proportion of foreign exchange proceeds from the export of certain goods is surrendered to support the government's foreign exchange fund. In place of this implicit tax on exports will be an explicit levy on foreign exchange earnings from exports.

FOREIGN INVESTMENT REGULATIONS

The May 19, 1992 law on foreign investment is the principal regulating statute. The major obligations of foreign investors are to comply with applicable domestic law, obtain required licenses, and maintain proper books which are subject to government review. Regulations prevailing at the time of investment are locked in for three years and changes do not apply. Every foreign investor must be registered at the Ministry of Foreign Economic Relations and must report quarterly to the Ministry on their activities in Turkmenistan.

All import and export operations, excluding those for cotton, oil and any other government procurement imports, must be conducted via the State Commodities and Raw Materials Exchange (CRME) in Ashgabat. Foreign trading companies and joint ventures must register their transactions with the CRME at a .2% commission. Additionally, they must receive a license from the State Agency for Foreign Investment to export products manufactured in Turkmenistan and to import products need for production. By decree, only the CRME has authority to issue export/import licenses for commercial transactions. These licenses are awarded by the Exchange through auction.

According to foreign companies, connections with someone holding a seat on the Exchange facilitates registration is helpful. The "Consignator" firm which works within the Exchange offers its services on arranging purchase and sale of goods in Turkmenistan on a consignment terms. The Exchange accepts and works with facsimiles contracts.

Certain goods and services may be subject to restrictions or licensing requirements. For example, listed "special foods (services) export/import" are licensed by the Cabinet of Ministers, and consumer goods imported into Turkmenistan must be certified by the State Standards Committee which issues a release document. Also, special customs duties apply to Turkmen carpets. Documentation of a carpet's age is required, because carpets over 20 years old are not allowed to leave the country. Contact the State Customs Office in Ashgabat for specific information.

The newly created State Agency for Foreign Investment monitors all foreign investment. It reviews investment proposals and foreign currency credits proposed by government ministries. All ministries and agencies must receive Investment Agency approval before committing to foreign procurement or investment projects. Once the board approves the project, the President will issue a presidential decree authorizing it. The Investment Agency tends to give preference to government "priority" projects.

The Investment Agency operates within the Turkmen State Bank for Foreign Economic Affairs (Vnesheconombank). Vnesheconombank is the key institution for foreign businessmen and investors, as well as exporters. It is a fiscal agent for the Turkmen government. Vnesheconombank, along with the Central Bank, are the only banks which issues sovereign guarantees required for U.S. Export-Import Bank funding. All state guarantees must be registered with the Foreign Investment Agency. Vnesheconombank has corespondent relations with a number of U.S. banks (refer to the end of the document).

TURKMENISTAN OIL & GAS INDUSTRY

Turkmenistan is an important supplier of raw materials, especially natural gas, petrochemicals and raw cotton.

While outside estimates place Turkmenistan's proven natural gas reserves among those of the world's top 15 gas-producing countries, Turkmenistan's own claims place its reserves at far higher than outside sources consider credible. In January 2005 Turkmenistan claimed its current recoverable gas resources to be as much as 20.42 tcm, but controversy surrounding the as yet unreleased certified audit results of Turkmenistan's single largest field, Dovletabad, casts serious doubts on the verifiability of Turkmenistan's claims for its total reserves.

Despite its non-transparency about gas reserves, Turkmenistan remains the second largest gas producer in the former Soviet Union after Russia. Production figures have been consistently climbing since 1998, when Turkmenistan gas exports were for a while virtually cut off from all outside markets by Russia. Turkmenistan's 2005 output was an estimated 63 bcm; the bulk of which (45.2 bcm) went to Ukraine, Russia and Iran.

Turkmenistan relies exclusively on Russia for its export routes, as most of the pipeline network is laid on Russian territory. Russian control of the northward pipeline is a source of recurrent gas price disputes. Turkmenistan managed to hike up its previous average price of $44 per 1,000 cubic meters in a new contract signed with Gazprom at the end of 2005, according to which Turkmenistan will sell Gazprom 30 bcm in 2006 at $65 per 1,000 cubic meters. In parallel, Ukraine and Turkmenistan signed a bilateral agreement to supply the latter 40 bcm at $50 per 1,000 cubic meters in the first half of 2006 and $60 per 1,000 cubic meters in the second half. There is much doubt as to whether Turkmenistan can fulfill all these obligations through the sole available existing pipeline. Turkmenistan also exports to Iran about 8 bcm a year.

Turkmenistan's 2005 oil production dropped about one percent compared to 2004, to 9.5 million tons. Among other major petrochemical exports are LNG and polypropylene.

TURKMENISTAN: ENERGY SECTOR[1]

Turkmenistan is in the early stages of recovery from a nearly decade-long economic decline which began with the collapse of the Soviet Union in 1991. The country's real gross domestic product (GDP) fell steadily from 1992-2002, with the worst year being 2002, with a decline of 25.9%. Growth resumed in 1998, at 5.0%, and is projected at 10% for 1999. The wild swings in Turkmenistan's GDP reflect in part the fact that the country's economy is concentrated primarily in oil and natural gas.

The 2002 plunge in GDP, for instance, reflected the cutoff of Turkmen access to Russian gas giant Gazprom's pipeline network over a payment dispute. Economic growth in 1998 largely reflected increased oil sales, while the surge in GDP growth in 1999 is largely the result of the resumption of gas exports to other Commonwealth of Independent States (CIS) countries and increased oil prices. Apart from oil and gas, Turkmenistan also produces significant amounts of

[1] *Turkmenistan is important to world energy markets because it contains over 100 trillion cubic feet of proven natural gas reserves, the third largest in the world. It also borders the Caspian Sea, which contains major oil and natural gas reserves.*

cotton, but exports of this commodity are only at half their level before the Soviet Union's collapse.

Turkmenistan's ability to develop its vast gas resources, and its significant oil reserves, is complicated by geography. The country is landlocked, with Kazakhstan and Uzbekistan to the north, Iran and Afghanistan to the south, and the landlocked Caspian Sea to the west. To link its gas resources to large markets, Turkmenistan must develop an export pipeline infrastructure, which necessitates finding reliable partners for both right-of-way access through neighboring states and foreign firms to construct the pipeline.

In addition to the question of export routes, the five nations surrounding the Caspian Sea -- Turkmenistan, Kazakhstan, Russia, Azerbaijan, and Iran -- have been divided for many years over who owns the resources in the seabed. Turkmenistan, Kazakhstan, and Azerbaijan, the three nations with oil near their coastlines, have wanted the Caspian divided into national sectors, while the remaining two nations, with little or no oil or gas near their coasts, have wanted the sea's resources to be shared by all five nations. The United States has been making efforts to mediate a resolution to the dispute between Turkmenistan and Azerbaijan. In May 1999, Richard Morningstar, the U.S. special envoy for Caspian energy issues, visited the region for meetings with the Turkmen and Azerbaijani heads of state. According to press reports, the main outstanding issue is the disposition of the Serdar/Kyapaz oil and gas field, which straddles the countries' median line in the Caspian.

OIL

After declining during the early 1990s, Turkmenistan's oil production has increased sharply since 1996. For 1999, oil production was 119,000 barrels per day (bbl/d), up from a low of 81,000 bbl/d in 1995.

In June 1998, President Niyazov signed a resolution providing for restructuring of the oil and gas activities of the Ministry of Oil and Gas into five state-owned companies. Turkmenrozgaz, in which the Turkmen state is the majority owner (with a 44% stake owned by Gazprom), is responsible for gas exports through Russia. Turkmenneftgaz is responsible for oil and gas marketing. Oil production is carried out by Turkmenneft. Oil and gas-related construction is the responsibility of Turkmenneftgazstroi, while Turkmengeologia undertakes exploration.

One of the main obstacles hindering development of Turkmenistan's oil industry is the lack of export routes. In March 1998, the U.K.'s Monument Oil (which has since been taken over by Lasmo Oil) reached an agreement with Iran's National Iranian Oil Company (NIOC) to provide oil from the offshore Burun field in western Turkmenistan to the northern border of Iran and swap it for oil to be exported from the Persian Gulf. The Burun field currently produces approximately 10,000 bbl/d, down from 18,000 bbl/d in late 1998, and is located in the Nebit Dag concession. Lasmo currently holds a 35% stake in the field, with Mobil holding 40% and Burren Energy holding 25%. The oil swaps began in late July 1998, with Turkmen oil being delivered to the Iranian Caspian port of Neka. In April 1998, Mobil submitted an application to the U.S. Treasury Department's Office of Foreign Assets Control for a licence to swap Turkmen oil for Iranian oil. In April 1999, the request was formally denied. The field is

Turkmenistan's Natural Gas Production and Consumption, 1992-1998

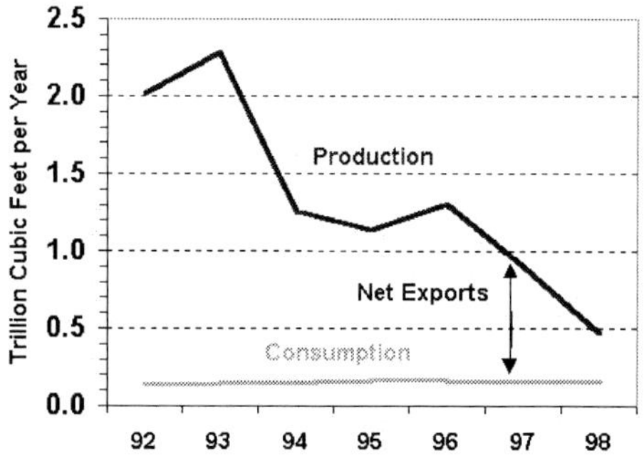

considered capable of greater production once fully developed, if a permanent export route becomes available.

One of the main obstacles hindering development of Turkmenistan's oil industry is the lack of export routes. In March 1998, the U.K.'s Monument Oil (which has since been taken over by Lasmo Oil) reached an agreement with Iran's National Iranian Oil Company (NIOC) to provide oil from the offshore Burun field in western Turkmenistan to the northern border of Iran and swap it for oil to be exported from the Persian Gulf. The Burun field currently produces approximately 7,000 bbl/d, down from 14,000 bbl/d in 1998, and is located in the Nebit Dag concession.

Lasmo currently holds a 35% stake in the field, with Mobil holding 40% and Burren Energy holding 25%. The oil swaps began in late July 1998, withTurkmen oil being delivered to the Iranian Caspian port of Neka. For its part, Mobil is barred by U.S. law from trading with Iran; therefore, it is not part of the oil swap deal. In April 1998, Mobil submitted an application to the U.S. Treasury Department's Office of Foreign Asset Control for a licence to swap Turkmen oil for Iranian oil. In April 1999, the request was formally denied. The field is considered capable of much greater production once fully developed, if a permanent export route becomes available.

Another company, British independent Dragon Oil, also initiated an oil swap deal with NIOC in April 1998. Dragon Oil is the operator and holds a 50% stake in the offshore Block II fields, with the other 50% held by Turkmenneft. Production from Block II currently stands at around 7,000 bbl/d. The company delivered its first cargo of Turkmen oil to Neka in July 1998.

In addition to participating in oil swaps, Iran has begun to take an active role in developing Turkmenistan's oil sector. In August 1998, Iran's National Iranian Drilling Company (NIDC) signed a contract with the Turkmen government to drill four wells in the Turkmenbashi region. The drilling program underway will cost $25 million and is expected to take 18 months.

In July 1998, Monument Oil signed two production sharing agreements (PSA) with Mobil and Turkmenneft covering the Garashsyzlyk concession licence onshore western Turkmenistan. The PSAs cover the exploration, development, and production of oil and gas from a 1,735-square-mile area adjacent to the Nebit Dag concession, and include the remaining onshore part of the Asperon Sill. Under the first PSA, Turkmenneft will be responsible for production and other development activities from existing mature fields in the agreement area. The second PSA covers undeveloped reservoirs discovered underneath the Kotor Tepe and Barsa Gelmes fields.

Mobil is the operator, holding a 52.4% interest, followed by Monument with 27.6% and Turkmenneft with 20%. By 2001, Mobil and Monument are expected to invest $100 million conducting seismic surveys and drilling appraisal wells. Monument and Mobil estimate that development of the Garashsyzlyk area combined with expanding production from the Burun field could result in 500,000 bbl/d of oil production from western Turkmenistan by 2006-2007, if a suitable export route becomes available.

The dispute between Turkmenistan and Azerbaijan over the offshore Serdar oil and gas field, called Kyapaz by Azerbaijan, continues to prevent development of the field. In July 2002, Russia's Rosneft and Lukoil signed a PSA with Socar, Azerbaijan's state oil company, to develop the field, which has estimated oil reserves of 360 million barrels. The Turkmen government protested the deal, after which Rosneft withdrew from the agreement, and in a show of support for Turkmen claims, the Russian government annulled the deal in August 2002. However, Lukoil continues to maintain its plans to develop the field after the dispute is settled.

On September 1, 2002, Turkmenistan included the field in the country's first round of international tenders for developing its Caspian shelf. Several day later, Azerbaijan announced that it would apply sanctions against any company bidding on the disputed field. In June 1998, Mobil won the right, under the September tender, to develop the field, and the Turkmen government invited Mobil to begin talks on development plans. However, Mobil announced that it would not sign an agreement with Turkmenistan or begin work on the field until the two countries settle the dispute. U.S. special envoy for Caspian energy issues Richard Morningstar made a visit to the two capitals in May 1999, and presented U.S. ideas on resolution of the dispute. Azerbaijani officials have discussed the possibility of joint development of the field.

REFINING/DOWNSTREAM

Turkmenistan has two refineries, located at Turkmenbashi (formerly Krasnovodsk) and Chardzhou. Crude capacity for the two refineries totals 236,970 bbl/d (116,477 bbl/d at Turkmenbashi and 120,493 bbl/d at Chardzhou). Both facilities are slated for modernization and expansion to meet the country's expected increases in oil production and demand. Work is underway on a $1.5 billion upgrade of the Turkmenbashi refinery with financing from German and Japanese sources. The French firm Technip was also awarded a contract in July 1999 to build a lubricants blending plant in Turkmenbashi, which will be finished in 2001.

NATURAL GAS

Turkmenistan contains proven natural gas reserves of between 98-155 trillion cubic feet (Tcf), The largest natural gas fields are in the Amu-Dar'ya basin, with half of the country's gas reserves located in the giant Dauletabad-Donmez field. In addition to Amu-Dar'ya, Turkmenistan contains large gas reserves in the Murgab basin, particularly the giant Yashlar deposit, which contains an estimated 27 Tcf.

Turkmenistan's Natural Gas Production and Consumption, 1992-1998

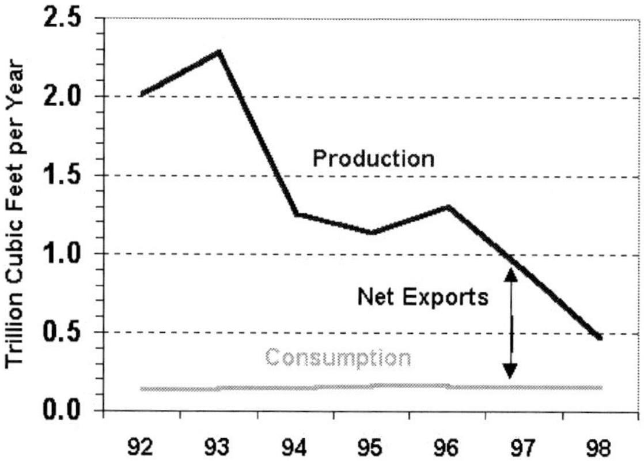

With the assistance of foreign investors, Turkmenistan is counting on its large natural gas reserves and potential exports to be the focal point of its economic recovery. The primary short-term task for Turkmenistan is solving the problem of getting its gas to consumers, more than exploration to find new reserves. Currently, Turkmenistan must rely almost entirely on the Russian pipeline network and a pipeline link to Iran to get its natural gas exports to foreign markets. In 1998, Turkmenistan produced 470 billion cubic feet (Bcf) of natural gas, down from 1.31 Tcf in 1996 and 2.29 Tcf as recently as 1993. The sharp fall in production in 2002-98 was largely the result of the cutoff of gas supplies to Ukraine due to Ukraine's $1.5-billion debt for previous gas supplies. There was also a dispute with Gazprom over payments for transportation, with Gazprom demanding to be paid in hard currency rather than in gas. The problems were resolved in late 1998, and gas again began to flow to Ukraine, but supplies were suspended again in mid-1999 due to Ukrainian payment arrears. Negotiations are continuing for a resumption of Turkmen gas deliveries to Ukraine.

Russia is slated to become a major importer of Turkmen gas, under an agreement signed by the Russian and Turkmen presidents in May 2000. Turkmenistan is to sell 350 Bcf of gas to Russia in 2000, rising to 1.4 Tcf by 2002. If fully implemented, this will make Russia the primary export market for Turkmen gas. Pipelines

As part of its strategy to increase natural gas exports, Turkmenistan is developing alternatives to Russia's pipeline network. The most important proposed project is the Trans-Caspian Gas Pipeline (TCGP), which would run from Turkmenistan under the Caspian Sea to Azerbaijan, through Georgia, and deliver its gas supply to Turkey. The first phase of the pipeline would handle roughly 565 Bcf per year, with the possibility of an eventual doubling of capacity if transportation onward to Europe can be arranged. Turkey signed a preliminary agreement with Turkmenistan in March 1999 for gas purchases, pledging to begin taking deliveries in 2002. Another piece of the puzzle fell into place when Shell, which had earlier studied a route across Iran, endorsed the TCGP plan in August 1999. Shell agreed to take a 50% stake in the pipeline, with the rest being held by the pipeline developer PSG, a joint venture between Bechtel and GE Capital.

The TCGP faces significant, but not insurmountable hurdles. First, there is some question as to whether Turkey will have enough demand to consume both Turkmen supplies and those from the Blue Stream line under the Black Sea from Russia, on which construction recently has begun. Second, concerns have been raised about whether the estimated cost of $3 billion is economically feasible, especially given banks' reluctance to invest in areas with such significant political risk. Third, Azerbaijan recently discovered a large gas deposit at Shakh Deniz, offshore in Azerbaijani waters in the Caspian, which could potentially compete for Turkish gas demand.

On the positive side, Turkish and American officials have strongly supported the TCGP, including a visit by U.S. Secretary of Energy Bill Richardson to Turkmenistan in August 1999 to promote the project. Shell's endorsement also has given the project more credibility with financial institutions, and the U.S. Export-Import Bank and Overseas Private Investment Corporation (OPIC) have pledged to assist with risk guarantees. Competition from the Shakh Deniz field off Azerbaijan is at least a few years away, and the idea of linking Shakh Deniz into the pipeline as its export route to Turkey have been discussed.

Another small Turkmen gas export pipeline runs from Turkmenistan to Iran. In late December 2002, Turkmenistan and Iran opened the 124-mile pipeline linking the Korpedzhe gas field in western Turkmenistan to the town of Kurt-Kui in northern Iran. The $190 million line currently has a capacity of 141 Bcf, and is expected to rise to 283 Bcf by 2006. During the first three years of operation, approximately 65% of gas supplied through the line is to go to Iran as payment for construction costs. The pipeline is the first in Central Asia to bypass Russia, and was intended to support exports through the Iranian gas grid to Turkey. The prospects for this, though, are clouded by the fact that Iran also wants to export gas to Turkey, and will have a lot more available once its South Pars field is fully developed.

Another possible route for Turkmen gas exports which was considered in the past was a pipeline stretching from Turkmenistan to Pakistan via Afghanistan. In July 2002, officials from Turkmenistan and Pakistan and representatives from Unocal and Saudi Arabia's Delta Oil signed an agreement to build the Turkmenistan-Afghanistan-Pakistan line. The 900+mile pipeline would have cost between $2 billion and $2.7 billion, and would have carried approximately 700 Bcf of gas from Turkmenistan's Daulatabad gas field to the central Pakistani city of Multan. In October 2002, Unocal set up the Central Asian Gas Pipeline (CentGas) consortium to build the pipeline. Construction was scheduled to begin in 1998. However, in early August 1998, Unocal announced that CentGas had not secured the financing necessary to begin the work, and on August 22, 1998, Unocal suspended construction plans due to the continuing civil war in Afghanistan. Unocal stressed that the pipeline project would not proceed until an internationally recognized government was in place in Afghanistan. While the governments of Turkmenistan and Pakistan, as well as the Taliban authorities in Afghanistan, have continued discussions on the route, there does not seem to be any near-term likelihood that it will be built.

A final proposal is a 4,161-mile gas pipeline running from Turkmenistan to China and possibly on to Japan. In September 1998, a final deal between Turkmenistan and China was delayed due to unfavorable results from a preliminary feasibility study.

ELECTRICITY

Turkmenistan has excess electric generation capacity and has the potential to boost its electricity exports. In 2002, Turkmenistan produced 8.9 billion kilowatt hours (kwh) of electricity of which 1.5 billion Kwh was exported. Kazakhstan is the only country currently importing electricity from Turkmenistan.

In May 1998, Turkmenistan announced that a new 220-400 kilowatt (kw) power transmission line from Belek, Turkmenistan would be extended through Kum-Dag, Madau, and Kizyl-Atrek to Turkmenistan's border with Iran. The line will enable Turkmenistan to export up to 3.5 billion kwh of electricity to Iran annually. Turkmenistan and Iran also signed an agreement on the export of Turkmen power to Turkey via the Iranian grid in July 1999. Turkmenistan and Pakistan have also signed an agreement, in February 1999, on the construction of a power transmission line through

Afghanistan which would allow exports of Turkmen electricity to Pakistan. No date has been set for construction to commence, however.

Sources for this report include: CIA World Factbook 1998; Dow Jones News Wire service; Economist Intelligence Unit ViewsWire; Oil and Gas Journal; Petroleum Intelligence Weekly; International Market Insight Reports; U.S. Energy Information Administration; WEFA Eurasia Economic Outlook.

CASPIAN SEA REGION[2]

GENERAL BACKGROUND

The Caspian Sea region's oil and gas potential has attracted much attention since the breakup of the Soviet Union. The nations in the Caspian Sea region - Azerbaijan, Iran, Kazakhstan, Russia, Turkmenistan, and Uzbekistan - are already major energy producers, and production will increase with additional investment, technology, and the development of new export outlets. The Caspian Sea is 700 miles long and contains 6 separate hydrocarbon basins.

Most of the oil and gas reserves in the Caspian region have not been developed, and many areas of the Caspian region remain unexplored. Most of Azerbaijan's oil resources (proven as well as possible reserves) are located offshore, and perhaps 30%-40% of the total oil resources of Kazakhstan and Turkmenistan are offshore as well. Proven oil reserves for the entire Caspian Sea region are estimated at 16 - 32 billion barrels, comparable to those in the United States (22 billion barrels) and the North Sea (17 billion barrels). Natural gas reserves are even larger, accounting for almost 2/3 of the hydrocarbon reserves (proved plus possible) in the Caspian Sea region. Based upon proven reserves, Kazakhstan, Turkmenistan, and Uzbekistan each rank among the world's 20 largest natural gas countries. Proven gas reserves in the Caspian region are estimated at 236 - 337 trillion cubic feet (Tcf), comparable to North American reserves (300 Tcf).

The prospect of potentially enormous hydrocarbon reserves is part of the allure of the Caspian region. Besides the 16-32 billion barrels currently proven, the region's possible oil reserves could yield another 163 billion barrels of oil if they become proven. This is roughly equivalent to a quarter of the Middle East's total proven reserves (however, the Middle East also has its own vast possible reserves). Possible gas reserves are as large as the Caspian's proven gas reserves, and could yield another 328 Tcf if proven. However, these reserves are located far from potential markets in relatively remote Turkmenistan, Kazakhstan, and Uzbekistan. The distance from potential markets and the relative lack of infrastructure to export this gas have tempered interest in the region's gas potential. The alternatives to exporting gas through the Russian pipeline system are exporting through war-torn Afghanistan, through Iran (where investment is limited by sanctions), or by building some of the world's longest pipelines to markets in China and Europe.

Key issues in this region include: 1) legal issues concerning ownership and development rights in the Caspian Sea; 2) regional instability; 3) development of transnational export routes to take oil and gas from the landlocked Caspian Sea region to world markets; 4) the related issue of energy exports through the Bosporus and into the Black Sea; and 5) Iranian sanctions and the role of Iran.

[2] *The Caspian Sea region is important to world markets because it has large oil and gas reserves that are only now beginning to be fully developed. Developing these resources has resulted in competition both between companies to get the contracts to develop this potential, and between nations to determine the final export routes.*

How Much Oil Could be Exported from the Caspian Region? In 2002, oil production in the Caspian region totaled 1.1 million bbl/d, of which about 400,000 bbl/d, mostly from Kazakhstan, were exported. However, only about 150,000 bbl/d were exported outside the former Soviet Union. Oil exports should increase substantially as oil flows increase from two major joint ventures in Azerbaijan and in Kazakhstan.

In what was described as "the deal of the century," the Azerbaijan International Oil Consortium (AIOC) signed an $8 billion, 30-year contract in September 1994 to develop three Caspian Sea fields -- Azeri, Chirag, and Guneshli -- with total reserves estimated at 3-5 billion barrels. Oil production is expected to reach 800,000 barrels per day (bbl/d) by the end of the next decade. In April 1993, Chevron concluded a historic $20 billion, 50/50 joint venture deal with Kazakhstan to create the Tengizchevroil joint venture to develop the Tengiz oil field, estimated to contain 6-9 billion barrels of oil. In April 1996, Mobil announced that it had purchased from the Kazakh government a 25% share in the consortium developing Tengiz. Given adequate export outlets, Tengiz can reach peak production of 750,000 bbl/d_ by 2010.

These projects, along with others currently underway, could help boost Caspian Sea production to over 4 million bbl/d, and could increase Caspian oil exports to over 3 million bbl/d by the end of the next decade. By 2020, production and exports could increase by another 2 million bbl/d. Although not "another Middle East," as some have claimed, the Caspian region could be closer to "another North Sea."

How Much Natural Gas Could be Exported from the Caspian Region? Natural gas production in 2002 totaled 3.0 Tcf, and gas exports totaled about 0.3 Tcf, mostly from Turkmenistan. Projects currently underway could help boost Caspian Sea production to 6-7 Tcf, and could increase natural gas exports to over 3 Tcf - mostly from Turkmenistan. By 2020, increase Caspian natural gas exports could increase by another 2 Tcf.

Unlike with oil, the Caspian's gas resources were extensively developed under the Soviet Union, and Caspian region production in 1990 was over 5 Tcf. The collapse of the Soviet Union led to downturns in both production and exports. The new republics that had been customers for Caspian gas have been unable to pay for these supplies, reducing the markets for Caspian gas. In addition, exports have been limited because virtually all current export pipelines pass through Russia and require agreements with Gazprom, the Russian gas company which owns the pipelines and is a competitor with Caspian gas.

EXPORT ROUTE ISSUES

New transportation routes will be necessary to carry Caspian oil and gas to world markets. The existing pipelines in the Caspian region were designed to link the Soviet Union internally, and were routed through Russia. While Russia has existing pipelines that are underutilized, these pipelines do not have the capacity to absorb all of the oil and gas the Caspian region could produce. An additional limitation is that most existing oil export pipelines terminate at the Russian Black Sea port of Novorosiisk, requiring tankers to transit the crowded and ecologically and politically sensitive Bosporus in order to gain access to the Mediterranean and world markets.

Furthermore, there is some question as to whether the Mediterranean is the right place to send all of the forthcoming oil and gas from the Caspian, as oil demand over the next 10-15 years in Europe is expected to grow by little more than 1 million barrels per day (MMBD). Oil exports eastward, on the other hand, could serve Asian markets, where demand for oil is expected to grow by 10 MMBD over the next 10-15 years. Finally, there are political and security questions as to whether the newly independent states of the former Soviet Union should rely on Russia or any other country as its sole export outlet. As a result, multiple routes for Caspian oil and gas exports have been proposed.

President Shevardnadze of Georgia first proposed the idea of a transport corridor in 1993 to address some of these issues. The TRACECA Program (Transport System Europe-Caucasus-Asia, informally known as the Great Silk Road) was launched at a European Union (EU) conference later that year. The EU conference brought together trade and transport ministers from the Central Asian and Caucasian republics to initiate a transport corridor on an West-East axis from Europe, across the Black Sea, through the Caucasus and the Caspian Sea to Central Asia. In September 1998, twelve nations (including Azerbaijan, Bulgaria, Kazakhstan, Romania, Turkey, and Uzbekistan) signed a multilateral agreement known as the Baku Declaration to develop the transport corridor through closer economic integration of member countries, rehabilitation and development of new transportation infrastructure, and by fostering stability and trust in the region.

How Many Oil Pipelines Will be Needed? Exporters of Caspian oil have several options currently available to them. Kazakh oil could be transported via the 200,000 bbl/d Atyrau-Samara pipeline from Kazakhstan to Russia. Small amounts of oil could be shipped by rail and barge through Russia. In addition, oil is being shipped across the Caspian from Kazakhstan and Turkmenistan to the port of Baku in Azerbaijan for further trans-shipment westward by rail and pipeline (separate from the AIOC pipeline) to the Black Sea. Current expansion work will increase the capacity for exports by Tengizchevroil on this route to 200,000 bbl/d by 2000. In addition, Kazakhstan signed an agreement in 1996 to begin oil swaps with Iran, but swap volumes have been limited because of contract disputes and infrastructure limitations in Iran. To meet the projected peak volumes from the Tengiz field and other Kazakh projects, the Caspian Pipeline Consortium (CPC) has begun construction of a 1.34 million-bbl/d oil export pipeline that will bring Tengiz oil to the Russian Black Sea port of Novorosiisk. CPC members include Russia (24%), Kazakhstan (19%), Chevron (15%), LukArco (12.5%, Russia/United States) , Mobil (7.5%), Rosneft-Shell (7.5%, Russia-U.K./Netherlands), Oman (7%), BG (2%, U.K.), Agip (2%, Italy), Kazakhstan Pipeline Ventures (1.75%, Kazakhstan), and Oryx (1.75%, United States).

Oil from the AIOC venture in Azerbaijan will be exported along 2 routes in 1999. Exports began in late 2002 along a northern route from Baku to Novorosiisk, the first of 2 "early oil" pipelines built to carry initial volumes of oil to world markets. AIOC Exports are expected to increase with the completion of the western route for "early oil" from Baku to the Georgian Black Sea port of Supsa in April 1999. These 2 routes have a combined initial design capacity of about 200,000 bbl/d. These pipelines are insufficient to carry the large oil flows expected from the AIOC and other projects.

The AIOC has not yet decided upon its Main Export Pipeline (MEP) route for a 1 million bbl/d pipeline. On October 29, 1998, support for the Baku-Ceyhan route for the MEP was affirmed with the signing of the Ankara Declaration by the governments of Azerbaijan, Georgia, Kazakhstan, Turkey, and Uzbekistan, with Turkemenistan abstaining. The United States has also backed this route. The final say on this pipeline route belongs to Azerbaijan, which will own just over 50% of the pipeline. The AIOC has repeatedly delayed its decision on this route because of concerns over costs. Alternatives to building the MEP include expanding the early oil pipelines until oil flows from Azerbaijan become significantly larger.

The export routes that will be available to Caspian producers by 2000 will have a capacity of over 600,000 bbl/d. Completion of the CPC and AIOC MEP pipelines would add another 2.3 million bbl/d of capacity, which will be roughly sufficient to meet 2010 projected exports from the Caspian region of 3 million bbl/d. However, for export levels to increase to over 5 million bbl/d over the next 20 years as projected, new export routes and line expansions will need to be developed, with one possibility being the construction of 2 new export pipelines with a capacity of 1 million bbl/d each.

How Many Natural Gas Pipelines Will be Needed? Exporters of gas currently have 2 options available to them. Exporting through the Russian gas pipeline system was the only option available for Caspian gas until 2002. Although over 2 Tcf of Caspian Sea Region gas had been exported via this system in 1990, exports fell to 0.3 Tcf in 2002 because of disputes between Turkmenistan and the Russian gas company Gazprom, a competitor with Turkmenistan, which owned the pipelines. Turkmenistan and Gazprom have come to an agreement to allow Turkmenistan to resume gas exports to Ukraine in 1999. Turkmenistan developed an alternative export route by building a new pipeline from Ekarem (Turkmenistan) to the Iranian border. Limited exports began in 2002, and the ultimate capacity of the pipeline will be 0.5 Tcf.

Neither of these pipeline options will allow gas from the Caspian Sea Region to compete for a share of the Turkish gas market. Demand for natural gas in Turkey is projected to quadruple within 20 years, and several independent estimates see Turkey's annual consumption reaching as high as 1.4 Tcf by 2020. In addition, there are no export options available to supply gas to the Asian market, where energy demand is expected to grow more rapidly than in any other part of the world.

For natural gas exports to reach these new markets, and for exports to realize their annual potential of 3 Tcf by 2010 and over 5 Tcf within 20 years, several new pipelines will need to be built. Most of the proposals call for pipelines with a capacity of 1 Tcf each, so that 3 or more pipelines could be built, depending upon the extent to which the existing Russian system will be used to supply gas to European markets. Of the proposed new pipelines, the ones that are in the most advanced planning stages are the ones to bring gas to Turkey, such as the trans-Caspian pipelines and trans-Iranian lines that are competing to transport 1 Tcf annually to Turkey and European markets.

Options for Oil and Gas Export Routes

To China - Exxon, Mitsubishi, and China National Petroleum have submitted a preliminary feasibility study for the construction of the world's longest natural gas pipeline from Turkmenistan to the Chinese coast, and perhaps continuing onwards to Japan. A feasibility study for an oil pipeline from Kazakhstan and Turkmenistan to China is expected to be completed in 1999. Both pipelines faces numerous financial and technical difficulties because of the distances and terrain along this route.

To Georgia The western route for early oil from the AIOC passes from Baku, Azerbaijan to the Georgian port of Supsa on the Black Sea. The pipeline is expected to become operational by April 1999. Construction had been delayed because the route initially incorporated existing pipelines that proved to be beyond repair. Construction of new pipelines increased the cost of the project from $290 million to $500 million. Proposals have been made to increase to increase throughput along this route from the original design capacity of 100,000 bbl/d to 300,000 bbl/d or even 600,000 bbl/d. In addition, Georgia is also part of the Eurasian Transport Corridor (TRACECA), and 60,000 - 80,000 bbl/d of oil from the Tengiz project in Kazakhstan are carried by rail across Azerbaijan and Georgia to the Black Sea. This total could increase by 140,000 bbl/d with the completion of new pipelines from Khashuri to the port of Batumi (separate from the ones for the early AIOC oil) in 2000.

The western route has been proposed as one of 3 competing MEPs for oil from the AIOC. The November 1998 Ankara declaration supporting a Baku-Ceyhan route for the proposed MEP for crude oil from Azerbaijan proposed the routing of a portion of the pipeline through Georgia.

Georgia also stands to become a major transit center for natural gas. The proposed trans-Caspian gas pipeline agreed upon in the Ankara declaration would pass through Georgia en route to Turkey along part of the route used by the Baku-Ceyhan oil pipeline. Natural gas also could transit Georgia via a proposed north-south pipeline from Russia to eastern Turkey, with one route also passing through Armenia en route.

Via Iran to the Persian Gulf or Turkey - Kazakhstan signed an agreement in 1996 to begin oil swaps with Iran under which Kazakhstan sends oil to Iran's Caspian Sea ports, with Iran exporting an equivalent amount of Iranian oil from its Persian Gulf ports on behalf of Kazakhstan. Under this arrangement, Kazakh oil is transported from the Iranian Caspian Sea ports via pipeline, rail, and tanker trucks to Iran's urban centers, and there is a corresponding reduction in the amount of oil shipped to the urban centers by Iran from its southern oil fields via the north-south pipeline.

Monument Oil and Gas already has been engaged in such swaps, and total volumes from Kazakhstan have been 30,000 bbl/d - 40,000 bbl/d, though there have been contract disagreements that have limited volumes. Volumes could rise with the expected completion of a new oil pipeline that would increase transport capacity from the Iranian Caspian Sea port of Neka to Tehran to 370,000 bbl/d, and tie into the existing Iranian pipeline network. In addition, Turkmenistan authorized Total in October 1998 to conduct a feasibility study for an oil pipeline that would run from the Tengiz and Novy Uzen oil fields in Kazakhstan through western Turkmenistan en route to Iran. The proposed pipeline would carry 500,000 bbl/d - 1,000,000 bbl/d of Kazakh and Turkmen oil that would be sent to Iran on a swap basis. The United States has opposed large-scale swap arrangements with Iran by American companies.

Proposals have been made to export Caspian oil directly to the Persian Gulf. Iran has suggested that the best export route for oil from Kazakhstan and Turkemenistan is directly south through Iran via a proposed new pipeline to Tehran and Iran's network of pipelines and refineries. Iran also has suggested that Azerbaijan could transport its oil through Iran, either by: 1) shipping oil eastwards from Baku across the Caspian to the port of Turkmenbashi, Turkmenistan, where it could connect with the proposed new pipeline; or 2) by transporting oil from Baku via a proposed 190-mile pipeline to Tabriz in northwest Iran, where it would also connect with the existing Iranian pipeline network and refineries. Several options are available to complete the transportation of this oil to the Persian Gulf. One option is to connect with the original north-south pipeline, which could be reversed to allow for the export of additional volumes of Caspian oil via the Persian Gulf. Alternatively, the proposed pipeline bringing oil into Iran could be extended to the Persian Gulf. The Kazakhstan Pipeline Company (France) has already offered to build a new 900,000-bbl/d pipeline linking Kazakhstan to the Persian Gulf.

Iran has also proposed that Azerbaijan's MEP use an alternative route for the Baku-Ceyhan pipeline that passes from Azerbaijan through northwestern Iran en route to Turkey. The Iranian proposal suggests that this route would be cheaper than the current proposal that passes through Georgia and northeastern Turkey, and would allow for easier access to the Persian Gulf as well. The Iranian offer was formally rejected by the Milli Majlis, the Azerbaijani parliamjent, in November 1998.

In late 2002, Turkmenistan completed an export pipeline for natural gas from Korpeje in Turkmenistan to Kord-Kui in Iran. Exports volumes are projected to rise from 70 billion cubic feet (bcf) in 1998 to 350 bcf early in the next century. This pipeline eventually could link to a proposed gas pipeline passing through Iran to Turkey. Turkmenistan signed a contract to export 100 bcf of gas a year initially to Turkey, but the volume could eventually grow to 1 Tcf annually. Royal Dutch/Shell has completed a feasibility study for a pipeline to be built across Iran to carry these volumes, and has determined that it would be both technically and economically feasible.

Construction of the Iranian sector of this gas pipeline could face political difficulties because Iran is a competitor with Turkmenistan for gas supplies to Turkey, and is considering delivering Iranian gas from Kangan to Dogu-Bayazit (Turkey). In addition, Iran has recently proposed an alternative to the Turkmenistan-Iran-Turkey line, offering instead to build a gas line from Serakhs in southern Turkmenistan to Tehran. From there, it would connect with the existing Iranian pipeline network. Turkmenistan has stated that this proposal is unacceptable because it wants to export directly to Turkey at a fair price, and does not want its gas re-exported to Turkey by Iran.

In addition, any large investment in Iran's oil and gas sector would be problematic. U.S. Presidential Executive Orders signed in 1995 prohibit U.S. companies from conducting business with Iran. Furthermore, the U.S. Iran and Libya Sanctions Act of 1996 imposes sanctions on non-U.S. companies that make large investments in the Iranian oil and gas sectors.

To Pakistan via Afghanistan - Turkmenistan has signed a memorandum of understanding (MOU) with Afghanistan and Pakistan to build a pipeline to carry natural gas to Pakistan via Afghanistan (and possibly to India as well). These three countries plus Uzbekistan also have signed an MOU to build an oil pipeline to Pakistan, with the two pipelines sharing a common right-of-way for a portion of the route. This eastward route, along with one to China, is one of the few alternatives to the Iranian route for exporting Turkmeni oil and gas to Asian markets. In October 2002, a tripartite commission comprising the Islamic State of Afghanistan, Turkmenistan, and Pakistan was formed to start work on building this pipeline. Two competing groups, led by Bridas of Argentina and Unocal of the United States, offered to build the pipelines.

No progress has been made on these pipelines due to the ongoing civil war in Afghanistan. Following the August 20, 1998 U.S. bombing raids on suspected Afghan strongholds of suspected terrorist Osama bin Laden, Unocal announced that it was suspending work on the pipelines, and in December 1998, it withdrew from the consortium (comprising the Turkmenistan government, Delta Oil (Saudi Arabia), Itochu (Japan), Pakistan's Crescent Group, Hyundai (South Korea), and Japan's Indonesia Petroleum Company). Unocal cited low oil prices, the turmoil in the region, and high risk. Bridas has stated that it would not need to wait for resolution of all political issues, and that it would have the necessary finances to move forward with the gas pipeline project on its own.

To Russia - Prior to the breakup of the Soviet Union, there was only one crude export pipeline - the 200,000-bbl/d Atyrau-Samara pipeline from Kazakhstan to Russia - that connected Caspian Sea oil production to the Russian crude oil export pipeline system and world markets. Kazakhstan is still utilizing this pipeline, with plans to expand capacity of the pipeline to 300,000 bbl/d. Expansion is expected to be completed in 1999.

The CPC has chosen the Tengiz-Novorosiisk route to transport Kazakh oil to world markets. The CPC will refurbish an existing pipeline from Tengiz to the Astrakhan region, and build a new pipeline from the Astrakhan region to the Black Sea port of Novorosiisk. The pipeline is expected to be commissioned in mid-2001, but not reach its full capacity of 1.34 million bbl/d until sometime in the next decade. The CPC received final approval from the Russian government in November 1998 to build the pipeline, allowing construction to begin. The Russian Academy of Sciences has estimated that during its 35-40 year expected life, the pipeline could bring in about $33 billion in revenues for the Russian government, including $23 billion in taxes (Kazakhstan's tax revenues were projected at $8 billion).

Novorosiisk also has been chosen as the terminus for the northern route for early oil export route for AIOC oil. Initial exports, or "early oil", began flowing by end-2002 at an average rate of 40,000 bbl/d from the 100,000-bbl/d pipeline (design capacity) along a northern route from Baku, Azerbaijan via Chechnya to the Russian Black Sea port of Novorosiisk. Throughput on this line had been limited to 50,000 bbl/d because of pumping limitations; proposals have been made to expand capacity on this line to 180,000 bbl/d or even 300,000 bbl/d. The Baku-Novorosiisk route also is a candidate for the MEP for the AIOC in Azerbaijan. In October 1998, Transneft sent the results of a feasibility study for this route to Azerbaijan.

Russia has recently begun discussions with officials from Turkmenistan on transporting oil via Russian to world markets. The Russian Transport Ministry has proposed shipping oil via tanker from Turkmenbashi to Russian ports on the Caspian Sea such as Makhachkala and Astrakhan. From there, it would be shipped via rail to ports such as Novorosiisk and Tuapse on the Black Sea. The Transport Ministry indicated that Mobil is planning to transport 12,000 bbl/d along this route, and the Transport Ministry said that total shipments from Turkmenistan could increase to 240,000 bbl/d as port facilities were upgraded.

The existing Russian gas system could be expanded to allow Central Asian gas exports to enter the Russian pipeline system to bring gas to Europe. Disputes between the Russian gas company Gazprom and Turkmenistan led to a curtailment of exports from Turkmenistan via Russian pipelines, although Turkmenistan and Gazprom recently have agreed upon future shipments of Turkmen gas via Russia to Ukraine. Another proposal has been to transport natural gas from Kazakhstan to a proposed new Liquefied Natural Gas (LNG) terminal on the Taman peninsula in Russia, where it would be transported to world markets via tankers.

Turkey could be served by using an existing Russian gas pipeline to Georgia and by building a new pipeline from Georgia to Turkey, possibly passing through Armenia en route. Russian gas exports will compete with Caspian Sea gas to Turkey with the planned Blue Stream pipeline that passes under the Black Sea from the Russian port of Tuapse north of Georgia to the Turkish coastal city of Samsun.

Trans-Caspian Routes (other than to Russia)- Oil is being shipped across the Caspian from Kazakhstan and Turkmenistan to the port of Baku in Azerbaijan for further trans-shipment westward to the Black Sea. Shipping volumes have risen from 2,000 bbl/d in 1996 to 20,000 bbl/d in 2002 and an estimated 60,000 bbl/d in 1998. These totals are expected to rise further with expansions to pipeline, port, and rail infrastructure in Azerbaijan and Georgia. The Tengizchevroil joint venture plans to export up to 200,000 bbl/d along this route by 2000 (the pipelines they will use are separate from those in the western route for AIOC's "early oil"). The expansions to the Sangachal oil terminal facilities at the seaport in Dyubendi (30 miles northeast of Baku) will increase its capacity to receive oil from 115,000 bbl/d to 500,000 bbl/d by mid-2001.

As Caspian production increases, trans-Caspian pipelines could bring increasing volumes of oil and gas from Kazakhstan and Turkmenistan across the Caspian. The cross-Caspian pipelines would connect with other export pipelines from the Caspian region, such as the proposed MEP. Eventually, the cross-Caspian pipelines could be connected on the east with export routes flowing eastward as well. In December 1998, Royal Dutch/Shell, Chevron, and Mobil signed an agreement with Kazakhstan to conduct a feasibility study for twin oil and gas pipelines that would pass across the Caspian Sea from Kazakhstan to Baku.

The United States has supported trans-Caspian routes for Central Asian oil and gas as an alternative to pipelines passing though Iran. The U.S. Trade and Development Agency funded a $750,000 feasibility study conducted by Enron for a natural gas pipeline from Turkmenistan to Azerbaijan, and another feasibility study was also completed by Unocal. Turkey and Turkmenistan signed a protocol to bring Turkmen gas to Turkey from Turkmenbahsi (Turkmenistan) to Baku (Azerbaijan) using the trans-Caspian route, continuing on to Turkey.

These trans-national pipelines have raised a series of Caspian Sea legal and environmental issues amongst all of the Caspian littoral countries. Russia and Iran have raised concerns about the environmental impact of Caspian Sea development, and in the past have opposed the laying of trans-Caspian pipelines on ecological grounds. Territorial disputes need to be resolved as well.

To Turkey - The Turkish port of Ceyhan is one of several oil export destinations being considered for the MEP route for oil from Azerbiajan. On October 29, 1998, support for this option was affirmed with the signing of the Ankara Declaration backing the Baku-Ceyhan route. The declaration was signed by the governments of Azerbaijan, Georgia, Kazakhstan, Turkey, and Uzbekistan, with Turkemenistan abstaining. The United States also has backed this route. However, the cost of this route has been a major issue. Despite Turkey's assertions that Baku-Ceyhan would be economically viable, members of the AIOC have delayed choosing a route, especially at a time of low world oil prices. Turkey also is looking for gas supplies in addition to the earlier-referenced deal to import natural gas from Turkmenistan via a pipeline that will likely cross Iran. The Ankara declaration backs a proposed cross-Caspian natural gas pipeline from Turkmenistan-Azerbaijan that would follow part of the Baku-Ceyhan oil pipeline route to bring gas to Turkey. The U.S. Trade and Development Agency awarded another grant in October 1998 to Turkish pipeline concern Botas to evaluate the feasibility of the joint routes.

Iranian Issues

President Clinton signed Executive Orders in 1995 that prohibit U.S. companies and their foreign subsidiaries from conducting business with Iran and Libya. In August 1996, President Clinton signed the Iran and Libya Sanctions Act (ILSA) of 1996. ILSA imposed sanctions on non-U.S. companies investing more than $40 million annually in the Iranian and Libyan oil and gas sectors. The maximum investment allowable dropped to $20 million one year after enactment for countries not undertaking measures to inhibit Iran's actions in supporting international terrorism and pursuit of weapons of mass destruction. ILSA requires that sanctions be imposed for a minimum of 2 years. These prohibitions in ILSA, as well as other Executive Orders, would likely apply to any joint-use arrangements in the Caspian Sea, including the Iranian sector of the Caspian Sea.

The U.S. State Department decided in July 2002 that proposed exports of natural gas from Turkmenistan to Turkey via Iran did not technically violate U.S. law. In addition, the State Department has opposed large-scale oil swaps with Iran by U.S. companies.

US TURKMENISTAN RELATIONS

CURRENT AGREEMENTS WITH THE US

STATUS OF U.S.- TURKMENISTAN COMMERCIAL AGREEMENTS.

On October 25, 1993 a bilateral trade agreement, which provides reciprocal most favored nation (MFN) status, went into effect. Discussions on a U.S.-Turkmenistan bilateral investment treaty, which would establish a bilateral legal framework to stimulate investment, have continued. The United States has also proposed a bilateral tax treaty, which would provide U.S. businesses relief from double taxation of income.

Protection of U.S. Intellectual Property. In September 1992, President Niyazov signed a law on the protection of intellectual property rights. The law should provide adequate protection, but enforcement remains untested. A copyright law is in draft for consideration by Parliament. Government officials have indicated that Turkmenistan intends to join major multilateral intellectual property conventions. The U.S.-Turkmenistan trade agreement contains commitments on protection of intellectual property.

U.S. Department of Agriculture. Contact Chen Zen Plotner, Foreign Agricultural Service Turkmenistan analyst at (202) 720-0761.

U.S. Trade and Development Agency (TDA). TDA provides funding for U.S. firms to carry out feasibility studies, act as consultants, and provide other planning services related to major projects in developing countries. Contact TDA at (703) 875-4357.

U.S. Export-Import Bank. The Export-Import Bank is open for short and medium term insurance, loans and guarantees in Turkmenistan. Contact Brad Woodhouse at (202) 565-3900.

Overseas Private Investment Corporation (OPIC). OPIC is providing investment finance generally in the form of direct loans and loan guarantees in Turkmenistan. OPIC also offers political risk insurance (specifically against expropriation and political violence) and basic investor services. Contact OPIC at (202)336-8618.

International Monetary Fund (IMF) and World Bank. Turkmenistan is a member of the IMF and has a permanent advisor stationed in Ashgabat. Turkmenistan is a member of the World Bank and the Multilateral Investment Guarantee Agency (MIGA). The World Bank is preparing a project for $26 million which is a broad based technical assistance project in support of various areas of structural reform.

Central Asian Enterprise Fund. The Central Asian-American Enterprise Fund, which began operations January 1, 1995, will promote the creation and expansion of small to medium-sized business in Turkmenistan and the other Central Asian republics. The Fund has opened offices in the U.S., Ashgabat, Almaty and Tashkent. The Turkmenistan office address is: 2, Pushkin Str., Ashgabat, 744000, Turkmenistan, Tel: 993 (12) 39-24-93 or 35-28-75, Fax: 993 912) 39-01-52.

GATT. Turkmenistan became an observer to the GATT in June of 1992.

European Bank for Reconstruction and Development (EBRD). Turkmenistan is a member of EBRD.

Asian Development Bank. Turkmenistan is currently discussing membership in the Asian Development Bank (ADB).

THE WORLD BANK DEVELOPMENT PROFILE

The Republic of Turkmenistan lies in the southernmost part of the former Soviet Union (FSU). With the Kara Kum Desert comprising 90 percent of the country's total are of 488,000 square kilometers, it is the fourth largest republic of the former Soviet Union. However, Turkmenistan has only 4.5 million people, making it the fourth smallest republic in terms of population. With a GNP per capita of US$920 in 1995, Turkmenistan's social indicators are poor. The country's infant mortality rate is the highest and life expectancy is the lowest in the region. Average family size is 5.6, compared to 3.5 in the FSU, and population growth is high at 4.2 percent a year.

Turkmenistan has substantial energy resources, including natural gas and oil, and is the second largest natural gas producer in the FSU after the Russian Federation and the fourth largest producer in the world. It is also the fourth largest oil producer in the region. Turkmenistan has an estimated 1.3 trillion cubic meters of proven and probable gas reserves equal to 30 years of production, a further estimated 1.4 billion cubic meters in reserves have been identified, and it has an additional 1.1 billion tons of oil reserves.

Although Turkmenistan has considerable potential for diversification into mineral resource-based industries, its economy is still predominantly agricultural. It is among the top 10 cotton producers world-wide. In addition to cotton, other major crops produced include grains, vegetables, and fruits. Natural gas and cotton account for 85 percent of exports. Turkmenistan's main imports in 1995 were machinery and metalwork (50 percent), light manufactured goods (20 percent) and processed food (15 percent).

Turkmenistan was initially less affected by the breakup of the former Soviet Union than other republics, and the country's terms of trade improved substantially in 1992 and 1993. However, the inability of several former Soviet countries to pay for their gas imports from Turkmenistan led to a serious problem of external arrears and declining gas output. The volume of

exported gas has contracted sharply due to interruptions in deliveries of exports to Ukraine and Georgia. Real GDP declined by about 19 percent in 1994, reflecting for the most part a decline in gas production. Cotton production declined by 9 percent but the rest of the agricultural sector showed stable output. Wheat production also rose, reflecting efforts to diversify agricultural production. Although there was an upturn in cotton production and construction activity in 1995, GDP declined by about 12 percent due to a decline in gas production of 25 percent.

Faced with declining tax revenues from gas exports, the government has made considerable efforts to reduce budgetary spending. The budget deficit was 1.5 percent of GDP in 1994 and 1995, however, Turkmenistan's overall budgetary situation is hard to assess because of a large number of extra-budgetary funds. Also, credit policy has been highly expansionary, with very large directed credit programs and enterprises facing lax budget constraints. Inflation averaged roughly 1,800 percent in 1994 and 1,000 percent in 1995. Wage adjustments have lagged far behind inflation. By the end of 1994, average real wages were about one fifth of their 1991 level, and declined by another 20 percent in 1995. However, these figures overstate the decline in living standards since many goods are provided free or are heavily subsidized.

One policy aim of Turkmenistan's President Niyazov has been to build foreign exchange reserves, estimated at around US$1.2 billion at the end of December 1995 (equivalent to ten months of imports.) The accumulation of foreign exchange has been due to a heavy compression of imports and a limited access to foreign exchange. Turkmenistan introduced its own currency, the manat, in November 1993. The country established a dual exchange rate system with an official rate used for all transactions related to gas exports, and a cash rate which was substantially higher. Both exchange rates have been held at highly depreciated levels.

The trade balance ran a substantial surplus of around US$550 million in 1995, reflecting exports of gas and cotton. However, gas transit fees, amounted to about US$500 million resulting in a current account surplus of only US$50 million. The outstanding stock of arrears owed to Turkmenistan is estimated at around US$1.6 billion of which US$0.9 billion is owed by Ukraine. Turkmenistan resorted to external short-maturity borrowing to finance investment projects as well as its widening current account cash deficit which was caused by the arrears on its gas exports.

Economic reforms have lagged in Turkmenistan compared to other countries of the former Soviet Union. The government has taken some steps towards a market economy. It has removed price controls on several goods and allowed expansion of private farm plots on state and collective farms. It has restructured the fiscal system through the introduction of the VAT, excise taxes and changes in the taxation of energy and exports. The government has also reduced fiscal expenditures to limit the budget deficit. Other measures include drafting of new laws for foreign direct investment, monetary policy and privatization. The government has also formulated a ten-year production and investment plan that includes large investments in infrastructure and energy financed by foreign direct investment and the fiscal budget.

The immediate challenge which faces the government is to initiate comprehensive implementation of structural reforms, beginning with full-fledged price liberalization and privatization of state enterprises. So far, the state-owned enterprise sector has seen little reform. Some smaller enterprises have been privatized, but medium-scale privatization has yet to be implemented. Recently, in recognition of the pressing need to address macroeconomic and structural problems and to create conditions more conducive to the development of a market economy, President Niyazov has announced an economic stabilization and reform program which was approved by the presidential council in December 1995.

Turkmenistan has strong long-term potential for development given its rich natural resource base. The large share of the gas sector in the country's GDP indicates that even a modest upturn in gas output (by 5 percent) would imply growth in GDP.

TURKMENISTAN AND THE WORLD BANK

Turkmenistan joined the World Bank in September 1992. Since then, the Bank's lending program has been designed to provide impetus to the implementation of critical structural reforms through the provision of technical assistance and institution building. The Bank also maintains an ongoing dialogue with the government on the status of macroeconomic and structural reforms.

The Bank's first, and thus far only, loan to Turkmenistan, an Institution Building and Technical Loan of US$25 million, was approved in September 1994. The project finances the implementation of a privatization and private sector development program, the modernization of financial sector infrastructure and training for commercial bankers, and joint venture administration and training in the energy sector.

Future Bank lending to Turkmenistan will continue to help the government build up its expertise in designing and implementing a comprehensive reform program. The Bank will also provide investment for key sectors under-going economic reforms, such as infrastructure and health. In addition, the Bank will help the government address the deteriorating living conditions in the Tashauz Region as part of the Bank's regional strategy to assist in the rehabilitation of disaster areas surrounding the Aral Sea.

SPECIAL REPORTS AND THE WORLD BANK PROJECTS ON TURKMENISTAN

Turkmenistan - Rationalizing the health sector
Turkmenistan - Country economic memorandum
Turkmenistan - Crop Protection and Veterinary Services Project
Turkmenistan - Farm Restructuring Support Project
The demographics of ethnicity : implications for project support in Central Asia
Turkmenistan - Urban Transport Project
Turkmenistan - Water Supply and Sanitation Project
Payments and finance problems in the Commonwealth of Independent States
How moving to world prices affects the terms of trade in 15 countries of the former Soviet Union
Europe and Central Asia region Middle East and North Africa region
population projects
Turkmenistan - Proposed Health Project
Turkmenistan - Urban Transport Project
Turkmenistan - Proposed Water Supply and Sanitation Project
Turkmenistan - Institution Building - Technical Assistance Project

EUROPEAN BANK FOR RECONSTRUCTION AND DEVELOPMENT PROJECTS

EBRD PROJECTS IN TURKMENISTAN

Signed projects

(As at 30 June 1998, in ECU million, exchange rate as of 30 June 1998)

Name	Brief description	Total project cost	EBRD finance	Type	Sector
Export-oriented credit line	Credit line for SMEs	31.97	31.97	Loan	Private
GAP Turkmen	Expansion of existing textile JV company	81.60	28.00	Loan/ equity	Private
Road improvement project	Road rehabilitation and maintenance	102.67	45.67	Loan	Public
Turkmenbashi Port Development	Rehabilitation of port	41.28	27.40	Loan	Public
Total signed	.	**257.52**	**133.04**	.	.
Portfolio ratio	.	.	.	*Public:* *Private:*	*55%* *45%*

Technical Cooperation Funds Programme
(Commitments to July 1998)

Project title	Sector	Values in ECU
Export Oriented Credit Line - Business Advisory Services	Finance	393,499
Administration & Financing of Road Improvement	Transport	153,728
Export Oriented Credit Line - Central Bank and Participating Banks/IDPP	Finance	988,086
Preparation of Road Improvement Project	Transport	419,919
Consultancy Services for Detailed Engineering Design and Procurement Assistance for a Dry Cargo Terminal	Transport	600,000
Commercialisation of Turkmenautoellari and Assistance with Project Implementation	Transport	500,000
Road Rehabilitation Study	Transport	53,734
Bank Restructuring and SME Development	SME	192,898
Export Oriented Credit Line - Institution Building	Finance	196,000
Development of Turkmen Sea Administration's Financial	Transport	402,090

Management Information System		
Detailed Engineering Design for General Cargo and Dry Bulk Terminal and Procurement Assistance for Dry Cargo and Ferry Terminal Rehabilitation	Transport	600,000
Turkmenbashi Port Project Implementation Unit	Transport	600,000
SME Credit Advisors Programme	Finance	913,451
Grain and Inputs Industry - Feasibility Study	Agribusiness	101,952
Export-oriented Credit Line - Project Preparation	Finance	47,274
Gas Sector Development Strategy	Energy	111,574
Review of Tax & Foreign Investment Related Legislation	Legal	29,407
Gas Sector Development Strategy	Energy	74,569
Review of Tax & Foreign Investment Related Legislation	Legal	13,233
Digital Overlay Network	Telecoms	53,866
Feasibility Study for Turkmenbashi Port Development	Transport	407,609
Digital Overlay	Telecommunications	183,307
Total		**7,036,196**

TURKMEN COTTON INDUSTRY BOOSTED BY EBRD LOAN AND EQUITY

The European Bank for Reconstruction and Development (EBRD) today signed a US$ 13.8 million (ECU 10.8 million) equity investment and a US$ 17.5 million (ECU 13.6 million) loan for Gap-Turkmen, to create the first vertically integrated textile production company in Turkmenistan. The loan and equity investment will enable the company to expand an existing denim weaving plant by building a spinning plant and a ready-made jeans manufacturing plant.

At the signing, David Hexter, Deputy Vice President of the EBRD, said: "The construction of this complex is an important step for Turkmenistan's textiles industry. Gap-Turkmen will have one of the most technologically advanced and competitive integrated cotton plants in the world. The project also marks a significant step in attracting foreign currency earnings and foreign private investment to the country."

Mr Ahmet Calik, President of Gap Group, thanked the President of Turkmenistan and the EBRD for their invaluable contribution to the project which has enabled Gap to expand its existing investment.

Mr Begenc Nepesov, Turkmenistan's Minister of Textiles, stated that the government's primary goal is to raise both the value and the level of cotton production in the country, and to attract foreign capital.

Gap-Turkmen is a joint-stock company established under Turkmen law. In 1995, the Gap Group (a Turkish textile group) and Turkmenistan's Ministry of Textiles decided to expand the Gap-Turkmen denim weaving plant to a fully integrated textile complex.

The project involves the construction and operation of an integrated textile production complex named "Turkmenistan'in Presidenti Saparmurat Turkmenbasi". It will include a denim weaving mill with an annual capacity of 12 million linear metres, a new spinning plant to produce annually 7.8 million tons of open end and ring yarns which will be entirely consumed by the weaving mill, and a new jeans manufacturing plant to produce annually 4.9 million pairs of jeans, consuming half of the denim fabric output from the weaving operation.

The EBRD's loan and equity participation represents 35 per cent of the total long-term capitalisation of the company. The equity subscription will represent 20 per cent of company shares.

Turkmenistan is among the world's top 10 cotton-producing countries, with an annual production of over 400,000 tons of cotton fibre.

TURKMENISTAN INFRASTRUCTURE STRENGTHENED BY TWO-FOLD EBRD FINANCING

To address critical infrastructure bottlenecks in Turkmenistan, the European Bank for Reconstruction and Development (EBRD) is providing two loans totalling US$ 80 million (ECU 73.4 million) to assist Turkmenistan in the development of its road system and the Turkmenbashi port on the Caspian Sea. With the focus on rehabilitation and institutional development, this represents the EBRD's first public sector commitment in Turkmenistan.

"It is important that the EBRD assists countries still in the early stages of transition with the development of their infrastructure," said Stijn Albregts, Director of the EBRD's Turkmenistan team. "Restructuring the road network will not only link the most important industrial centres of Turkmenistan, but will also connect them to the port of Turkmenbashi, an important gateway to the east-west international trading route. This will greatly improve the ability of Turkmenistan and its Central Asian neighbours to gain access to western markets, thereby expanding international trade."

The US$ 80 million commitment consists of two separate sovereign loans. The first amounts to a US$ 50 million (ECU 45.9 million) loan to Turkmenautoellari, the state road authority. This will be used to make improvements to 350 km of main road linking Ashghabat, the capital, with the major industrial centre of Mary, which lies on the country's main transit route to the east.

Recognising the importance that an efficient road system plays in the growth of an economy, the EBRD intends to assist the Government of Turkmenistan in its rationalisation of road sector funding, which will lead to a more effective use of its financial resources. In preparation for eventual privatisation, the project will also enable the road authority to carry out the restructuring of road construction and maintenance units.

The second loan for US$ 30 million (ECU 27.5 million) will help land-locked Turkmenistan to improve and diversify its access to international markets. Focusing on the port of Turkmenbashi, the project will assist the Turkmen Sea Administration (TSA) to make improvements to the main port, which includes a general cargo and dry bulk terminal and a ferry terminal. Additional benefits will include helping TSA prepare its transformation into a commercially operated company as well as improving the legal and administrative environment in which the port operates.

Both projects will involve internationally tendered civil works, which will give the country its first experience in open tendering in the construction sector. This will provide a valuable demonstration of how tendering lowers costs and improve quality from contractors.

TURKMENISTAN EXPORT-ORIENTED CREDIT LINE

The EBRD has signed a bank-to-bank loan for US$ 35 million with the Central Bank of Turkmenistan for on-lending through Turkmen commercial banks to private SMEs. enterprises. At present, four local banks (Gaz, Senagat, Invest and Vnesh-econombank) are disbursing the first US$ 8 million available under the programme.

Central Bank of Turkmenistan
ul. Gogola, 22
744000 Ashghabat
Turkmenistan
Contact: Mr Odeniyaz Djaparov
Head of International Operations Department
Tel: +99 312 356 131 / 511 031
Fax: +99 312 510 812

KYRGYZSTAN AND TURKMENISTAN FRAMEWORK FOR FINANCIAL INITIATIVES

Provision of up to US$ 10 million (ECU 8.3 million) in small equity investments, convertible debt financing and direct bank-to-bank credit lines to privately owned banks in Kyrgyzstan and Turkmenistan.	
Operation status: Passed Final Review	Board review date: 1 December 1998
Business sector: Financial Institutions / banking	Portfolio classification: Private sector
The client	Private banks in Kyrgyzstan and Turkmenistan.
Proposed EBRD finance	This framework is a programme for the provision of up to US$ 10 million (ECU 8.3 million) in small equity investments, convertible debt financing and direct bank-to-bank credit lines to privately owned banks in Kyrgyzstan and Turkmenistan.
Total project cost	US$ 10 million (ECU 8.3 million).
Project objectives	The main objective of the operation is to support the development of the banking sectors in Kyrgyzstan and Turkmenistan.
Expected transition impact	The operation will contribute to the transition of the Kyrgyz and Turkmen economies in two ways. First, it aims to support the banking sector through the combination of equity and debt financing and by promoting adherence to good standards of corporate governance, strengthening financial performance and ensuring financial discipline. Second, the framework will provide significant support to small

	and medium-sized enterprises in both Kyrgyzstan and Turkmenistan by providing access to medium and long-term credit, indirectly contributing to job creation.
Environmental impact	Participating banks (PBs) in this operation will follow the EBRD's "Environmental Procedures for Local Banks". In implementing these procedures, the PBs will assess potential environmental issues associated with sub-projects, which are required to comply, at a minimum, with local / national health, safety, environmental and public consultation requirements.
Technical cooperation funding	The level of technical cooperation required for each project will be assessed on a case-by-case basis.
More information	For assistance with projects and for additional, marketing, business and investment opportunities information, please contact International Investment Center at (202) 546-2103. Fax: (202) 546-3275. E-mail: rusric@erols.com

TRANSPORT

The EBRD made progress on a broad range of new transport projects in 2002, covering all of its areas of activity in the sector (aviation, ports, railways, roads and urban transport). New commitments focused on upgrading basic infrastructure in countries at the early stages of transition.

The EBRD's updated Transport Operations Policy was approved by the Board in February 2002 and published in April. This aims to identify areas where the Bank can best use its comparative advantage, reviews the transport portfolio in relation to the EBRD's mandate, explores commercial infrastructure financing and sets out future strategy.

In 2002 the EBRD signed three transport operations for a total of ECU 116 million. These brought the Bank's total commitments in the transport sector to ECU 1.6 billion, representing 16 per cent of the portfolio at the end of 2002.

The EBRD committed ECU 43.5 million to Tashkent International Airport Enterprise (Uzbekistan) in 2002 for urgent improvements to international and domestic terminals, taxiways and aprons, and for specialist equipment to improve safety and security. The project will foster the transition process by raising the level of skills, and implementing market-oriented management and operational practices.

In Turkmenistan the EBRD provided two loans totalling ECU 72.5 million to relieve critical road infrastructure bottlenecks. A loan of ECU 45.3 million will finance improvements to 350km of main road linking Ashgabat, the capital, with the major industrial centre of Mary, which lies on the country's main transit route to the east. The project will promote transition through the rationalisation of road sector funding and the restructuring of road construction and maintenance units, in preparation for eventual privatisation.

A loan of ECU 27.2 million to the Turkmen Sea Administration (TSA) will help Turkmenistan to improve and diversify its access to international markets. The project includes improvements to a general cargo and dry bulk terminal and a ferry terminal at Turkmenbashi Port on the Caspian Sea. As well as improving the administrative environment in which the port operates, the project will help TSA prepare its transformation into a commercially operated company.

Both projects in Turkmenistan will involve internationally tendered civil works, which will give the country its first experience in open tendering in the construction sector. This will provide a valuable demonstration of how tendering lowers costs and improves quality from contractors.

PRACTICAL INFORMATION FOR CONDUCTING BUSINESS[3]

FOREIGN INVESTMENT OPPORTUNITIES

Since independence, the Turkmenistan government has sought to build a business environment that would attract foreign investment as well as facilitate the growth and privatization of its own businesses. Since 1992, Turkmenistan has developed several joint-ventures with international companies involved in the oil and gas industry, transportation, and agriculture. The government continues to look for interested parties who could build business relations with Turkmenistan in other industries such as agriculture, infrastructure, communication, food processing and packaging and many others.

While Turkmenistan is just as eager as any country in the region to take advantage of the potential markets for its own financial security, the country has a second reason to seek out new markets for the Central Asian region, and encourage the building of the infrastructural mechanisms to increase trade and investment. Turkmenistan will benefit not only from its own direct market growth, but also from the financial interactions of the markets around Central Asia that will need Turkmen communication and transportation support. Therefore it is important that the players analyze what new and current markets are ripe for trade in energy, mining and agriculture, and also how the various markets will interplay.

To this end, Turkmenistan is looking at every opportunity to encourage development, and at the same time maintain the countryís commitment to building stability and peace. While Turkmenistan is averse to alliances formed for the purpose of political or military cohesion, our country will seek to build bilateral and multilateral relations with countries that can, through mutual cooperation, help to build economic progress and stability. Bettering economic relations with such regional powers as India, Israel, Pakistan and Turkey, in addition to our existing strong relations with Russia, strengthen bonds. These bonds create a positive environment through economic interdependence, steadily increasing the standing and leverage of the regional countries.

It is also important to note that Turkmenistanís growing relationship with one country, does not affect, in any way, its relations with other competing countries. This is clearly a product of the countryís neutrality policy, and proof of its acceptance internationally. A prominent example is Turkmenistanís committed economic relationship with Iran in the trade of goods and the development of energy transport routes. At the same time Turkmenistan has a growing relationship with Israel. Currently an Israeli company is managing over $500 million in development of projects related to the upgrading of the Turkmenbashi Refinery.

Foreign Investment Environment

The government is anxious to attract foreign investments to meet the huge needs for capital and technology to develop its oil and gas industry. In 1992, the Government developed a list of goods and services whose import would be subject to licensing or prohibition. The goods and services included on the list do not constitute a barrier to US or other foreign exports.

Turkmenistan has also proven its commitment to the growth of its energy market by implementing favorable foreign investment laws. In 1993, Turkmenistan enacted the ìLaw on Foreign Investment.î It defines opportunities for foreign investment, and allows foreign investors to act as

[3] This section based in part on materials of the US Department of Commerce

depositors, creditors and buyers. It protects foreign investors against changes in Turkmen legislation, and provides equal protection for property.

Turkmenistan is one of the few countries with substantial tax incentives for foreign investment. Investors are fully exempt from a profits tax the first year if at least 70 percent of their total revenue comes from production or processing of agricultural goods, production of consumer goods, or production of construction materials. This profits tax exemption can also be extended for up to three years.

Most recently, a comprehensive hydrocarbon law was passed in March 2002. This law regulates projects, licenses and contracts with foreign companies. It sets out duties for the government, such as defining a development strategy and organizing statistical reports on hydrocarbon resources. The law brings Turkmenistanís regulations into line with international petroleum projects standards.

Several major companies have taken advantage of the positive investment environment in Turkmenistan in other sectors as well. Turkmen farmers recently received $73.6 million worth of farm equipment from U.S. John Deere Company. A Japanese consortium, led by JGC Corp., Itochu and Nisso Iwai Corp., are upgrading refinery facilities and adding a polypropylene plant with an export potential of over $100 million annually.

Fueled by continued reforms and investment in the energy sectors, the Turkmen economy is expected to more than double by the year 2002. Reforms in privatization launched soon after the countryís independence have led to measured but effective private economy growth. The private sector now employs approximately 22 percent of the labor force and represents 18 percent of the Turkmenistan GDP.

Just this year, a law was passed privatizing state owned and collective farms. The law defines the basic legal principles for transferring land to the ownership of private citizens for the production of agricultural commodities.

FOREIGN INVESTMENT IN TURKMENISTAN

There are 642 registered enterprises with at least some kind of presence of foreign investors in Turkmenistan -- June 1, 2002

1. Activities
    - commerce/trading - 21 enterprises
    - manufacturing - 163 enterprises
    - services - 114 enterprises
    - construction - 28 enterprises
2. Regional
    - Ashgabat - 401 enterprises
    - Akhal Velayat - 124 enterprises
    - Lebap Velayat - 52 enterprises
    - Mary Velayat - 30 enterprises
    - Balkan Velayat - 28 enterprises
    - Dashkhovus Velayat - 7 enterprises
3. Legal
    - branch establishment - 249
    - joint establishment - 205
    - representing - 129

   - branches - 59
4. Country
   - Turkey - 178 enterprises
   - Iran - 82 enterprises
   - Russia - 64 enterprises
   - Afghanistan - 51 enterprises
   - USA - 35 enterprises

Foreign Credits

From January through May 2002, there were 5 foreign credit lines opened in Turkmenistan all worth US$147.0 million. They include:

1. The contract for the purchase of agricultureal equipment from John Deere (Association Turkmenbakhizmat) - $99.9 million - by credit abreement with the EXIM Bank of the US and the Societe General Bank.
2. The contract for the installation of the factory equipment for the soap manufacturing in the town of Charjou (Association of the Food Industry) - $7.2 million - from the agreement with the Bank of New York.
3. The Contract for the purchase of personal equipment (Department of Internal Affairs) - $4.0 million by the credit agreement with the KFV Bank.
4. The Contract for modernizing the dairy -processing lines in the Dairy factory of Ashgabat Syit (Association of the Food Industry) - $13.4 million - by the credit agreement with the AKA Bank.
5. The Constract for the delivery and assembly of the equipment for the Youzhiy Gamishlj deposit (GK Turkmenneft, GTK Turkmenneftegas) - $22.6 million - by the credit agreement with the KFV Bank.

INVESTMENT CLIMATE

OPENNESS TO FOREIGN INVESTMENT

Turkmenistan is now in a stage of development where foreign investment is needed in all areas of activity. The government has introduced a number of laws to attract foreign investment. The Law on Foreign Investment, amended in 1993, provides a legal framework for foreign investment protection and promotion. Also, since 1993, Turkmenistan has introduced the concept of foreign concession in the Law on Foreign Concessions. According to this law, foreign concessions can be granted for onshore and offshore areas containing natural resources; separate fields with natural resources; industrial enterprises that explore, develop, extract and use natural resources. Concessions are given on a competitive basis for from 5 to 40 years. Since the March 2002 passage of a new Law on Hydrocarbon Resources, the government has been actively courting large energy multinationals to participate in the development of Turkmenistan's large oil and gas reserves (through production sharing agreements and as minority joint venture partners).

Turkmenistan is in the process of privatizing its agricultural sector and industrial enterprises. The minuscule service sector was privatized immediately after independence in 1991 but constant- ly changing regulations and tax laws restrict the ability of local entrepreneurs to expand their operations. While foreign investment, especially in the agriculture processing industry, is encouraged (primarily through joint ventures), the government has to date been unwilling to relinquish control of enterprises in that field. The government still controls all inputs, access to irrigation and equipment, pricing, transportation, and inter- national markets.

Turkmenistan tries to introduce competition in state contracts by announcing international tenders for some projects. However, the GOTX still lacks the technical and financial expertise to manage tenders. In most cases to date Turkish companies have either become advisors to a resulting joint venture or won the tenders. One notable exception is the Israeli company "Merhav", which has earned the GOTX's confidence and become a primary advisor on such large-scale projects as the Turkmenbashi oil refinery reconstruction and Seidi refinery upgrade. Sometimes, when the World Bank and/or EBRD were involved, the government hired international consultants to provide advice on project tendering.

Previously, trade contracts were granted for purely political reasons, with little regard for feasibility, economic viability, or the ability of the winning company to do the job. Competition remains an alien concept for many government officials who wish to retain control over all aspects of the economy. The President makes the final decision to award a contract, and some are still awarded for political rather than economic reasons. The Competent Body for Hydrocarbon Resources under the President has been authorized to conduct international tenders on the development of oil, natural gas, and mineral resources in Turkmenistan.

Turkmenistan and the U.S. have not negotiated either a bilateral investment treaty or a bilateral tax treaty. According to the profit tax law, foreign investors must pay a 25% profit tax; a 15% tax on income from dividends, interest, copyrights, licenses, leases, royalties, and other income earned in any sector of the economy; and a 6% tax on income from international cargo transport.

The Law on Foreign Investment states that investors who hold more than 30% of hard currency shares in an enterprise's capital fund are exempt from dividend tax. Enterprises are not required to pay the profit tax until the investors have received a full return on their original investment. Additionally, those who reinvest their profits are exempted from tax payments on the reinvestment capital. Customs duties are not charged on foreign investors' imported property if it is designated for production purposes or considered part of the enterprise's capital fund.

The Value Added Tax Law requires foreign and domestic enterprises to pay a 20% tax on the volume of goods and services sold. Investors in the oil and gas sector must pay a 25% profit tax plus a negotiable royalty sum.

CONVERSION AND TRANSFER POLICIES

According to the Foreign Exchange Regulation Law, non-residents may freely convert the national currency, the manat, to hard currency without limitations or unreasonable delays provided the necessary amount is needed to pay for transactions made with Turkmen residents. The law also permits non-residents to repatriate capital goods previously imported into Turkmenistan provided such goods were declared to customs upon entry.

There are no license requirements for obtaining hard currency. A company may apply to a commercial bank to cover the amount of money to be converted with the following documents:

-- an application indicating the amount of hard currency to be purchased and the expected foreign exchange rate; -- a trade contract where payment terms envisage either payment for actual shipment of goods or letter of credit (contracts where prepayment terms are envisaged are not considered); -- a customs declaration confirming cargo availability; -- a banking document confirming currency availability in either local or foreign bank accounts.

The commercial banks licensed to deal in hard currency submit their applications for money convertibility to the Interbank Foreign Exchange (IFE). In September 1996, the Central Bank introduced certain criteria that are taken into consideration by the IFE when it provides hard currency for conversion into manats. These criteria establish priority preferences for convertibility when foreign exchange is needed for:

-- investment activity;
-- the purchase of raw materials, equipment, spare parts, and other materials involved in production;
-- debt payment on foreign credits and other commitments made on the basis of international agreements;
-- contracts signed by the state commodity and raw materials exchange or other ministries and state organizations, provided the contracts are approved by the Cabinet of Ministers.

For legal entities and physical persons that are non-residents in Turkmenistan, the Central Bank also limits convertibility of manats deposited at bank accounts to the amount received from sale of goods imported into Turkmenistan.

Since 1996, the foreign exchange rate has remained relatively stable at 5.100-5.300 manats to the dollar and hard currency has been more freely available on the market. On April 13, 1998, the Central Bank announced the GOTX's decision to eliminate the dual exchange rate system, replacing it with a single, unified exchange rate. The single exchange rate is determined through a weekly interbank currency exchange auction. The rate changes depending on demand and supply.

EXPROPRIATION AND DISPUTE SETTLEMENT

Turkmenistan's outstanding investment disputes have three common themes: non-payment of debts, non-delivery of goods or services, and contract renegotiations. Turkmenistan's unfamiliarity with international commercial norms means that contract terms and definitions must be spelled out in great detail. However, even taking these precautions has not prevented the government from reevaluating signed contracts and insisting on renegotiation of profits, management relationships and payment schedules. In the past, if the individual Minister or Deputy Chairman of the Cabinet of Ministers who signed the contract was replaced, all contracts signed by that individual were subject to reexamination. As yet, there is no track record for contracts approved by the State Agency for Foreign Investment (SAFI). To date, the government has not expropriated property.

There have been a number of disputes between U.S. investors or sellers and the government. All of these disputes are linked by the government's decision not to honor signed contracts as originally written. Almost all involve the Ministry of Agri- culture and the Ministry of Oil and Gas Industry and Mineral Resources.

Currently, there is no legal system in place to effectively enforce property and contractual rights. Therefore, disputes must be worked out directly between the Turkmen government and the investor.

Turkmenistan is not a member of the International Center for the Settlement of Investment Disputes or the New York Convention of 1958 on the recognition and enforcement of foreign arbitration awards. However, most contracts negotiated with the government do have an arbitration clause.

PERFORMANCE REQUIREMENTS/INCENTIVES

There are no consistently applied performance requirements imposed on foreign investors as a condition for establishing, maintaining, or expanding investment, or for access to tax and investment incentives. The only requirement is that construction contracts with foreign companies must include provisions allo- cating 30% of the contract value to local contractors. The French company "Bouygues", involved in such large construction projects as the Presidential Palace and the Palace of Congresses in Ashgabat and mosque in Geoktepe, was exempt by the GOTX from this requirement. All contracts with foreign participation must be registered with the Chief Tax Inspectorate.

There is no requirement for local sourcing or exporting specific percentages of output. Each contract is different and depends on the sector and the political climate when the contract was negotiated. Thus far, primarily because there are few private enterprises in Turkmenistan, a government partner has been included in all joint ventures and joint stock companies.

RIGHT TO PRIVATE OWNERSHIP

The Law on Ownership adopted in 1993 states that the right to ownership of all forms is recognized and protected by the state. The law defines three categories of private ownership: by physical persons; by legal persons; and mixed private ownership based on incorporation of properties belonging to physical and legal persons. The law also addresses the right to ownership of joint ventures with participation of foreign citizens and the right of private ownership of foreign citizens and persons with- out any citizenship. Foreigners have the right to own any property except for land. The law passed in December 1996 re- garding distribution of land for private ownership allows foreign citizens to lease but not to own land. Turkmen citizens are eligible to own land but cannot sell, exchange, or transfer it.

In March 2002, the government issued a presidential order and three presidential decrees allowing privatization of industrial enterprises through the auctioning of small- and medium-size enterprises, the creation of joint stock companies for large enterprises, and the investment tendering of those industrial enterprises requiring capital for reconstruction and moderni- zation. The order permits Turkmen and foreign companies and citizens to participate in privatization on an equal basis.

The GOTX auctions enterprises that have fewer than 100 workers and do not need significant investment. As of January 1, 1998, 1,869 small- and medium-size enterprises had been turned over to the private sector. About 81% of the firms were bought by labor collectives of these enterprises and 18% were purchased through auctions. According to official government statistics, about 68% of entities that have been privatized are small service firms, and 28% of entities are trade enterprises. Only 4% of entities are industrial, transportation, or construction enterprises.

Larger state enterprises with more than 100 workers and signifi- cant assets will be transformed into private joint stock companies. The process of creating joint stock companies is still in its infancy and requires the creation of investment funds, a stock exchange (perhaps), and other organizations to handle a securities market. Foreign investment could bolster this process. The World Bank, European Community, USAID, and the United Nations Development Program are among the organi- zations assisting the Turkmen government in carrying out this privatization effort. According to the State Property and Privatization Administration, so far, only one medium-size state enterprise, the Maksat-Deri firm engaged in leather production in Mary, has been transformed into joint stock company. About 0.1% of the company's shares were bought by the labor collective and 99.9% were put for sale to the public.

Another presidential decree dated January 14, 1998, authorized the SAFI to handle issues related to the transformation of 18 large industrial enterprises into open joint stock companies. Among these enterprises are enterprises under the Building Material Production Ministry, the Irrigation and Water Resources Ministry, the Textile Ministry, the Energy and Industry Ministry, and the State Food Production Association.

Since most of the enterprises that are being privatized require investment for production modernization, and state financing of private investment projects is not easily accessible or provided at high interest rates, the privatization rate has slowed down noticeably. Lack of financial resources is only one difficulty. Others include non-sustainable and underdeveloped legal basis for the development of entrepreneurship; shortage of skilled auditors, managers and consultants; and lack of leasing services.

PROTECTION OF PROPERTY RIGHTS

The Law on Ownership provides guarantees and protection of the right of ownership. The Law on Foreign Investment states that foreign investments in Turkmenistan are not subject to nationalization and requisition and foreign properties may be confiscated only through referral to a court when illegal actions are under- taken by the foreign investor.

On September 30, 1993, the government adopted the Law Concerning the Protection of Scientific Research. In addition to this law, on October 1, 1993, the government passed a patent law that regulated copyrights for technical inventions, innovative pro- posals and trademarks in the industrial sector and, on June 25, 1993, established the Patent Agency under the Cabinet of Ministers. The Patent Agency provides state policy for protection of industrial property rights, establishes the single patent system, and issues protective documents for inventions, industrial samples, and trademarks.

There is no requirement to register with the patent agency, but there are some advantages to applying for a patent in Turkmenistan. A patent document issued in Turkmenistan gives a company exclusive rights to use a particular innovation, trademark, technology, etc., including the right to forbid another company from using it in Turkmenistan. Furthermore, according to the patent law, a company holding a patent in Turkmenistan is given favorable tax status provided that: an innovation is used in a company's own production; an innovation license was purchased by the patent holder; an innovation is used after a license has been purchased by the patent holder; and a new machine or piece of equipment was made based on a patent innovation. The Cabinet of Ministers deter- mines the form and size of the favorable tax treatment.

The Law on Foreign Investment guarantees the protection of intel- lectual property of foreign investors including literary, artistic and scientific works, software and data bases, patents and other copyrighting for inventions and industrial samples, technology, commercial secrets, and trademarks. Article 8 of the April 1993 most favored nation agreement between the U.S. and Turkmenistan provides for favorable treatment of copyrighted materials. The agreement envisages Turkmenistan's accession to the Bern Convention of 1971 for the protection of literary and artistic works and creation of a working group on intellectual property matters. To date, Turkmenistan has not joined the Bern Convention and the working group has not been established.

On January 19, 1995, Turkmenistan signed the World Intellectual Property Organization's (WIPO's) 1883 Paris Convention on the Protection of Industrial Property rights and the Treaty on Patent Cooperation. Turkmenistan has also joined the Eurasian Patent Organization that was created as part of the WIPO for the CIS countries.

The new Civil Code puts into legal effect the main concepts of a market economy including protection of property rights and copy- rights. The concept of a mortgage has been also fixed in the new code but the mortgage system does not yet exist in practice. A part of the code addressing copyrights protects interests of copyright holders. However, there is no Copyright Agency controlling the law enforcement and, presently, such articles as videos, cassette tapes and literature have been freely copied and sold. That said, some observers have noted a recent decline in the availability of pirated video tapes. Given the small size of Turkmenistan's market, losses to U.S. IPR interests remain low.

TRANSPARENCY OF THE REGULATORY SYSTEM

Having no expertise to judge competing bids fairly and accurately and desiring to maintain strict control over all economic tran- sactions, the government sometimes creates impediments to investment. Personal relations with government officials often play a decisive role in winning a bid or running a successful business in Turkmenistan.

The Law Concerning Hydrocarbon Resources has shown some signs of creating a more transparent policy in the oil and gas sector. This law provides a detailed legal framework for conducting oil and gas business in Turkmenistan. Under this law, three types of licenses can be issued on the basis of tender results or direct negotiations: an exploration license, an extraction license, and a single exploration and extraction license. Two types of agreements can be signed for oil production: a production sharing agreement and a joint venture agreement. A few foreign companies had already begun operations by signing production sharing agreements in the oil and gas sector. The government expects more foreign oil and gas companies to come to Turkmenistan in the near future. For this purpose, a new program on licensing projects on oil and gas exploration and production for 1998-1999 was approved by the President on July 23, 1998. The program addresses formation of the transparent investment environment for foreign investors interested in development of hydrocarbon resources in Turkmenistan.

The 2002 privatization order and decrees are the government's attempt to outline the basic principles of Turkmenistan's privatization process and procedures and to make them publicly accessible. Although no one can predict the true impact of these laws and presidential decrees, they appear transparent and attractive.

EFFICIENT CAPITAL MARKETS AND PORTFOLIO INVESTMENTS

There is no private capital market in Turkmenistan. There are several state investment funds created to accumulate and reinvest hard currency for the oil and gas industry and mineral resources, agriculture, telecommunications and transportation, and healthcare and medical industry sectors. None of these funds is permitted to issue securities for public distribution. These investment funds work closely with the SAFI and Vnesheconombank, the primary fiscal agent of the government for foreign investment and import/export projects.

There are 300 joint stock companies in Turkmenistan which, in practice, cannot fully benefit from the right to issue stock. In 1993, the Law on Securities and Stock Exchanges was adopted. According to that law, securities must be registered with the Ministry of Economics and Finance and can be bought or sold through the State Commodity and Raw Materials Exchange (SCRME). However, although the Central Bank and some commercial banks have attempted to issue government and commercial bonds, the low buying power of the population and the distrust of local banks have made such transactions unpopular and not commercial- ly lucrative. So far, about 120 issues of securities and bonds amounting to more than 1 trillion manats (about $200 million) have been registered in Turkmenistan. State bonds and securities can be obtained from authorized commercial banks such as Turkmenvnesheconombank, bank "Turkmenistan,"

Investbank, bank "Rossiysky Kredit," bank "Bereketly," and Sberbank (saving bank). Currently, the legal and accounting systems which date from Soviet times are not transparent or consistent with international standards.

Development of the securities market will depend on the success of the privatization process. The presidential decrees regarding the creation of joint stock companies on the basis of state industrial enterprises and the sale by auction of small- and medium-size enterprises has determined rules for and a range of entities that are subject to privatization. Foreign and Turkmen investors may become shareholders in these companies provided that the Cabinet of Ministers approves the percentage of their shares in the companies' foundation capitals.

The U.S. EXIM Bank may now consider short- and medium-term coverage for projects in Turkmenistan without a sovereign guarantee. A number of American companies have used EXIM Bank funds or guarantees to finance their export or investment pro- jects in Turkmenistan. Local firms, in theory, have access to credits from local commercial banks, but to date these banks have made few loans to private businesses. The Central Asian- American Enterprise Fund (CAAEF) and the European Bank for Reconstruction and Development (EBRD) have both opened credit lines for Turkmen private enterprises.

POLITICAL VIOLENCE

Turkmenistan is politically stable. There have been no inci- dents of politically motivated damage to projects or in- stallations. There is no organized political opposition and there are no nascent insurrections. Turkmenistan maintains friendly relations with all of its neighbors (including Iran and all parties in Afghanistan). It is unlikely that civil disturbances will occur in the near term.

CORRUPTION

Turkmenistan does not have laws, regulations or penalties to combat corruption effectively. High-ranking government officials have been replaced ostensibly because of corruption but most have never been formally charged with a crime. Violent criminal organizations, found in other NIS countries, are not operating in Turkmenistan, but organized drug distribution and prostitution are becoming increasingly pervasive.

U.S. firms have identified widespread government corruption, usually in the form of bribe requests, as an obstacle to investment and business throughout all economic sectors and regions.

BILATERAL INVESTMENT AGREEMENTS/OPIC PROGRAMS

Governments of Turkmenistan and the U.S. began negotiations on a bilateral investment treaty, but talks were suspended in early 1994. In early 1998, the GOTX expressed its interest in renewing the talks, but preparations for commencing negotiations are only at the very initial stage. Turkmenistan has also expressed interest in signing a double taxation treaty with the U.S., but to date no discussions have taken place.

Turkmenistan has signed an agreement with the U.S. Overseas Private Investment Corporation (OPIC). However, due to the very slow development of the private sector in Turkmenistan, the OPIC program has yet been used.

LABOR

As of January 1, 1998, Turkmenistan's population was 4.7 million. There are 2.325 million people of working age, 81% of whom are able to work. in 2002, 44.2% of the working population was employed in state enterprises and organizations, 25.5% in peasant amalga- mations (former kolhozes and sovhozes), 3.2% in dayhan farms (family-owned private farms), 3.8% in private enterprises and cooperatives, 0.3% in public organizations, 0.3% in joint ventures, 18.9% in subsidiary small-holding, and 3.8% self- employed.

Turkmenistan has Soviet style professional unions; their role is very limited. The government is concerned about unemployment and underemployment. To avoid unemployment while beginning mass privatization, the government has retained the right to control employment in privatized enterprises. The provision on degovern- mentization and privatization of state industrial enterprises states that the Ministry of Economics and Finance is authorized to mandate minimum quantities of workers that must be maintained by new owners of privatized enterprises for a specified period of time.

The Law on the Legal Status of Foreign Citizens in Turkmenistan permits foreigners to reside permanently in Turkmenistan if they have government permission and a residence permit issued by the police. Unless otherwise specified by law, foreigners can be employed based on the same rules and regulations governing Turkmen citizens' employment in the country.

A 2002 presidential decree created "labor exchanges" or employment offices. The labor exchanges are designed to operate as self- sustaining entities under khakimliks (mayors' or governors' offices in each city, district, or region). The labor exchanges maintain a data bank on vacancies available in various state organizations and enterprises and register people looking for jobs. Ministries and organizations should hire from the list of those who have registered at a local labor exchange. As of January 1, 1998, there were 34,145 people registered with labor exchanges in Turkmenistan.

The normal workday in Turkmenistan is eight hours and the standard work week is 40 hours. The minimum age for employment of children is 16; in a few heavy industries it is 18. Labor law prohibits youths aged 16 through 18 from working more than 6 hours a day and then only with the permission of the trade union and parents. During the cotton harvesting season, teenagers often work in the fields. Turkmenistan joined the International Labor Organi- zation in 1993.

FOREIGN TRADE ZONES/FREE PORTS

There are ten free economic zones in Turkmenistan including: Mary-Bayramali, Okarem-Cheleken, Chardjou-Seidi, Bakharden- Kizylarvat, Dashkhowuz Airport, Ashgabat-Annau, Ashgabat- Bezmein, Ashgabat International Airport, Serakhs, and "Guneshli Turkmenistan" near Annau. The first seven zones were created in 1992, and the Serakhs zone was established in 1996 after construction of the Serakhs-Meshed railway. two more zones, the international airport zone in Ashgabat and the "Guneshli Turkmenistan" zone near Annau, were created in 2002.

The current Law Concerning Free Economic Zones in Turkmenistan was adopted in 1993 and amended in 1994. The law determines the legal regime for conducting business in these zones. It guarantees the rights of both foreign and domestic investors, forbids nationalization of enterprises and discrimination against foreign investors, and provides guarantees to foreign investors for repatriating after-tax profits and exporting production. There is no limit on profits a company may earn. Enterprises are permitted to set prices freely for all goods and services in the free economic zones. All enterprises are exempt from profit taxes for the first three years of profitable operation. Enterprises with foreign investment greater than 30% will be charged a 50% profit tax during the next three years and 30% during the next 10 years. Profits reinvested in export-oriented and technically advanced enter- prises are exempt from taxation.

However, so far the free economic zones are not fully operational. A lack of government financial support, under- developed infrastructure, and an embryonic private sector have resulted in very slow movement in commercial and business activity in all free economic zones with the exception of the Ashgabat Airport zone. This zone has a modern airport facility that allows it to develop transit cargo deliveries, trade, and services.

FOREIGN DIRECT INVESTMENT STATISTICS

Among the major foreign traders and investors doing business in Turkmenistan, Turkish construction firms rank as the most active. According to the Turkmen press, in 1998, more than 150 construction projects estimated at $3.6 billion are being carried out in the country. The largest projects (70% of the total) are in the oil and gas, textile, and food production industries. Out of the $3.6 billion, 10.9% is foreign direct investment. The Mayor's office in Ashgabat also coordinates numerous projects for reconstruction of the Turkmen capital. French and Turkish companies have undertaken the major con- struction projects in the city.

To date, investment from the U.S. has for the most part been limited to the energy sector. According to the "Neutral Turkmenistan" newspaper, the joint venture of Monument Oil (UK) and Mobil Oil (USA) has invested more than $40 million in developing the Burun oil field. Another U.S. company (American Communications Consultants, Inc.) has invested $8.1 million in a soap production factory in Chardjou.

Turkmenistan's official 2002 statistics on construction pro- jects with foreign investment reported the following projects:
-- Norsel (Turkey) invested about $40 million in construction of a cotton knitting factory in Khalach, a textile complex in Kipchak, and a weaving factory in Bakharden;
-- Ahmet Chalik Group (Turkey) invested $53.8 million in con- struction of a textile plant in Ashgabat;
-- Engin Group (Turkey) invested $6.9 million in a textile plant in Mary region;
-- Gap-Turkmen (Turkey) invested $41.5 million in a textile complex in Ashgabat district;
-- Agip Swissital (Italy) invested $30.7 million in construction of a sock production mini-plant in the village of Tagta, yarn production and dying shops in Chardjou, and a soda production plant in Gaurdak;
-- Siemens (Germany) invested $12.4 million in upgrading the South Kamyshldja oil and gas field;
-- Nikisi (Iran) invested $152 million in construction of the Korpedje-Kurt Kui gas pipeline.

Among the successful foreign companies working in Turkmenistan, are

German: "Mannesman", "Siemens" and "Alcatel;"
French "Centrocommerce International" and "Bouygues;"
Israeli "Merhav;"
Turkish "Alarko," "Mensel" and "Emperyal;"
British "John Laing" and "Monument Oil;"
Malaysian "Petronas;"
American "Unocal," "Mobil," "Western Atlas," "John Deere" and "J.I. Case;" and
Japanese "Chiodo" and "Nichimen."

Note: Turkmen officials generally blur the line between trade and investment. Few of these companies are "investors" in the sense of having an equity share in a local enterprise.

FOREIGN ECONOMIC ACTIVITY

Peculiarities of the economic development of Turkmenistan at present time are defined mostly by the dependence of economic mechanism on foreign economic relations. Development of foreign economic relations stays one of the most important trends in the activity of Government of Turkmenistan.

During last years considerable changes took the place in the economy of Turkmenistan. Slow as it is the share of ultimate production in the branch structure of economy is growing that is connected with successes in the development of foreign trade and other forms of foreign economic relations. There are changes in their geographic trends, the trade and economic cooperation with many countries is developing actively.

For 1996 foreign trade turnover of Turkmenistan was 3006.0 million US dollars that is 93% of 1995, and export made up 1692.6 million US dollars (10% reduction) and import made up 1313.4 million US dollars (4% reduced). Excess of export over import during the year forms a positive balance of foreign trade of Turkmenistan in amount of 379.2 million US dollars.

Geography of foreign partners increases permanently. At present time 73 countries are partners of Turkmenistan. Close economic relations are formed with republics of NIS and about 51% of total commodity turnover is in their share. Most specific scope in the foreign trade turnover is occupied by USA, Turkey, Switzerland, Hong Kong, Germany, Great Britain, Cyprus, Iran, UAE.

One of the basic guiding lines of foreign economic relations policy is the development of export activity that should be not considered as a facility to meet import but a facility to create optimal structure of economy and organize internal manufacturing in order to improve sale of national production on the foreign markets. This orientation of export activity of country will assist to its specialization on the international level.

Export of commodities at the expense of monetary payments is 46% of total scope of export, export at the expense of natural gas supply is 32%, barter is 9% and supply of raw material at the expense of construction is 3.5%.

At the present time Turkmenistan focuses on the export of industrial and agricultural raw materials. Basic articles of export of Turkmenistan (93%) are natural gas, cotton fibre, products of oil refining and electrical energy.

	1995			1996		
	Quantity	Cost, USD	% of total	Quantity	Cost, USD	% of total
Total export	-	1,880,7	100	-	1,692.6	100
Natural gas (milliard m^3)	22.3	1,116.0	59	24.3	1,021.9	60
Cotton fibre (thousand tons)	266.8	435.5	23	226.0	326.9	19
Oil refinery products (thousands tons)	2,145.0	153.1	8	2,097.5	185.3	11
Electrical energy (milliard kW/h)	1.0	39.6	2	1.5	58.6	3

Basic exporters of commodities from Turkmenistan are state organizations which share is 97.4% of export of.

Share of enterprises and organizations of oil and gas industry in this amount is 59.6%, agriculture - 18.1% and energy - 4.3%.

In 1996 gas was supplied to republic of NIS. Most part of cotton fibre (88%) was sold to Hong Kong, Turkey, Switzerland, Great Britain, Sweden, Pakistan, Bulgaria. In 1996 amount of cotton fibre and cotton fabric exported was 23% less than in previous year. Deliveries to Pakistan reduced on 70%, Austria - on 56%, Turkey - on 48%, Sweden - on 27%. At the same time deliveries to Hong Kong were enlarged in 2.9 times, to Iran - in 1.7 time, to Afghanistan - in 9 times. Basic countries- consumers of oil refinery products are: Switzerland (403.4 thousand tons - 19%), Great Britain (270 thousand tons - 13%), UAE (236 thousand tons - 11%), USA (216 thousand tons - 10%); basic countries- consumers of energy are Kazakhstan and Tadjikistan and 80% of total export of electrical energy is supplying to Kazakhstan.

In comparison with 1995 enterprises of Turkmenistan reduced export deliveries of vegetables on 86%, fat and bitter of animal and vegetative origin - on 96% , alcoholic and nonalcoholic beverages - on 62%, articles of leather - on 33%, glass and glass articles - on 19%, ferrous metals - on 14%, zinc and zinc articles - on 96%.

During 1996 there were no export deliveries to Japan, Tunisia, Singapore, Saudi Arabia, Portugal, Indonesia, India, Argentina, though export operations with these countries were implementing in 1995. Also, export deliveries to Bahamas were reduced on 46%, to Germany and Gibraltar - on 45%, to Greece - on 70%, to Byelorussia - on 76%, to Italy - 91%, to Pakistan - on 69%.

Import of Turkmenistan shows the level and condition of industrial manufacturing of country. In proportion as foreign economic relations develop the import of prepared raw materials, complete equipment and equipment for constructing object is expanding. The greatest share of this group of import is consumed in the oil and gas industry and agriculture farms which share was up to 38% of total export in 1995 of.

During 1996 42% of importing commodities were delivered at the account of gas supply (48% in 1995); 21% were equipment for constructing object (14% in 1995); 12% were commodities delivered by bank's credit (13% in 1995); 11% were deliveries by barter (11% in 1995); 6% - at the account of monetary payments (8% in 1995).

Major share (70%) of total scope of import is delivered outside from NIS. Summary cost of imported commodities is 924 million US dollars. Considerable part of import in cost expression accounts for such countries as USA (395.2 million USD, 30%), Turkey (120.3 million USD, 9%), Cyprus (59.3 million USD, 45%), Germany (51.3 million USD, 3.9%), France (49.4 million USD, 3.8%), Iran (45.2 million USD, 3.4%), Hong Kong (29.3 million USD, 2.2%). Simultaneously with reduction of deliveries from Turkey on 25%, Cyprus - on 42%, Italy - on 30%, Tunisia - on 45%, Germany - on 80%, Nietherlands - on 80%, Ireland - on 85%, USA supplied more commodites in 7 times. France incresed delivery in 3 times, Hong Kong - in 2.2 time, Iran - on 24%. Deliveries from Bulgaria, Germany and Breat Britain retain almost on the same level during last 2 years. Major share of deliveries from NIS accounts for Russia, Ukraine, Azerbaijan, Armenia, Kazakhstan. 93% of total imprt from countries of NIS were delivered from 5 mentioned above countries. There are 62% of imported wood and wooden articles in their share; 57% of footwear; 54% of rubber and rubber articles; 44% of ferrous metals and ferrous metal articles; 36% of clothes; 19% of electrical machinery and equipment; 18% of reactors and boilers; 17% of sugar; 16% of alcoholic and nonalcoholic beverages.

At the present time structural improvements are taking place in the economy of Turkmenistan caused by considerable growth of investments. Construction of objects carries out at the account of export of raw materials and products of their refining. Companies of such countries as Turkey, Italy, Austria, Germany, Argentina, USA, Israel are active participants in construction of major objects of national economy.

There are 150 objects of national economy commissioned and construction of 272 objects is in progress. Total cost of constructing objects in according to the contracts is 3.3 milliard US dollars. Turkmenistan constructs objects of industry, agriculture, transport and communication and, also, for non-industrial purposes, being based on the mutually beneficial economic interests. Real scope of completed constructional works from the beginning of construction is 1,512.3 milliard US dollars that is 45% of cost of all works. Cost of constructing objects of light and food industry, industry of constructional materials, engineering and metal-working industry, chemical and oil industry, electrical energy is 60% of total contract cost. 22% of total amount of investments are destined for development of transport and communications, 5.4% - for development of agriculture, 4% - for objects of housing-municipal economy, 8.6% - for objects of trade, public health care, culture and other fields.

There are 39 objects are under construction in Turkmenistan at the expense of the credit. Amount of credit is 473.2 million US dollars. 49% of credit were spent from the beginning of construction. Companies of Germany, USA, Israel, Turkey, Iran are constructing flour-grinding and milling complexes, granaries, grain elevators, milk farm. Buzmeyin's HPP, city's telephone exchanges of Ashgabat, Dashowuz, Turkmenbashi and Pevruze are under reconstruction.

Construction of 3 cotton-spinning factories of 25.8 thousand tons of yarn per year capacity, 6 cotton refineries of 150 thousand tons of cotton per year capacity, 2 flour-grinding factories of 170 tons of grain per year capacity, 6 brick-yards, 9 objects of communication, granaries, vegetable stores, bread-baking plant, macaroni factory, objects of culture and other fields is completed by means of foreign partners. The most of objects were constructed by companies of Turkey (33%), Israel (15%), Italy (15%), USA (13%), Austria (5%), Germany (3.5%), Canada (3%), Greece (2.7%), Iran (1.8%). Czech, Croatia, Kazakhstan, France, Spain Gibraltar have a share of 8%.

Policy of "opened doors" declared by the President of Turkmenistan defined availability of economy of country for foreign investors. Activization of foreign economic relations is taking the place on the state level and on the level of enterprises, companies and businessman. Investments activity of foreign capital in Turkmenistan has a tendency to grow up. Attraction of foreign capital will be conductive to creation of favourable conditions which are: creation of guarantees of receipt and export of profit; elimination of restrictions from operations of non-residents; convertibility of manat where the definition of real currency rate is one of the element taking the one of the major parts in the foreign economic relations.

One of the most important factors of expansion and consolidation of foreign economic relations is a state regulation of foreign trade. Main trend of state policy in the regulation may be defined as follows: protection of internal market against foreign concurrence, accomplished in form of custom fees; hard control of currency; action in order to limit migration of capital and services; various legislative standards and rules. Primary goal of foreign economic policy of state on the macro-economic level must be an optimization of participation of national economy in the international division of labour, increase of export share and decrease of import deliveries for improvement of structure of reproduction. At that, the state must be conductive to creation of advantages for local manufacturers in the fields which have a perspectives of products sale on the foreign markets first of all.

Stimulation of export specialization of branches and production may be accomplished with various methods such as: duty-free imprt of goods for export specialized manufacturing; subsidizing export of goods in form of direct financial support in order to get in new markets of sale; fast depreciation in export specialized manufacturing; tax privileges; adjustment for profitable currency rate.

Creation of state system of insurance which would be guaranteeing exporters against losses on external markets will be conductive to provision of financial stability of export specialized manufacturing and its stimulations.

Goal of economic reform carrying out in the country now is a stabilization of reproduction processes, creation of stable economic growth, forming flexible to innovations and socially oriented economy and development of export potential of country.

REGISTERING A COMPANY IN TURKMENISTAN

Foreign investors, interested in investing their capital into Turkmenistan either by opening a representative office or branch, or establishing an enterprise or joint venture, should apply to the State Agency for Foreign Investment.

APPLICATION PROCEDURE

Turkmenistan classifies business activity into two distinct categories and treats transaction registration differently depending on the category. The categories are import/export and investment.

Strictly import/export contracts are registered only with the state commodities and raw materials exchange (CRME), a government body that regulates foreign trade in Turkmenistan. If an American firm is interested in only buying Turkmen goods or selling American products in Turkmenistan and not creating an office or joint venture, the firm registers only with the CRME to buy or sell.

However, if, in addition to importing and/or exporting, a foreign company intends to "invest" in Turkmenistan -- create a joint venture with a Turkmen firm or another foreign firm or create a branch or affiliated office in Turkmenistan, with the idea of investing capital, technology or expertise in Turkmenistan -- the firm must register with the State Agency for Foreign Investment (SAFI), as well as the CRME. The SAFI analyzes a project's feasibility and is the agency that register the foreign company in Turkmenistan.

FREE ECONOMIC ZONES

Free economic zones have been created in the republic to attract more foreign capital. Foreign investors operating in these zones have the right to transfer, deposit and export hard currency without restrictions. Investors may earn unlimited profits, repatriate after-tax profits, and export their products. Also, enterprises may freely set prices of their goods and services within the free trade zone. Enterprises in which foreigners hold more than 30 percent will be charged 50 percent profit tax during the next three years and 30 percent during the next ten years. Reinvested profits are exempt from taxation. All enterprises are exempt from profit taxes for the first three years of profitable operation. For details on the location of these free economic zones, contact the Turkmen Ministry of Foreign Economic Relations directly.

By presidential decree, foreign investors are freely able to repatriate profits and exchange national currency, manats, for dollars at the exchange rate established by regular central bank auctions. Due to Turkmenistan's hard currency shortage, investors may sometimes experience difficulty exchanging money.

At present, there is no legal system in place to enforce property and contractual rights. In the event of a dispute between investors and the government, the problem must be worked out directly between the two parties.

CURRENCY

Turkmenistan's new national currency, the manat, was introduced on November 1, 1993. On December 14, 1994, President Niyazov issued a decree requiring all companies operating in Turkmenistan to conduct transactions in the manat as of December 20, except in specific cases approved by the President. On September 19, 1995, the Central Bank announced new official and commercial exchange rates for the manat against the dollar. The official exchange rate for government transactions changed from 75 manats/usd to 200 manats/usd. The commercial rate changed from 195 manats/usd to 500 manats/usd. The black market rate fell briefly from a high of 850 manats/usd immediately after the announcement was made, but has since climbed back to 720 manats/usd.

Foreign businesses can benefit from provisions allowing direct purchase of national currency through local banks, though Turkmen banks usually experience a lack of liquidity both in manats and in dollars.

The texts of existing laws on foreign investment, taxes, privatization, and ownership are available in translation from the National Technical Information Service. These laws may be ordered by calling (703) 487-4650.

LEADING SECTORS FOR U.S. EXPORTS AND INVESTMENTS

BEST PROSPECTS FOR NON-AGRICULTURAL PRODUCTS

OIL AND GAS INDUSTRY: EXPLORATION, DEVELOPMENT SERVICES, AND EQUIPMENT

ITA Industry Code: OGS, OGM

Turkmenistan has the world's fourth largest known natural gas reserves, after Russia, the U.S. and Iran, with estimated reserves totaling 13 to 21 trillion cubic meters of gas. In 1992, Turkmenistan produced 84 billion cubic meters of gas, but only half of that amount was produced in 1996. Faced with limited export pipeline options and non-paying customers, gas production fell even further in 2002 to 13,284 billion cubic meters. A new but small gas pipeline to Iran built in 2002 currently allows Turkmenistan to export around 3 billion cubic meters of gas per year (although the throughput capacity of the line is 8 billion cubic meters per year). Turkmenistan is actively pursuing a project to construct a pipeline to Turkey via the Caspian Sea, Azerbaijan and Georgia. In February 1999, the Government chose Pipeline Solution Group International (PSG), a joint venture between two U.S. companies, Bechtel and GE Capital, to lead a consortium on development, construction, and management of the Trans-Caspian pipeline. An agreement concerning the sale/purchase of Turkmen natural gas has been signed between the Turkmenistan and Turkey. Turkmenistan is also exploring options for exporting gas to China and Pakistan.

Turkmenistan has significant oil reserves amounting to 6 to 8 billion tons. Turkmenistan produced 6,280 thousand tons of oil in 1998 and around 3,500 thousand tons of oil during the first six months of 1999. There are two oil refineries in the country: the Turkmenbashi refinery and the Seidi refinery. The Turkmenbashi refinery, where most Turkmen oil is being refined to meet domestic needs in petroleum products, is currently being upgraded. The Seidi refinery, which is currently running at from 6% to 8% of capacity, will also be reconstructed.

The GOTX is looking for foreign investment to explore and develop its oil and gas industry and export routes to hard currency markets. Eight oil and gas resource areas have been made available for joint venture projects and production sharing. The Government has enacted a hydrocarbons law and a program on licensing projects on exploration and production of hydrocarbon resources in Turkmenistan; both contain guidelines for licensing oil and gas investment projects, production sharing agreements, and joint ventures with foreign companies.

The Government is also interested in developing offshore oil fields in the Caspian Sea. An international tender for bidding on Caspian Sea offshore oil field development was held in 2002. However, unresolved dispute with Azerbaijan on the Serdar oil field has discouraged the winners of the tender from developing their concessions. Currently, Western Atlas does a geological study of the shallow water area and the Karabogazgol gulf in the Caspian Sea. An international tender on the right to explore and produce oil in the Caspian Sea is expected to be announced by the Government at the end of 1999.

Electrical Energy: Development, Equipment and Services

ITA Industry Code: PGE

Turkmenistan is self-sufficient in electricity. In 1996, production of electrical power amounted to 10.1 billion kilowatts of electricity; in 1998, Turkmenistan produced 9.28 billion kilowatt-hours. (Reportedly, present capacity is 14 to 17 billion kilowatts annually.) Approximately 15% to 17% of the electrical power produced in Turkmenistan is exported to its neighbors, often in barter arrangements. A new transmission line of 320 kilometers with a capacity of 200 to 500 megawatt-hours stretching to northern Iran (Nebitdag-Aliabad) will be put into operation this year. As part of the energy grid system connecting neighboring countries, the line will permit the export of Turkmen electrical energy to such countries as Turkey, Armenia, Azerbaijan and Georgia.

Turkmenistan has to import its electrical power equipment. The Ministry of Energy and Industry is interested in increasing the capacity and improving the efficiency of electricity production. Also, to expand its electrical power export opportunities, the GOTX is interested in constructing an electrical power line across Afghanistan to Pakistan. Production of electrical equipment, cables, electric bulbs and other products has been planned by the GOTX as well.

Chemical/Mining Industry: Development, Equipment and Services

ITA Industry Code: CHM, MIN

Turkmenistan possesses significant mineral resources, most of which have not been fully developed. There are 10 chemical enterprises involved in the production of mineral fertilizers, iodine and bromine, carbon, sulfites, gypsum, and other minerals. Most of the chemical production facilities are in need of rehabilitation. The Government considers the upgrade and increase of iodine production and the expansion of carbomide and defoliant production as priority projects.

Mining and other types of chemical manufacturing industries have not been developed in Turkmenistan. To meet domestic needs in various metals and expand export opportunities for domestically processed chemicals and minerals, the GOTX would like to develop such industries as magnesium oxide, aluminum, and mineral fiber production.

TRANSPORTATION: INFRASTRUCTURE CONSTRUCTION, DISTRIBUTION AND SERVICES

ITA Industry Code: AUT, APS, CON, TRN

The GOTX has embarked on a large-scale program to upgrade its air, rail and road transportation networks. Since independence, Turkmenistan has built a modern international airport and purchased six Boeing aircraft to service international routes. A second runway designed for heavy aircraft was completed in 1998. Thompson, a French company, has completed installation of air traffic control system at the Ashgabat International airport and was granted a second contract for the installation of air traffic control system in the Turkmenbashi airport by the year 2000.

In 1996, the 300-kilometer Tedjen-Serakhs-Meshed railroad opened, linking the Central Asian states to the Persian Gulf. The 215 kilometer Turkmenabad-Kerki-Kerkichi railway, which will connect the right bank of Amudarya with the national railway network and will end Turkmenistan's dependence on the Uzbek railroad, is being laid by the State Turkmendemiryollary company. As part of this project, the new Kerki railway bridge via the Amudarya river will be erected by May 2000 by the Ukrainian company "Ukrtransstroy". Construction of two more rail connections (Kazanjik-Kizylatrek-Bender Turkmen (Iran) and Turkmenbashi-Yeraliyevo (Kazakhstan)) to link other CIS countries with the Persian Gulf has begun. The governments of Turkmenistan, Uzbekistan, Azerbaijan and Georgia have signed an agreement to upgrade a rail link to the Black Sea. Preparatory work has been done to upgrade the road system including the Ashgabat-Mary and Ashgabat-Turkmenbashi highways, and the Turkmenbashi sea port is planned to be reconstructed.

In 1994, the Government auctioned its late-model public taxicabs, encouraging development of private taxi services. The next step in the privatization of transportation enterprises will include privatization of small enterprises engaged in transportation and repair services. Besides investment in the infrastructure of transportation, the GOTX foresees increased investment in locomotives, aircraft, trucks, and cars into the next century.

COMMUNICATIONS: EQUIPMENT AND SERVICES

ITA Industry Code: TEL, TES

Turkmenistan inherited an archaic, deteriorating telecommunications network. In 1994, a U.S. telecommunications consulting firm with funding from TDA developed a 10-year Master Plan for Turkmenistan's telecommunications sector. Based on the plan, the Government has started gradual upgrading of its old communications system by building new digital telephone stations in Ashgabat, Turkmenabad, Nebitdag and Dashoguz. Two German companies, Siemens and Alcatel, are involved in implementation of these projects. These companies have been awarded contracts to construct two more digital telephone stations in Ashgabat, one station in Mary and another in Turkmenbashi.

The Government is also interested in upgrading its telecommunications infrastructure in rural localities, seeking low-interest financing.

Turkmenistan is the site of a 708-kilometer portion of the Transasian-European fiber optic telecommunications line initiated by the European Union. The line extends from Frankfurt,

Germany, to Shanghai, China. The Turkmen portion of this line was built by the Iranian Telecommunications Company in 1998.

Development of a telecommunications infrastructure in this country has provided the basis for the development of Internet and other information services. The State Turkmentelecom Company and MCI (USA) have signed an agreement to provide Turkmenistan with direct access to the Internet and a direct telephone connection between the U.S. and Turkmenistan.

ENVIRONMENTAL TECHNOLOGY AND SERVICES

ITA Industry Code: POL

Turkmenistan possesses about 25 billion cubic meters of water resources of which 98 percent is surface water. The Amudarya River supplies 22 billion cubic meters of water annually. Other major rivers are the Murgab, Tedjen and Atrek rivers -- all which dry up during the summer months. All the rivers flow along borders with neighboring countries with which Turkmenistan has signed water sharing agreements. The Karakum Canal (1,300 kilometers in length) connects the Amudarya River with the western areas of Turkmenistan and provides irrigation water for 1 million hectares of Turkmenistan's estimated 1.77 million hectares of arable land. Inefficient flood irrigation techniques, heavily silted water and high evaporation rates from the open canal result in widespread salinization and hamper efforts to maximize agricultural production. The Government has expanded acreage under cultivation for wheat production and plans to increase irrigation water supply through the Karakum Canal. To do that, repair of the Karakum Canal is needed. Irrigation pumping systems along the river also need major upgrading.

The Amudarya River is also a primary source of potable water for the most of Turkmenistan. Due to the overuse of chemical and mineral fertilizers in agricultural production and imperfect water collection and drainage system, this river supplies very poor quality potable water. The Dashoguz region is the most vulnerable region of Turkmenistan, suffering ecologically unsafe irrigation and potable water problems due to its proximity to the Aral Sea as well as to the extremely contaminated water of the lower Amudarya.

The significant rise in recent years of the water level in the Caspian Sea has heightened environmental concerns about the oil fields and pipelines in western Turkmenistan. The Caspian Sea has expanded by as much as 150 meters inland, flooding oil terminals, ports and oil fields, although the GOTX says the Caspian began to recede in 2002. Non-environmentally friendly drilling techniques and storage facilities used by local enterprises are threatening the area with potential environmental disasters in the coming years. Water and waste treatment are areas where the GOTX sees a significant need for improvement.

HEALTH CARE AND MEDICAL INDUSTRY

ITA Industry Code: MED

After the collapse of the Soviet Union, Turkmenistan inherited a health care system which included just one pharmaceutical plant in Ashgabat that produced a few medicines (primarily iodine and analgetic pills) and several clinics and hospitals providing very poor medical services. The Turkmenderman-Adjanta pharmaceutical plant, a Turkmen-Indian joint venture, was built last year to produce annually up to 75 million capsules for 20 million injections, various ointments, medical salts, and toothpaste. A mini-plant for infusion solution production was recently commissioned and the Ashgabat pharmaceutical plant has been upgraded. The National Institute of Medicaments was recently created to develop new technology for medicament production based on raw materials available in Turkmenistan. The Institute will be fitted with laboratory equipment and other medical tools to conduct scientific research.

Siemens, a German company, built the International Medical Center in Ashgabat. Almost all other medical cure and treatment facilities existing in Turkmenistan, especially those located out of Ashgabat, require renovation and upgrading. The Government plans to build new clinics and diagnostic medical centers in each province.

BEST PROSPECTS FOR AGRICULTURAL PRODUCTS, EQUIPMENT AND SERVICES

Agriculture, especially cotton production, has historically been the country's second largest source of foreign exchange earnings after the oil and gas sector. Turkmenistan used to produce as much as 1.2 million tons of cotton annually. Despite unfavorable weather conditions, outdated equipment, and lack of a water supply, manpower, and key inputs, the 2002 cotton harvest increased to 630,200 tons in comparison with 436,000 tons of cotton harvested in 1996.

The Government intends to become self-sufficient in wheat production. In 2002, Turkmenistan produced 707,000 tons of wheat, well below the state production target of 1.2 million tons. 1998 figures state that production reached 1.24 million tons of wheat and 1.5 million tons in 1999. Current consumption is estimated at 1.2 million tons.

Although Turkmenistan produces seasonal fruits, vegetables, rice, wheat and maize, it imports many of its foodstuffs. The food processing industry is extremely underdeveloped. A shortage of modern storage facilities aggravates existing procurement system problems in agriculture.

The Government took its first steps toward agricultural privatization in December 1996. Private farmers were allowed to lease land, and will be able to acquire ownership if they keep using the land for agricultural production and meet output targets. However, these "private landowners" will have no right to sell, exchange or give away the land. Foreigners can only lease land. Various state agricultural associations are gradually transforming their relationships with farmers from state orders to a contract-based system. The government is also interested in distributing plots of land not currently under cultivation to private farmers to develop crop production.

AGRICULTURAL EQUIPMENT AND SERVICESIRRIGATION EQUIPMENT AND TECHNOLOGY; DRY LAND FARMING

Technology and Seeds

- Harvesting machinery
- Haying and mowing machinery
- Wheel tractors
- Dairy equipment
- Poultry equipment
- Other machinery and parts

American companies have already established a strong presence supplying farm machinery, tractors, combines and cotton pickers to replace outdated equipment. These contracts also include provisions for service and spare parts centers. This area will continue to be a promising market.

- Sprayers-agricultural
- Pumps and equipment

Out of 48.8 million hectares of Turkmenistan's territory, 0.04% constitutes arable land of which 70% is irrigated. Inefficient irrigation techniques and equipment have limited Turkmenistan's ability to expand its arable land to increase agricultural production and yields. The Karakum Canal connects the Amudarya River with southern and western Turkmenistan and has been the only source of irrigation water for those regions. There are three water reservoirs built along the Karakum Canal, as well as 115 pumps, dams, dikes and other facilities. Most of the facilities require reconstruction. The Government also plans to implement several projects in irrigation area:

- construction of a new Shorkelskiy water reservoir and two canals in the Zeidskiy water reservoir,
- extend the Karakum Canal to the Kizylkay water reservoir in the Kizylatrek district and beyond to Turkmenbashi, and
- reconstruct the Ozyorniy and Daryalykskiy water collectors.

These projects generate opportunities for investment in and sales of pumping equipment, and of irrigation systems and services.

- Planting and fertilizing machinery
- Plows and cultivators

Turkmenistan has the lowest level of agricultural productivity among all the countries of Central Asia. The necessary investments to develop dry land farming technology and create sound seed stocks have not been made in the past. Now, the country is experiencing a shortage of seeds and modern technologies. The inexperience of private farmers in land cultivation also leads to a failure to increase crop harvests.

In addition, Turkmenistan requires an infusion of new cotton seed stock to ensure the continued quality of its cotton harvest and wheat seeds which will increase yield and be resistant to extended periods of drought. The potential exists for American technology and research to address these needs.

FOOD PROCESSING AND PACKAGING EQUIPMENT

- **Packaging equipment**
- **Processing equipment**

The Government wants to develop its agricultural processing facilities to reduce dependence on imported food. The Government has been involved in numerous construction contracts in agriculture and food processing in the past, some of which have not been completed because of financial difficulties. Several projects have been stopped and, as a result, the equipment delivered to Turkmenistan has not been put into operation.

The Government welcomes proposals that include the entire construction/production process for food processing -- from the construction of a manufacturing facility to production to marketing. SAFI would prefer to consider proposals that use local raw materials in the following projects:

- Dairy processing and packaging
- Meat processing and canning
- Sausage production
- Cheese production
- Chicken production and processing

- Fruit and vegetable processing and canning
- Spice production
- Beer production
- Beverage production
- Wine production
- Agricultural waste processing.

POTENTIAL INVESTMENT OPPORTUNITIES

Implementation of the projects from the extensive list below will depend on project feasibility and the availability of budgetary resources or private investment:

1. Oil and Gas Ministry

a) Construction of oil and gas pipelines to transport Turkmen natural gas to Turkey, and, eventually, to Europe, Pakistan and China.

- Trans-Caspian gas pipeline construction project (1,800 km) to transport natural gas from eastern Turkmenistan via the Caspian Sea, Azerbaijan and Georgia to Turkey (Erzurum). The projected capacity of the pipeline is 16 to 30 billion cm of gas per year and estimated cost is USD 2 to 3 billion.

- Turkmenistan-China-Japan gas pipeline construction project with a capacity of 30 billion cm of gas per year and estimated cost of USD 11 billion.

- Turkmenistan-Afghanistan-Pakistan gas pipeline construction project is planned to carry up to 20 billion cm of gas per year; estimated cost is around USD 2 billion.

b) Upgrading the Seidi oil refinery to an overall annual capacity of 6 million tons of oil, including diesel fuel hydroprocessing with an annual capacity of 2,000 tons of fuel and utilization of 100,000 tons of gas annually; project estimated cost is USD 300 million.

c) Construction of a gas and chemical production complex in Seidi with an annual capacity of 200,000 tons of polyethylene; project estimated cost is USD 800 million.

d) The GOTX conducted a tender for the development of offshore oil fields in the Caspian Sea. An opportunity for an increase in the export of U.S. oil and gas equipment and services exists.

e) Installation of gas collector at the 94 kilometer Beshkyzyl-Yelkui-Uchadji route; estimated cost is USD 50 million.

f) Rehabilitation of the 42 kilometer Vyshka-Belek trunk oil Pipeline; estimated cost is USD 3 million.

g) Construction of the 135 kilometer Okarem-Vyshka trunk oil Pipeline; estimated cost is USD 11,5 million.

h) Construction of a production facility for the Administration on Capital Repair of Wells under the State Turkmenoil Company; estimated cost is USD 700,000.

i) Development of oil fields at Eastern Cheleken, Northern Erdekli, and Southern Kamyshldja; estimated cost is USD 30 million for each oil field.

j) Rehabilitation of the Shatut, Ekerem, and Nebitlidje oil Fields; estimated cost is USD 50-60 million.

2. MINISTRY OF ENERGY AND INDUSTRY

ELECTRICAL ENERGY PROJECTS:

a) Construction of a 1,150 kilometer electrical line across Afghanistan to Pakistan (Mary-Mazari Sharif-Kabul-Peshawar) with a carrying capacity of 500 kilovolts; estimated cost is USD 288 million.

b) Construction of a 220 kilovolt electrical substation in Nebitdag with a capacity of 2x63 megawatts; estimated cost is USD 2 million.

c) Upgrade of the Seidi thermoelectric power generation plant to a capacity of 1x80 megawatts to meet regional demand for electricity; estimated cost is USD 35 million.

d) Construction of a 500 megawatt capacity thermoelectric plant in Kyzylatrek; estimated cost is USD 350 million.

e) Construction of a thermoelectrical plant in Dashoguz with a capacity of 2x125 megawatts; estimated cost is USD 175 million.

f) Construction of three 220 kilovolt substations in Serakhs, Kerki, and Farab with a capacity of 2x63 megawatts; estimated cost is USD 2 million for each substation.

g) Construction of two 500 kilovolt substations in Dashoguz and Seidi with a capacity of 2x167 megawatts; estimated cost is USD 3.5 million.

h) Reconstruction of the Turkmenbashi thermoelectrical plant with a capacity of 1x125 megawatts; estimated cost is USD 62 million.

h) Reconstruction of the Ashgabat electrical cable production plant with a capacity of 5,000 kilometers of cable a year; estimated cost is USD 30 million.

CHEMICAL PRODUCTION PROJECTS:

a) Construction of an iodine and bromine production plant at the Boyadag field located 55 kilometers from Nebitdag is estimated at USD 15 million. The concentration of iodine is 35 grams per cubic meter and bromine is 380 grams per cubic meter. The projected annual capacity of the plant is from 100 to 250 tons of iodine and 2,000 tons of bromine.

b) Turnkey construction of the Turkmenabad carbomide production plant near the Turkmenabad chemical plant with a capacity of 350,000 tons of carbomide and 333,000 tons of ammonia annually; estimated cost is USD 250 million.

c) Construction of the Mary carbomide production plant with an annual capacity of 1.5 million tons of mineral fertilizers; estimated cost is USD 390 million.

d) Construction of chemical production facilities at the Karabogazsulfate enterprise in Bekdash including:

- magnesium and magnesium oxide production with annual capacities of 5,000 tons of magnesium and 25,000 tons of magnesium oxide;
- epsomite production with annual capacity of 75,000 tons of epsomite;
- caustic soda and chlorine production with annual capacity of 10,000 tons of caustic soda and 9,000 tons of chlorine;
- sulphite and sodium sulphide production with annual capacity of 2,000 tons of each product;
- chemical reagent production with annual capacity of 5,000 tons of reagents;
- non-chlorine potash magnesium production or shenit fertilizer production with annual capacity of 70,000 tons of fertilizers;
- lithium carbonate production with annual capacity of 5,000 tons;
- boron magnesium concentrate production with annual capacity of 10,000 tons;
- potassium sulphate production with annual capacity of 50,000 tons;
- magnesium sulphate production with annual capacity of 2,000 tons; and
- sodium sulphate production with annual capacity of 50,000 tons.

e) Construction of a potash fertilizer production plant in Gaurdak in Lebap Velayat. Projected annual capacity of the plant will be 150,000 tons of calcinated soda, 50,000 tons of caustic soda, and 30,000 tons of sodium bicarbonate. Project estimated cost is n/a.

f) Construction of a strontium carbonate production plant in the village of Gaurdak, Lebap Velayat, that will produce 20,000 tons. Project estimated cost is n/a.

g) Construction of a methanol, formaldehyde and urea-formaldehyde resin production facility with annual capacity of 100,000 tons of methanol. Project estimated cost is n/a.

g) Construction of the "Extra" salt production facility at the Turkmenabad chemical plant with a capacity of 10,000 tons of salt; estimated cost is USD 2.5 million.

h) Construction of a calcium bromide production facility at the Cheleken chemical plant with a capacity of 1,000 tons; estimated cost is USD 500,000.

OTHER INDUSTRIAL PROJECTS:

a) Construction of a pulp and paper production plant in Bezmein with a capacity of 40,000 tons of each product; estimated cost is USD 136 million.

b) Construction of an aluminum production complex in the Mary Velayat includes the following three projects: an alunite mining facility with an annual capacity of 2 million tons of alunite (USD 100 million project cost); an alumina production facility with an annual capacity of 300,000 tons of alumina (USD 250 million project cost); and an aluminum smelter with an annual capacity of 150,000 tons of aluminum (USD 350 million project cost).

c) Construction of a paint production plant in Turkmenabad with an annual capacity of 5,000 tons; estimated cost is USD 7 million.

d) Construction of a ruberoid production plant with an annual capacity of one million square meters of ruberoid; estimated cost is USD 1.5 million.

e) Construction of a school appliance production facility with an annual capacity of 50 conditional sets; estimated cost is USD 16 million.

f) Construction of an immersing pump (ECV-8 and ECV-12 types) production facility at the Mary machine building plant with an annual capacity of 2,000 units; estimated cost is USD 1 million.

g) Construction of a rubber and technical item production facility in Ashgabat with an annual capacity of 50 tons; estimated cost is USD 500,000.

h) Construction of a technological line for assembling washing machines at the Arzuv plant in Ashgabat with an annual capacity of 10,000 units; estimated cost is USD 600,000.

i) Construction of a computer production plant with an annual capacity of 12,000 computers; estimated cost is USD 25 million.

3. State Association for Food Production and Processing

a) Reconstruction of vegetable oil production plants in Bayramali, Turkmenabad and Dashoguz; estimated cost is USD 268 million.

b) Reconstruction of the Ashgabat confectionary factory "Gundogar" to expand production capacity of biscuits and cakes up to 9,600 tons and chocolate up to 5,600 tons; estimated cost is USD 15.6 million.

c) Construction of a margarine and mayonnaise production Facility in Ahal Velayat with an annual capacity of 3,000 tons of margarine and 2,000 tons of mayonnaise; estimated cost is n/a.

d) Construction of a cardboard production facility for meat, dairy and other food products in Ashgabat with an annual capacity of 5,000 tons; estimated cost is USD 10 million.

4. State Association for Bread Production

a) Construction of a grain mill complex in Mary with a daily capacity of 200 tons of grain; estimated capacity is USD 15 million.

b) Construction of an elevator for a raw rice storage in Dashoguz with a daily capacity of 50,000 tons; estimated cost is USD 5 million.

c) Reconstruction of the flour mills with elevators in Turkmenabad and Mary each with a daily capacity of 250 tons of grain; estimated cost is USD 30 million for each mill with elevator.

d) Reconstruction of a mill with an elevator in Dashoguz with a daily capacity of 500 tons of grain; estimated cost is USD 30 million.

e) Construction of a bread production plant in Ashgabat with a daily capacity of 30 tons of bread; estimated cost is USD 10 million.

f) Reconstruction of the Ashgabat Bread Enterprise with a daily capacity of 25 tons of bread; estimated cost is USD 5 million.

5. Ministry of Communications

a) The project on the development of the National Data Transfer Network and reconstruction of the telegraphic net system will cover Ashgabat and the four other velayat capitals; estimated cost is USD 3 million.

b) Development of the 280 kilometer Turkmenabad-Kerki-Gaurdak communications line; estimated cost is USD 3 million.

c) Development of the 260 kilometer Bayramali-Kushka communications line; estimated cost is USD 3 million.

d) Construction of the 130 kilometer Tedjen-Serakhs radio relay line; estimated cost is USD 700,000.

e) Reconstruction of Turkmenistan's radio and television broadcasting stations and ultra-short wave frequency transformers; estimated cost is USD 12 million.

f) Reconstruction and modernization of the postal mail network; estimated cost is USD 5 million.

g) Development of the second phase of the 653 kilometer Ashgabat-Turkmenbashi fiber-optic communications line; estimated cost is USD 24 million.

6. State Company "Turkmenautoyollary" (highway construction)

a) Rehabilitation and expansion of the highway from Turkmenabad to Mary to Ashgabat to Turkmenbashi:

- Ashgabat-Turkmenbashi length: 560 km.

- Ashgabat-Mary length: 352 km. The European Bank for Reconstruction and Development (EBRD) has approved a loan to finance this project; estimated cost is $75 million.

- Mary-Turkmenabad length: 230 km.

a) Construction of a bridge for trains and motor vehicles over the Amudarya River in Kerki.

c) Reconstruction of the Turkmenabad bridge for trains and motor vehicles.

7. STATE RAILWAY ADMINISTRATION

Construction of four railway lines: Kazanjik-Kizylatrek: length 245 km; Kazanjik-Kizylkaya: length 170 km; Turkmenbashi-Kuulisol-Bekdash: length 400 km.

8. STATE STEAMSHIP ADMINISTRATION

a) Reconstruction of the seaport at Turkmenbashi and moorings at Kuulisol and Ufra. The TDA has funded a feasibility study for a seaport modernization project, and EBRD has approved financing for this estimated USD 30 million project.

b) Construction of a tanker is estimated at USD 11 million.

c) Construction of an oil pier with 235 berths is estimated at USD 700,000.

d) Construction of a floating dock with a capacity of 5,000 tons is estimated at USD 5 million.

9. Khakimlik of Balkan Velayat

Due to GOTX plans to expand oil and gas and other industries' operations in the Balkan Velayat, the issue of improving the water supply has become vital for this region. Caspian Sea water desalinization and purification is considered a high priority for Turkmenistan. To receive detailed information on this project, companies should also approach SAFI.

10. MINISTRY OF TRANSPORTATION

a) International cargo delivery development (resulting from the agreement to develop transit trade between the ECO member-states). This project will include the purchase of about 200 heavy trucks and service infrastructure development worth $20 million. The extension of a credit line or truck leasing are the financing options being considered.

b) Expansion of Turkmenistan's fleet of dump trucks (resulting from Turkmenistan's need for highway construction and development). The GOTX is interested in purchasing or leasing dump trucks.

c) Construction of automobile service facilities (called Caravan-Sarai) along highways throughout Turkmenistan. This project includes construction of motels, service stations and automobile spare parts stores and the provision of telephone and fax communications, insurance and medical services.

d) Conversion of gasoline-powered vehicles to natural gas with the construction of a natural gas conversion facility with a monthly capacity of 100 to 5,000 vehicles.

e) Construction of a chassis production facility that can assemble vehicles and trucks using universal chassis. The projected annual capacity of the plant is 1,000 to 5,000 light trucks and 500 to 900 medium capacity trucks.

f) Tire rehabilitation facility designed to help meet the country's annual demand for 2 million tires. The Ashgabat automobile repair plant will house a tire rehabilitation shop with an annual capacity of 100,000 tires.

g) Storage battery production development will require purchase of storage battery production technology and equipment to be installed in the Mary automobile repair plant. The projected annual capacity of the equipment is 80,000 batteries.

h) Production of automobile spare parts, including windshields, belts and other parts.

11. MINISTRY OF TEXTILE INDUSTRY

a) Reconstruction of the Ashgabat silk production plant to increase annual production capacity to 60 tons of raw silk.

b) Reconstruction of the Ashgabat shoe production factory to expand annual shoe production to 3 million pairs.

c) Reconstruction of the Bezmein carpet production plant to increase the annual production capacity to 2.45 million square meters of carpet. A wool washing shop is also needed to process 2,000 tons of wool.

d) Reconstruction of the Nebitdag hosiery factory to increase the annual production capacity to 30 million hosiery items.

e) Reconstruction of the Turkmenabad knitted goods factory to increase the annual production capacity to 12.7 million pieces. The factory plans to produce fabric made of synthetic thread, curtains and laces.

f) Completion of construction of the Seidi cotton fabric factory to produce up to 7,000 tons of cotton fabric annually.

g) Completion of construction of the Yolotan cotton fabric factory to produce annually up to 5,000 tons of fabric annually.

12. STATE TOURIST CORPORATION

Plans to develop tours, tourist services and recreational facilities are part of the state's program for tourism development. Foreign investments are expected to be the catalyst for this sector. Starwood Hotels and Resorts, Inc., a U.S. company, has become a ten year operator of the Grand Hotel "Turkmen" which includes the Sheraton Grand Turkmen Hotel and the Four Points Ak Altyn Plaza Hotel.

Potential exists for developing a recreational zone on the Turkmen side of the Caspian Sea.

It should be noted that, to date, Turkish construction companies have been the primary competitors for most hotel construction projects implemented in Turkmenistan.

13. MINISTRY OF HEALTH CARE AND MEDICAL INDUSTRY

a) Construction of a medical item production plant in Ashgabat
with an annual capacity of 2,300 tons of cotton, 240 tons of tampons, and 470 tons of children's padding; estimated cost is USD 19 million.

b) Reconstruction of liquorice root processing facility at the
Turkmenabad liquorice production enterprise "Buyan" with an annual capacity of 300 tons of extract, 50 tons of glycerin, and 100 tons of flavinoids; estimated cost is USD 6 million.

c) Construction of a mini-plant for the production of medical tablets and pills in Dashoguz, Mary, Nebitdag, and Turkmenabad with an annual capacity of 50 million tablets and pills; estimated cost is USD 2 million for each mini-plant.

d) Reconstruction of the Ashgabat chemical and pharmaceutical plant "Saglyk" with an annual capacity of 300 million tablets and 18 million bottles; estimated cost is USD 8 million.

e) Construction of clinics with diagnostic centers in Ashgabat, Dashoguz, Mary, Nebitdag, and Turkmenabad with a capacity of 25 beds in each clinic; estimated cost is USD 20 million.

f) Construction of the Scientific and Research Institute of Oncology in Ashgabat with 250 beds and 300 visiting patients per shift; estimated cost is USD 35 million.

g) Construction of a tuberculosis clinic with 200 beds and a polyclinic for 300 visiting patients per shift in Ashgabat; estimated cost is USD 25 million.

h) Construction of a catgut production facility in Ashgabat with an annual capacity of 2 million ampoules; estimated cost is USD 7 million.

There is considerable foreign competition from the German firm Siemens in the medical equipment and services sector.

U.S. companies interested in the opportunity to export American medical supplies to Turkmenistan should contact the Ministry of Health Care and Medical Industry at the following address:

Mr. Kurbankuli Berdymukhamedov, Minister
Ministry of Health Care and Medical Industry
90 Makhtumkuli Street, Ashgabat, Turkmenistan 744000
Tel: (993)(12) 35-10-63, 35-58-33, or 35-45-21
Fax: (993)(12) 35-50-32

14. Ministry of Agriculture and Water Resources

a) Construction of the Zeid water reservoir with an annual capacity of 2,520 million cubic meters of water; estimated cost is USD 144.7 million.

b) Reconstruction of the Karakum Canal to extend it up to 1,100 kilometers in length and to increase its annual capacity up to 610 cubic meters of water; estimated cost is USD 26.8 million.

c) Construction of the Madau water reservoir in Kizylatrek etrap with an annual capacity of 250 million cubic meters; estimated cost is USD 119.5 million.

d) Reconstruction of pumping station No. 7 at the Karakum Canal for 5,100 hectares with an annual capacity of 6 cubic meters of water per second; estimated cost is USD 80 million.

e) Reconstruction of the Ozyorniy and Daryalykskiy collectors in Dashoguz Velayat at 442,200 hectares; estimated cost is USD 80 million.

f) Construction of a 785 kilometer Trans-Turkmen water collector; estimated cost is USD 427 million.

g) Construction of a pumping station at the Zahmet-Turkmengala machine canal with an annual capacity of 50 cubic meters of water per second; estimated cost is USD 5 million.

h) Installation of a divider unit at the 15th kilometer of the Karakum Canal and the SK-2 canal with an annual capacity of from 400 to 500 cubic meters of water per second; estimated cost is USD 3 million.

i) Construction of the basic structure of the Karakum Canal with an annual capacity of 980 cubic meters of water per second; estimated cost is USD 37.2 million.

j) Construction of two partitioning units at the 326th and 456th kilometers of the Karakum Canal with the capacity of 727 and 580 cubic meters of water per second, respectively; estimated cost is USD 35.4 million and USD 31.9 million, respectively.

k) Project cost for irrigation of 34,000 hectares of land in southwest Turkmenistan; estimated cost is USD 425 million.

l) Reconstruction of the pumping station No. 21 at the Karakum Canal with a capacity of 11 cubic meters of water per second; estimated cost is USD 7.8 million.

m) Reconstruction of the pumping station at the 672nd kilometer of the Karakum Canal with a capacity of 6.7 cubic meters of water per second; estimated cost is USD 12.4 million.

n) Reconstruction of the 270 kilometer south-western branch line of the Karakum Canal with a capacity of 30 cubic meters of water per second; estimated cost is USD 83.7 million.

o) Construction of the Serakhs machine canal in Ahal Velayat with a capacity of 15 cubic meters of water per second; estimated cost is USD 39 million.

p) Construction of pumping stations "Gaurdak-1" and Gaurdak-2" in Lebap Velayat, each with a capacity of 16 cubic meters of water per second; estimated cost is USD 21.6 million.

q) Construction of the Meana-Chacha pumping station with a capacity of 2.25 cubic meters of water per second; estimated cost is USD 31.5 million.

r) Construction of the Bis pumping station with a capacity of 3.45 cubic meters of water per second; estimated cost is USD 15 million.

s) Construction of four pumping stations in Lebap Velayat
and two pumping stations in Dashoguz Velayat each with a capacity of 45 cubic meters of water per second; estimated cost is USD 15 million.

t) Strengthening the Murgap and the Tedjen Rivers to prevent
flash flooding; estimated cost is USD 35 million.

Comment

The above mentioned projects reflect the GOTX's thinking concerning priority areas. Implementation will be determined by availability of internal budgetary resources and external financing. Nevertheless, U.S. investors should seriously consider appropriate projects in Turkmenistan.

The Government of the United States acknowledges the contribution that outward foreign direct investment can make to the U.S. economy. U.S. foreign direct investment is increasingly viewed as a complement or even a necessary component of trade. Nearly sixty percent of total U.S. exports originate with American firms with investments abroad. Recognizing the benefits that U.S. outward investment brings to the U.S. economy, the Government of the United States undertakes initiatives, such as Overseas Private Investment Corporation (OPIC) programs, bilateral investment treaty negotiations and business facilitation programs, that support U.S. investors.

MARKETING PRODUCTS AND SERVICES

Doing business in Turkmenistan requires patience, persistence and personal contacts with officials at a high level in the Government. The GOTX wishes to encourage foreign investment and business, but the current legal and regulatory regimes do not conform to international business standards. The commercial code is not yet adopted; most local officials are unfamiliar with western business practices and internationally accepted norms; and business is often a matter of personal influence and politics.

Many marketing methods employed in the West do not work well here. Successful companies in Turkmenistan have established personal contact with GOTX officials either through representative offices or repeated visits. Smaller or lesser-known companies must establish their bona fides before being accepted. Large-scale contracts are signed at the presidential level and often require the travel to Ashgabat of the company's president or CEO to close the deal. Follow-up visits are also critical. Communication through fax and telephone are helpful but are no substitute for personal contact. There are locally-based distributors representing U.S. companies, but most are foreign companies themselves (usually Turkish) that have established offices in Ashgabat since Turkmenistan's independence. A list of potential distributors is available from the Commercial Section at the Embassy. Turkmenistan is not familiar with the concept of franchising, therefore, it is not yet practiced here.

Almost all companies investing in Turkmenistan form joint ventures. Since there is limited privatization, joint ventures generally include government partners. There is no standard form for a joint venture agreement (except in the oil and gas sector); each agreement is negotiated individually, approved by the Cabinet of Ministers, and finalized by presidential decree.

DISTRIBUTION AND SALES CHANNELS

Turkmenistan inherited a Soviet-style distribution system with a centralized distribution network, state orders, and state controlled prices. Gradually, the GOTX has liberalized prices for consumer goods, poor quality locally produced flour is sold at fixed, rationed, subsidized prices through state stores. In August 1994, the State Commodity and Raw Materials Exchange (SCRME) was established to regulate foreign and domestic trading and partially insulate the internal market from foreign competition during the country's gradual transition to a free market.

For this purpose, the presidential decree establishing the SCRME required that foreign trade transactions made on the basis of clearing agreements, trade credits, barter contracts, joint venture capital import/export, charitable activity, and other transactions be reviewed and registered by the SCRME. The process of registration takes, on average, one week, although in some cases the period is longer. After the approval of a contract, a fee for contract registration of 0.2% of the value of import or export transaction must be paid by both the seller and the buyer (50% of the sum goes to the general government budget and 50% stays at the SCRME). The following are exempt from payments of contract registration fees:

- enterprises and organizations importing grain, children's food, food products to be sold at regulated state prices, and medical equipment and medicine; and
- goods imported on the basis of contracts funded by the state budget.

Barter contracts require the approval of the Cabinet of Ministers. According to Article 47 of the Law on Hydrocarbon Resources, all materials and equipment used in petroleum operations are exempt from registration with the SCRME and exempt from customs duties.

Registration of trade contracts is not automatic. If the SCRME finds that the articles of a contract are contradictory, or documentation is not complete, or prices set up in the contract can negatively affect a consumer market, then the contract will not be registered. Prices stated in the contract are subject to scrutiny by the SCRME and are compared with world market prices. If a contract requires an advance payment by a Turkmen partner, then the SCRME will require a guarantee issued by a solid foreign bank. Otherwise, registration of the contract can be rejected.

Besides registering contracts, the SCRME conducts auctions and trade transactions for both consumer goods and raw materials. The SCRME also has the authority to auction securities although a true securities market does not yet exist in Turkmenistan.

The SCRME itself does not function as a trader or an intermediary at auctions. It plays no role in the distribution of consumer goods that are produced locally for domestic consumption. These goods are distributed through a state wholesale network or direct transactions.

The Trade and Foreign Economic Relations Ministry determines and the SCRME announces restrictions on export from Turkmenistan. Usually, restrictions apply to goods that are in short supply in Turkmenistan.

Turkmen Customs maintains a list of goods that cannot be imported into Turkmenistan, including handmade wool rugs of the Koshma type, yurtas, handmade carpets, and astrakhan wool.

INFORMATION ON TYPICAL PRODUCT PRICING STRUCTURES

The Turkmen market is small, and economic and natural factors affect the pricing of goods. First, transportation costs can double, even triple the price of goods imported. Also, the small population size (5.0 million people, according to Government statistics) and limited income (the average salary in the state sector is $16 to $40 per month) also limits marketing possibilities. Finally, excise taxes levied on some imported products and goods and a value added tax of 20% affect prices. Due to an average monthly inflation rate of 3% and a fluctuating black market foreign exchange rate (in July 1999 it ranged between 13,000 manats to 16,000 manats per U.S. dollar), prices are steadily rising.

USE OF AGENTS AND DISTRIBUTORS, FINDING A PARTNER

A U.S. firm looking for a local partner will encounter three options: Turkmen state enterprises; small Turkmen private firms, largely involved in trading, and Turkish firms that have established trade, construction, and production businesses in Turkmenistan. So far, Turkish firms have been instrumental in promoting American and European companies' businesses in the Turkmen market, distributing goods and services, providing construction services for trade contracts involving turn-key sale of equipment, running representative offices, and other forms of business activities. In addition, Iranian, Japanese and some European distributors have established wholesale and retail enterprises in Turkmenistan (especially in Ashgabat), introducing to the local market a wider range of goods not previously available to consumers. However, given the limited number of these distributors, prices are relatively high. Very few U.S. consumer goods are currently available on the local market, and many that do appear are trans-shipped from Dubai. The low buying power of the population and the import substitution policy in agriculture pursued by the government serve to limit the number of foreign distributors in Turkmenistan. To promote U.S. exports to Turkmenistan, U.S. companies should be prepared to take a "hands on" approach to locating potential distributors and training them in effective sales techniques.

The Commercial Section of the U.S. Embassy in Ashgabat provides a number of useful programs to help develop contacts. They include:
- Gold Key Service, which arranges meetings for a U.S. company representative's visit to Turkmenistan;
- BISNIS "Search for Partners" which provides contact information on Turkmen companies looking for a U.S. partner; and
- BISNIS "Trade Opportunities", which helps establish contacts with Turkmen companies seeking to buy U.S. products.

In all transactions, U.S. companies must carefully investigate potential local partners and exercise due diligence when doing business with local firms.

FRANCHISING

So far, no franchises have been sold in Turkmenistan. However, since many Turkmen small- and medium-size enterprises do not have sufficient capital to establish solid businesses, the franchising concept in such areas as fast food, dry cleaning/laundry services, and hotels and motels might become accepted.

DIRECT MARKETING

There are very few foreign companies that practice direct marketing in Turkmenistan. Though it is a consumer-tailored approach to market, door-to-door, mailing, and other techniques of direct marketing have not become a popular practice among the population. One reason is extremely low purchasing power of consumers. Inadditiopn, direct marketing is not part of the local tradition.

JOINT VENTURES AND LICENSING

The GOTX encourages the formation of joint ventures with Turkmen state and private companies when a long-term foreign investment project or commercial transaction is negotiated. There have been about 278 joint ventures registered in Turkmenistan, most of which (more than 170) are located in Ashgabat. Usually, joint ventures are organized into a limited liability partnership, complete or mixed company, or joint stock company.

THERE ARE LICENSING REQUIREMENTS FOR A NUMBER OF ACTIVITIES IN TURKMENISTAN:

- oil and gas exploration and production are licensed by the Competent Body on Hydrocarbon Resources Development;
- gambling, slot machines, and tourist businesses are licensed by the State Tourist Corporation, "Turkmensiyakhat";
- tourism services are licensed by Turkmensiyakhat;
- culture and art businesses are licensed by the Ministry of Culture;
- cinema and video-cassette distribution is licensed by the State Movie and Video Company;
- publishing and sales of publishing products are licensed by the State Company "Metbugat" with Cabinet of Ministers and the Interior Ministry approval;
- wholesale and retail trade is licensed by the Ministry of Trade and Foreign Economic Relations;
- production and processing of meat and dairy products, animal fat and butter, beer and beverages and confectionery products are licensed by the State Association of Food Production;
- seed production is licensed by the Ministry of Agriculture;
- sheep, goat, camel wool, astrakhan wool and leather production and processing are licensed by the State Turkmenmallary Association of Cattlebreeding Joint Stock Partnerships;

- sale of medical and pharmaceutical products and services is licensed by the Ministry of Health Care and Medical Industry;
- fish farming is licensed by the Administration of Fish Preservation of the State Fish Committee;
- importation of alcohol is licensed by the Ministry of Trade and Foreign Economic Relations;
- banking activity is licensed by the Central Bank of Turkmenistan;
- legal advising activity is licensed by the Ministry of Justice;
- insurance, reinsurance, broker activity, and operations with bonds are licensed by the Ministry of Economics and Finance;
- educational activities are licensed by the Ministry of Education;
- cargo and passenger transportation services are licensed by the Ministry of Transport;
- auditing activities are licensed by the Ministry of Economics and Finance;
- sea transportation services for cargo and passenger deliveries at the Caspian sea are licensed by the State Sea Steamship company.

Licensing requirements vary from one sector to another. However, there are a number of common documents must be submitted: foundation documents, certificate of registration, standard application, and license fee. Additional documents are required to demonstrate that the applicant has appropriate qualification to perform the proposed activity. The time to obtain a license should not exceed 30 days, according to decrees. The term of the license is usually three years. Most licenses may be obtained from either central or regional authorities. For certain licenses, a permit from the Sanitary and Epidemiological Inspectorate, Fire Inspectorate, and/or State Standard Inspectorate is required. Foreign investors are required to submit the same documents as domestic investors in order to obtain licenses.

SELLING FACTORS AND TECHNIQUES

The Turkmen population has some national peculiarities related to food products, women's dresses, home appliances, and other factors related to climatic conditions and cultural traditions. For instance, preserved or semi-ready food products are not very popular in Turkmenistan because the majority of the population have small farms and produce fresh natural products. Second-hand clothing is also not popular and will have a long shelf life in Turkmenistan.

Quality products do matter in Turkmenistan but most consumers cannot afford to pay high prices. There is significant competition to U.S. goods from Turkish and European products that enjoy a geographic advantage.

STEPS TO ESTABLISHING AN OFFICE

A new amendment to the Law concerning Profit Tax outlines the definition of a representative office of a foreign company doing business in Turkmenistan whose activities will be subject to profit tax payment. The definition of a representative office includes "(1) a branch office, department, administrative office, bureau, agency, factory, production shop; (2) mines, oil and gas wells and/or other stationary and movable facilities used for natural resource development and extraction; and (3) a construction site, or mounting and assembling shop that operates for more than six months." The amendment states that the following activities of foreign companies in Turkmenistan will not be considered "a representative office subject to profit tax payment" including: (1) demonstration and storage of goods belonging to a foreign company; (2) storage of goods and items that belong to a foreign entity with the purpose of goods processing by another entity for their further exporting them from Turkmenistan; (3) purchase of goods and products; and (4) collection of information for a foreign entity and other kinds of assistance necessary for signing a contract.

To open a representative office in Ashgabat, a foreign company should first obtain registration from the State Agency for Foreign Investment.

A foreign company opening a representative office must register with the Registration Department of the State Agency for Foreign Investment (SAFI). The following documents are required for registration of a foreign company representative office:

1. An application with the description of the goal of the company's activity in Turkmenistan, background information about the firm, and a short survey of its latest activity.
2. Written confirmation about the availability of a legal address (lease or other document).
3. Statement about the representative office approved by a company's CEO (2 copies in Russian and Turkmen languages).
4. Power of attorney.
5. Background information about the head of the representative office in Turkmenistan with a photograph (3x4 size).
6. A copy of the charter of the foreign firm, certified by a consulate of Turkmenistan abroad or the Foreign Ministry of Turkmenistan.
7. Official registration document of the foreign investor from the investor's residence (an original). This document must be notarized.
8. A document from a bank in the country where the foreign investor resides (an original) giving the financial status of the foreign investor.

All documents must be originals that are stamped and sealed, translated into Russian and Turkmen, and submitted in the language of the country where the foreign investor resides. (No faxes are accepted.) Copies of translations must be certified by the agency that makes the translation. When submitting the documents to the Registration Department, copies of all the documents must be certified. The foreign investor pays $3,000 for registration of its representative office in Turkmenistan.

All the above mentioned documents are required for registration of a foreign company branch office with the Registration Department. The only exception is submission of a business plan for enterprises involved in production, processing and/or construction activities.

For more information, contact:

Registration Department
State Agency for Foreign Investment
53 Azadi Street, Ashgabat, Turkmenistan 744000
Tel:(993)(12) 39-62-07, Fax:(993)(12) 35-04-11,12

Foreign investors interested in investing in Turkmenistan by establishing a joint venture (which to this point is the method used by most foreign companies), must also register their particular investment projects with SAFI. To evaluate a foreign investment project, SAFI requires the following information:

- General information about the project;
- A marketing analysis;
- Raw materials supply analysis;
- Location of the facility and the environmental effect;
- Technology to be used;
- Management plan;
- Labor resources to be used;

- Project implementation schedule; and
- Financial analysis and investment appraisal.

For more information, contact:

Investment Project Appraisal and Registration Department
State Agency for Foreign Investment
53, Azadi Street, Ashgabat, Turkmenistan 744000
Tel/Fax:(993)(12) 35-04-12, 35-02-31, 35-04-15

To register a joint venture, a foreign company must provide the following documents:

1. An application with the description of the goal of the company's activity in Turkmenistan, background information about the firm and a short survey of its latest activity.
2. Written confirmation about the availability of a legal address (lease or other document).
3. A charter of the newly created enterprise approved by the Board of Directors (two copies in Russian and Turkmen).
4. Two copies of an establishment agreement approved by protocol of the Board of Directors.
5. Business plan approved by the Board of Directors for those enterprises that will be involved in production, processing and/or construction activities.
6. Power of attorney.
7. Short background information about the head of the enterprise (two photographs must be attached).
8. A copy of the charter of the foreign firm notarized by a consulate of Turkmenistan abroad or the Ministry of Foreign Affairs of Turkmenistan.
9. Official registration document of the foreign investor from the investor's residence (an original). This document must be notarized by a consulate of Turkmenistan abroad or the Ministry of Foreign Affairs of Turkmenistan.
10. Original banking documents certifying the solvency of the firm.

All the documents are submitted in the language of the country of the foreign investor's residence. They must be originals, stamped and sealed (no faxes are accepted), translated into Turkmen and Russian and certified by an agency that is recognized as producing accurate translations (for example, the Turkmenistan Chamber of Commerce). The charge is usually $5 per page to translate and certify the translation is accurate.

SAFI charges registration fees that vary depending on the type of activity. A company that produces raw materials, consumer goods, equipment and so on must pay $2,000. A company that is not engaged in production but in services and other activities must pay $3,000. To extend the term of registration, the fee is $1,500 (the original registration is valid for two years and then must be renewed).

SAFI may reject a company's registration on the grounds of non-feasibility of the investment project to be implemented in Turkmenistan.

A company may rent space in:

- business centers or hotels, or
- a building that belongs to a ministry, state organization or state/private enterprise.

Current rules prohibit renting space in private apartments, state-owned apartments and houses, and unfinished construction sites.

After a company has chosen office space, it must submit an application to the local Khakimlik (mayor's office) for approval for the legal address of the representative office. The application must be accompanied by the following documents:

- short description of the company's activity and the goals for opening a representative office in Turkmenistan;
- a lease (rental lease or letter of guarantee);
- proof of power of attorney for the head of the representative office; and
- short background information about the head of the office (a photograph must be attached).

A fee for registration is charged by the Khakimlik. For more information on opening presence in Ashgabat, contact:

Department of Foreign Economic Relations
Khakimlik of Ashgabat
22 Neutral Turkmenistan Street
Ashgabat, Turkmenistan 744000
Tel:(993)(12) 39-04-24, Fax:(993)(12) 35-67-00

Foreign entities that have registered their representative offices in Ashgabat and do business in Turkmenistan must quarterly transfer 0.5% of their balance profit into the State Fund for development of the city of Ashgabat.

ADVERTISING AND TRADE PROMOTION

Commercial advertising in Turkmenistan is controlled by the Government. Mass media offers very few options for advertising: two or three newspapers and TV and radio broadcasting. The mayors (khakims) of the cities and towns issue permission for billboards, neon signs and other outdoor advertisements. A new law concerning health protection is currently being developed by the Ministry of Healthcare and Medical Industry. One of the articles of this law will address the issues regarding the banning use of alcohol and tobacco advertisements. The draft law will be submitted to the Turkmen Parliament later this year for approval. However, local authorities are restricting the placement of alcohol and tobacco advertisements outdoors in response to growing public opinion against advertising these products. Bars and casinos are also not allowed to advertise. Foreign firms do not need permission from the Government to advertise except for companies involved in educational or medical activities; they require permission from the Ministry of Education or the Ministry of Healthcare and Medical Industry.

Radio and Television Advertising. The National Television and Radio Company (NTRC) provides advertising services for both resident and non-resident companies doing business in Turkmenistan and accepts completed commercials as well as offering its own production facilities. There are two Turkmen channels, TMT and TMT-1, and one Russian channel, ORT, where commercials are placed.

The NTRC charges foreign companies airing TV commercials on TMT and TMT-1 channels 1,350,000 manat per minute. The price includes a 20% value added tax and a 5% advertisement tax (the overall tax is 25%). To air commercials on the ORT channel, NTRC charges foreign companies 1,480,000 manat per minute including a 25% tax. All charges are made only in the national currency. Discounts are provided depending on a length of a commercial. (The July 1999 official foreign exchange rate is 5,200 manat per one U.S. dollar.)

The charge for making TV commercials by the NTRC varies depending on the complexity of the production process and is different for resident and non-resident foreign companies. The prices may also be negotiated and discounts are provided.

The charge for airing radio advertisements is 260,000 manat per minute for foreign companies. A 25% tax is included in the price. Producing a radio advertisement it costs 4,000 manat per word plus a 25% tax for foreign companies.

Advertisements can be placed from 9 a.m. till 6 p.m. (with a lunch break from 1 p.m. till 2 p.m.) Monday through Friday. To place an advertisement, contact:

TMT Reklama Enterprise
3 Molla Nepes Street
Ashgabat, Turkmenistan 744000
Tel: (993)(12) 35-15-15 or 39-46-94, or 39-86-62
Tel/Fax: (993)(12) 39-47-22

Print Advertising. The two newspapers with the highest circulation in the country are "Neutral Turkmenistan" in Russian and "Turkmenistan" in Turkmen. Each distributes around 40,000 copies a day. The advertising office "Turkmenpressservice" places advertisements in both newspapers. The newspapers sell advertising space payable in manat .

U.S. companies resident in Turkmenistan may place advertisements in these newspapers at the following prices: 2,500,000 manat including 20% value added tax for one-half of a page, 1,300,000 manat for one-fourth of a page, 700,000 manat for one-eighth of a page, and 400,000 manat for one-sixteenth of a page.

Advertisements can be placed during working hours from 10 a.m. till 5 p.m., Monday through Friday, and on Saturday from 11 a.m. till 2 p.m. To place an advertisement, contact:

Mr. Konstantin Zavistovski, Advertisement Manager (speaks Russian)
Turkmenpressservice Office
2nd Floor, Room 234
20 Atabayev Street
Ashgabat, Turkmenistan 744000
Tel/Fax: (993)(12) 35-40-10
Tel: (993)(12) 46-84-55

The Akasya Ltd. firm, a private company, also provides a range of advertising services in Turkmenistan. It publishes ads in its own "Biznes Reklama" newspaper in the Turkmen language, arranges TV advertising and produces billboards. The firm may be contacted at the following address:

Mr. Warol Bekdash, Director (speaks Turkish and English)
Akasya Ltd.
54-A Makhtumkuli Street
Ashgabat, Turkmenistan 744000
Tel/Fax:(993)(12)47-18-64

The Vestnik advertising newspaper offers advertising services in Turkmen and Russian languages at 1,800 - 2,400 manat per square centimeter plus a 25% tax and can be reached at:

Mrs. Regana Balaban, Chief Editor
Vestnik Newspaper
First Floor, Room 39
20 Atabaev Street
Ashgabat, Turkmenistan 744000
Tel/Fax: 46-84-70, 46-84-43

Pricing Products

Since 1991, the GOTX has been in the process of liberalizing prices for food products and services. Prices for almost all food products have been freed with the exception of flour available at subsidized prices and sold only to low-income families, families with children under sixteen, students and pensioners. Locally produced coarse-ground salt is available for free.

The GOTX continues to subsidize prices for utility services provided to the Turkmen population including gas, electricity, heating and water. Prices for the utility services provided to commercial entities are higher than for the population. Public transportation and telecommunications services are also heavily subsidized. To provide access to certain products and services by Turkmen citizens and entities and to protect them from foreign competition, the GOTX has been maintaining dual prices for these products and services reflecting a difference in prices set up for local residents and foreigners. Such products and services include air, rail, and inter-city bus transportation, telecommunications, admission fees to museums and exhibitions, gasoline station services, and building materials and fertilizers produced locally. Foreigners are charged in dollars while local residents pay state-subsidized prices.

Prices for goods sold by state enterprises are initially set by sectoral ministries and later approved by the SCRME through contract registration. About 80% of production in Turkmenistan comes from state enterprises.

According to the Law of Turkmenistan on Enterprises, an enterprise shall sell its products, services and production wastes at prices established independently or on a contract basis, or, if stipulated by Turkmen legislation, in accordance with state prices. State regulation of prices is permitted for those products and services that dominate the market. The list of such products and services is determined by the Government. At the same time, the Law of Turkmenistan concerning investment activities sets forth principles of pricing. It provides that the value of products and/or services produced during investment activity is defined on the basis of contract prices and/or prices negotiated through trade and/or auctions. The value of construction services that are financed by the Turkmenistan's state budget is defined on the basis of estimated and indexation.

SALES SERVICE AND CUSTOMER SUPPORT

Upon independence after the breakup of the a former Soviet Union, Turkmenistan inherited a system of very poor sales services provided along with poor quality goods and products at relatively low prices. The first foreign trading companies that entered the Turkmen market in 1991 were pioneers who introduced the practice of competing via quality sales services and prices. Foreign trading companies, primarily Turkish, have been teaching local labor the ways of western standard sales services.

There are no widespread customer support practices used in Turkmenistan. Foreign trading companies and their local distributors provide such customer support services as one-year product guarantees, goods deliveries, and custom-tailored orders for goods and services.

SELLING TO THE GOVERNMENT

Turkmenistan's economy remains largely government owned and controlled. In some sectors, such as oil and gas, electrical energy, and telecommunications, the Government plans to play a controlling role for the foreseeable future. As the privatization process advances, private companies will make up more of the market, but in the short term, most procurement will be done by the GOTX.

So far, most U.S. business activity in Turkmenistan has centered on development of the energy sector and on the sale of U.S. goods to the Government. According to the State Institute of Statistics and Forecasting, in 1998, the export of Turkmen goods to the U.S. was valued at USD 873,600 and the import of U.S. goods into Turkmenistan at USD 73 million. The U.S. exports such goods as food, agricultural equipment, iron products, vehicles, electronic equipment and spare parts, aircraft, helicopters and spare parts, medicine and medical equipment, chemical products, building materials, furniture and other goods to Turkmenistan. So far, direct U.S. investment in the country has been limited. However, it is expected that U.S investment in the oil and gas sector will increase in the near future.

In April 1996, the State Agency for Foreign Investment (SAFI) was established to perform multiple functions related to foreign investment projects as well as large trade credit transactions. SAFI determines the priority given to projects involving foreign traders and investors, evaluates business proposals, reports to the President about the basic aspects of projects under consideration to obtain his approval, arranges international tenders, registers foreign traders and investors, and monitors the implementation of projects. In addition, four State Funds for Development (petroleum and mineral resources; agriculture; transportation and telecommunications; health care and medical industry; and education) have been created to allocate foreign exchange earned by these industries to priority investment projects. To ensure sufficient funding for a particular investment project, SAFI and the Funds cooperate in regulating financial commitments made by Turkmen partners involved in foreign investment projects. A Presidential decree ordered that all trade and investment projects that need foreign credits must receive SAFI's approval before applying for financial support.

Import and export transactions carried out within investment projects and trade credit contracts must be registered with SAFI, the appropriate Fund and the SCRME.

PROTECTING YOUR PRODUCT FROM IPR INFRINGEMENT

On March 1, 1999 the GOTX adopted a Civil Code that regulates IPR ownership in the areas of science, literature, and arts, as well as audio and video record production and distribution. A patent law and a law on legal protection of algorithms, software, databases, and topology of integrated microcircuits have been in effect since 1993 and 1994, respectively. The Patent Agency under the Cabinet of Ministers oversees patent law enforcement only for industrial innovations. No separate state agency supervises IPR issues. Should a case arise, all inquires must be made to the Cabinet of Ministers.

To date, IPR infringement in Turkmenistan has not caused significant losses to U.S. holders of intellectual property rights.

NEED FOR A LOCAL ATTORNEY

There is a lack of skilled legal consulting and auditing services in Turkmenistan. Lack of knowledge of western legal systems, absence of any experience in working with U.S. law firms, limited experience with international law, an undeveloped legal system, and other factors such as the absence of skilled English-speaking lawyers, contribute to this lack.

The State Economic Court of Turkmenistan deals with economic disputes occurring between Turkmen enterprises. Cases with foreign company participation are also in the competence of the Court. However, it is recommended that a U.S. company stipulate international arbitration in any contract when considering doing business in Turkmenistan.

Performing Due Diligence and Checking Bona Fides of Banks, Agents, and Customers

The Government has always been very cautious in establishing business relations with new and little-known foreign companies. Normally, it prefers to deal with well-known names and brands. With only limited experience in locating business partners and suppliers, the government has often relied on an intermediary, usually a small Turkish or American firm, to help find quality products and services overseas.

To gain the trust and confidence of Turkmen Government, small and medium-sized foreign firms must first prove their intentions to do serious long-term business in Turkmenistan. That can mean opening a representative office in Ashgabat, signing a long-term investment contract, or negotiating a state concession for foreign investment.

TRADE AND PROJECT FINANCING

DESCRIPTION OF THE BANKING SYSTEM

The banking system in Turkmenistan is based on a number of basic laws addressing the financial and monetary policy of the state, including the Law on the Central Bank of Turkmenistan, the Law on Commercial Banks and Banking Activity, the Law on Foreign Exchange Regulation, and the Law on the Monetary Unit of Turkmenistan. The banking system consists of the State Central Bank of Turkmenistan; five state banks: the State Bank for Foreign Economic Affairs (also known as Vnesheconombank), the State Commercial Bank "Turkmenistan", the State Commercial Investbank, the State Commercial Daykhanbank, and the State Savings Bank (Sberbank); 4 joint stock commercial banks, and two joint banks with foreign participation. There are the Iranian Commercial Bank "Saderat" and a representative office of Deutsche Bank operating in Ashgabat.

The Central Bank is the National Bank and acts on behalf of the government. According to the Law on the Central Bank, the Bank is independent from any state power and administrative bodies. It is responsible for formulating and conducting monetary and foreign exchange policy; licensing banking activity; supervision and regulation of the banking system; management of international financial reserves of the country; and development of the efficient banking settlement system. The Central Bank is the banker, advisor and fiscal agent of the Cabinet of Ministers. In addition, the Bank is charged with setting interest rates and for administering subsidies to the priority sectors of the economy. The Central Bank is also responsible for running the weekly currency exchange auctions in cooperation with the Foreign Exchange Committee chaired by the Deputy Chairman of the Cabinet of Ministers for Banking and Foreign Exchange. The Interbank Commission, chaired by the same Deputy Chairman, controls foreign exchange circulation and distribution and regulates the activities of commercial banks. The Central Bank is responsible for the supervision of commercial banks. It has implemented a cautious licensing policy and has also closed a number of smaller banks in recent years. The Bank has introduced regulations on banking supervision including: a) a minimum capital requirement of 500 million manat for smaller banks and from 500 million manat to 1 billion manat for larger banks. Branches of foreign banks have a minimum capital requirement of USD 1 million; b) a capital adequacy requirement of 8% of risk-weighed assets, defined in line with internationally accepted standards; c) a liquidity ratio of 30% of liabilities, to be held in cash deposits with the Central Bank, loans receivable within 30 days, or treasury bills; d) a concentration risk ratio, limiting loans to a single borrower to 20% of paid-up capital; and e) loan classification and extension rules based on the duration for which the loan repayment is overdue. The Central Bank received technical assistance in bank supervision from the World Bank and the International Monetary Fund in 2002-1998.

The State Bank for Foreign Economic Affairs (Vnesheconombank) is the key institution for foreign businessmen and investors, as well as local exporters. It dominates import/export and investment operations and is a member of the International Payment Cards Association. The Vnesheconombank has signed an agreement with Standard and Poors concerning awarding Turkmenistan an international sovereign credit rating. Vnesheconombank is the primary fiscal agent for the GOTX that secures financing for all government commercial transactions and handles all foreign exchange operations. Vnesheconombank closely works with SAFI and the state development funds. In 1998, the bank's total assets amounted to USD 1.26 billion. It is the only bank in Turkmenistan that works with VISA cards.

State Commercial Turkmenistan Bank, Investbank, and Daykhanbank focus on certain areas of economic activity; in particular, Turkmenistan Bank deals with financial operations made in social infrastructure; Investbank deals with industrial project financing; and Daykhanbank deals with agricultural transactions. All state entities are ordered to work only with state commercial banks.

Most of the Turkmen commercial banks are small- and medium-sized with almost 100% of the shares in their founding capital belonging to various state enterprises. In addition, the Government has a 50% share in any joint venture with a foreign bank. All banks, including foreign banks, may operate only if they are licensed by the Central Bank of Turkmenistan. Three state commercial banks, the Joint Stock Commercial Senagat Bank, the International Joint Stock Bank of Turkmenistan for Reconstruction, Development and Promotion of Entrepreneurship, the Joint Stock Commercial Garashsyzlyk Bank, the Turkish-Turkmen Joint Commercial Bank, the Russian-Turkmen Joint Stock "Rossiysky Kredit" Bank, and Sberbank have licenses from the Central Bank enabling them to carry out foreign exchange operations.

Turkmenistan has no tradable financial instruments and no non-bank financial institutions, although insurance companies are gradually developing. The commercial banks play only a minor role in financial intermediation and continue to function more as administrators of public sector financial transactions. Manat credits are financed primarily by the Central Bank and are short-term. There continues to be a general lack of confidence in local banks.

FOREIGN EXCHANGE CONTROLS AFFECTING TRADE

In the past, foreign companies doing business in Turkmenistan had difficulty converting the national currency into hard currency. Some companies could not even receive manat coverage for a transaction made in Turkmenistan because of a shortage of both local and hard currency. Therefore, most trade transactions in the past were made on a barter basis (usually, payments were made in cotton). Now, all barter transactions are controlled by the Cabinet of Ministers.

In 2002, the foreign exchange rate became single and unified at 5,300 manat against the dollar and was stable until July 1998. At that time, a gap began to develop between the official rate and the black market rate, which peaked at 19,000 manat per dollar in April 1999 and has been fluctuating between 14,000 and 15,000 manat in July. All domestic trade is done in manat. Foreign companies may convert the manat into hard currency through their commercial banks. There are certain criteria that are taken into consideration when the Central Bank provides foreign

exchange through its Interbank Currency Exchange to meet the commercial banks' needs in hard currency. (See paragraph "Conversion and Transfer Policies" in the Investment Climate Statement.)
The Central Bank licenses foreign exchange operations by commercial banks and guarantees the security of foreign investors' deposits, stocks, securities and other payment documents kept in commercial banks.

General Financing Availability and Terms of Payment

The Central Bank extends credits in manat to the government and banks, and in manat and foreign currency to non-budget ministries and state enterprises. Most of these credits are interest free. The internal financial market in Turkmenistan is heavily supported by the state: state entities hold majority shares in most Turkmen commercial banks. However, due to the tough monetary policy of the Central Bank and general improvements made in banking services, most of the banks have increased their own capital. As a result, commercial banks have activated project or trade financing services. However, there are difficulties that prevent commercial banks from expanding their investment activities. Among the difficulties are a lack of stimulus for long-term investment; inexperience of heads of enterprises in management, and, at times, their failure to honor contracts; lack of a well-established mechanism of debt payment by enterprises; and a shortage of skilled banking specialists. High interest rates for credits are a significant obstacle for local entrepreneurs in expanding their commercial activities.

A few Turkmen commercial banks are experienced in working with letters of credit (Turkmenbank, Investbank, and Senagat Bank). To date, this method of payment has been the safest one. Payment based on actual shipment of goods or work performance is another method used in Turkmenistan. The Government does not allow commercial banks to service transactions on a prepayment term.

To finance large commercial projects involving foreign and Turkmen state companies, the Government uses foreign credits extended by foreign governments and international financial institutions. Vnesheconombank handles all transactions involving foreign credits.

Types of Export and Project Financing and Insurance Available to U.S. Companies

1. The Export-Import Bank of the United States (U.S. EXIM Bank) is an independent U.S. government agency that provides support for U.S. exports through export credit insurance, loan guarantees, direct loans, working capital guarantees, and project financing. The Bank assists only the export of goods and services with at least 50% U.S. content. Under medium- and long-term programs, if the U.S. export product contains foreign-made components, EXIM Bank will cover up to 100% of the U.S. content, provided EXIM Bank's support does not exceed 85% of the export price. Short- and medium-term export credit insurance and project financing are available to Turkmenistan. So far, for short-term transactions, EXIM Bank has been requiring an ILC or guarantee from the Vnesheconombank and extended $424 million to Turkmenistan. In April 1998, EXIM Bank signed a framework agreement on financing creditworthy projects in Turkmenistan. The agreement envisages that the Bank will provide financing for export projects involving private companies without requiring government guarantees, but to date all financing has required government guarantees.

2. The Overseas Private Investment Corporation (OPIC) is a self-sustaining independent agency of the U.S. government that promotes economic growth in developing countries by encouraging U.S. private investment. OPIC facilitates U.S. investment through the following basic programs: financing of investments through direct loans and loan guaranties; insuring investments against political risks; and providing a variety of investor services. In 1993, Turkmenistan signed an OPIC

agreement but, to date, there has been little U.S. direct investment in Turkmenistan and no OPIC program involvement.

3. The International Finance Corporation (IFC), an independent member of the World Bank Group, is the largest source of direct project financing for private investment in developing countries. In the CIS countries, IFC normally invests in projects with a total cost greater than $25 million and requires that a project generate hard currency. In 1996, Turkmenistan joined the International Finance Corporation, but is not a member of the Multilateral Investment Guarantee Agency.

4. The U.S. Trade and Development Agency (TDA) is an independent U.S. government agency that provides non-reimbursable grants for U.S. firms to carry out feasibility studies for both public and private sector projects. In Turkmenistan, TDA has extended grants in the oil and gas, minerals and telecommunications sectors.

5. The European Bank for Reconstruction and Development (EBRD) is a multilateral financial institution that lends and invests exclusively in the countries of Central and Eastern Europe. The bank provides advice, loans, equity investments and debt guarantees in order to foster the transition toward open market-oriented economies and to promote private and entrepreneurial initiative. In Turkmenistan, EBRD has opened a $35 million credit line available for small- and medium-size project financing. The bank has invested its equity in a textile production complex, and arranged tenders for a number of projects in Turkmenistan.

6. Central-Asian American Enterprise Fund (CAAEF) has an office in Ashgabat which provides assistance to businesses through three primary activities: direct investment program including direct investments and loans to qualified private enterprises and start-up ventures; joint ventures; and small business loan program. The Fund's investments range from a minimum of USD 100,000 to a maximum of USD 5,000,000 with both transactions combining both loans and equity. CAAEF also offers various forms of technical assistance, including business plan development, to new private businesses.

7. The U.S. Caspian Finance Center was opened in Ankara, Turkey, to assist American companies to enter the energy rich market of the Caspian region. The center handles businesses of three U.S. trade and finance agencies: U.S. TDA, U.S. EXIM Bank, and OPIC. Working with the commercial and economic officers of the Departments of Commerce and State, the multi-agency trade finance team offers services designed to maintain U.S. commercial interests in the region and better position U.S. firms over foreign competition.

TYPES OF PROJECTS RECEIVING FINANCING SUPPORT

Turkmen official 1998 statistics state that only 2% of total credit extended in the national currency to local state and private enterprises by Turkmen commercial banks were for a term of 5 to 7 years and 98% were short term (from one month to 3 years). It should be noted that, so far, state enterprises have dominated the economic structure of Turkmenistan. Therefore, most credits have been granted to state enterprises. Short-term credits have been provided to primarily small- and medium-size state and private enterprises. About 28.4% of short-term credits covered agricultural production projects, 25.3% industrial production, 6.6% trade transactions, and 2% construction projects.

EBRD has extended an ECU 32 million credit line for small and medium-size enterprises since 1996. It provides hard currency term financing through selected participating banks including Investbank, Senagat Bank, and Garashsyzlyk Bank. Priority is given to industrial, agricultural, textile and various service development projects.

During 1998 and the first half of 1999, Central Asian-American Enterprise Fund disbursed USD 4.3 million to private Turkmen firms through local banks including Daykhanbank, Investbank, Senagat Bank, and Turkmenistan Bank. The CAAEF provides financial support (the preferred size is from USD 50,000 to USD 300,000) to businesses involved in primarily food processing, consumer goods production, services, and light manufacturing.

LIST OF BANKS WITH CORRESPONDENT U.S. BANKING ARRANGEMENTS

Central Bank - Chase Manhattan, New York
- Citibank N.A., New York
- Deutsche Bank, New York

Vnesheconombank - American Express Bank Ltd., New York
- Bank of America Int'l, New York
- Bankers Trust Company, New York
- Bank of New York, New York
- Chase Manhattan Bank, New York
- Chemical Bank, New York
- Citibank N.A., New York
- Credit Lyonnais, New York
- Republic National Bank of New York, New York

Investbank - Bank of America Int'l, New York
- Chase Manhattan Bank, New York
- Citibank N.A., New York and Frankfurt/Main, Germany

Turkmenbank - Citibank N.A., New York
- Bankers Trust Company, New York

Daykhan Bank - Citibank N.A., New York
- Bank of New York, New York
- Chase Manhattan Bank, New York

TURKMENISTANS CUSTOMS: IMPORTANT INFORMATION

FOREIGN TRADE ZONES/FREE PORTS

The Law on Economic Zones for Free Entrepreneurship was enacted in 1993. The law guarantees the rights of businesses — foreign and domestic — to operate in these zones without profit ceilings. The law forbids the nationalization of enterprises operating in the zones and discrimination against foreign investors. Other rights guaranteed include:

-- Preferential tax status, including exemption from profit tax if profits are reinvested in export-oriented, advanced technology enterprises,
-- Repatriation of after-tax profits,
-- Exemption from customs duties, except on product of foreign origin,
-- Export of products, and
-- Set product prices.

There are ten zones in Turkmenistan: Mary-Bayramaly, Ekerem-Hazar, Turkmenabat-Seydi, Bakharly-Serdar, Ashgabat-Anew, Ashgabat-Abadan, Serakhs, Guneshli, Ashgabat International Airport, and Dashoguz Airport. The zones have not been successful in drawing increased economic activity. Despite the legal guarantees, the government continues to meddle in business decisions even for firms located in these zones. The zones have not been financially supported by the government and lack infrastructure, such as advanced telecommunications, to attract businesses. The infrastructure at Ashgabat International Airport is more developed and has modern cargo transit facilities.

CUSTOMS AND DUTIES

Technically, Turkmenistan does not levy tariffs except on imports by individuals. However, in practice, the excise tax system applies higher rates to imported goods than domestic, effectively putting an unspoken tariff in place. Additionally, certain domestic products are exempted from the value-added tax (VAT) and, by special presidential decree, government regulatory agencies have the power to go into certain markets and determine the prices of domestically produced goods and the prices for which importers pay for foreign products. Certain imports from countries outside the rural area are prohibited or require a license. Turkmenistan is not a member of any free trade agreements and is not a member of the Commonwealth of Independent States customs union. It has signed trilateral agreements with Iran and Ukraine, Iran and Armenia, Iran and Bangladesh, and Iran and the Philippines and is pursuing more such agreements. Turkmenistan has most-favored nation status with the United States and Austria. Duties run from 10% to 100%, the average being 30%.

BASIC TRADE REGULATIONS AND STANDARDS

TRADE BARRIERS, INCLUDING TARIFF AND NON-TARIFF BARRIERS

Turkmenistan does not officially apply tariffs to imported goods, with the exception of import by individuals. However, in effect the current excise tax regime sets up excise taxes for certain imported goods but not for their corresponding domestic ones and the excise tax rates for imported goods are higher than those applied on the same domestic products.

Turkmenistan maintains a significant number of non-tariff barriers to trade. Among them is the trade contract and investment project registration requirement. Foreign companies must register with the SCRME and SAFI, the main bodies regulating foreign trade and investment. In addition, there are other agencies that also require registration of contracts and projects for various purposes including Khakimliks (mayor offices), the State Tax Inspectorate, and some sectoral ministries.

The SCRME often creates difficulties for both local and foreign traders. A special Presidential Decree has authorized the SCRME to regulate prices for goods produced in Turkmenistan and exported from the country, and to control implementation of export contracts. The SCRME also sets up prices at which local businesses are allowed to purchase goods from foreign markets and requires them to sell products at prices (not more not less) fixed in contracts registered with this body. Otherwise, businesses can be fined. Such requirements often lead to the import of products and services of low quality. The SCRME also requires goods to be received in country before they can be paid for.

Entities with foreign involvement are required to file documents for registration as legal entities in addition to those set forth for entities without foreign participation. Also, projects with foreign company involvement must obtain authorization from SAFI while projects without foreign participation are not subject to this authorization process. Registration with SAFI is normally a time-consuming process that creates delays in getting goods and services to consumers.

The commercial tax structure which includes the Law on Profit Tax, the Law on VAT, and the Law on Wage Fund Excess Levy, puts foreign investors at a disadvantage relative to domestic investors by making various exemptions applicable to domestic businesses and taxing foreign investors as to certain sources of income. The Law on VAT provides VAT exemptions to a number of domestic companies producing a wide variety of products. On the other hand, such exemptions are not provided to the same imported products. (Note: Beginning July 1, 1998, state and non-state enterprises and agricultural entities are exempted from value added tax payment on part of the profit received from export of goods and services.)

Article 37 of the Law on Hydrocarbon Resources requires contractors in the oil and gas sector to provide preferences to equipment, materials, and finished products made in Turkmenistan if they are competitive in terms of quality, price, operating parameters, and delivery conditions. Such a requirement may create an impediment to foreign investors and traders.

CUSTOMS REGULATIONS

Foreign companies doing business in Turkmenistan consider the Turkmen customs clearance process very complicated, in terms of paper work, and lengthy (sometimes up to 2 months). Requests for bribes have been a typical occurrence in day-to-day customs operations.

To pass through customs, an importer of goods must submit the following documents:

- A trade contract registered with the SCRME. The contract should contain information about quantities and costs in hard currency that will be the basis for the customs valuation;

- A bill of lading with similar information on qualities and costs;

- A customs cargo declaration form that can be obtained in the Ashgabat-Expertisa firm of the Chamber of Commerce of Turkmenistan at the following address:
"Ashgabat-Expertisa" Firm

36 Shevchenko Street
Ashgabat, Turkmenistan 744000
Tel: (993)(12) 47-17-97

- A conformance certificate confirming the quality of delivered goods. The certificate can be obtained from the State Standards Inspectorate at the address below:
State Chief Standards Inspectorate
14 Seidi Street
Ashgabat, Turkmenistan 744000
Tel: (993)(12) 51-14-94, 51-14-32
Fax: (993)(12) 51-04-98

- A certificate of origin.

- A Central Bank document confirming a money transfer for purchasing goods or an irrevocable Letter of Credit.

The customs cargo declaration and bill of lading are only accepted in English or Russian. Other documents can be in Russian. Translated copies must be certified by the Chamber of Commerce. The fee for certification ranges from USD 1 to 2 per page. Faxes and copies are not accepted as official documents by the customs authority.

During the customs clearance process, Customs charges a service fee of 0.2% of the contract cost and 20% of the value added tax assessed on the customs service fee sum.

TARIFF RATES

A March 19, 1999 Presidential decree introduced a 5 percent customs duty for goods imported into Turkmenistan by individuals. The duty is charged against values determined by Turkmen Customs on the basis of world and domestic price information provided quarterly by the State Institute for Statistics and Prognosis. Duties are not charged on goods that have been exported previously from Turkmenistan, declared at Customs and re-imported into the country. Customs also does not charge duty on goods imported as part of passenger personal luggage though the total value of goods included in the passenger personal luggage should not exceed an amount determined by Customs. Food items except for alcohol and tobacco products, medicine and medical items, school appliances, and children's goods are not subject to the customs duties.

Turkmen Customs levies excises on a limited number of exported goods. The list includes:

(1) Pure wool and partial wool yarn USD 100 per ton
(2) Cattle leather:
- leather from cows, camels, bulls, USD 100 per ton
etc.
- leather from sheep and goats USD 0.50 per piece
- non-standard leather USD 50 per ton
(3) Ammonia saltpeter USD 100 per ton
(4) Superphosphate * USD 100 per ton
(5) Ammonium phosphate * USD 100 per ton
(6) Ammonium sulphate * USD 100 per ton
(7) Turkmen sheep-dogs (license USD 300 per dog

required from the Nature Protection
Ministry)

*) Note: All marked products are exempt from excises when sold for hard currency through the State Commodity and Raw Materials Exchange.

Import Taxes Including Value Added Taxes, Purchase Taxes, Uplifts and Surcharges, and Provincial Taxes

In 1996 the Government introduced Customs excises for four categories of goods including alcohol, vehicles, tobacco products, and jewelry made of precious and semi-precious stones and metals. Gradually, the list of goods subject to customs excises has grown to more than one hundred categories of goods. The Government officially claims that there are no customs tariffs charged for export/import of goods by juridical entities, however Turkmen Customs does, in fact, charge customs excises for export/import transactions in accordance with Presidential decrees regulating export/import operations. A Presidential decree of August 18, 1999 approved the updated list of goods subject to excise taxes. This list is effective October 1, 1999.

When considering importing or exporting goods from Turkmenistan, the following should be noted:
- the importation of alcohol into Turkmenistan is licensed by the Ministry of Trade and Foreign Economic Relations;
- goods and products imported in accordance with intergovernmental agreements, governmental decrees and orders, and for the implementation of projects and contracts, including those involving foreign investment, state loans, humanitarian assistance, and products and/or raw materials that are reworked or to which value is added in Turkmenistan, are exempt from excises.
- excises are paid in the national currency, the manat, at a foreign exchange rate determined by the Central Bank of Turkmenistan on the date of contract registration with the State Commodity and Raw Materials Exchange.

According to customs' instruction of February 10, 2002, excises on imports are computed on the basis of one of the following:
(a) the physical volume or weight of goods (in which case the excise rate is set in U.S. dollars); or
(b) trade contract value (in which case the rate is expressed as a percentage), provided the resulting tax equals or exceeds the amount of tax customs would collect under (a).

The following goods imported into Turkmenistan are subject to customs excises:

(1) Eggs 10%
(2) Natural honey 30%
(3) Fresh or cooled potatoes 10%
(4) Tomatoes, peppers, eggplants, cabbage,
cucumbers, onion, garlic 100%
(5) Carrot, turnip, red beet 50%
(6) Legumes 10%
(7) Other vegetables including fresh or 10%
cooled, non-cooked or cooked,
preserved for short time life, dried
wholes or sliced ones
(8) Fruit and nuts 20%
(9) Lemons 50%
(10) Grapes 100%

(11) Watermelons, melons, gourds 100%
(12) Coffee 20%
(13) Wheat (except for seed wheat and 50%, but not less that USD
hard sorts imported by enterprises of 0.12 per kilo
Turkmengalaonumlery company)
(14) Wheat flour 50%, but not less than USD
0.17 per kilo
(15) Other types of wheat except for 10%
wheat and wheat-rye flour
(16) Cereals 10%
(17) Potato flour, cereal, flakes, and 10%
granules
(18) Oil-bearing seeds and fruit and other 10%
seeds and fruit (except for officinal)
(19) Vegetable oils 10%
(20) Confectionery 10%
(21) Chewing gum USD 0.01 per one piece
(22) Cocoa and derivatives 10%
(23) Pasta 50%, but not less than USD
0.50 per kilo
(24) Ready made products of vegetables, 30%
fruit, and nuts
(25) Ice cream 50%, but not less than USD
1.50 per kilo
(26) Mineral water except mineral water 100%
used for medical purposes
(27) Potable water USD 0.2 per liter
(28) Non-alcoholic beverages 50%, but not less than
USD 0.2 per liter
(29) Beer USD 0.50 per liter
(30) Grape wines including USD 1.50 per liter
strong wines, vermouth, and
other grape wines
(31) Ethyl spirit except for spirit USD 4.00 per liter
imported by enterprises of the
State Food Association of Turkmenistan
And the Turkmen Union of Consumer
Cooperation
(32) Alcohol, liquors, and other drinks USD 2.50 per liter
(33) Vinegar and its substitutes 30%
(34) Ground sulphur and brimestone 30%
(35) Cigars including cigars with cut 20%, but not less that USD
ends cigarillos and their substitutes 0.10 per pack
except cigarettes without filters
(36) Tobacco and its substitutes USD 0.25 per pack
(37) Coarse-ground salt 30%
(38) Sea salt 50%
(39) Gypseous and anhydride stone 30%
(40) Cement (M-300 and M-400 types) USD 10 per ton
(41) Natural magnesium sulphate 30%
(epsomit)
(42) Ozocerite 20%
(43) Oil coke 30%
(44) Bitumen 30%

(45) Technical iodine (A type) 30%
(46) Tetrabrominedifeninololpropan 30%
(47) Ferro bromide 20%
(48) Technical carbon K-354 30%
(49) Oxygen 20%
(50) Potassium iodide 30%
(51) Technical sulfur acid 20%
(52) Technical sulfur acid 20%
(53) Carbon dioxide 20%
(54) Technical magnesium chloride 30%
(bishofit)
(55) Sodium sulphate (A and B type) 30%
(56) Aluminum sulphate 20%
(57) Glauber's salt 50%
(58) Tan extracts and dying tannins and 10%
derivatives
(59) Essential oils, perfume, cosmetics, 10%
and other body care products
(60) Soap bars and other washing means
except for "Belizna" bleach 10% but not less than
USD 0.2 per kilo
(61) "Belizna" bleach 30%
(62) Albumen, modified starch, glue, and 10%
ferments except for technical salt
(63) Technical salt 30%
(64) Photo and film products 10%
(65) Plastic products 20%
(66) Rubber items 20%
(67) Leather except for fur and sheep 10%
and lamb skin
(68) Leather goods: saddles and harness, 30%
and travelling items
(69) Natural and artificial fur and fur 20%
items except for astrakhan fur coats
(70) Astrakhan fur coats 100%
(71) Silkworm cocoons 50%
(72) Raw silk 50%
(73) Sheep wool except Sardjinskaya, 50%
Merenosnaya and Angora wool
(74) Cotton yarn (all sizes) 100%
(75) Cotton fabric (coarse calico) 100%
(76) Denim fabric 100%
(77) Cotton wool except for medical 100%
cotton wool
(78) Quilted cotton wool for furniture 50%
(79) Cotton sheet wadding 50%
(80) Hand made carpets, koshmas and other 150%
floor covers
(81) Yurtas 150%
(82) Machine-made wool carpets, rugs 50%
and carpet items
(83) Machine-made partial wool carpets, 50%
rugs and carpet items
(84) Machine-made synthetic carpets, 50%

rugs and carpet items
(85) Strips of cotton carpets 50%
(86) Special fabrics, fabrics with nap, 10%
laces, and tapestry
(87) Textile materials, impregnated, 10%
with coating, or duplicated fabrics
processed with special materials
(88) Knitted cotton fabric of all types 100%
(89) Knitted garments except for knitted 20%
cotton garments for adults, knitted
cotton underwear, knitted cotton
women's pajamas, knitted cotton
men's jersey and sweaters, and
children's garment
(90) Cotton underwear 50%
(91) Knitted cotton women's pajamas 50%
(92) Knitted cotton men's jersey or 50%
sweaters
(93) Knitted cotton outer-clothing for 100%
adults except for high-bulk yarn
(94) Textile garment except for special 20%
garment made of cotton and denim
fabrics, denim trousers, cotton robes,
cotton mittens, and children's clothing
(95) Cotton and denim clothing used for 100%
industrial and agricultural work
except for clothing made of tarpaulin
material and other fabrics processed
with special materials
(96) Denim trousers 50%
(97) Cotton robes except for terry robes 100%
(98) Cotton mittens 100%
(99) Other ready made textile items, sets, 20%
second hand clothing, and rags except
for cotton bed clothing
(100) 100% cotton bed clothes 50%
(101) Beach shoes made of polyvenilcloride 50%
and Asian galoshes moulded of rubber
(except for varnished and gummed
galoshes)
(102) Shoes 20%
(103) Head-dresses and accessories 10%
(104) Umbrellas, walking sticks, whips, and 10%
accessories
(105) Processed feather and down, feather 20%
and down items, artificial flowers
(106) Items made of stone, gypsum, cement, 10%
asbestos, mica and other similar
materials except for slates
(107) Slate USD 20 per one thousand
of conditional slab
(108) Ceramic items 10%
(109) Window glass with 3-4 millimeter USD 1 per square meter
thickness except for shaded, reinforced

and patterned glass
(110) Crystal items 20%
(111) Jewelry made of precious and semi- 25%
precious stones and metals, plated with
precious metals, or natural and
cultivated pearls or precious and
semi-precious stones
(112) Cauldrons with a capacity of up 100 50%
liters
(113) Enameled bowls with a capacity of 30%
up to 2 liters
(114) Enameled mugs with a capacity of 30%
0.4 to 1 liter
(115) Gas stoves 20%
(116) Aluminum teapots 50%
(117) Saws of PMP00183 type 100%
(118) Saws of 4AP05002 type 100%
(119) Pouring equipment of USN-175 type 10%
(120) Equipment of USN-175 and USNPn-175 30%
(121) Internal combustion engine designed USD 0.15 per cubic centimeter
for vehicles of 8703 type of engine capacity
(122) Engine spare parts for vehicles of 10%
8703 type
(123) Fans (VG-70, VG-50, ZVG-25, VG-70 30%
without engine, and VG-50 without
engine types)
(124) Rotor (V16VG-70 type) 30%
(124) Air conditioning system with fan 10%
installed in it
(125) Dough, pastry mixing equipment 20%
(TMM-1M)
(126) Cream mixing machines of MV-60 20%
and MV-35 types
(127) Drilling equipment (BPR-70) 10%
(128) Electrical batteries 15%
(129) Electromechanical home appliances 10%
(130) Electrical equipment used for internal 10%
combustion engines
(131) Electrical telephone and telegraph 10%
equipment for wire communications
(132) Tape-recorders 10%
(133) Video-recorders and video-players 10%
(134) Receivers for radio-telephone and 10%
radio-telegraph communications
(135) Television receivers including 10%
video-monitors and video-projectors
(136) Lamp holders, sockets, switch 30%
outlets
(137) Non-isolated cord for electricity
transmission lines 30%
(138) Cord for connection with electrical 30%
appliances
(139) Cable for signalization and block 30%
system

(140) Conductors, cord, one-strand cable 30%
with plastic isolation
and section of 50 to 120 square
millimeters, radio cord, control cable,
adjusting cord, cable and cord for
radiofication and communications,
non-isolated supply cord, telephone
cable
(141) Sleeve and piston for engine A-01 50%
(142) Oil heaters PP-0.63 50%
(143) Automobiles:
- with engine capacity up to 2,000 cc USD 0.25 per one cc of engine capacity
- with engine capacity 2,000 cc or USD 0.60 per one cc of
greater engine capacity
(144) Chassis 15%
(145) Body including cab for cars of 8703 15%
type
(146) Spare parts and equipment for cars of 15%
8703 type
(147) Motor cycle and motorized bicycle 15%
(148) Trailers 15%
(149) Yacht, boats and gigs 10%
(150) Photo camera, photo flash, and photo 10%
equipment
(151) Copying machines 10%
(152) Watch, watch belts, and bracelets 10%
(153) Furniture 10%
(154) Mattress, blanket, and cotton pillow 100%
(155) Arts, collection items, and antiquary 50%

*) Note that spirits imported by the State Food Association and Turkmen Union of Consumer Cooperation (Turkmenpotrebsoyuz), except for spirits imported by these organizations on consignment basis and/or as products and/or raw materials that are reworked or to which value is added in Turkmenistan, are not subject to excises.

Foreign and domestic legal entities and individuals must pay Value Added Tax for the import and export of goods. The VAT rate for import/export is 20%. According to regulations, the following goods are exempt from payment of VAT:

- goods for official use by foreign diplomatic representations or similar organizations and for private use of the diplomatic and administrative-operating staff of these representations as well, including the members of their families who live with them;
- goods sold by manufacturing enterprises or associations of blind and deaf people;
- goods produced and sold by the medical-productive workshops within psychiatric hospitals and public organizations of disabled people;
- goods produced and sold by enterprises, organizations and institutions where the number of disabled people is not less than 50% of total staff;
- enterprises and organizations of all types of property at all stages of production and sale (excluding export delivery) of flour, bread, rolls and buns, macaroni, grouts, including rice, mixed feed, milk, sour milk products, curds, sour cream, cream, brynza, cheese, ice-cream, oil butter, meat and meat products, including tinned foods, sausage products of all kinds, fish products (excluding delicacy ones), confectionery, baby food, salt, tea, sugar, and medicaments.

VAT applies on the total value of the registered contract plus customs excise taxes, and plus customs processing fee.

IMPORT/EXPORT LICENSE REQUIREMENTS

Issued in November 1994, a presidential decree outlines two separate sets of goods whose import and/or export must be licensed by the President and the Cabinet of Ministers. The following is the list of goods where import or export is controlled by the President:

1. Arms and military equipment and special items used for military production and services;
2. Gunpowder, explosive substances, explosive and pyrotechnic devices;
3. Radioactive materials, technology, equipment and installations, special non-nuclear materials and radioactive wastes;
4. Precious metals and alloys, ores, scrap material and wastes;
5. Precious stones and items including wastes, powder, recuperation of precious stones, pearls and amber;
6. Narcotics;
7. Special kinds of raw materials, equipment, technology and scientific information used for arms and military equipment production;
8. Materials, equipment and technology ostensibly produced for peaceful purposes but which may be used for production of nuclear, chemical and other kinds of weapons of mass destruction;
9. Investment abroad;
10. Export of scientific and research works, expertise and innovations; and
11. Poisons (except those that are included in the list below).

The Cabinet of Ministers licenses export or import of the following goods:

1. Chemicals;
2. Poisons;
3. Industrial wastes;
4. Turkmen national jewelry;
5. Cultural valuables;
6. Ancient printed products and manuscripts;
7. Archaeological findings;
8. Numismatics;
9. Art pieces;
10. Collections of materials on mineralogy and biology;
11. Central Asian sheep-dogs;
12. Ahalteke horses;
13. Pedigreed cattle;
14. Wild animals;
15. Wild plants, bones of fossil animals, ivory, horns, hoofs, corals and other such materials; and
16. Information about energy resources and minerals broken down according to regions and fields located throughout the territory of Turkmenistan and within the continental shelf and offshore zone.

The Ministry of Trade and Resources issues licenses for the import of alcohol.

The Precious Stone and Metal Fund under the Central Bank of Turkmenistan provides licenses for export and/or import of precious stones and metals.

SPECIAL IMPORT/EXPORT REQUIREMENTS AND CERTIFICATIONS

The SCRME is authorized to issue import/export licenses for all commercial transactions involving foreign participation.

To register direct trade contracts not involved in auctioning at the SCRME, three original copies of the contract along with a product quality certificate and a document confirming product availability must be submitted to the SCRME.

Goods that are auctioned at the SCRME can be exported from or imported into Turkmenistan without licensing.

To register a contract for selling or purchasing goods at the SCRME, an application should be submitted at least five days prior to the sale or purchase. The application must contain information about the goods: quantity, price, place of origin and current location, terms of delivery and payment and the seller's contact information. In addition, the following documents must be submitted: a product quality certificate issued by the producer of goods offered for sale; a written confirmation of product availability issued by the seller; and a guarantee document containing the date and terms for delivery of goods in Turkmenistan. A buyer must present a bank confirmation of sufficient funds to cover the cost of the goods.

Contracts concluded on the basis of clearing agreements, trade credits and investment barters (as well as those entailing the import of a part of joint venture capital goods, and charitable donations) must also be registered with the SCRME.

With the exception of cotton, all goods imported into and exported from Turkmenistan must be certified as adhering to quality standards determined by the State Chief Standards Inspectorate. The process of obtaining the certificate of conformity is complicated and requires testing of imported and exported goods by the Standards Inspectorate. A fee up to 0.5% of the total value of goods to be certified is collected. The time to obtain a certificate of conformity ranges form 7 days to 30 days depending on the type of product and the time required for testing. Imported goods are placed in a bonded warehouse until the certificate of conformity is obtained.

All certificates issued by certificate bodies accredited by other CIS countries for goods originating in that CIS country are accepted by Turkmenistan. Those countries that signed a bilateral agreement on acceptance of national state certificates may enjoy mutually simplified procedures on issuing conformance certificates for imported/exported goods. There is no such agreement signed between Turkmenistan and the U.S. The fee for recognition of a foreign certificate is USD 25 (paid in manats).

A certificate of origin is required for all imported and exported goods. The customs authorities accept certificates of origin for import if they are issued by designated bodies of the exporting country (e.g. Chamber of Commerce).

Beginning May 1, 1998, the GOTX introduced a sanitary certification requirement for imported food products. The State Sanitary and Epidemiological Inspectorate (SSEI) was assigned to oversee enforcement. Radiological, radiochemical and chemical tests of imported food products must be made by the SSEI which then issues certificates provided that an appropriate document confirming product quality and issued by the country of product origin is presented. If such a document is not available, imported food products will be tested in the Central Laboratory of Hygiene and Epidemiology.

Raw and ginned cotton to be exported from Turkmenistan is certified by the Cotton Inspectorate under the State Cotton Association.

Turkmenistan does not have any Preshipment Inspection arrangement.

LABELING REQUIREMENTS

So far, Turkmenistan has not introduced any restrictive packaging or labeling standard rules. However, due to the hot climatic conditions in summer, the government requires that labels for all food products, especially perishables, contain production and expiration dates. Also, the conformance certificates for food products must be accompanied with the product description in Russian language. Spirits and wines must be in glass bottles (plastic bottles are not accepted).

PROHIBITED IMPORTS

The Government has developed a list of goods that cannot be imported into Turkmenistan. The list includes the following items:

(1) Handmade wool rugs (named Koshma)
(2) Yurtas
(3) Handmade carpets
(4) Astrakhan pelts

FREE TRADE ZONES/WAREHOUSES

According to the Law on Free Economic Zones, a special customs regime that includes duty free treatment for goods and property imported into and exported from free economic zones, with the exception of exported goods of foreign origin, is provided in the free economic zones. All goods and properties must be declared when imported into or exported from free economic zones.

MEMBERSHIP IN FREE TRADE AGREEMENTS

Turkmenistan is not a member of any free trade arrangements and is not a member of the CIS Customs Union. It has signed trilateral trade agreements with Iran and the Ukraine, Iran and Armenia, Iran and Bangladesh, Iran and the Philippines, and Iran and India and is interested in concluding more such trilateral agreements. In 1993, Turkmenistan signed and ratified a Most Favored Nation Trade Agreement with the United States, however, a dual tax treaty and bilateral investment treaty have not been signed yet. Turkmenistan is not a member of the World Trade Organization.

CUSTOMS CONTACT INFORMATION

Mr. Meret Khalovezov, Chairman
State Customs
7 Sona Muradova Street
Ashgabat, Turkmenistan 744000
Tel: (993)(12)47-02-21, 47-04-56
Fax: (993)(12)47-04-77

Mr. Kurbangeldy Durdyev, Head
Ashgabat Customs Office (automobile and railway cargo deliveries)
7 Sona Muradova Street

Ashgabat, Turkmenistan 744000
Tel: (993)(12) 47-05-00, 47-02-09
Fax: (993)(12) 47-00-45

Customs Post "Ashgabat-Cargo"
Tel: (993)(12) 32-18-97, 32-16-47, 32-20-95

Customs Post "Khova Yollary" (air transportation)
Ashgabat Airport
Tel: (993)(12) 33-00-98, 51-14-73, 51-01-59
Fax: (993)(12) 51-01-59, 51-01-25

TRADE BARRIERS, INCLUDING TARIFFS, NON-TARIFF BARRIERS AND IMPORT TAXES

The GOTX imposes excise taxes on certain goods imported into and exported from Turkmenistan. In February 1998, a Presidential Decree approved an updated list of those goods.

When considering importing or exporting goods from Turkmenistan, the following should be considered:

-- the importation of alcohol into Turkmenistan is licensed by the Ministry of Trade and Resources; -- goods and products imported in accordance with intergovern- mental agreements, governmental decrees and orders, and for the implementation of projects and contracts, including those involving foreign investment, state loans, and humanitarian assistance, are exempt from excise taxes. In addition, the raw materials and/or semi-finished products imported into Turkmenistan with a purpose of further processing as well as finished and/or semi-finished goods and products made of these raw materials and exported from Turkmenistan are also exempt from excise taxes. -- excises are paid in the national currency, the manat, at a foreign exchange rate determined by the Central Bank of Turkmenistan on the date of contract registration with the State Commodity and Raw Materials Exchange.

According to customs rules issued on February 10, 2002, excise taxes on imports are computed on the basis of one of the following:

(a) the physical volume or weight of goods (in which case the excise rate is set in U.S. dollars); or
(b) trade contract value (in which case the excise rate is expressed as a percentage), provided the resulting tax equals or exceeds the amount of tax customs would collect under (a).

The following goods imported into Turkmenistan are subject to excise taxes:

(1) Beer $0.50 per liter
(2) Grape wines including strong wines $1.00 per liter
(3) Vermouth, other grape wines $1.50 per liter
(4) Alcohol, liquors, other drinks $1.50 per liter
(5) Coarse-ground salt 30% of contract price
(6) Mineral water except mineral water 100% used for medical purposes
(7) Beverages: from September through March 50% from April through August 30%
(8) Ice cream 50%, but not less than $1.50 per kilo, beginning June 1, 1998
(9) Macaroni 50%, but not less than 0.50 per kilo
(10) Tomato paste 30%

(11) Preserved tomatoes 50%
(12) Tomato juice 50%
(13) Pickled, sour cabbage 50%
(14) Cherry-plum, plum, apple compotes 30%
(15) Apple, plum, cherry-plum jam 30%
(16) Apple, carrot, pumpkin, melon jam 50%
(17) Pickled eggplants 30%
(18) Pickled beets 30%
(19) Watermelons, melons, gourds 100%
(20) Grapes 100%
(21) Fresh vegetables including tomatoes, peppers, eggplants, cabbage, cucumbers, onion, garlic 100%
(22) Lemons 50%
(23) Cigars including cigars with cut ends, cigarillos and their substitutes except cigarettes without filters 20%, but not less than $0.10 per pack
(24) Tobacco and its substitutes $0.25 per pack
(25) Jewelry made of precious and semi- precious stones and metals, plated with precious metals, or natural and cultivated pearls or precious and semi-precious stones 10%
(26) Automobiles: -- with engine capacity up to 2,000 cc $0.25 per one cc of engine capacity -- with engine capacity 2,000 cc or greater $0.35 per one cc of engine capacity
(27) Cotton fabric (coarse calico) 100% (28) Denim fabric 100%
(29) Cotton yarn (all sizes) 100%
(30) Knitted cotton fabric 100%
(31) Knitted cotton garments 100%
(32) Knitted cotton men's jersey or sweaters 30%
(33) Knitted cotton women's pajamas 30%
(34) Cotton robes except for terry robes 100%
(35) Cotton terry towels 20% (36) 100% cotton bed linens 50%
(37) Cotton underwear 50%
(38) Denim trousers 50%
(39) Mattresses, blankets, cotton pillows 100%
(40) Cotton mittens 100%
(41) Cotton and denim clothing used for industrial and agricultural work except for clothing made of tarpaulin material or other fabrics processed with special materials 100%
(42) Cotton wool except for medical cotton wool 100% wool
(43) Cotton sheet wadding 50%
(44) Quilted cotton wool for furniture 50%
(45) Strips of cotton carpets 50%
(46) Machine-made wool carpets, rugs and carpet items 50% (47) Machine-made partial wool carpets, rugs and carpet items 50%
(48) Machine-made synthetic carpets, rugs and carpet items 50%
(49) Astrakhan fur coats 100%
(50) Sheep wool except sardjinskaya, merenosnaya and angora wool 50%
(51) Raw silk 50%
(52) Silkworm cocoons 50%
(53) Lamp holders, sockets, switch outlets 30%
(54) Window glass with 3-4 milli- meter thickness except for shaded, reinforced and patterned glass $1 per square
(55) Cauldrons with 3,5,9,15,25, 50 and 100 liter capacity 50%
(56) Aluminum teapots 50%
(57) Enameled bowls with a capacity of up to 2 liters 30%
(58) Enameled mugs with a capacity of 0.4 to 1 liter 30%
(59) Gas stoves 20%
(60) Saws of PMP00183 type 100%

(61) Saws of 4AP05002 type 100%
(62) Cream mixing machines of MV-60 and MV-35 types 20%
(63) Pouring equipment (USN-175 type) 10%
(64) Drilling equipment (BPR-70) 10%
(65) Dough, pastry mixing equipment (TMM-1M) 20%
(66) Carbon dioxide 20%
(67) Technical sulfur acid 20%
(68) Aluminum sulfate 20%
(69) Oxygen 20%
(70) Ferro bromide 20%
(71) Ozocerite 20%
(72) Technical carbon K-354 30%
(73) Sodium sulfate (A and B type) 30%
(74) Technical magnesium chloride (bishofit) 30%
(75) Natural magnesium sulfate (epsomit) 30%
(76) Glauber's salt 50%
(77) Potassium iodide 30%
(78) Technical iodine (A type) 30%
(79) Tetrabrominedifeninololpropan 30%
(80) "Belizna" bleach 30%
(81) Sea salt 50%
(82) Gypseous and anhydride stone 30%
(83) Oil coke 30%
(84) Bitumen 30%
(85) Sulfur 30% (86) Technical salt 30%
(87) Fans (VG-70, VG-50, ZVG-25 types) 30% (88) Equipment (USN-175 type) 30%
(89) Rotor (V16VG-70 type) 30%
(90) Conductors (types: APV-4, APV-6, APV-12 APV-16, APV-25, APV-35, APV-50, APPV-2*4) 30%
(91) Cord 30% (92) Cable (types: AVVG-2*4, AVVG-3*4, AVVG-4*4, AVVG-4*6, ACCG-4*10, AVVG-4*16, AVVG-4*25, AVVG-4*35 15%
(93) Radio cord PRPPM-2*0.9 15%
(94) Control cable AKVVG-4*2.5 15%
(95) Cement (M-300 and M-400 types) $5 per ton
(96) Slate $20 per one thousand of conditional slab

THE GOVERNMENT LEVIES EXCISE TAXES ON A LIMITED NUMBER OF EXPORTED GOODS.

The list includes:

(1) Pure wool and partial wool yarn $100 per ton
(2) Cattle leather: -- leather from cows, camels, bulls, etc. $100 per ton -- leather from sheep and goats $0.50 per piece -- non-standard leather $50 per ton
(3) Ammonia saltpeter $100 per ton
(4) Superphosphate * $100 per ton
(5) Ammonium phosphate * $100 per ton
(6) Ammonium sulphate * $100 per ton
(7) Turkmen sheep-dogs (license required from the Nature Protection Ministry) $300 per dog

) Note: all marked products are exempt from excise taxes when sold for hard currency through the State Commodity and Raw Materials Exchange. Trade contracts for the export of these products, if registered with the SCRME before March 1, 1998, are also exempt from excise tax payments.

CUSTOMS VALUATION

To pass through customs, an importer of goods must submit the following documents: -- A trade contract registered with the SCRME. The contract should contain information about quantities and costs in hard currency that will be the basis for the customs valuation; -- A bill of lading with similar information on qualities and costs; -- A customs declaration form that can be obtained in the Ashgabat-Expertisa firm of the Chamber of Commerce of Turkmenistan at the following address:

"Ashgabat-Expertisa" Firm 17 Baymukhamed Batyrov Street Ashgabat, Turkmenistan 744000 Tel: [9](9312) 35-13-52, 35-53-26

-- A conformance certificate confirming the quality of delivered goods. The certificate can be obtained from the State Standards Inspectorate at the address below:

State Chief Standards Inspectorate 14 Seidi Street Ashgabat, Turkmenistan 744000 Tel: [9](9312) 51-14-94, 51-14-32 Fax: [9](9312) 51-04-98

The Cotton Inspectorate under the State Cotton Association issues a separate conformance certificate for cotton exported from Turkmenistan. -- A Central Bank document confirming a money transfer for pur- chasing goods or an irrevocable Letter of Credit.

During the customs clearance process, Customs charges a service fee of 0.2% of the contract cost and 20% of the value added tax assessed on the customs service fee sum.

THE CABINET OF MINISTERS LICENSES EXPORT OR IMPORT OF THE FOLLOWING GOODS:

1. Chemicals;
2. Poisons;
3. Industrial wastes;
4. Turkmen national jewelry;
5. Cultural valuables;
6. Ancient printed products and manuscripts;
7. Archaeological findings;
8. Numismatics;
9. Art pieces;
10. Collections of materials on mineralogy and biology;
11. Middle Asian sheep-dog; 12. Ahalteke horses;
13. Pedigree cattle;
14. Wild animals;
15. Wild plants, bones of fossil animals, ivory, horns, hoofs, corals and other such materials; and
16. Information about energy resources and minerals broken down according to regions and fields located throughout the territory of Turkmenistan and within the continental shelf and offshore zone.

The Ministry of Trade and Resources issues licenses for the import of alcohol. The Precious Stone and Metal Fund under the Central Bank of Turkmenistan provides licenses for export or import of precious stones and metals.

To promote the export of Turkmen goods, a special Presidential Decree has authorized the State Commodity and Raw Materials Exchange to regulate prices for goods produced in Turkmenistan and exported from the country, and to control implementation of export contracts. Also, beginning July 1, 1998, state and non-state enterprises and agricultural entities are exempted from value added tax payment on part of the profit received from export of goods and services.

IMPORT/EXPORT DOCUMENTATION REQUIREMENTS

The SCRME is authorized to issue import/export licenses for all commercial transactions involving foreign participation.

To register direct trade contracts that are not involved in auctioning at the SCRME, three original copies of the contract along with a product quality certificate and a document confirming product availability must be submitted to the SCRME.

Those goods that are auctioned at the SCRME can be exported from or imported into Turkmenistan without licensing.

To register a contract for selling or purchasing goods at the SCRME, an application should be submitted at least five days prior to the sale or purchase. The application must contain information about the goods: quantity, prices, place of origin and current location, terms of delivery and payment and the seller's contact information. In addition, the following documents must also be submitted: a product quality certificate issued by the producer of goods offered for sale; a written confirmation of product avail- ability issued by the seller; and a guarantee document containing the date and terms for delivery of goods in Turkmenistan. A buyer must present a bank confirmation of sufficient funds to cover the cost of the goods.

Contracts and treaties concluded on the basis of clearing agree- ments, trade credits and investment barters (as well as those entailing the import of a part of joint venture capital goods, and charitable donations) must also be registered with the SCRME.

TEMPORARY ENTRY

According to Turkmenistan's Law on Foreign Investment, goods and properties that are imported temporarily and used for personal needs are exempted from customs duty payments. (Note that there are no customs duties levied in Turkmenistan.) The GOTX has been developing regulations on temporary entry requirements which will probably be in effect in 1998.

Current rules on temporary entry require that excise taxes be levied on goods and properties that will be used in Turkmenistan for one year and then exported from the country. However, the excise taxes levied will be paid back upon exporting the goods from Turkmenistan.

STANDARDS, LABELING AND MARKING REQUIREMENTS

Turkmenistan joined the International Standard Association in 1991, and, in 1992, began to adhere to the Interstate Council on Standard, Metrology and Certification that covers CIS countries. Also, Turkmenistan became a member of the International Standard Organi- zation (ISO) in 1993 and signed bilateral agreements on cooperation with the National Standard Agencies of Turkey and Iran. Inter- governmental agreements on standards, metrology and certification have been signed with Uzbekistan, Armenia and Georgia. Presently, the Turkmen conformance certificate is accepted in 14 countries.

Turkmenistan has developed "national standards" for locally produced goods. Since Turkmenistan is a member of the ISO, Turkmen national standards are developed to meet international standards requirements. As part of the CIS, Turkmenistan has accepted General Interstate Standards (GOST) and Technical Standards (TS), developed in accordance with an agreement reached between 12 CIS countries. Most of the GOST standards incorporate former Soviet Union standards.

With the exception of cotton, all goods imported into and exported from Turkmenistan must be certified as adhering to quality standards determined by the State Chief Standards Inspectorate. Those countries that signed bilateral agreement on acceptance of national state certificates may enjoy mutually simplified procedures on issuing conformance certificates for imported/exported goods. There is no such agreement signed between Turkmenistan and the U.S. So far, Turkmenistan has not introduced any restrictive packaging or labeling standard rules. However, due to the hot climatic conditions in summer, the government requires that labels for all food products, especially perishables, must contain production and expiration dates. Also, the conformance certificates for food products must be accompanied with the product description in Russian language.

Beginning May 1, 1998, the GOTX introduced a sanitary certification requirement for food products imported into Turkmenistan. The State Sanitary and Epidemiological Inspectorate (SSEI) was assigned to oversee enforcement. The radiological, radiochemical and chemical tests of imported food products must be made by the SSEI which then issues certificates provided that an appropriate document confirming product quality and issued by the country of product origin is presented. If such a document is not available, imported food products will be tested in the Central Laboratory of Hygiene and Epidemiology.

Raw and ginned cotton to be exported from Turkmenistan is certified by the Cotton Inspectorate under the State Cotton Association.

ENTRY/EXIT REQUIREMENTS

American citizens must have a valid passport and visa to enter and exit Turkmenistan. To apply for a visa, all U.S. citizens must complete an application and have a letter of invitation approved by the State Agency for the Registration of Foreigners (SARF) in Ashgabat. An individual or organization in Turkmenistan must submit the letter of invitation on behalf of an American citizen to the SARF. The SARF requires at least ten working days for approval. The U.S. Embassy in Ashgabat does not issue letters of invitation to citizens interested in private travel to Turkmenistan. Applications for a Turkmen visa can be submitted to the Turkmen Embassy in Washington, D.C. or directly to the SARF in Ashgabat. A traveler with a stamped and approved invitation letter may also obtain a visa at the Ashgabat International Airport upon arrival in Turkmenistan.

The price for the visa will vary according to the intended length of stay. For an additional charge the SARF can extend a visa in Ashgabat from its initial validity. Any traveler arriving without a visa or without the needed documents to obtain a visa will be denied entry and may be held at the airport or border until the traveler has secured transportation out of Turkmenistan. Travelers departing Turkmenistan must have a valid visa or they will be denied exit until they extend the validity of the visa. In addition, U.S. citizens traveling in Turkmenistan should be aware that they may need special permission from the SARF to travel to areas of the country that have been restricted by the Government of Turkmenistan.

Upon arrival at an airport or border entry point, foreigners will be charged $10 for an immigration card issued by Turkmen authorities. All foreigners are required to carry this immigration card for the duration of their stay in Turkmenistan. Authorities upon departure will collect the immigration card.

There are also local Turkmen registration requirements. Americans who plan to stay more than three working days in Turkmenistan must register with the SARF. SARF offices are located in all of Turkmenistan's five major cities: Ashgabat, Dashoguz, Mary, Turkmenabat and Turkmenbashi. One day prior to departure, foreigners must return to an SARF office to register their departure. Foreigners who fail to register their departure may be prevented from leaving until they have done so. The penalties for remaining in Turkmenistan with an expired visa and for failing to register with SARF include fines and arrest. Foreigners may also be deported and not allowed to return to Turkmenistan for up to five years. American citizens in Turkmenistan are strongly urged to ensure that their Turkmen visas do not expire and that they register with SARF upon arrival and upon departure.

Visitors holding tourist visas organized by a travel agency must stay in hotels; other visitors may stay in private accommodations whose owner must register the visitor's presence.

SAFETY AND SECURITY

Those considering travel to Turkmenistan should take the country's proximity to regions of past and current instability into account before making any plans. The Government of Turkmenistan has designated many areas throughout the country as "restricted zones," particularly the border areas next to Iran, Uzbekistan, and Afghanistan, the entire region of Dashoguz, Dashoguz city, and areas of the Caspian coast. Travel to these areas is forbidden without special permission from the Government of Turkmenistan. Turkmen Air, the national airline, will not sell a ticket to any traveler who intends to travel to a "restricted zone" without proof of permission from the Government. Travelers who wish to visit a "restricted zone" must have a valid passport and visa and must apply to the Ministry of Foreign Affairs for permission. There is a minimum processing time of 10 working days.

Visible police and military presence in Turkmenistan is common. Both uniformed and plainclothes officials frequently ask to see passports, visas, migration cards, and SARF registrations. Travelers should ask to see identification if they are not certain that the person requesting the information is an official. In addition to the questioning of foreigners, home and vehicle searches are common. Security personnel maintain checkpoints on major roads.

Security personnel may at times place foreign visitors under surveillance. Hotel rooms, telephones, and fax machines may be monitored, and personal possessions in hotel rooms may be searched. Taking photographs of anything that could be perceived as being of military or security interest, such as government buildings, may result in problems with authorities.

Supporters of extremist groups such as the Islamic Movement of Uzbekistan, Al-Qaeda, and the Eastern Turkistan Islamic Movement remain active in Central Asia. These groups have expressed anti-U.S. sentiments and may attempt to target U.S. Government or private interests in the region, including in Turkmenistan. Terrorists do not distinguish between official and civilian targets. Because of increased security at official U.S. facilities, terrorists are seeking softer civilian targets such as residential areas, clubs, restaurants, places of worship, hotels, schools, outdoor recreation events, resorts, beaches, maritime facilities, and commercial aircraft.

For additional regional security information concerning Central Asia, U.S. citizens should refer to the Public Announcements for Central Asia and the Kyrgyz Republic, the Travel Warning for Uzbekistan, and the Consular Information Sheets, for Kazakhstan, the Kyrgyz Republic, Tajikistan and Uzbekistan. The U.S. Embassy in each of these countries can provide up-to-date information about local crime and safety issues. Information about how to contact each Embassy directly is available on the Internet at the Consular Affairs home page, http://www.travel.state.gov

STANDING GUARD OVER THE NATIONAL INTERESTS AND STABILITY

In the first year of independence – on November 4, 1991 the President of Turkmenistan issued the decree "On the Customs Committee under the Government of Turkmenistan". The history of the establishment and development of the national customs services began on that day. In the following years a number of the statutory acts and the Customs Code of Turkmenistan were adopted.

From the earliest days of independence the priority tasks of the customs services of Turkmenistan were defined as to ensure the protection of national economic interests, to strengthen the law and order in the customs territories and to train well-qualified customs specialists.

Nowadays, the State Customs Service of Turkmenistan includes over 1,000 officers, 8 customs agencies and about 50 custom offices and check-points.

The aims of the national customs services stipulated in the legislative and statutory acts are to take measures to prevent contraband and violation of the customs rules. With this aim in view the special agencies charged with organizing and monitoring this activity were established. The officials exercising the customs supervision of goods and transport vehicles on the borders and examination at the custom authorities in the destinations play the crucial role in impediment to contraband and violation of the customs rules. The officers' practical experience and professional training as well as technical equipment of customs offices condition progress in the field.

The key priorities of the national customs services are to apply advanced information technologies and improve the material and technical and methodological base of personnel training. The training courses are established under the State Customs Service of Turkmenistan to improve the professional level of Turkmen customs officers. The specialists of the national customs agencies made the trips to the USA, Great Britain, Germany, Austria, Belgium, Japan, China and other countries to study the international customs practice and to participate in the international symposiums and seminars.

Implementing the conception on Turkmenistan's foreign-economic activity the State Customs Service elaborated the package of the statutory acts in compliance with the new tariff legislation focusing on the technique, rules, provisions and regulations on the customs procedure of inspecting foreign commodities and other goods exported (imported) by citizens.

Being aware of the importance of establishing co-operation with customs agencies in other countries Turkmenistan concluded a number of the agreements regulating international customs relations, concerted efforts in the struggle against the violations of customs rules, contraband and other customs issues.

The legal basis of the fight against terrorism in Turkmenistan is represented by the Constitution of Turkmenistan, the decisions of Halk Maslakhaty, the Criminal Code, the Law of Turkmenistan "On Terrorism", other laws, the resolutions and decrees of the President of Turkmenistan, the universally recognized principles and norms of the international law, the international treaties as well as the statutory acts of the respective government agencies adopted in compliance with the international requirements.

The technological schemes and methodical recommendations used for inspecting vehicles and commodities, training customs officials in the inspection methods, analyzing the means of concealing and trafficking contraband were elaborated. The projects on extensive technical assistance to the customs agencies in preventing contraband trade are implemented in the country.

To reform the national customs system through simplifying and harmonizing the customs procedures, introducing the advanced inspection methods, improving the technical equipment level, developing information and telecommunication infrastructure is the key aspects of the customs policy in Turkmenistan.

The customs agencies are supplied with radiation control devices and office equipment, the border control points and short-term customs warehouses are equipped with the units for controlling the flow of people and goods (including personal effects and hazardous items) in and out of the country. It is planned to equip the customs services with the systems of controlling and inspecting heavy haulers and containers, to design the telecommunication network, to apply computer-aided monitoring systems.

Nowadays, the customs services of Turkmenistan inspect all imported commodities along with reserving the effective instruments of handling operations regarding the violations of the customs rules.

In particular, the resolutions of the President of Turkmenistan stipulate for the heavy investments in the development of the State Customs Service. Up-to-date means of controlling vehicles, commodities and luggage are procured. These include X-ray television systems, mobile X-ray devices, sets of the tools for revealing contraband, stationary metal detectors, etc.

The well-qualified customs officials from the USA, Great Britain, Germany, France conduct the seminars to train the officials of the customs services of Turkmenistan in the methods of detecting drugs transported by different types of vehicles, the rules of the use of technical control devices and detection of the types of drugs, etc.

The customs environment makes progress, and Turkmenistan fulfills and will fulfill the tasks of the protection of the national interests in collaboration and close interaction with the customs services of the Asian region and the European community.

Turkmenistan signed a number of the interdepartmental agreements with Azerbaijan, Kazakhstan, Kyrgyzstan, Tajikistan and Uzbekistan: “On Mutual Acknowledgement of Customs Documents and Customs Provisions”, “On Illegal Trafficking of Narcotic Drugs and Psychotropic Substances”, “On Arrest and Restitution of Illegally Exported Cultural Heritage”, “On Unified Passenger Customs Entries”, etc. Turkmenistan is a member of the World Customs Organisation which manages the information on the decisions on the topical customs issues.

The achievements of the Turkmen customs services were distinguished by international experts. The State Customs Service of Turkmenistan and local customs services endeavour to make transit routes running through Turkmenistan the roads of peace, friendship, political stability and international co-operation.

Orazberdy MULKIEV,
Senior inspector of the State Customs Service of Turkmenistan

SELECTED CUSTOMS REGULATIONS

LAW OF TURKMENISTAN ON THE FOREIGN CURRENCY CONTROL

The present Law determines the general principles of implementation the foreign currency operations in the domestic economic turnover and in the international settlements of Turkmenistan, powers and functions of the authorities concerning the foreign currency control and management of foreign currency finances; the present Law determines the rights and responsibilities of residents and non-residents in respect of possession, use and management of foreign currency values; directions of foreign currency control and responsibility for violation of foreign exchange legislation.

SECTION I. GENERAL PROVISIONS

Article 1. Terms definition

The terms used in the present Law mean the following:
1. "Foreign currency values":
- foreign currency;
- securities - payment documents (cheques, promissory notes, bills of exchange, letters of credit etc.) and fund values (stocks, bonds, etc.) in foreign currency;
- precious metals - gold, silver, platinum and other metals of platinum group (palladium, iridium, rhodium, ruthenium and osmium) in any kind and condition excluding jewellery and other household clauses made of these metals and scrap of these clauses;
- natural gems - raw and manufactured (diamonds, cut diamonds, rubies, sapphires as well as pearl) - excluding jewellery made of such gems and scrap of these clauses.

вЂњCurrency of TurkmenistanвЂќ - manats in circulation in a form of bank-notes and coins of the Central Bank as well as withdrawn or to be withdrawn but remaining subject to exchange into circulating bank-notes; funds in manats on accounts with banks and other credit institutions of Turkmenistan.

"Foreign currency"- bank-notes and coins in circulation that are the legal tender on the territory of a relevant foreign state as well as withdrawn or to be withdrawn but remaining subject to the exchange into bank-notes in circulation; funds in foreign currencies and international monetary or settlement units on accounts.

"Residents":
- physical persons permanently residing on in Turkmenistan including those temporarily residing abroad;
- legal entities, as well as subjects that do not have the status of a legal entity located in Turkmenistan, registered in Turkmenistan, including enterprises with the participation of foreign investments;
- diplomatic, trade and other official representative offices of Turkmenistan abroad as well as other representative offices of enterprises and organisations of Turkmenistan abroad not involved in economic or other commercial activities;
- officers of international organisations residing in Turkmenistan and working as international officers.

"Non-residents":
- physical and legal entities as well as subjects having no status of a legal entity, residing both on the territory of Turkmenistan and abroad and not being the residents of Turkmenistan;

"Foreign currency operations"- operations involving:
- the transfer of the rights of property on foreign currency values;
- the use of foreign currency or payment documents in foreign currency as a means of payment;
- import and transfer to Turkmenistan from abroad and export and transfer from Turkmenistan to foreign states foreign currency values, as well as performance of international money transfers.

Foreign currency operations are subdivided into current operations and operations involving movement of capital.

"Current foreign currency operations"
- operations on purchase and sale of foreign currency values, goods and services;
- transfers to and from foreign states of interests, dividends and other income from bank deposits, credits, investments and other financial operations;
- transfers of non-trade means including transfers of salaries, pensions, alimony, inheritance and other similar operations.

"Foreign currency operations involving movement of capital":
- investments including purchase and sale of securities;
- giving and obtaining credits;
- attraction and placement of funds on deposits and accounts;

- any transfers of cash and securities to and from abroad;
"Cash"- means of payment in a form of bank-notes, coins, traveller cheques and other similar means of payment.
"Non-cash"- bank accounts and clauses in transit.
"Authorised banks"- banks that have obtained a licence of the Central Bank for holding foreign currency operations.

Article 2. Regulation functions

The Central Bank of Turkmenistan shall issue and apply regulation documents under the present Law pursuant to the authority granted to it.

Article 3. Delegation of authority

The Central Bank of Turkmenistan is entitled to delegate some of its powers to the authorised banks.

SECTION II. MAIN PRINCIPLES FOR FOREIGN EXCHANGE CONTROL

Article 4. Exchange rates

The procedure of determining exchange rates shall be established by the Central Bank of Turkmenistan. The exchange rates determined by the established procedure are applied to all foreign currency operations in Turkmenistan.

Article 5. Authorised banks

All the foreign currency operations in Turkmenistan shall be performed through the authorised banks. Each authorised bank, acting as an intermediary for its customers performing exchange operations, shall secure the observance of the legislation.
An authorised bank may freely buy and sell foreign currency in Turkmenistan and abroad in accordance with the procedures set by the Central Bank of Turkmenistan.

Article 6. Currency of Turkmenistan

The only legal tender on the territory of Turkmenistan is manat.

Article 7. Transfer of cash

Import or export of cash are subject to being declared at the Customs Station at entrance and exit. Foreign currency cash bought from the authorised banks of Turkmenistan as well as the currency declared at the entrance shall be exported without any restrictions. Import of foreign currency cash is not restricted.
The procedure and terms of import and export of foreign currency values and the national currency of Turkmenistan shall be determined by the Customs Code of Turkmenistan and regulations of the Central Bank of Turkmenistan.

Article 8. Current foreign currency operations

Any resident is entitled to convert the currency of Turkmenistan into foreign currency without any restrictions or groundless delays with the purpose of performing current operations in the time the required date of their performance has come, pursuant to the procedures set by the Central Bank of Turkmenistan.
Non-residents are entitled to convert the currency of Turkmenistan into foreign currency without any

restrictions or groundless delays provided that the amounts being asked for are required for the transfer of revenue obtained as a result of the operations with the residents of Turkmenistan.
Residents are entitled to perform current foreign currency operations through authorised banks without any restrictions in accordance with procedures set by the Central Bank of Turkmenistan.

Article 9. Operations involving movement of capital

Residents - physical persons who have obtained foreign currency from the current non-trade operations and who keep it on deposits with the banks of Turkmenistan are entitled to carry out operations associated with movement of capital without any restrictions and groundless delays and in the order established by the Central Bank of Turkmenistan.
Non - residents are entitled, without any restrictions and groundless delays, to export capital which was before imported into the territory of Turkmenistan and declared in compliance with the Customs legislation.

Article 10. Claims on repatriation

Residents - recipients of foreign currency earned from current operations and operations on movement of capital with non-residents shall be obliged to transfer or import all foreign currency proceeds into Turkmenistan.
The Central Bank of Turkmenistan shall determine procedures and amounts of the obligatory sale of foreign currency proceeds for residents.
Foreign currency received by the authorised banks shall be sold to the Central Bank in accordance with its regulations.
Collection charges and commissions relating directly to an export transaction, and other similar costs and fees may be paid out of current receipts and are subject to the provisions of the given article.
Physical persons - residents may open foreign currency accounts and deposits abroad and keep foreign currency on such accounts and deposits for the period of their stay abroad.

Article 11. Acquisition of foreign currency by the Cabinet of Ministers

The Cabinet of Ministers has a priority right for acquiring foreign currency from the Central Bank of Turkmenistan or any authorised bank.

Article 12. Restrictions on transfer of non-cash funds

The Central Bank of Turkmenistan has the right to restrict the transfer of non-cash funds for the provision by Turkmenistan of its international obligations in accordance with the Charter of the United Nations Organisation.

Article 13. Exchange rate risk

The Central Bank of Turkmenistan shall not cover exchange rate risk and give no other subsidies on foreign currency operations or any other relevant actions.

SECTION III. THE LICENSING OF AUTHORIZED BANKS

Article 14. The licensing of authorised banks

The Central Bank of Turkmenistan is entitled on any conditions and with any restrictions to grant to any bank the right to perform foreign currency operations in accordance with the present Law and regulations issued on its basis.

Article 15. Restrictions and deprivation of licence

1. The Central Bank of Turkmenistan may restrict the right to perform foreign currency operations or deprive an authorised bank of this right in case it does not follow the provisions of the granted licence, the present Law or regulations issued on its basis.
2. The Central Bank may cancel any licence or permission in case it is notified of the facts and conditions that could have made the issue of a licence or permission impossible, should such facts and conditions have been known at the moment of consideration of a relevant application.

SECTION IV. INFORMATION AND SANCTIONS

Article 16. Information

Any physical persons and legal entities, on demand of the Central Bank of Turkmenistan, are obliged to submit declarations, accounts statements and other documents enabling the Central Bank to control observance of the present Law.

Article 17. Appeal against decisions

Physical persons and legal entities failing to obtain a licence for the performance of foreign currency operations may appeal against this decision in court.

Article 18. Sanctions

Deliberate and non-deliberate non-observance, violation as well as an attempt of violation or non-observance of the present Law provisions, regulations or any other decisions of the Central Bank of Turkmenistan adopted on the basis of the present Law shall be subject to the responsibility according to the current legislation of Turkmenistan.
Sanctions are applied to: owners and heads of enterprises, legal representatives of the owners, members of the bodies designated for performing functions of official representatives of legal entities, parties authorised to represent relevant interests in joint ventures, as well as persons performing or authorised to perform duties of management or supervision of an enterprise or part of an enterprise of another person under his own responsibility, in case of violation of the present Law by deliberate or non-deliberate failure to fulfil its control functions.

EGULATIONS ON TURKMENISTAN PRESIDENT DECREES "MEASURES TO IMPROVE TURKMENISTAN TAX SYSTEM"

No 4828 dated September, 8, 2000 and "SUPPLEMENTARY VALUE-ADDED TAX REMISSIONS" No 5207 dated April, 10, 2001 TO BE APPLIED REGARDING VALUE-ADDED TAX EVALUATION AND ASSIGNMENT

The present Regulations have been worked out in accordance with Turkmenistan President Decrees "Measures to improve Turkmenistan Tax system" No 4828 dated September, 8, 2000 and "Supplementary tax remissions to value-added tax" No 5207 dated April, 10, 2001 on value-added tax to be estimated and assigned by the payment source for goods imported to Turkmenistan, as well as for foreign legal entities, performing operations and rendering services in Turkmenistan.

Section I. Value-added tax calculation and assignment for goods imported

Article 1. General provisions

1. The value-added tax is to be applied to goods, imported by Turkmenistan legal entities, foreign legal entities and individual subdivisions thereof (representative offices and branches) to the territory of Turkmenistan. The value-added tax for goods being imported to the territory of Turkmenistan is to be imposed while customs formalities are being effected. These Regulations also cover enterprises, which are taxed upon the simplified system. The simplified taxation system subjects are specified in Turkmenistan Law "Income tax" Article 6 [1].

2. The value-added tax for goods imported is to be imposed by the customs authorities before or at the moment the customs formalities are being effected.

3. The value-added tax is to be imposed in the national currency of Turkmenistan and assigned to Turkmenistan Central Budget.

4. The amount of value-added tax, paid while customs formalities of goods imported (raw stuff or materials) are being effected, is to be taken into consideration, when value-added tax is calculated with regard to items being produced from raw stuff and materials stated in the established procedure.
The value-added tax for the wholesale and retail enterprises, which are engaged in supplying and merchandizing business, is to be also estimated for goods imported thereby while calculating the value-added tax following sale of goods imported related to value-added tax on goods being sold. If the goods specified are free of value-added tax being sold at the territory of Turkmenistan, thus, the value-added tax related to goods, which have been sold, are to be referred to the trading costs.

5. The legislative regulations, envisaging tax remissions to individual tax payers, which have been adopted before, are valid for the period such tax remissions are in force.

Article 2. VAT payers for goods imported

1. Turkmenistan legal entities, foreign legal entities and individual divisions thereof (representative offices and branches), importing cargoes, are considered to be payers of value-added tax related to goods being imported to Turkmenistan.

2. The legal entities, acting as contractors and subcontractors in accordance with Turkmenistan Law "On hydrocarbon resources" are not to be treated as value-added tax payers related to goods, being imported to Turkmenistan customs territory for petroleum operations to be held. If legal entities, acting as contractors and subcontractors in accordance with Turkmenistan Law "On hydrocarbon resources", effect import of cargoes to the customs territory of Turkmenistan, which are not intended for petroleum operations, a value-added tax is to be imposed by procedure, established by the present Regulations.

3. While cargoes are being imported by legal entities, a value-added tax is to be paid by declarant or any other entity, being in charge of assigning value-added tax jointly with other customs fees, namely, before or at the moment of customs formalities are being effected.

Article 3. An object to be imposed on a value-added tax and goods import tax basis

1. Goods being imported to Turkmenistan customs territory are to be considered as object to impose a value-added tax on.

A value-added tax is not to be imposed on below specified goods being imported to the territory of Turkmenistan while customs clearance is being effected:

- goods stated in the specific List (Annex No 1 to the present Regulations);
- goods being imported in accordance with intergovernmental agreements, governmental decrees, as well as within frameworks of the international humanitarian, fiscal and technical assistance projects and programs;
- goods being imported upon clearing operations against cargo supplies for the natural gas and electric power.

2. Customs value of those goods is to serve as a tax basis to impose a value-added tax for goods, being imported to the customs territory of Turkmenistan, taking excise into consideration for goods being treated as excise ones.
A tax basis to calculate value-added tax for goods being imported is to be estimated per each type of goods being imported and represents a total amount to be assigned for all goods being imported.
The goods value estimated on the basis of a price, which has been really paid or to be paid or to be indemnified against trade-in supplies in accordance with the foreign transaction conditions, taking delivery costs into consideration (forwarding, handling, insurance), is considered to be customs value of goods, being imported in accordance with contracts, which have been registered by Turkmenistan Raw Materials and Commodity Exchange.
If the contracts to import cargoes are not available, the customs value is to be stated, taking the market (wholesale) prices for identical (similar) good being imported into consideration.
The goods customs value in a foreign currency is to be estimated in manats per the rate of the Central Bank of Turkmenistan on the date when goods imported to the customs territory of Turkmenistan are customs cleared.

Article 4. Procedure to calculate and terms to pay value-added tax

1. The value-added tax to be assigned to budget for goods being imported is to be stated (calculated and defined) by the customs body, which is effecting customs clearance, taking into consideration a tax basis, which is to be stated in accordance with article 3.2. of the present Regulations and 20 percentage value-added tax stated.
2. The value-added tax is to enter deposit account of customs body, which supervises entry thereof in accordance with bank statements. If the funds do not enter a deposit account within three working days, since the payment order has been submitted, the customs is to submit data for these amounts to be imposed by the State Tax Inspectorate for their further entry to the deposit account of customs, which has effected customs clearance.
3. The value-added tax, which entered the customs deposit accounts, is to be assigned by the banks to Turkmenistan Centralized Budget the latest next date.
4. Upon the payer request the customs body may allow value-added tax to be paid later within one month being guaranteed by the authorized bank and penalty fee to be imposed in the established procedure.
5. If the payer or authorized bank failed to fulfill guarantee obligations thereof in accordance with a value-added tax payment delay allowed, the customs body is to notify the Central Bank of Turkmenistan of VAT as well as a penalty fee per each day of delay, including date of payment, to be imposed in any way from the authorized bank, which has issued a guarantee obligation.

Amounts, being imposed by the Central Bank of Turkmenistan in any way, are to enter a deposit account of the customs body, which was effecting customs formalities, for further assignment to Turkmenistan Centralized Budget.

Article 5. Procedure to reimburse preliminary payments

1. Turkmenistan Customs Authorities are to resolute on value-added tax, which has been imposed, being repaid in cases as follows:

- a value-added tax has been wrongly calculated, including that one caused by modification of a foreign trade (contractual) goods value;
- the Customs Authorities have imposed a value-added tax in accordance with customs regime.

The tax basis modification is to be exercised only if it is proved by the relevant documentation.
The value-added tax payer may claim repayment of surpluses, being assigned or imposed, from the Customs Authorities within 1 year since assignments have been effected or imposed.

2. For a value-added tax to be repaid its is required to submit documents as follows to the Customs Authorities:

- a payer application for value-added tax, which has been assigned or imposed, to be repaid;
- a cargo customs declaration made by the Customs Authorities, which serves as a basis for a value added tax to be estimated;
- a payment order of a value-added tax being paid, confirmed by the bank statement, proving acceptance and payment effected.

It is required to submit supplementary documents, confirming the amount paid as being overpaid and wrongly estimated in order for overpaid or wrongly estimated value-added tax amounts to be reimbursed.

3. The Customs Authorities are to submit to Turkmenistan Administration of Economy & Finance at the place, where the tax has been paid, a statement on the value-added tax overpaid or overimposed to be reimbursed.

4. The Ministry of Economy and Finance is to notify the tax and customs authorities at the place, where the tax has been paid, of its decision to reimburse value-added tax being overpaid, overimposed or make set-off taking future tax payments to import goods into consideration.

5. The value-added tax overpaid or overimposed is to be reimburesed in the national currency of Turkmenistan by the rate, stated by the Central Bank of Turkmenistan to account and impose customs fees at the moment of a tax being paid.

Article 6. Peculiarities to estimate and settle value-added tax at various customs regimes

1. Regulations on customs regimes are to state correspondence of a proper customs regime identified for goods.

2. The value-added tax is not to be paid while the goods are crossing Turkmenistan customs boundary in accordance with customs regimes as follows: transit, customs warehouse, free trade shop, free customs zone, free warehouse or destruction.

3. The value-added tax is to be imposed in accordance with the established procedure, if there is import of goods, which are to be processed at the customs area or upon customs control.
When ready-made products made of imported give-and take stuff are exported, a value-added tax, which has been paid for give-and-take stuff and refers to a ready-made production lot being exported, is to be paid back in accordance with the established procedure.

4. When goods are imported at the temporary customs regime, the tax is to be imposed in accordance with the established procedure, as well as for goods

released at the free circulation regime. When temporarily imported goods are exported from Turkmenistan, a tax being paid or imposed is to be reimbursed in accordance with the established procedure, provided that a temporary staying thereof at the territory of Turkmenistan does not exceed six months after being imported.

5. When the foreign goods, which have been declared to be re-exported, are imported to Turkmenistan customs territory, a value-added tax is to be imposed in accordance with customs regime for goods to be released for free circulation. When goods, which have been declared to the Customs Authorities to be re-exported, are being exported outside Turkmenistan, a value-added tax paid or imposed is to be paid back in accordance with an export real volume, provided that staying thereof at the territory of Turkmenistan does not exceed six months after being imported.

6. If the payer does not follow terms and conditions of the customs regime, he is to pay a value-added tax in accordance with the customs regime to release goods for a free circulation regime, as well as fine to be estimated from the period the goods are imported till the moment the tax is paid, inclusive.

Article 7. Payer responsibility and tax authorities monitoring

1. The payer is responsible for a value-added tax to be correct and paid in time.
2. Entities are to undertake responsibility in accordance with Turkmenistan legislation for the present Regulations to be infringed.
3. Turkmenistan Head National Inspectorate is to make monitoring of a value-added tax to be full and assigned to the State budget in time.

Section II. A value-added tax to be imposed from foreign entities by the payment source

1. The foreign legal entities, which perform operations and render services via representative offices thereof, located at the territory of Turkmenistan, are to assign value-added tax independently, free of tax being imposed by the payment source.
A value-added tax is not to be imposed from the foreign legal entities, who are considered to be contractors and subcontractors in accordance with Turkmenistan Law "On hydrocarbon resources" related to petroleum works done and services rendered. If the legal entities being trated as contractors and subcontractors in accordance with Turkmenistan Law "On hydrocarbon resources" perform operations or render services, which are not related to petroleum operations, a value-added tax is to be imposed in the procedure, specified by the present Regulations.

2. A place, where a legal entity has been established or branch or representative office thereof has been located and through which operations are done and services rendered, is considered to be a place to perform operations and render services, besides those ones specified in paragraphs 8.3 and 8.4 of the present Regulations.

3. The place to perform operations and render services is considered to be as follows:

a) a place to perform operations and services related to real assets, where these assets are located;
b) a place to perform operations and services related to personal assets, where these

works are really done and services rendered;
c) a real place to render services in the sphere of culture, arts, education, physical culture or sport or in any other similar scope of activity;
d) a place, where real freights are exercised, taking distances covered into consideration (except international freights by air or water carriers) for freight services rendered;
e) a place of dispatch for those carriers, where catering services ar the air and water carriers are rendered while international freights are performed.
4. If the service buyer is located at one state and the seller - in another one, then a place, where a legal entity, acting as a service buyer, has been established or where the branch or representative office thereof is located, is considered to be a place to render services as follows:
a) to delegate or provide any rights, including disposal of intellectual property objects and other non-property rights, to transfer into a property or to assign patents, licencies, trade marks, copyrights or any similar rights;
b) to delegate or give a rights, including those ones to dispose intellectual property items and other personal non-proprietary rights, to delegate into a property or to assign patents, licences, trade marks, copy rights or other similar ones;
c) to make advertisement;
d) to provide consultative, juridical, book-keeping, engineering services, as well as to manage, to proceed data and provide information and to hold geological surveys. The engineering services cover particular items as follows: engineering-consultative services, pre-project and project services (working out of feasibility studies, project design and similar services);
e) to provide balance sheet, banking and insurance ones, re-insurance inclusive, except rendering services on the safe rentals;
f) to provide a personnel;
g) services, rendered by an agent, who is acting on behalf and in the name of other entity, if they secure that one services stated above;
h) to lease movable tangible property, except all vehicle types of legal entities, whose basic business is to render transport services;
i) to refrain (fully or partially) from exercising above stated services upon obligations undertaken.
5. In order to estimate a value-added-tax, a place as follows is considered to be a place to sell goods:

- goods location at the moment they are taken over to the buyer, provided they are not being shipped or transported;
- goods location at the moment they started to be shipped or transported, provided they are being shipped or transported by the supplier, buyer or any other entity;
- a place of goods being installed, mounted or assemblied, provided they are not able to be delivered to the buyer by any other way, except being dismantled ot diassemblied, caused by the technical, technological or any other reasons, while an installation, mounting or assembly are being made by these goods supplier or on his behalf.

6. Turkmenistan legal entities, entrepreneurs free of forming a legal entity, who are registered in accordance with Turkmenistan legislation, branches and representative offices, as well as permanent representatives of the foreign legal entities, located at the territory of Turkmenistan, are to be treated as sources, who are to be taxed, as works and services are dircctly rendered thereto.
7. The value-added tax is to be withdrawn from the foreign legal entities at 16,67% rate from the payment total amount each time, when payment is effected.
The value-added tax is to be deducted from any amounts (advanced, scheduled, upon real performance of works (services), etc.), which are paid to a foreign legal entity upon

agreement or contract conditions. If there is any barter (goods exchange) operations, the tax is to be paid in a similar way.
8. If a foreign legal entity has paid a value-added tax at the territory of Turkmenistan, following fulfilment of any agreement (contract) to perform works or render services, regarding purchasing stuff, materials, services or works, which value is to be treated as production and trading costs, then set-off or repayment thereof is to be effected in a way, specified by Turkmenistan Ministry of Economy and Finance.
9. The value-added tax estimation is to be submitted by entities, who are withholding tax from a payment source in accordance with annex No 2 to the present Regulations by the 20-th of a month following a reported one. The value-adde tax is to be assigned the latest 5 days after the tax has been withheld.

ANNEX NO 1 TO REGULATIONS ON TURKMENISTAN PRESIDENT DECREES "MEASURES TO IMPROVE TURKMENISTAN TAX SYSTEM"

No 4828 dated September, 8, 2000
and "SUPPLEMENTARY VALUE-ADDED TAX REMISSIONS" No 5207 dated April, 10, 2001 TO BE APPLIED REGARDING
VALUE-ADDED TAX EVALUATION AND ASSIGNMENT
List
of goods being imported to Turkmenistan and exempt from a value-added tax while customs clearance

1. Drugs, medical items, prosthetic-orthopedic items, specific vehicles for invalids.
2. Currency, money, banknotes, being legal payment facilities (provided they are not imported for numismatics), securities.
3. A property legitimated.
4. A property being imported, caused by requisition or confiscation.
5. Goods, being imported by the foreign diplomatic and representative offices of a similar status, located at the territory of Turkmenistan, for being officially or personally disposed by the diplomatic or administative-technical staff of those representtaive offices, family members inclusive.*
6. Goods, which are paid for by Turkmenistan Currency Reserve.
7. Goods, which are to be owned by the state, provided a tax payer refuses therefrom.
8. Machines, mechanisms, equipment, vehicles, spare parts thereto and production technical tools.**
9. Machines, mechanisms, equipment, vehicles, spare parts thereto and production technical tools.**
10. Chemical fertilizers, chemical items, lubricants, being implemented for the oil/gas and agricultural complex needs.**
11. Construction and finishing materials required to proceed construction operations (repair, reconstruction, modernization) of objects, being implemented in accordance with
12. Turkmenistan President resolutions. Turkmenistan Ministry of Construction and Building Materials Industry is to approve expediency of supplies thereof, taking technical, quality, esthetic peculiarities and value into consideration. **

---

* Remission specified is applied only if a similar remission is stated for the diplomatic and similar Turkmenistan representative offices operating abroad or being personally disposed by the diplomatic or administrative-technical staff of those representative offices, family members inclusive.
** The remissions stated are in force since April, 1, 2001.

ANNEX No 2
TO REGULATIONS ON TURKMENISTAN PRESIDENT DECREES "MEASURES TO IMPROVE TURKMENISTAN TAX SYSTEM" No 4828 dated September, 8, 2000

and "SUPPLEMENTARY VALUE-ADDED TAX REMISSIONS" No 5207 dated April, 10, 2001 TO BE APPLIED REGARDING
VALUE-ADDED TAX EVALUATION AND ASSIGNMENT

<table>
<tr><td>1</td><td colspan="4">Value-added tax evaluation to be withheld by the payment source from the foreign legal entities within
_______________ 200__</td></tr>
<tr><td>2</td><td colspan="4">To ____________________Tax Inspectorate</td></tr>
<tr><td>3</td><td colspan="4">Enterprise full name:</td></tr>
<tr><td>4</td><td colspan="4">Legal address:</td></tr>
<tr><td>5</td><td colspan="4">Residential address:</td></tr>
<tr><td>6</td><td colspan="4">Uniform State Register of Legal Entities Code:</td></tr>
<tr><td>7</td><td colspan="4">Identification Tax Code:</td></tr>
<tr><td>8</td><td colspan="4">Tel.:</td></tr>
<tr><td>9</td><td colspan="4">Surname, name & patronymic of an official, being in charge to make tax estimation:</td></tr>
<tr><td rowspan="4">10</td><td rowspan="2">Full name of a foreign Legal entity, stating a Residential country</td><td rowspan="2">Amount to be paid for works done or services rendered</td><td colspan="2">Value-added tax</td></tr>
<tr><td>VAT rate</td><td>VAT estimated (line 2x3)* (in thous.manats)</td></tr>
<tr><td>1</td><td>2</td><td>3</td><td>4</td></tr>
<tr><td colspan="4"></td></tr>
<tr><td>11</td><td colspan="4">TOTAL: X</td></tr>
<tr><td>12</td><td colspan="4">Postage date:</td></tr>
<tr><td>13</td><td colspan="4">Date of receipt:</td></tr>
<tr><td>14</td><td colspan="4">Signatures of authorized persons:

Enterprise Chairman: Principal Accountant:</td></tr>
<tr><td>15</td><td colspan="4">Tax inspector remarks and notes:</td></tr>
<tr><td>16</td><td colspan="4">Date of preliminary audit: Signature:</td></tr>
</table>

IMPORTANT LAWS AND REGULATIONS AFFECTING EXPORT-IMPORT AND CUSTOMS OPERATION

BASIC LAWS AND REGULATIONS AFFECTING BUSINESS ACTIVITY

1. LAW OF TURKMENISTAN ON CHAMBER OF COMMERCETHE PRESIDENT OF TURKMENISTAN SAPARMURAT TURKMENBASHI, (Ashgabat, October, 8, 1993)
2. LAW OF TURKMENISTAN ON ENTEPRENEURIAL ACTIVITY IN TURKMENISTAN
3. LAW OF TURKMENISTAN ON FOREIGN ECONOMIC ACTIVITIES IN
4. LAW OF TURKMENISTAN ON THE CENTRAL BANK OF TURKMENISTAN[4]
5. List of Goods Subject to Excise Tax
6. New Laws and Regulations on Privitization
7. NEW Regulations on exporting and importing goods by the individual
8. Overview of the Copy Right and Patent System
9. Petroleum Law of Turkmenistan 2002
10. Privatization of Industrial Enterprises
11. Registering Your Company with the State Agency for Foreign Investment
12. Registration of Foreign Investors in Turkmenistan
13. STATUTE ON THE PROCEDURE OF STATE REGISTRATION OF THE INTERPRISES(INSTITUTIONS, ORGANIZATIONS) CARRYING FOREIGN INVESTMENTS AND REGISTRATION OF BRANCHES AND REPRESENTATIONS OF THE FOREIGN FIRMS
14. Taxes for Foreign Investors
15. The Law of Turkmenistan on Foreign Concessions
16. The Law of Turkmenistan on Foreign Investments
17. THE LAW OF TURKMENISTAN ON FREE ECONOMIC ZONES
18. TURKMENISTANPRESIDENT OF TURKMENISTAN S. NIYAZOV, Adopted in May 19, 1992 (With changes and amendments by Mejlis of April 12, 1993)

THE LAW OF TURKMENISTAN ON FOREIGN CONCESSIONS

The present law shall define organisational, economic and legal conditions of establishment and activities of foreign concessions in Turkmenistan.

SECTION I. GENERAL PROVISIONS

Article 1. The concept of a foreign concession
A concession is the permission of the state to carry out a specific type of business activity on the territory of Turkmenistan granted to foreign legal entities and physical persons.
A concession shall provide for the right given by the state to a foreign legal entity or a physical person - a concessionaire - to use plots of land, natural resources, enterprises and other assets on the basis of an agreement for a specified period of time and in return for a payment.

Article 2. The legal regulation of foreign concessions
1. Legal relations resulting from Concession agreements shall be regulated by the present Law and other legislative acts of Turkmenistan.
2. The legislation of Turkmenistan determines territories, objects of the state property, types of enterprises and other assets the concession of which is limited or prohibited.

[4] Available upon request

3. If the international agreements signed by Turkmenistan set forth another provisions than those contained in this Law, the provisions of international agreements shall be applicable.

Article 3. The basic principles of concession activity
Concession activity in Turkmenistan is carried out by the following principles:
- contribution to solving economic objectives of Turkmenistan, attraction of foreign investments, structural economic reforms and introduction of advanced technologies;
- rational use of natural resources, provision of ecological, sanitary and hygienic safety;
- provision of the production of goods meeting the requirements of industrial standards established in Turkmenistan;
- involvement in the social development of the territories where concession activity is carried out;
- assistance by the authorities and governmental agencies of Turkmenistan to concessionaires in achieving the objectives set out in concession agreements.

Article 4. Terms of granting a concession
1. A Concession shall be granted on a tender basis. The terms and procedure for the competition shall be determined by the Cabinet of Ministers of Turkmenistan. When granting objects for concession the publicity shall be provided.
2. A concession shall be terminable, repayable and contractual. 3. Concession projects and programs as well as feasibility studies shall be subject to the state expert examination including their environmental. sanitary and hygienic qualifications.
Participants of a Concession agreement shall have the right to arrange for an additional expert examination on their own.

Article 5. Objects of concession activity
1. The right for exploration, development, production or operation of natural resources as well as for carrying out any other type of business activity shall be guaranteed to a concessionaire in all spheres and types of activity not prohibited by the legislation of Turkmenistan.
The objects of concession activity shall be:
- plots of land and territories with their natural resources;
- water surfaces with their natural resources;
- individual deposits of natural resources;
- industrial objects intended for the exploration, development, production or exploitation of natural resources;
- other objects.

2. Concession activity causing damage to the legally protected rights and interests of the citizens and the state and not meeting the requirements of ecological, sanitary and hygienic norms, radiological, fire and explosion safely standards, shall be prohibited.

Article 6. Subjects of concession activity
1. The subjects of a concession agreement (contract) shall be the state of Turkmenistan duly represented by the authorised bodies, and foreign legal entities and physical persons as well as foreign states (concessionaires).

2. A concessionaire - the general contractor - is granted the right to engage subcontractors for implementation of works in accordance with a concession agreement. Agreements signed with subcontractors must not contradict the provisions of a concession contract.

SECTION II. THE ESTABLISHMENT AND ACTIVITY OF CONCESSION ENTERPRISES

Article 7. The Procedure for granting a Concession
1. The Cabinet of Ministers of Turkmenistan shall approve priority sectors for concession activities by branches of industry, territories and objects.

2. An application for granting a concession enclosed by the documents verifying the applicant's professional qualifications and technological potentials of an applicant and his guarantors confirmed by a bank as well as the feasibility study along with the results of an expert examination and the request from an executive body of the velayat where the concession object is located, shall be submitted to a state property administration agency.

3. After checking the submitted documents and selecting applications on a competitive basis the state property administration agency shall sign a concession agreement.

4. The Cabinet of Ministers of Turkmenistan shall specify the objects, concession agreements on which shall be subject to mandatory approval by this highest executive body.

5. Concession agreements shall be registered within ten days after being signed and approved by an executive body in the location of a concession object. Within ten days the registration agency that has completed a registration shall notify of the fact of registration the tax inspectorate and forward the formation to an authorised agency for inclusion in the State register.

6. A concession agreement shall be come into force from the day of receipt of the state registration certificate issued by the holder of the General state registrar of enterprises and organisations.

Article 8. The contents of a concession agreement
A concession agreement shall contain the information on:
- the subjects of the agreement;
- concession object and objectives;
- borders of the territory within the frameworks of which a concession shall be granted;
- the list of the assets conceded and their value;
- the rights and responsibilities of the parties;
- terms of payment;
- procedure for selling ready made products on the domestic and foreign markets;
- procedure for import of raw materials, component parts;
- the customs terms;
- procedure of insurance;
- validity period of a contract, procedure of its amendments, extension and termination;
- requirements for environmental protection and restoration, safeguarding historical and cultural monuments, natural landscapes, flora and fauna;
- concessionaire's obligations to submit new information obtained as a result of concession activity, including geological exploration data, to the grantor f the concession;
- terms of hiring labour force;
- procedure for settling disputes, each party's responsibility for violation of the agreement;
- minimum requirement of the capital invested into the business;
- level of prices for concession products for the domestic and foreign markets;
- terms and procedure for the return of concession objects upon expiration of the agreement term, or for any other reason;
- each party's financial guarantees, legal addresses and bank requisites;
- legal, economic and organisational consequences in cases of emergency and contingency;
- procedure and terms of inspection, control for implementation of a concession agreement;
- other items of importance the contracting parties.

Article 9. Concession payment and taxes
Procedure and amounts of concession payments and taxes by foreign legal entities and physical persons are specified by the current legislation of Turkmenistan.

Article 10. Terms of concession agreements
1. A concession agreement shall be signed for the period from 5 to 40 years. In exceptional cases an agreement may be signed for 5 years. Upon expiration of the period specified in the agreement the latter may be renewed as agreed between the parties. Terms and conditions of an agreement being renewed may be altered.

2. Upon expiration of the period of a concession agreement the concession objects shall be returned to the State body that has granted the concession.

Article 11. Changes in the terms and cancellation of a concession agreement
1. Changes in the terms of a concession agreement or pre-term cancellation may take place by the mutual agreement of parties or in the legal order.

2. The liquidation of a concession shall be carried out in accordance with the procedure stipulated by the agreement, or by mutual agreement between the parties; in case of discord between the parties or bankruptcy of a concession enterprise liquidation shall be carried out by a court.

3. The fact of liquidating a concession shall be registered by the agency that has registered the concession agreement.

4. The concession shall be considered liquidated from the date of its exclusion from the Unified State Register of Enterprises and Organisations of all forms of property and management.

Article 12. Inheritance of concession rights
Inheritance of concession rights shall be carried out in accordance with the laws of Turkmenistan.

Article 13. Insurance
1. Risks of a concession enterprise shall be insured by mutual agreement between a concessionaire and the granter of a concession.

2. The social insurance of the staff of concession enterprises shall be regulated by the legislation of Turkmenistan, and for foreign employees - by individual labour agreements (contracts) by transfer of payments to the corresponding funds in the countries of their permanent residence.

Article 14. Accounting and reporting
1. Concession enterprises carry out accounting and statistical reports of their activity in accordance with the current laws of Turkmenistan.

2. The translation of foreign currency into the monetary units used in Turkmenistan for the purpose of accounting and calculating the book value of assets shall be carried out in compliance with the rules established by the Central Bank of Turkmenistan.

SECTION III. REGULATION OF CONCESSION RELATIONS

Article 15. The rights of the state body granting a concession
The State body of Turkmenistan that granted a concession has the right to:
- have a share in the concession's profits;

- to purchase the concession's products;
- to control the performance of the concession agreement;
- authorise the concessionaire to use and exploit natural by-resources. The list of mineral resources not subject to exploration as natural by-resources shall be determined by the Cabinet of Ministers of Turkmenistan.

Article 16. The obligations of the state body granting a concession
The state body that has granted a concession must:
- observe all the terms of the concession agreement;
- give the concessionaire exclusive rights to exploit and to use a concession object;
- must not publish and render to third persons information on commercial and production activities, obtained from the concessionaire, without his consent;
- guarantee that any alteration of terms of the concession agreement shall not be admitted without concessionaire's consent;
- compensate for the concessionaire's expenses in case of pre-term cancellation of the agreement on the grantor's initiative;
- compensate for the concessionaire's losses resulting from violating the agreement through someone else's fault;
- guarantee the right to export a stipulated share of the output and hard currency profit on conditions provided for by the concession agreement, or by additional agreements.

Article 17. The concessionaire's rights
A concessionaire shall have the right:
- to carry out business activity as stipulated by the concession agreement;
- to use on the terms set up for enterprises in Turkmenistan a plot of land, piped water, energy, communications, to construct on the concession territory buildings, structures, approach roads, highways, wire and telephone lines.
- to open representations, branches and offices in compliance with the legislation of Turkmenistan;
- to hire personnel from among the citizens of Turkmenistan in accordance with the labour legislation of Turkmenistan as well as personnel from among the citizens of other countries;
- to import, for the purpose of providing for the production process and labour force, instruments, overalls and foodstuff without the right to resell or use them outside the concession territory;
- to establish consortia;
- to appeal to the court against illegal actions by state administrative bodies and their officials.

Article 18. The obligations of a concessionaire
A concessionaire shall be obliged to observe the terms of the concession agreement and work strictly accordance with the legislation of Turkmenistan.

Article 19. Procedure for settling disputes
Disputes of a concessionaire with state bodies, enterprises, public organisations, other legal entities and citizens of Turkmenistan as well as disputes between concessionaires with each other related to their activity shall be solved in the courts of Turkmenistan if otherwise not stipulated by international agreement.

Article 20. The responsibilities of parties
The parties that signed concession agreements shall be responsible for its non-observance in the way established by the legislation of Turkmenistan and provided for by concession agreements.

THE LAW OF TURKMENISTAN ON FOREIGN INVESTMENTS IN TURKMENISTAN

This Law determines legal, economic and organisational bases of realisation of foreign investments on the territory of Turkmenistan and is aimed at attraction and efficacious use in national economy of foreign advanced technologies, managerial experience, material and financial resources and at formation of open market economy.

SECTION I. GENERAL PROVISIONS

Article 1. Foreign investments By foreign investments there are meant all kinds of property and intellectual values, which are invested by foreign investors into the objects of entrepreneurial and other activities on the territory of Turkmenistan in the form of:
- foreign currency, other currency values, currency valid on the territory of Turkmenistan;
- movable and immovable property (buildings, constructions, equipment and other material values) and property rights related to them;
- shares, bonds, other securities or forms of participation in enterprises;
- money requirements or rights of requirements of contract obligations execution, which are of value;
- any rights of intellectual property having value, including copyrights, rights on inventions, trade marks, firm names, industrial samples, "know-how" and others;
- right on economic activities, including exploration, extraction, output of mine or exploitation of natural resources, received by law or agreement;
- paid services;
- other kinds of investments not prohibited by the legislation of Turkmenistan.

Foreign investors have the right to make investments in the forms of partial participation in enterprises of Turkmenistan, creation of enterprises which completely belong to foreign investors, or acquisition of functioning enterprises, acquisition of movable and immovable property including houses, apartments, premises, equipment, transport facilities and other objects of property not prohibited by the legislation of Turkmenistan by means of direct acquisition of property or in the form of shares, bonds, other securities, acquisition of independence or the right to use lands and concessions with the participation of legal entities or physical persons of Turkmenistan for the use of natural resources on the territory of Turkmenistan, acquisition of other property rights.

Article 2. Foreign investors The following persons can be the foreign investors in Turkmenistan:
- foreign legal entities including international organizations and associations and also the states;
- foreign physical persons (foreign citizens or persons without citizenship).

Article 3. Enterprises with foreign investments Enterprise with foreign investments is acknowledged and effect of the present law covers any form of enterprise founded in accordance with the legislation of Turkmenistan in case when the foreign investor possesses within the period of calendar year not less than 20 percent of declared charter capital on an average or a part the absolute value of which is established by the Cabinet of Ministers of Turkmenistan.

Article 4. Legal regulation of foreign investments Relations connected with foreign investments in Turkmenistan are regulated by the Law "On investment activities in Turkmenistan", by this Law and also by other legislative acts of Turkmenistan functioning on the territory of Turkmenistan and international agreements.

In case if an international contract or agreement signed by Turkmenistan determines different rules than those of the legislative acts of Turkmenistan, the rules of international contract or agreement are used.

Article 5. Government policy in the sphere of foreign investments Elaboration and implementation of the policy of Turkmenistan aimed at attraction and use of foreign investments, co-ordination of investment activities, the assistance to foreign investors in their activities on the territory of Turkmenistan are performed by the Cabinet of Ministers of Turkmenistan or by the authorised body.

SECTION II. CREATION OF LEGAL ENTITIES WITH FOREIGN PARTICIPATION AND THEIR ACTIVITIES

Article 6. The creation of legal entities with foreign participation By a legal entity with foreign participation any legal entity in Turkmenistan is meant, entrepreneurial activities of which are invested by subjects noted in article 2 of the present law, and foreign enterprises which are under jurisdiction of Turkmenistan. Legal entities with foreign participation are created on conditions and in the order determined by the laws on enterprises, entrepreneurial activities, stock associations, by this law and other normative acts of Turkmenistan.

Article 7. Activities of legal entities with foreign participation Legal entities with foreign participation may perform any kinds of activities not prohibited by the legislation of Turkmenistan. Special kinds of activities, which are determined by the Cabinet of Ministers of Turkmenistan, may be carried out by legal entities with foreign participation only with special permission.

Article 8. State registration State registration of legal entities with foreign participation is carried out in the order established by the Cabinet of Ministers of Turkmenistan. In order to be registered the legal entities should submit the following documents:
- application of the participants (founders);
- permission to make investments into the economy of Turkmenistan;
- agreement on the terms of establishing a joint venture;
- Charter (regulations);
- the document certifying financial position of the foreign investor.

The agreement and the charter are to be submitted in two copies verified by notary in the state language as well as in the language of original documents.

The authority responsible for state registration has no right to require any other documents except those mentioned above in this law and has no right to refuse the founder in accepting his documents for registration. The resolution on registration or on rejection of registration is taken within two weeks after the foundation documents have been submitted.

An enterprise is rejected in state registration in writing and rejection is possible in case of violation by a founder of the procedure of establishing an enterprise set by the legislation of Turkmenistan and also in case of non-compliance of the founding documents with the requirements of this law.

The authority that has registered an enterprise with foreign participation within three days sends the verified copies of foundation documents for enterprises to be included into the State Register of Enterprises and to the Taxation Department of the location place of enterprise.

Enterprises with foreign participation obtain the right of legal entity after being included into the State Register of Enterprises. The information on including it in State Register of Enterprise is published by the legal entity.

Article 9. Foundation documents of legal entity with foreign participation Foundation documents of legal entity with foreign participation must determine the subject and purposes of activities, the amount of the charter fund, share participation, the order of liquidation of a legal entity and also the other regulations provided by the legislation of Turkmenistan.

All the additions and amendments to the foundation documents of already registered enterprises with foreign investments and their branches are also subject to the state registration. Additions and amendments to the foundation documents come into force only after their registration and with the written consent of the authority that issued the permission to make investments in the economy of Turkmenistan.

Article 10. Appraisal of investment objects Investment projects and programmes, technical-economic calculations on the construction of objects are subject to the obligatory state expert examination including the compliance with the standards of seismic firmness, fire-burn security, ecological and sanitary requirements.

An investor at his discretion can carry out expert examination of the projects additionally, involving state and other expert organisations on a contract basis.

Article 11. Limitation of foreign investing Foreign investing is not allowed into the objects creation and use of which does not meet the requirements of sanitary, ecological and other standards set by the legislation of Turkmenistan.

Article 12. Responsibility of foreign investors The foreign investors are responsible for their actions violating the legislation of Turkmenistan up to the holding up of their activities on the territory of Turkmenistan by the resolution of Cabinet of Ministers.

Article 13. Requirements to production of foreign investors The quality of foreign investors' production and provided services must correspond to the standards accepted in Turkmenistan. The legal entity with foreign participation can independently determine the terms of realisation of production (work, services), including prices on it.

Article 14. Associations of legal entities with foreign participation Legal entities with foreign participation may voluntarily join into unions, associations, concerns, industrial, regional and other associations in the order and on terms provided by the legislative acts of Turkmenistan.

Article 15. Customs privileges Property imported in Turkmenistan as the contribution of a foreign investor into the charter fund of legal entities with foreign participation, and also property intended for their own material production are exempted from customs duty and the tax on import.

Property brought to Turkmenistan by foreign employees of legal entities with foreign participation for personal needs is exempted from customs duty.

Article 16. Export and import of production Legal entities with foreign participation which have more than 30% of foreign investments in hard currency in the charter fund have the right to export goods (works and services) of their own production without license and in the volume adequate to the foreign investor's share in the charter fund on the basis of the certificate issued by the authorised body. Legal entities with foreign participation have the right to import goods (works, services) for their own economic activities without license.

The order of attribution of goods (works, services) to the goods of own production of legal entities with foreign participation is established by the Cabinet of Ministers of Turkmenistan.

After the payment of taxes and duties stipulated by the legislation of Turkmenistan, the currency income of the legal entity with foreign participation from the export of it's own production is left at it's disposal.

Article 17. Taxation Legal entities with foreign participation pay taxes on profit in the amount and in the order determined by the legislation of Turkmenistan. For the period of the recovery of initial investments the foreign investor who has invested the share of more than 30% of hard currency in the charter fund of an enterprise is exempted from the tax on dividends and the enterprise is exempted from the tax on profit.

Enterprises with foreign participation directing their profit to re-investment are exempted from the taxation in the sphere directed to reinvestment after the recovery of initial investments.

The other privileges for the legal entities with foreign participation may be established by the Cabinet of Ministers of Turkmenistan.

Control of regularity of tax payments, financial and commercial activities is implemented by the tax authorities and authorised organisations of Turkmenistan.

Article 18. Book-keeping report and accounts Book-keeping (statistical) report and accounts of legal entities with foreign participation on the territory of Turkmenistan are recorded according to the rules adopted in Turkmenistan. Balance appraisal and property accounting of legal entities with foreign participation are carried out in the way of re-calculation of foreign currency into the money unit of Turkmenistan according to the special rate of the Central Bank of Turkmenistan.

Article 19. Obligations security Property of the legal entity with foreign participation including attracted borrowed funds, property rights including rights for buildings, constructions, equipment, except rights of possession of land and other natural resources can be used as security for all kinds of obligations.

Mortgaged property can be sold by the mortgage holder for the money unit of Turkmenistan and for foreign currency including auctions, to other legal entities and physical persons.

SECTION III. STATE GUARANTEES OF FOREIGN INVESTMENTS PROTECTION

Article 20. Legal regimen of foreign investments Foreign investments on the territory of Turkmenistan have legal protection provided by the this Law, other legislative acts and international agreements applicable on the territory of Turkmenistan. Legal regimen of foreign investments and foreign investors activities directed to the investments implementation cannot be less favourable than regimen for property, property rights and investment activities of legal entities and citizens of Turkmenistan. In case of the change of legislation concerning foreign investments, a foreign investor can require that the law that was in force at the moment of investment registration must be used for the period of 10 years.

Article 21. Guarantees of property of foreign investors Foreign investments in Turkmenistan are not subject to nationalization and requisition. The property of foreign investor can be confiscated in case of perpetration by the investor of illegal actions and only in the court order.

Article 22. Guarantees of the property transference right Foreign investors and foreign employees are given the guaranteed right of free property transference abroad. The order of transference through the border of currency, payment documents, securities is determined by the legislation of Turkmenistan on currency regulation.

Article 23. Guarantees of the use of foreign investor's profit After paying taxes the profit of the foreign investor remains at his disposal and can be re-invested on the territory of Turkmenistan. Foreign investors have the right to open current and settlement accounts in banks of Turkmenistan in the currency of Turkmenistan and currencies of other states. A foreign investor has the right to use the currency of Turkmenistan for acquisition of foreign currency at the domestic currency market.

Article 24. Guarantees of the restitution of foreign investor's property In case of termination of investment activities a foreign investor has the right for the restitution of his investments not later than within 6 months and also restitution of income in the form of money and goods on the real market price.

Article 25. Protection of the rights on intellectual property of foreign investors The legislation of Turkmenistan provides implementation and protection of the rights for intellectual property of foreign investors including copyright for fiction, scientific works, programmes for computers and data base, patents and other rights for inventions and industrial samples, "know-how," commercial secrets, service and trade marks, firm names and protection of these rights from unfair competition.

Article 26. Money compensation of damages and indemnification for losses of foreign investors Foreign investors have the right to claim in the court order for money compensation of damages and indemnification for losses resulting from illegal actions of authorities or its officials. The amount of damages and losses is determined according to the current market prices or on the basis of appraisals of independent auditors.

The damages are compensated and losses are indemnified in the currency used for the investment or in another currency acceptable for the investor. From the moment of effect of the right for compensation and until the compensation payment period the interests are added.

SECTION IV. LABOUR AND SOCIAL RELATIONS OF LEGAL ENTITIES WITH FOREIGN PARTICIPATION GOVERNED BY LAW

Article 27. Regulation of legal labour relations in enterprises with foreign participation Legal labour relations of enterprises with foreign participation, including items of social development and health protection of the staff are regulated by collective and individual agreements (contracts) in accordance with the legislation of Turkmenistan and international standards. The staff of workers and employees of the legal entity with foreign participation and it's administration may also include foreign citizens.

Article 28. Social insurance and security Social insurance and security of employees of the legal entity with foreign participation (with the exception of pensions security for foreign employees) are regulated by the legislation of Turkmenistan.

The legal entity with foreign participation makes allocations for the state social insurance and pension security of their workers at the rates established for enterprises of Turkmenistan.

Allocations for the state social insurance of foreign employees of the legal entity are made by an enterprise only in case if these workers want to use the proper forms of social insurance on the territory of Turkmenistan. Payments for pension security of foreign employees of enterprise are transferred to the proper funds in countries of their permanent residence place in the currency and on the terms of these countries.

Article 29. Regulation of the right for intellectual property at the enterprise with foreign investments The right for intellectual property between the legal entity with foreign participation and an employee is regulated by the agreement between them. The agreement points the obligation of the legal entity to provide for the financial, industrial and social security of an employee in response to his concession to the right of the patent possession.

If such an agreement was not signed the patent is issued to the author of the invention and the legal entity may use this invention on the terms stipulated in the agreement with the author - the owner of the patent. The patent on the invention, industrial sample and trade mark is issued to the legal entity by proper authorities after the submission of the mentioned agreement.

Article 30. Insurance of property and risks Insurance of the property and risks of legal entity with foreign participation is implemented at its discretion if it is not stipulated by the current legislation on the territory of Turkmenistan.

SECTION V. LIQUIDATION OF THE LEGAL ENTITY WITH FOREIGN PARTICIPATION AND SOLUTION OF ARGUMENTS

Article 31. Liquidation of legal entity with foreign participation Liquidation of the legal entity with foreign participation, it's branches (representations) is carried out in the order and in the cases pointed in the foundation documents and according to the legislation of Turkmenistan.

In case if the founders have not contributed 50% of the initially declared charter capital within one year since the date of putting an enterprise in the State Register of Enterprises, the banks of Turkmenistan terminate performing operations on the accounts of such enterprises and inform on this fact the authorities that registered this enterprise for adopting a decision on it's liquidation.

Registration of liquidation of the legal entity with foreign participation is implemented by the registration body on the basis of the statement of liquidation commission and liquidation balance approved by the auditing organization. When liquidating the enterprise with foreign participation, its accumulated assets are subject to taxation according to their real cost.

The legal entity with foreign participation is liquidated after the expiration of 30 days period, after publishing it by the legal entity in press.

The enterprise with foreign participation is excluded from the State Register after its liquidation.

Article 32. Solution of disputes of the foreign investor Disputes of the foreign investor with legal entities and physical persons are subject to the trials in courts of Turkmenistan or in arbitration by agreement of the parties.

In case if the international agreement of Turkmenistan stipulates the other rules of disputes' consideration, the rules of international agreement are applied.

LAW ON PETROLEUM RESOURCES

The Present Law is elaborated by the President of Turkmenistan Sparmurat Niyazov on the basis of the Constitution of Turkmensitan, taking into consideration the national interests of Turkmenistan and its people, and is directed toward securing rational and effective exploitation of the Petroleum resources and the protection of the natural wealth of Turkmenistan for future generations.

CHAPTER 1 GENERAL PROVISIONS, ARTICLE 1, DEFINITIONS

In this Law the definitions listed hereunder shall have the following meanings:

"Block" - areal section on land or on water which is partially or completely located in the territory under the jurisdiction of Turkmenistan and designated as such on a specially compiled map of Blocks.

"Internal water basins" - lakes, artificial water reservoirs and other surface water circumvented by land under the jurisdiction of Turkmenistan.

"Production Operations" - all types of operations for recovery of Petroleum, its saving, treating, handling, storing, transporting, metering, delivery and marketing as well as operations connected with primary and secondary production and other kinds of activities connected with these operations.

"Contract" - agreement entered into between a Contractor (Contractors) and the Competent Body or Concern for the conduct of Petroleum Operations.

"Contract Area" - the area delineated and defined by geographical coordinates, as described in the Appendices to a Contract, within which a Contractor is allowed to conduct Petroleum Operations.

"Competent Body" - State Body, to which the Cabinet of Ministers delegates powers, to issue Licenses and enter into the Contracts with the Contractors.

"Concern" - an operating structure of the Petroleum Sector of Turkmenistan, conducting Petroleum Operations on its own account or in a Joint Venture or in other forms.

"License" - the legal instrument instituted in the form of legal act and issued by the Competent Body and granting the right to carry out all or certain types of Petroleum Operations.

"Person" - a physical or legal person.

"Commercial Discovery" - a discovery of Petroleum, which, after consideration of all relevant data and of the operative, technical and economical factors could be developed commercially.

"Petroleum Operations" - all Exploration and Production Operations and related operations for treating, metering, saving, storing, marketing, delivery and transportation of Petroleum and its derivatives as well as other operations connected to the implementation of a Contract.

"Normal Atmospheric Pressure and Temperature" - pressure of 1,01325 atmospheres and temperature of 60 degrees Fahrenheit.

"License Holder" - a Physical or a Legal Person being granted a License pursuant to the present Law.

"Contractor" - a Physical or a Legal Person being a License Holder and having entered into a Contract with the Competent Body or the Concern pursuant to the present Law.

"Natural Gas" - hydrocarbons, which are in the gaseous state at Normal Atmospheric Temperature and Pressure associated or non-associated to Crude Oil.

"Exploration Operations" - geological, geophysical, aerial and other surveys, the drilling of such shotholes, core holes, stratigraphic tests and other wells for the discovery of Petroleum and the purchase as well as the leasing of materials and equipment therefor.

"Parent Company" - a Legal Person which owns more than 50% of the voting shares of the Contractor and which controls him at the general meetings.

"Affiliate" - a Legal Person which executes control over the Contracting Party or is controlled by such Contracting Party, or is controlled by an other Legal Person which at the same time executes control over the Contracting Party. For the purposes of this definition the control is understood as the power to define strategy of the Legal Person or the Contracting Party though direct or indirect ownership of more than 50% of the voting shares.

"Joint Venture" - the activity carried out by an aggregation of Persons, without constitution of a new legal entity, jointly participating in the supply of technical and financial resources for the implementation of the Contract entered into between the Competent Body and such aggregation.

"Contracting Parties" - the Competent Body or the Concern and a Contractor at the moment of entering into a Contract.

"Crude Oil" - any hydrocarbons, including distillates and condensates extracted from Natural Gas, which at Normal Atmospheric Pressure and Temperature, are in liquid state at the well head or oil/gas separator.

"Model Contract" - standard form of an agreement elaborated by the Competent Body for drafting a Contract and entering into a Contract with a Contractor.

"Petroleum" - Crude Oil and Natural Gas as well as all components derived therefrom or produced therewith.

ARTICLE 2. SPHERE OF APPLICATION OF THE PRESENT LAW

The present Law regulates relations arising in the course of conduct of Petroleum Operations in the territory under the jurisdiction of Turkmenistan, including sea and internal water basins, issuance of the Licenses, entering into and implementation of the Contracts on conduct of such Operations, and regulates powers, rights and obligations of State Entities as well as of the Companies, Enterprises and Organisations carrying out Petroleum Operations.

Should the legislation of Turkmenistan contain rules conflicting with those contemplated herein the provisions of this Law shall apply.

Should an international treaty to which Turkmenistan is a signatory party set rules different from rules contemplated herein, then the rules of the international treaty shall apply.

ARTICLE 3. OWNERSHIP OF PETROLEUM

Petroleum in its natural state in or upon the land in the territory of Turkmenistan is the exclusive property of Turkmenistan.

Competence for ownership, exploitation and disposal of Petroleum is granted to the Cabinet of Ministers (the Government) of Turkmenistan pursuant to the provisions of this Law.

CHAPTER 2. COMPETENCE OF THE CABINET OF MINISTERS (THE GOVERNMENT) OF TURKMENISTAN, THE COMPETENT BODY AND THE CONCERN IN THE SPHERE OF EXPLOITATION OF PETROLEUM RESOURCES

Article 4. Competence of the Cabinet of Ministers (the Government) of TurkmenistanThe Cabinet of Ministers (the Government) of Turkmenistan within the field of exploitation of Petroleum resources and the conduct of Petroleum Operations:

- defines the strategy for exploitation, further expansion of the productivity of Petroleum reserves as well the rates of its production;
- sets the order of priority for the exploitation of Petroleum resources and the rules of protection thereof.
- takes measures for the natural environment, public life and health protection, ensuring healthy and safe labour conditions in the conduct of Petroleum Operations;
- organises statistic reports on Petroleum reserves;
- sets restrictions for the conduct of Petroleum Operations in certain areas with the purpose of saving holy sites, historical and cultural monuments and the like, being important for the safeguard and development of the traditional values and culture of the Turkmen people;
- exercises other powers granted to it by the Laws and the acts of the President of Turkmenistan.

ARTICLE 5. COMPETENCE OF THE COMPETENT BODY

The Competent Body in the field of exploitation of Petroleum reserves and the conduct of Petroleum Operations:

- under the assignment by the Cabinet of Ministers (the Government) of Turkmenistan sets uniform rules for the development of Petroleum fields which shall comply with the uniform standards of the international practice for the conduct of Petroleum Operations;
- carries out the activity for preparation of a tender to be held in compliance with the rules set by this Law and other legislative acts of Turkmenistan and publishes terms, conditions and procedure for holding a tender;
- works out a Model Contract and gives it for consideration to Legal and Physical entities interested to obtain a License;
- carries out negotiations with a License applicant;
- carries out negotiations with a potential License Holder and Contractor about the terms and conditions of a Contract;
- issues the Licenses pursuant to this Law;
- signs a Contract;
- provides for registration of the Contract within fiveteen (15) days from the date of its signature;
- executes control over the conduct of Petroleum Operations and their compliance with the laws as well as with the terms of the License and the Contract;
- suspends and revokes a License pursuant to this Law;
- upon the nomination by the Cabinet of Ministers (the Government) and jointly with the Contractor carries out negotiations and enters into agreements with relevant authorities of other States concerning the construction and operation of transportation facilities for the transportation of the produced Petroleum through their territory and also concerning the utilisation of such transportation facilities, being available and used in these Countries;
- submits annual reports to the Cabinet of Ministers (the Government) of Turkmenistan on the implementation of Contracts;
- exercises other powers attributed to him by the laws and the acts of the President of Turkmenistan.

The Competent Body is entitled to require the License Holder and the Contractor to submit a bank guarantee or the guarantee of its Parent Company. Granting of the License and entering into the Contract may be subject to providing such guarantees.

The Competent Body in the exercise of its powers shall comply with the national interests of Turkmenistan.

ARTICLE 6. COMPETENCE OF THE CONCERN

The Concern assists the Competent Body in the exercise of its powers.

The Concern is entitled to sign Contracts, conduct on its own account Petroleum Operations in specific sites of the Turkmen territory, to act as a member of Joint Ventures as well as an entity authorised to execute control over the conduct of Petroleum Operations in accordance with the established order.

CHAPTER 3. LICENSING OF PETROLEUM OPERATIONS

Article 7. Types of LicensesThe present Law determines the following types of Licenses:

Exploration License; Production License; combined Exploration and Production License.

ARTICLE 8. METHODS FOR GRANTING A LICENSES

An Exploration or a Production License or a combined Exploration and Production License shall be granted on the basis of a tender or direct negotiations carried out by the Competent Body with the License applicant.

The method for granting a License shall be determined by the Cabinet of Ministers (the Government) of Turkmenistan.

ARTICLE 9. MAIN CONDITIONS FOR HOLDING A TENDER

A tender could be open or with a short list of bidders.

Tender conditions are published or delivered to the potential bidders not later than 90 days prior to the tender starting date.

A tendering procedure consists of 2 phases: submission of the application to prequalify and the submission of the bidding proposal.

All Persons wishing to prequalify are entitled to obtain an information related to the procedure and conditions for holding a tender.

A notice for holding a tender should contain the following information on:

- timing and location of the tender and on the deadline forsubmission of applications;
- main conditions for prequalification;
- location and description of the Blocks, offered for conduct of Petroleum Operations.

An application for prequalification should contain:

- name of the applicant, its address, its nationality (for legal persons) or citizenship (for physical persons);
- data on applicant`s shareholders, its directors and authorised representatives which shall represent it upon holding the tender or conducting the negotiations, as well as upon the granting

of the License;
- data on applicants`s technical, managerial, organisational and financial capabilities.

An application shall be accepted for consideration after the payment by the applicant of a tender fee, the amount of which is determined by the Competent Body.

Upon the compliance with the conditions for submission of applications, it shall be accepted for participation to a tender, and the applicant shall be notified to this effect within one month from the date of its filing.

Prequalified applicants shall be notified about the second phase of the tender. Such notification should contain an information on the cost of the package with technical and legal documents, on the deadline for paying such cost and on the main conditions for determination of the tender winner.

ARTICLE 10. BIDDING PROPOSAL

An applicant, within the deadlines set by terms of the tender, and in compliance with the requirements set therein, shall compile a bidding proposal and submit it to the Competent Body.

A bidding proposal shall be regarded as an application for the grant of an Exploration or a Production License or a combined Exploration and Production License, as the case may be.

ARTICLE 11. EVALUATION OF BIDDING PROPOSALS

The Competent Body shall form a commission of experts for the evaluation of technical, financial and organisational capabilities of the applicants and their bidding proposals.

The winner of the tender is determined on the basis of a combination of the following criteria:

- the commencement date of the operations and the work implementation pace;
- the expected date for start-up of Production and the projected time to attain the peak production (in the case of the issuance of a Production or a combined Exploration and Production License);
- the minimum commitments of an applicant in terms of conduct of geological and geophysical operations and exploratory drilling as well as appraisal and development drilling (in the case of the issuance of a combined Exploration and Production License) and of the expenditures for the conduct of aforesaid operations;
- compliance with the requirements for the protection of natural environment and subterranean resources and the safe conduct of operations;
- a projection of revenues for Turkmenistan during the Contract validity.

ARTICLE 12. APPLICATION FOR THE GRANT OF A LICENSE

An application for the grant of an Exploration License shall contain:

- name of the applicant, its address, nationality (for Legal Persons) and citizenship (for Physical Persons);
- data on applicants` shareholders, its directors and authorised representatives which shall represent it upon holding a tender or conduct of negotiations as well as upon granting a License;
- data on applicant`s technical, managerial, organisational and financial capabilities;
- information on previous activities of the applicant, including a list of the States where he has conducted Petroleum Operations during the last five years, and also a balance sheet for the said period;
- proposals of the applicant in respect to the conduct of Petroleum Operations, including minimum

commitments with indication of quantity of work and expenses for its implementation;
- obligations of the applicant concerning natural environment protection including replanting and reclamation of the Contract Area;
- numbers of the Blocks applied for by an applicant;
- sources of financing of Petroleum Operations;
- the time period the Exploration License is applied for.

In case of a Commercial Discovery the Exploration License Holder shall have an exclusive right to be granted a Production License subject to the submission of an application therefore.

An application for a Production License shall contain:

- data on the results of the Exploration Operations;
- official notification of the Commercial Discovery including relevant data and conclusions;
- a detailed plan for the development of the Commercial Discovery with the indication of recoverable Petroleum reserves;
- an expected start-up date for the development of the Commercial Discovery and the expected date for the start-up of the production of Petroleum;
- an estimated profile of production and expected date for attaining its peak production;
- an estimated calculation of the expenditures, associated with the development and production operations and of the proceeds from the sales of Petroleum;
- an analysis of the economic viability of the Commercial Discovery;
- a projected cash flow for Turkmenistan and recovery for capital investments into the development of an operational and social infrastructure of the Contract Area.

An application for a grant of a combined Exploration and Production License shall contain conditions required for the application for a grant of an Exploration and a Production License.

ARTICLE 13. TERMS AND PROCEDURES FOR THE ISSUANCE OF LICENSES

A License shall be issued to a Person to which the right to conduct Petroleum Operations shall be granted as the result from a tender or direct negotiations.

A License shall be issued upon reaching an agreement on the terms of the relevant Contract and concurrently to its conclusion.

The License issuance procedure shall be determined in compliance with the rules set forth by the present Law and other regulatory legal acts of Turkmenistan adopted in accordance with the present Law.

A License shall be issued to Foreign Physical and Legal Persons who register in Turkmenistan as an individual entrepreneur or open a branch in Turkmenistan of a foreign Legal Person or register as a member of Joint Venture.

ARTICLE 14. PURPOSE OF A LICENSE

No person is entitled to conduct Petroleum Operations without a relevant License. A License Holder is entitled to conduct only those kinds of Petroleum Operations which are specified in the License.

The terms of the Contract shall comply with the terms of the License.

ARTICLE 15. LICENSING BODY

The issuance of the Licenses giving the right to conduct Petroleum Operations is carried out by the Competent Body after its approval by the Decree of the President of Turkmenistan.

Article 16. Content of an Exploration License

An Exploration License should contain:

- data on the License grantee;
- type of Petroleum Operations the License is issued for;
- delimitation of the Contract Area through the indication of the geographical coordinates;
- License validity period;
- type of the Contract entered into between the Contracting Parties;
- commitments of the Contractor to comply with the requirements for the protection of the natural environment;
- conditions for the extension of the License validity period;
- other similar elements, as may be determined by the Competent Body.

ARTICLE 17. CONTENT OF A PRODUCTION LICENSE

A Production License should contain:

- data on the License grantee;
- type of the Petroleum Operations the License is issued for;
- delimitation of the part of the Contract Area which encompasses the Commercial Discovery;
- License validity period and conditions for its extensions;
- confirmation of the applicability of the Contract entered into by the Contracting Parties;
- commitments of the License Holder to comply with the requirements of natural environment protection;
- other similar elements as may be determined by the Competent Body.

A combined Exploration and Production License should contain all the conditions contained in an Exploration and a Production Licenses.

ARTICLE 18. LICENSE VALIDITY PERIODS

An Exploration License shall be granted for the period of up to 6 years.

An Exploration License Holder shall have the right to extend the License validity period subject to the fulfilment of the work program and other commitments stipulated in the License and the Contract.

The validity period of an Exploration License may be extended twice with duration of each extension period of up to 2 years.

A Production License shall be granted for the period of 20 years. The validity period of a Production License may be extended for the period of 5 years, if the License Holder applies for the extension of the License not earlier than 2 years and not later than 1 year prior to the Production License expiry date.

An application for the extension of the License validity periods shall be examined not later than in one month from the date of their submission to the Competent Body.

A combined Exploration and Production License shall be granted for a period, which includes the Exploration License validity period and the Production License validity period, including their possible extensions.

The License validity period is counted from the date of its simultaneous registration with the Contract in the authorised bodies.

ARTICLE 19. RIGHTS OF A LICENSE HOLDER

An Exploration License Holder shall have an exclusive right to carry out an Exploration of Petroleum and required kinds of Petroleum Operations connected to the Exploration pursuant to this Law and the terms of a License and provided for in the Contract.

A Production License Holder shall pursuant to the present Law and the terms of the License, have the exclusive rights:

- to carry out Exploration development and Production Operations in that parts of the Contract Area, which are specified in the content of the License;
- to sell or otherwise dispose of its share of Petroleum;
- to carry out such operations and works inside and outside the Contract Area as required for or connected to the issues provided for in the section 2 of this Article 21.

ARTICLE 20. TERMINATION OF THE LICENSE

A License shall terminate:

- upon expiration of the License validity periods or extensions thereof;
- if it is revoked in accordance with the present Law;
- in the event of the termination of the Contract pursuant to the provisions provided therein.

ARTICLE 21. SUSPENSION OF A LICENSE

The validity of a License shall be suspended by the Competent Body in the event when the License Holder:

- conducts Petroleum Operations not provided for in the License;
- carries out the activities within the framework of the License, but not under the program provided for in the Contract;
- in the course of its activities systematically violates the legislation of Turkmenistan in respect with the protection of subterranean resources and of natural environment and of safe conduct of Petroleum Operations.

In the event of suspension of the License validity, the Competent Body shall notify in written the License Holder of the reasons for such suspension and shall set a reasonable deadline for their elimination.

Upon the elimination by the License Holder of the reasons which have caused the License suspension, its validity shall be immediately restored and the License Holder shall be notified in writing to that effect.

The suspension of the License validity shall entail the suspension of the Contract entered into on the basis of said License. The validity of the Contract shall be restored at the same time as the License validity is restored.

ARTICLE 22. REVOCATION OF A LICENSE

The Competent Body shall have the right to revoke the issued License in the following cases:

- when the License Holder refuses to eliminate the causes that have resulted in taking the decision to suspend the License or if he fails to eliminate such causes within the fixed deadline;
- upon discovery of the fact of a deliberate submission to the Competent Body of false information which has materially affected the latter' s decision to issue a License to such person;
- in the event of a deliberate infringement by the License Holder of the deadline for the signing and registration of the Contract as well as the commencement date for conduct of Petroleum Operations stipulated in the Contract;
- in other cases provided for in this Law.

Revocation of the License shall entail the cancellation of the Contract entered into on its basis.

CHAPTER 4. CONTRACTS

ARTICLE 23. TYPES OF CONTRACTS

For carrying out Petroleum Operations in Turkmenistan the following types of Contracts shall be adopted:

- Production Sharing Contract;
- Joint Venture Contract.

Under a Production Sharing Contract the Concern and/or the Competent Body shall sign the Contract on behalf of the Turkmen side. Under such type of the Contract also the Concern shall have the right to act in the role of Contractor.

Under a Joint Venture Contract the Concern or any other entity designated by the Government shall participate as one party to the Joint Venture.

Depending on the nature of the specific Petroleum Operations and other circumstances, a combination of the aforementioned types of Contracts and other types of contracts are allowed.

ARTICLE 24. VALIDITY PERIODS AND TERMS OF A CONTRACT

The validity period and terms of a Contract shall be defined by the agreement between the Parties in conformity with the present Law and the License, and also taking into account provisions of the Model Contract.

ARTICLE 25. SIGNING OF CONTRACTS AND REGISTRATION PROCEDURE

It is a mandatory procedure that the Contract shall be agreed upon with State Entities in charge of health protection and sanitation, ecology, subterranean resources protection and safe conduct of Petroleum Operations. The time for such agreement shall not exceed 15 days from the date of filing of the contractual documents by the relevant entities. The absence of the agreement of the aforesaid entities within the fixed deadline shall not constitute an impediment for the registration of the Contract.

A Contract shall be registered in the competent entities designated by the Cabinet of Ministers (the Government) of Turkmenistan.

A Contract shall enter into force from the date of its registration in the competent entities.

ARTICLE 26. ANNULMENT OF A CONTRACT

A contract shall be rendered null and void in case of revocation of the License granted to the Contractor.

ARTICLE 27

. Amendments to and termination of the Contract Amendments to the terms of the Contract can be made only upon written consent by the Contracting Parties provided that such terms are consistent with requirements of the License and the present Law.

A Contractor and the Competent Body may terminate the Contract on the grounds and in accordance with the procedure provided for in the Contract.

Revocation of the License shall entail termination of the Contract.

The parties shall not be released from the discharge of current obligations which remain outstanding at the time of delivery of the notice on termination of the Contract.

In the event of premature termination of the Contract the Contractor shall, unless otherwise provided for in the Contract, have the right to freely dispose of the assets owned by him. In this case the Competent Body shall have the priority right to an acquisition of such assets.

The issues concerning the transfer of ownership of such assets belonging to the Contractor, during the Contract validity as well as upon its expiration, are stipulated in the Contract.

A Contractor shall leave the Contract Area in the condition which corresponds to the duly approved rules for conduct of Petroleum Operations and the protection of subterranean resources and natural environment.

CHAPTER 5. CONDUCT OF PETROLEUM OPERATIONS

ARTICLE 28. CONDITIONS FOR THE CONDUCT OF PETROLEUM OPERATIONS

Conditions for the conduct of Petroleum Operations including a work program and a budget for expenditures for its implementation shall be specified in the Contract.

If the Exploration results in a Commercial Discovery of Petroleum, the Contractor shall be obliged to notify the Competent Body of such discovery, to carry out an appraisal of the field including an appraisal of its reserves and prepare a report on whether the latter constitutes a Commercial Discovery. The deadline for the notification of the discovery, the results of the field appraisal and the preparation of a report on whether the field constitutes a Commercial Discovery shall be defined in the Contract.

If a Commercial Discovery is achieved the Contractor shall have the right to full recovery of its expenses related to the conduct of Petroleum Operations, the amount of which shall not exceed an amount of proceeds for its Petroleum entitlement share.

If, upon the expiration of the Exploration License validity or its extension periods no Commercial Discovery is achieved, a Contractor shall have no right to recover its investments. In this case, the validity of the License and the Contract shall terminate.

In the event, that the Contractor deems that the field doesn`t constitute a Commercial Discovery or fails to proceed with the development of the Commercial Discovery, Contractor shall be obliged to relinquish that part of the Contract Area, which encompasses such field.

ARTICLE 29. UNIT DEVELOPMENT OF A FIELD

Unit Development of a field means coordination between two or more Contractors carrying out their activity for the development of the same field which lies on the adjoining Contract Areas.

Contractors may enter into written agreements between themselves on unit development of the field, such agreement being subject to the approval by the Competent Body.

If Contractor (Contractors) fails to enter into an agreement with another Contractor (Contractors), or, if Contractor is not in agreement with the unit development plan, the Competent Body is entitled to bind him (them) to enter such agreement, or to direct preparation of such plan by an independent expert and its following mandatory implementation. In the event of failing to comply with the Competent Body`s directions, the Production License issued for such field shall be revoked, and the relevant area shall be withdrawn from the exploitation by the Contractor (Contractors).

ARTICLE 30. ARTIFICIAL ISLANDS, DAMS AND STRUCTURES

The construction, operation and use of artificial islands, dams and other structures installed for the purpose of conduct of Petroleum Operations at sea, shall be carried out on the basis of the permission issued to the Contractor by the Competent Body, subject to the protection by the Contractor of natural environment and bioresources.

A safety zone shall be established around such artificial islands, dams and other structures which shall extend to a distance of 500 meters from each point of their external boundaries.

Location of the artificial islands, dams and other structures shall not constitute an impediment to the customary sea routes of significance for navigation and fishing activities.

Contractors or subcontractors in charge of the construction, maintenance and operation of artificial islands, dams and other structures shall ensure their safeguard and constant availability of warning facilities, signalling their location.

Abandoned or unused artificial islands, dams and other structures shall, if they cannot be used for other purposes, be dismantled in such a manner, that they do not constitute a hazard for human safety and an impediment to the navigation and fishing activities.

Article 31. Discharge and burial of wastes associated with the conduct of Petroleum Operations

Discharge into and burial in the sea of wastes associated with the conduct of Petroleum Operations shall not be allowed.

Discharge of industrial waters into the sea shall be allowed only on the condition of their pre-treatment in order to bring them down to the permissible levels of impurity.

ARTICLE 32. TURKMENISTAN`S RIGHT TO PURCHASE PETROLEUM

The Cabinet of Ministers (the Government) of Turkmenistan shall have the priority right to purchase, at the proportionate basis, Petroleum from the entitlement share of foreign or Turkmen contractors of the private form of property, in order to satisfy the internal market requirements, and, on the condition that such requirements were not satisfied by full utilisation of the Turkmenistan`s entitlement share of Petroleum.

The maximum amounts of the Petroleum purchased, pricing procedure, form of the payment and the payment currency shall be specified in the Contract.

ARTICLE 33. REQUISITION OF PETROLEUM AND ITS COMPENSATION

In the event of war, natural hazard or other circumstances, specified by the legislation on emergency situations, the Cabinet of Ministers (the Government) of Turkmenistan shall have the right to requisition Petroleum belonging to the Contractor.

The requisition shall be carried out to such an extent as is necessary to satisfy the needs of Turkmenistan during the period when such emergency situation remain.

The Government of Turkmenistan shall guarantee the compensation of the requisitioned Petroleum either in kind or by payment of its value in freely convertible currency at the international market price.

ARTICLE 34. STATE CONTROL OVER THE CONDUCT OF PETROLEUM OPERATIONS

State control over the conduct of Petroleum Operations shall be carried out by the Competent Body and other state entities (within their competence) in accordance with the current legislation of Turkmenistan. The officers of such entities shall be obliged to secure the confidentiality of any information received during an inspection.

ARTICLE 35. MEASUREMENT OF PETROLEUM PRODUCED

The Contractor shall carry out measuring and weighing of Petroleum, produced or saved in the Contract Area, at regular time intervals, specified in the Contract, with the application of methods adopted in the international practice for conduct of Petroleum Operations.

Application of other methods for measurement or weighing of Petroleum as well as appliances and equipment used for such purposes by the Contractor, shall be done only upon the written consent of the Competent Body.

The Competent Body shall have the right, systematically and at specified time intervals, to direct that the equipment or appliance used for weighing and measurement of Petroleum be tested.

If any Petroleum weighing or measuring equipment or appliance, upon its test or examination, found to be false or unjust, such equipment or appliance shall, if it is impossible to determine the time at which such equipment or appliance became false or unjust, be deemed to have been false or unjust during a period which is represented by half of the period from the last date upon which the equipment and appliances were tested and found to be in good order to the date upon which such equipment and appliance were found to be false or unjust. Adjustment to all relevant terms under a contract shall be then effected.

CHAPTER 6. RIGHTS AND OBLIGATIONS OF A CONTRACTOR

Article 36. Rights of a contractorContractor shall have the right:

- to use the Contract Area for carrying out the activities specified in the Contract and in the License;
- to construct inside and outside the Contract Area facilities of operative, logistic and social infrastructures necessary for the conduct of Exploration and Production Operations, and also to use, upon agreement with the owners, facilities and communications of general use inside as well as outside the Contract Area;
-to avail itself of the services of sub-contractors in performing certain types of Petroleum Operations;
- to freely dispose of its Petroleum entitlement share in Turkmenistan as well as in other States, subject to the special agreement with such States;
-to carry out, with the right of first refusal, negotiations in respect with the extension of the Contract validity period above the periods provided for in the part 4 of Article 18
- to surrender all or part of its rights and to terminate its activities in accordance with terms specified in the Contract.

Article 37. Obligations of a Contractor In the course of implementation of a Contract the Contractor shall be obliged:

- to adopt the most efficient methods and technologies for the conduct of Petroleum Operations, based on standards of the international practice for the conduct of Petroleum Operations.
- to conduct Petroleum Operations in strict compliance with this Law, terms of the Contract and the License, to comply with the requirements pertaining to the protection of natural environment and subterranean resources;
- to control the flow and prevent the waste or escape of Petroleum inside or outside the Contract Area; - to prevent damage of productive strata, caused by water or other matter entering into Petroleum reservoirs;
- to take measures to prevent pollution of any water spring, river, canal, irrigation system, lake, sea by the escape of Petroleum, salt water, drilling mud, chemical additives or any other waste product or effluent. In case if pollution occurs, Contractor shall treat or disperse it in an ecologically acceptable manner;
- to give preference to the equipment, materials and finished products produced in Turkmenistan, if they are competitive in terms of quality, price, operating parameters and delivery conditions;
- to give preference to Turkmen citizens in hiring personnel for the conduct of Petroleum Operations and to provide for training programs of such personnel in accordance with the terms of the Contract;
- to provide free access to the necessary documents, information and the sites of operations to the authorised representatives and officers of the Cabinet of Ministers (the Government) of Turkmenistan and of the Competent Body;
- to make payment of taxes and other mandatory payments in due time;
- to participate in the development of social infrastructure in accordance with the Contract;
- to restore, at its own account, parts of land and other natural cites which have been damaged in connection with the conduct of Petroleum Operations to the condition acceptable for their further utilisation.

Contractor shall be liable for the damages resulting from risks connected with the conduct of Petroleum Operations. The enumeration of such risks is given in Article 52.

CHAPTER 7. MAIN PIPELINE

ARTICLE 38. OWNERSHIP OF THE MAIN PIPELINE

Main Pipeline means an engineering facility consisting of the main (linear) part of the pipelines systems and associated on-land facilities, communications and equipment designated for transportation of Petroleum from the place of production (treatment) to the place of transfer to another transportation, refining and consumption facilities.

Construction, financing, operation and maintenance of the Main Pipeline shall be carried out by a specially established company, the owners of which can be the Government, Contractor, independent investors or jointly aforesaid entities and persons.

ARTICLE 39. TRANSPORTATION TARIFF

Transportation tariff shall be set and charged by the Pipeline Company

ARTICLE 40. CONSTRUCTION OF MAIN PIPELINE

Main Pipeline shall be planned and constructed in such a way as to allow a throughput capacity, necessary for handling and transportation to land or seaboard terminals of Petroleum, estimated in accordance with medium and long term projections of production.

In the event that an extra throughput capacity is available in the Main Pipeline, and subject to the payment of relevant transportation tariff, independent producers may use such capacity for the transportation of their Petroleum production.

ARTICLE 41. MAINTENANCE OF THE MAIN PIPELINE

The maintenance of the Main Pipeline and its associated facilities shall be carried out in conformity with the norms for maintenance, safety and security applied in the international practice for conduct of Petroleum Operations. A control over the application of such norms shall be executed by the Cabinet of Ministers (the Government) of Turkmenistan and the Competent Body.

The owner (owners) of the Main Pipeline jointly with the Governmental Bodies of the States, which territories are crossed by the pipeline, shall elaborate the plan for joint control over the safe operation of the Main Pipeline and prevention of eventual accidents and emergencies.

A conduct of any operations or actions within the security zone of the Main Pipeline, set by owners, shall be prohibited.

Construction of any objects and facilities, which are not related to the pipeline and its purpose, shall be prohibited within the minimum distance from the Main Pipeline, set in conformity with the construction standards and safety norms, applicable in Turkmenistan.

ARTICLE 42. CONSTRUCTION, LAYING AND OPERATION OF SUBMARINE PIPELINES AND CABLES

Construction, laying and operation of submarine pipelines and cables shall be carried out in conformity with the safety and natural environment protection rules applied in the international practice for conduct of Petroleum Operations in respect of such types of activities.

CHAPTER 8. NATURAL ENVIRONMENT PROTECTION

ARTICLE 43. STATUS OF NATURAL ENVIRONMENT PROTECTION MEASURES

Natural environment and health protection measures for the population and the Contractors` personnel are the obligatory condition for planning and carrying out any types of Petroleum Operations.

ARTICLE 44. ECOLOGICAL GROUNDS FOR CONDUCT OF PETROLEUM OPERATIONS

Before starting a conduct of Petroleum Operations a Contractor shall submit to the special competent State entities a plan for the natural environment protection measures that he intends to adopt in the implementation of its work program.

Conclusion of the special Competent Body shall be given in writing within 30 days of the date of submission of the aforesaid plan and shall be applied by the Contractor to the extent to which it is compatible with the conduct of the planned activity and relevant planned expenditures. In case of absence within the fixed deadline of the decision of the special competent bodies the Contractor shall have the right to start implementation of the aforesaid plan.

ARTICLE 45. MONITORING

Before starting the conduct of Petroleum Operations and for the entire period of their conduct, a Contractor shall set up a monitoring system for obtaining comprehensive current information on changes occurring in the natural environment and on the nature of environmental impact of the Petroleum Operations conducted, with the purpose of taking necessary measures to eliminate and reduce the negative impact on the natural environment and ensure ecologically safe conduct of Petroleum Operations.

CHAPTER 9. FINANCIAL AND FISCAL REGIME

ARTICLE 46. CURRENCY TRANSACTIONS

The procedure for carrying out currency transactions by the Contractor and sub-contractor shall be determined by the current legislation of Turkmenistan and specified in the Contract.

Proceeds accruing to the Contractor from the sale of its Petroleum entitlement share may be deposited on the accounts in Turkmen banks as well as in foreign banks. In doing so, the Contractor shall submit statements of such accounts to the competent entities of Turkmenistan for control in accordance with the current legislation of Turkmenistan.

Contractor shall have the right to open and maintain accounts in national currency of Turkmenistan and foreign currency in banks in the territory of Turkmenistan.

ARTICLE 47. CUSTOMS REGIME

Customs regime shall be applied in accordance with the legislation of Turkmenistan.

All materials and equipment used in the conduct of Petroleum Operations shall be exempted from custom duties and the registration at the State Commodity Exchange of Turkmenistan.

Contractor shall not be exempted from the payment of custom duties and other payments for the conduct of operations other than Petroleum Operations.

ARTICLE 48. TAXES AND PAYMENTS

In the conduct of Petroleum Operations the Contractor shall pay only the following taxes and levies:

- a tax on profit at the rate established by the legislation of Turkmenistan. Procedure for determination of the taxable profit shall be provided for in the Contract.
- a royalty on Petroleum production at the rate specified in the Contract.

Payment of the bonus in form of lump-sum may be provided for in the Contract at the rate specified therein. A bonus may be paid upon the signing of the Contract and upon achievement of certain Petroleum production level specified in the Contract.

In the event that new taxes or levies are introduced subsequently to the date of entering into a Contract, a Contractor shall pay only those which are substituting taxes and levies paid by him. In such a case, an overall amount of due payments shall not exceed the amount of taxes and levies imposed on the Contractor as for the time the Contract is entered into.

Payment of taxes and levies envisaged in the present Law and the Contract shall not release Contractor from the payment of other taxes and levies due for the activities other than Petroleum Operations.

A sub-contractor shall pay profit tax at the same rate as imposed on the Contractor and no other taxes than the Contractor.

Employees of contractor and of its subcontractors shall pay income tax in accordance with the legislation of Turkmenistan and provisions of the Contract.

In the event of amendments to the legislation of Turkmenistan, which was applicable at the time when the Contract was entered into, including amendments due to the changes to the international treaties to which Turkmenistan is a signatory party, the Contractor and the Competent Body shall consider an issue of introducing the amendments into the Contract in order to secure balance in the interests of the Contracting Parties and economic results, which were expected by them in accordance with the terms of the Contact at the time the Contract was entered into.

ARTICLE 49. BOOKKEEPING AND AUDITING

Contractor (sub-contractor) shall maintain bookkeeping and submit accounting in compliance with the legislation of Turkmenistan in respect with the salaries and social security of the Turkmen employees.

For the purpose of recording Contractor`s costs and revenues, as well as for calculation of the taxable profit, bookkeeping and accounting shall be maintained in compliance with the international practice for bookkeeping and accounting applied in the conduct of Petroleum Operations and in accordance with the Contract provisions. For the purposes of foregoing a freely convertible currency shall be used as the monetary unit of the bookkeeping.

National currency shall be used for the purpose of periodical and annual reporting through the translation of foreign currency at the official exchange rate of the Central Bank of Turkmenistan.

Auditing of the financial and economic activity of the Contractor (subcontractors) shall be carried out by the Competent Body or other State entity designated by the Government, at the time intervals, specified in the Contract. The aforementioned entities shall be entitled to avail themselves of the services of independent auditing firms.

CHAPTER 10. LEGAL TERMS

ARTICLE 50. ASSIGNMENT OF THE CONTRACTOR`S RIGHTS AND OBLIGATIONS

Contractor may assign all or part of its rights and obligations under the License and the Contract to the other interested party, with the prior written consent of the Competent Body.

Contractor shall be entitled to assign all or part of its rights and obligations under the License and the Contract to an Affiliate or one of its members (in case of the multi-membered Contractor), with no consent required, subject to the submission of the document, endorsed by assignor, such document stating the joint liability of the Contractor for all the actions of the assignee.

As long as Contractor retains any participation interest in the License and the Contract, such Contractor and the assignee of its rights and obligations, shall bear joint responsibility under the Contract.

Expenses associated with the assignment of rights and obligations shall be borne by the Contractor.

ARTICLE 51. OWNERSHIP OF INFORMATION ON SUBTERRANEAN RESOURCES

Ownership of geological and geophysical information, data on Petroleum reserves and all other information obtained or prepared by the Contractor in the course of conduct of Petroleum Operations, shall belong to the Government. Such information shall not include proprietary rights and secrets of the Contractor.

ARTICLE 52. INSURANCE

Contractors shall be obliged to obtain and maintain an insurance as follows:

- all risks insurance, covering all plant, equipment, buildings and other property of the Contractor, used or intended for use in the conduct of Petroleum Operations;
- insurance, covering eventual loss of Petroleum and its by-products up to the point in time and location at which the title is transferred from Contractor to the Competent Body (in respect to the Competent Body`s entitlement share of production) or other persons;
- insurance, covering clean-up costs for damage to the natural environment, including pollution of the air, water, surface and subsurface soil under and in the Contract Area;
- general liability insurance, covering property damage and life and health harm resulted from or in connection with the conduct of Petroleum Operations;
- control-of-well insurance, covering control of well and redrill costs caused by accidents to wells in the Contract Area.
- health, life and accidents insurance, covering the insurance for employees and other persons, engaged by the Contractor for the conduct of Petroleum Operations; - such other types of insurance, as would be applied by the Contractor in compliance with the international practice for conduct of Petroleum Operations;
- such other insurance required by the current legislation of Turkmenistan on obligatory types of insurance.

Contractor shall be obliged to require sub-contractors, which activities are connected to the conduct of Petroleum Operations, to obtain and maintain insurance in such forms and amounts stipulated by the relevant contracts of sub-contractors.

ARTICLE 53. EMPLOYMENT RELATIONS

The employment legal relations of the Contractors with its employees are regulated by the legislation of Turkmenistan, collective or individual employment contracts.

Employment contracts of the Contractor with foreign employees may contain special provisions in accordance with the international practice for entering such contracts. In such case, the level of guarantees of labour rights of foreign employees should not be lower than the level of guarantees, provided for by the legislation of Turkmenistan.

ARTICLE 54. SOCIAL INSURANCE AND SOCIAL SECURITY

Social insurance and social security of the employees, which have entered into the employment legal relations with Contractor (except for the pensions provisions of foreign employees), are regulated by the legislation of Turkmenistan.

Contractor may contributes to the State social insurance in respect of foreign employees only in such cases when latter wish to enjoy social benefits in the territory of Turkmenistan.

Pension provisions and provisions on other kinds of social security of foreign employees are regulated by employment contracts, and shall comply with the legislation of the States of their permanent residence.

ARTICLE 55. GUARANTEES OF CONTRACTORS` RIGHTS

Contractor shall be guaranteed the protection of its rights in accordance with the principles of international law, legislation of Turkmenistan, the License and the Contract.

ARTICLE 58. RESOLUTION OF DISPUTES

Disputes associated with the issuance, refusal to issue, suspension or revocation of the License, as well as those related to the implementation of the Contract, shall be possibly resolved by way of negotiations, including the involvement of independent international experts, or in accordance with dispute resolution procedures previously agreed in the Contract.

In the event that disputes cannot be resolved in accordance with the provisions of part 1 of this Article within 3 months from the moment of a written communication from either part to the other, either party may, with prior written notification to the other party, refer to international arbitration bodies, determined by the parties in the Contract.

All other disputes, including disputes between the Contractor and Legal Persons and citizens of Turkmenistan, shall be resolved by competent judicial bodies of Turkmenistan, unless otherwise provided for in the agreement of the parties.

ARTICLE 59. FORCE MAJOR

Failure by the Contractor to fulfil the terms of the License and (or) the Contract or to comply with the requirements of the legislation shall not constitute their infringement if such actions are caused by war, act of war, military conflicts, natural hazard or other events, beyond the will and actions of the Contractor, or by other causes, envisaged in the Contract as circumstances of Force-Majeur.

In the event of failure to fulfil terms of the License and/or the Contract, the Contractor shall be obliged to immediately inform the Competent Body in that respect with indication of causes for such circumstances to arise.

Validity periods of the License and of the Contract shall be extended for periods during which the Contractor did not exercise its rights and obligations in compliance with the present Law, the License and the Contract due to the circumstances of Force-Majeure.

In the event that circumstances of Force-Majeur endure for more than 1 year, either party has the right to propose to the other to terminate the Contract. Upon reaching agreement by the Parties the Contract shall terminate.

In the event that the circumstances of Force-Majeur remain during a period of more than 2 years, either party has the right to unilaterally terminate the Contract with prior notification to the other party.

In the event that the Contractor did not recover its costs connected to the conduct of Petroleum Operations the Contract may be terminated at the Contractor` option.

The force of this Article shall not apply on the requirement of payments to be made in due time, as provided for by this Law, the License and the Contract.

CHAPTER 10. FINAL PROVISIONS

ARTICLE 60. INFORMATION REQUIRED BY THE COMPETENT BODY

The Competent Body shall have the right to summon the Contractor in writing to furnish an information and data related to Petroleum Operations, such data including also world price of Petroleum, in the event that the Competent Body has the ground to believe that the Contractor is in possession of such information or data, which information and data have not be submitted to the Competent Body in accordance with the provisions of the Law and terms of the Contract. Contractor shall be obliged to provide such information.

ARTICLE 61. POWERS OF THE COMPETENT BODY AND AUTHORISED OFFICERS

In order to ensure control over the compliance with present Law and fulfilment of the terms of the Contract, the Competent Body and authorised officers shall have the right to:
- enter any area, structure, vehicle being used in connection with the conduct of Petroleum Operations;
- to carry out an inspection or testing of the equipment or appliance being used in the conduct of Petroleum Operations;
- to extract samples of Petroleum or other substances from any area where Petroleum Operations are being conducted, with the purpose of their analysis or testing, or for use as evidence upon the violation of the Law or infringement of the terms of the Contract;
- carry out an inspection of the documents, relating to the Petroleum Operations, make extracts from and make copies of such documents;
- give directions and introduce restrictions on the activities of Contractor, related to securing safety and health protection of the Contractor`s personnel and of the population;
- carry out any necessary examination and inquiry in respect with the issues of compliance, by the Contractor, with the laws, other regulatory acts and terms of the Contract.

In the exercise of its powers the Competent Body or its authorised officers may involve other persons as experts.

Contractor shall be obliged to supply necessary help and assistance to the Competent Body or an authorised officer in the execution of their powers.

ARTICLE 60. CONFIDENTIALITY OF INFORMATION

Neither party has the right to publish, disclose or transfer any information, which is considered confidential and is related To Petroleum Operations, to a third party, without prior written consent of the other Contracting Party.

Confidential information may be supplied to legal counsels, accountants, other consultants, underwriters, lenders, subcontractors, shipping companies, subject to a prior written undertaking from such persons not to disclose the information received.

ARTICLE 61. INDEMNITY OF TURKMENISTAN AND THE CABINET OF MINISTERS OF TURKMENISTAN

A License Holder and Contractor shall keep the Government indemnified against all actions, claims and demands which may be brought or made against the Government by reason of anything done by such License Holder and the Contractor, in the exercise of the latter`s rights and obligations under the Law, the License and the Contract.

TAX SYSTEM AND LEGISLATION IN TURKMENISTAN

THE TAX CODE IS BEING REVISED AND CURRENT TAX LEGISLATION IS BASED ON SEVERAL TAX LAWS AND REGULATIONS AMENDED BY PRESIDENTIAL DECREES. LEGISLATION OF IMPORTANCE TO THE FOREIGN INVESTOR INCLUDES VALUE ADDED,PROFIT AND PROPERTY TAXATION, SPECIAL TAXATION FOR SMALL ENTERPRISES AND FAVORABLE TAXATION IN FREE ECONOMIC ZONES. ALSO, FOREIGN INVESTORS SHOULD BE AWARE THAT THEY ARE REQUIRED TO REGISTER WITH THE STATE CHIEF TAX INSPECTORATE BEFORE BEGINNING OPERATIONS. FOR CONTACT INFORMATION, SEE PARAGRAPH 19.

STATE TAX SERVICE

3. CREATED IN JANUARY 1992, THE STATE TAX SERVICE OF TURKMENISTAN CONSISTS OF THE STATE CHIEF TAX INSPECTORATE (SCTI), HEADQUARTED IN ASHGABAT, AND TAX INSPECTORATES LOCATED IN THE REGIONS, DISTRICTS AND CITIES OF TURKMENISTAN. THE TAX SERVICE OVERSEES TAX LEGISLATION ENFORCEMENT AND THE PAYMENT OF TAXES BY STATE AND PRIVATE ENTERPRISES AND ORGANIZATIONS OPERATING IN TURKMENISTAN AS WELL AS INDIVIDUALS INVOLVED IN BUSINESS ACTIVITY. ALL FAX PAYMENTS COLLECTED BY THE STATE TAX SERVICE GO TO THE STATE BUDGET AND SOCIAL FUNDS (PENSION FUND AND SOCIAL SECURITY FUND). THE SCTI REPORTS DIRECTLY TO THE PRESIDENT OF TURKMENISTAN.

4. THE STATE TAX SERVICE IS AUTHORIZED TO:

- CHECK ALL NECESSARY DOCUMENTATION RELATED TO TAX PAYMENTS MADE BY TURKMEN OR FOREIGN COMPANIES OR INDIVIOUALS OPERATING BUSINESSES IN TURKMENISTAN;
- REQUIRE ANY NECESSARY REPORTS REGARDING THE FINANCIAL STATUS OF A COMPANY'S ACTIVITY;
- VERIFY FHE EXISTENCE OF ANY OFFICE SPACE, PRODUCTION FACILITY, WAREHOUSE SPACE OR OTHER ASSET BELONGING TO A COMPANY;
- MONITOR ANY PAYMENT DEFAULTS MADE BY A COMPINY AND ISSUE INSTRUCTIONS ON HOW TO CORRECT IW;
- WITHDRAW DOCUMENTATION CONFIRMING INTENTIONALLY MADE TAX PAYMENT DEFAULTS SUCH AS HIDING REAL INCOME OR ASSETS;
- SUSPEND A COMPANY'S ABILITY TO MAKE BANK TRANSFERS IN CASES IN WHICH THE TAX INSPECTION TEAM IS PREVENTED FROM INVESTIGATING A COMPANY'S ACTIVITIES;
- WITHDRAW OVERDUE TAXES FROM A LOCAL BANK ACCOUNT WHEN

A COMPANY FAILS TO PAY IN A TIMELY MANNER. A FINE OF 0.3 PERCENT IS CHARGED FOR EACH DAY TAXES ARE OVERDUE;
- ORDER LAW ENFORCEMENT OFFICIALS TO FREEZE A COMPANY'S ASSETS AND BRING A SUIT AGAINST THE COMPANY.

REGISTRATION OF FOREIGN INVESTORS

5. IN JULY 2002, A PRESIDENTIAL DECREE DESIGNED TO STRENGTHEN TAX COMPLIANCE INTRODUCED A REQUIREMENT THAT FOREIGN INVESTORS INVOLVED IN CONSTRUCTION, CONSUMER GOODS PRODUCTION, PROVISION OF SERVICES AND/OR OTHER ACTIVITIES IN TURKMENISTAN REGISTER WITH THE SCTI AND RECEIVE A TAX CODE NUMBER. OTHERWISE, A PENALTY OF 2 PERCENT OF THE CONTRACT PRICE WILL BE CHARGED. IF A SPECIAL PRESIDENTIAL DECREE EXEMPTS A COMPANY'S ACTIVITY IN TURKMENISTAN FROM TAXATION, THE COMPANY MUST STILL REGISTER WITH THE SCTI. THOSE FOREIGN COMPANIES THAT ONLY EXPORT FROM AND/OR IMPORT GOODS INTO TURKMENISTAN ARE NOT REQUIRED TO REGISTER.

(NOTE: FOREIGN COMPANIES THAT INVEST IN TURKMENISTAN MUST ALSO REGISTER WITH THE STATE AGENCY FOR FOREIGN INVESTMENT (SAFI). THOSE COMPANIES THAT ONLY EXPORT AND/OR IMPORT GOODS MUST REGISTER ONLY WITH THE STATE COMMODITIES AND RAW MATERIALS EXCHANGE

TAX LEGISLATION

6. ACCORDING TO THE SCTI, A NEW TAX CODE THAT WILL UNIFY TAX REGULAFIONS AND PROCEDURES IS NOW BEING DEVELOPED. TAX LEGISLATION OF INTEREST TO THE FOREIGN INVESTOR INCLUDES LAWS ON VALUE ADDED AND PROFIT TAXES, FOREIGN INVESTMENT (ARTICLE 17), FREE ECONOMIC ZONES (ARTICLE 9), SECURITIES TAX, A PRESIDENTIAL DECREE CONCERNING SIMPLIFICATION OF TAX LEGISLATION FOR SMALL ENTERPRISES, AND OTHER REGULATIONS THAT CURRENTLY AMEND AND/OR SUPPLEMENT EXISTING TAX LEGISLATION.

VALUE ADDED TAX

7. FOREIGN COMPANIES OR INTERNATIONAL CONSORTIA, THEIR BRANCHES OR REPRESENTATIVE OFFICES, AND FOREIGN INDIVIDUALS REGISTERED AND ENGAGED IN PRODUCTION AND/OR COMMERCIAL ACTIVITY IN TURKMENISTAN ARE SUBJECT TO A VALUE ADDED FAX (VAT) OF 20 PERCENT.

ALL TAXES ARE LEVIED IN THE TURKMEN NATIONAL CURRENCY, THE MANAT. FOREIGN EXCHANGE INCOME IS TRANSFERRED INTO MANATS AT THE CURRENT BANK FOREIGN EXCHANGE RATE.

THE VAT MUST BE PAID EITHER EVERY 10 DAYS (IF PAYMENT IS MORE THAN 5 MILLION MANATS), MONTHLY (IF PAYMENT IS BETWEEN 2.5 AND 5 MILLION MANATS), OR QUARTERLY (IF PAYMENT IS LESS THAN 2.5 MILLION MANATS). THE VAT IS NOT LEVIED ON A NUMBER OF ACTIVITIES INCLUDING TRANSIT CARGO TRANSPORTATION SERVICES; CITY PASSENGER TRANSPORTATION SERVICES (EXCEP, FOR TAXIS); APARTMENT RENTAL;

INSURANCE SERVICES; MONEY TRANSFER SERVICES EXCEPT FOR PAYMENTS MADE FOR BROKER AND INTERMEDIARY SERVICES; SECURITIES SERVICES; INDUSTRIAL

PROPERTY COPYRIGHT OPERATIONS; SALES
OF MEDICINE, MEDICAL ITEMS AND EQUIPMENT, AND MEDICAL SERVICES, AND SOME OTHER OPERATIONS AND SERVICES.

PROFIT TAX

8. FOREIGN INVESTORS AND THEIR BRANCHES AND REPRESENTATIVE OFFICES INVOLVED IN PRODUCTION AND/OR COMMERCIAL ACTIVITY IN TURKMENISTAN ARE SUBJECT TO A 25 PERCENT PROFIT TAX. THOSE ENGAGED IN OPERATING COMMODITY, STOCK OR LABOR EXCHANGES, OR BROKERAGE AND INTERMEDIARY ACTIVITIES ARE CHARGED A PROFIT TAX OF 45 PERCENT. THE PROFIT TAX IS PAID ONCE A YEAR.

9. NEWLY-CREATED ENTERPRISES ARE EXEMPT FROM PROFIT TAX PAYMENTS DURING THE FIRST YEAR OF PROFITABLE OPERATION IF 70 PERCENT OF THE PROFIT IS DERIVED FROM PRODUCTION OF AGRICULTURAL PRODUCTS, CONSUMER GOODS, AND/OR BUILDING MATERIALS. DURING THE SECOND YEAR OF PROFITABLE OPERATION, SUCH ENTERPRISES ARE CHARGED 50 PERCENT OF THE PROFIT TAX. HOWEVER, THIS PRIVILEGE IS NOT EXTENDED TO THOSE ENTERPRISES THAT:

- LEASE STATE-OWNED EQUIPMENT;
- ARE CREATED ON THE BASIS OF ABOLISHED SFATE ENTERPRISES;
- ARE NEWLY PRIVATIZED;
- ARE JOINT STOCK ENTERPRISES WITH STATE EQUITY PARTICIPATION EXCEEDING 50 PERCENT.

10. RELIGIOUS ORGANIZATIONS; BUSINESSES THAT EMPLOY HANDICAPPED INDIVIDUALS (NOT LESS THAN 50 PERCENT OF THE TOTAL NUMBER OF EMPLOYEES) AND/OR ARE RELATED TO THE PRODUCTION OF HANDICAP ITEMS; ENTITIES ENGAGED IN EDUCATIONAL ACFIVITIES APPROVED BY THE CABINET OF MINISTERS ARE ALSO EXEMPTED FROM PROFIT RAX PAYMENTS.

IN ADDITION, A FOREIGN ENTERPRISE THAT INVESTS MORE THAN 30 PERCENT OF A JOINT VENTURE'S WORKING CAPITAL IN HARD CURRENCY IS EXEMPTED FROM PROFIT TAX PAYMENTS FOR THE TIME PERIOD THE ENTERPRISE IS RECOVERING ITS INITIAL INVESTMENT. THIS PERIOD CANNOT BE LONGER THAN IS ESTIMATED IN TECHNICAL DOCUMENFATION ASSOCIATED WITH THE ENTERPRISE'S CONTRACT.

11. THOSE SUBJECT TO PROFIT TAX INCLUDE ANY FOREIGN FIRM OR ORGANIZATION THAT IS REGISTERED IN ITS HOME COUNTRY AND OPERATES IN TURKMENISTAN THROUGH A REPRESENTATIVE OFFICE. AN EXCEPTION IS MADE ONLY FOR SUCH ACTIVITIES AS:

- USE OF FACILITIES ONLY FOR GOODS STORAGE ANO/OR EXHIBITION;
- STORAGE OF GOODS PROCURED ONLY FOR THE PURPOSE OF CARRYING OUT FURTHER PROCESSING OF THOSE GOODS;
- KEEPING A PERMANENT STORAGE SPACE ONLY FOR GOODS AND/OR RAW MATERIALS PURCHASED IN TURKMENISTAN, AND/OR COLLECTION OF INFORMATION THAT IS PERMITTED BY TURKMEN LEGISLATION FOR COLLECTION;
- MAINTENANCE OF A PERMANENT OFFICE SPACE ONLY FOR THE PURPOSE OF HAVING PREPARATORY AND/OR AUXILIARY WORK DONE IN TURKMENISTAN.

PROPERTY TAX

12. A PROPERTY TAX OF 1 PERCENT FOR A ONE-YEAR PERIOD IS CHARGED FOR ASSETS BELONGING TO AN ENTERPRISE, INCLUDING VEHICLES AND UNFINISHED CONSTRUCTION PROJECTS.

ENTERPRISES WITH FOREIGN INVESTMENT AND THEIR BRANCHES OPERATING IN TURKMENISTAN, REPRESENTATIVE OFFICES OF FOREIGN COMPANIES ENGAGED IN PROJECTS RELATED TO NATURAL
RESOURCES DEVELOPMENT AND TURNKEY CONSTRUCTION, AND OTHER REPRESENTATIVE OFFICES AND INDIVIDUALS REPRESENTING A FOREIGN COMPANY ARE SUBJECT TO PROPERTY TAXES. PROPERTY
TAX MAY ALSO BE PAID IN THE FOLLOWING MANNER: FIRST QUARTER, AT A 25 PERCENT RATE; FIRST HALF OF THE YEAR, AT A 50 PERCENT RATE; FIRST THREE QUARTERS OF THE YEAR, AT A 75 PERCENT RATE.

EXCESS PAYROLL TAX

13. TO REGULATE WAGE PAYMENTS IN CORRESPONDENCE WITH A SCOPE OF WORK AND WORK RESULTS, THE GOTX ESTABLISHED AN EXCESS PAYROLL TAX. THIS TAX IS LEVIED FROM THE AMOUNT OF THAT PART OF THE OVERALL SALARY FUND THAT EXCEEDS A NON-TAXABLE SALARY FUND. THE TAX EQUALS TO 50 PERCENT. THE NON-TAXABLE SALARY FUND IS CALCULATED ON THE BASIS OF THE FOLLOWING COMPONENTS:

- AN ENTERPRISE PAYROLL LIST;
- A BENCHMARK OF THE COUNTRY'S OFFICIAL MONTHLY AVERAGE SALARY; AND
- COEFFICIENTS THAT VARY DEPENDING ON A SECTOR OF THE TURKMEN ECONOMY.

THE NON-TAXABLE OVERALL SALARY FUND MAY VARY DEPENDING ON AN ECONOMIC EFFICIENCY OF AN ENTERPRISE.

14. THE FOLLOWING ENTERPRISES ARE EXEMPT FROM THE EXCESS PAYROLL TAX PAYMENT:

- ENTERPRISES INVOLVED IN PLANT-GROWING AND CATTLEBREEDING;
- ENTERPRISES OPERATING IN THE FREE ECONOMIC ZONES; AND
- CASINOS, AUDIO- AND VIDEO-RENTAL BUSINESSES, AND SLOT-MACHINE BUSINESSES.

OTHER TAXES

15. INCOME, DIVIDENDS AND INTEREST EARNED FROM SECURITIES, BONDS AND ROYALTIES (EXCEPT FOR STATE BONDS AND SECURITIES) AS WELL AS FROM PROFIT SHARING PARTICIPATION IN OTHER ENTERPRISES OPERATING IN TURKMENISTAN ARE ASSESSED A PROFIT TAX OF 15 PERCENT.

16. A PROFIT TAX OF 60 PERCENT IS LEVIED ON INCOME EARNED FROM OPERATING CASINOS, AUDIO AND VILEO RENTAL BUSINESSES, SLOT-MACHINEBUSINESSES, AND SPONSORING CONCERTS AND PUBLIC ENTERTAINMENT EVENTS WITH PARTICIPATION OF MORE THAN 2,000 PEOPLE.

FAVORABLE TAXATION IN FREE ECONOMIC ZONES

17. TURKMEN AND FOREIGN COMPANIES THAT BEGIN OPERATIONS IN THE FREE ECONOMIC ZONES IN TURKMENISTAN ARE EXEMPT FROM PROFIT TAXES FOR THE FIRST THREE YEARS OF OPERATION.

AN ENTERPRISE WITH FOREIGN INVESTORS WHOSE INVESTMENT WAS MORE THAN 30 PERCENT IN HARD CURRENCY (NO EQUIPMENT AND TECHNOLOGY ARE CONSIDEREO) IS CHARGED 50 PERCENT OF THE PROFIT TAX RATE DURING THE FOLLOWING THREE YEARS AND 30 PERCENT DURING THE SUBSEQUENT 10 YEARS OF OPERATION. THE PROPERTY TAX IS CHARGED AT HALF THE REGULAR RATE DURING THE FIRST FIVE YEARS.

18. PROFIT REINVESTED IN EXPORT-ORIENTED PRODUCTION (NOT LESS THAN 70 PERCENT OF PRODUCTION TO BE EXPORTED) AND/OR STATE-OF-THE-ART TECHNOLOGY, SCIENTIFIC RESEARCH, ENVIRONMENTAL PROTECTION, SPECIALIST TRAINING, OR INFRASTRUCTURE DEVELOPMENT WITHIN THE FREE ECONOMIC ZONES IS EXEMPT FROM TAX PAYMENTS.

19. THERE ARE OTHER TAX PRIVILEGES FOR TURKMEN AND FOREIGN COMPANIES AND INDIVIDUALS DOING BUSINESS IN THE FREE ECONOMIC ZONES. SEE ARTICLE 9 OF THE LAW OF TURKMENISTAN CONCERNING FREE ECONOMIC ZONES.FORMER USSR-U.S. DUAL TAXATION CONVENTION

20. TURKMENISTAN HAS NOT YET SIGNED A DUAL TAXATION TREATY WITH THE U.S. THEREFORE, THE GOTX RELIES ON THE DUAL TAXATION CONVENTION THAT WAS SIGNED BETWEEN THE FORMER USSR AND THE U.S. ON JANUARY 28, 1976. SINCE THE COLLAPSE OF THE USSR, PRACTICALLY SPEAKING, THIS DOCUMENT HAS HAD NO LEGAL POWER.

THE LAW OF TURKMENISTAN ON FREE ECONOMIC ZONES

The present Law determines general legal and economic principles of the establishment and functioning of free economic zones, regulates the relations between the subjects of economic activity operating on the territory of a free economic zone.

The law aims at ensuring the development of the regional economic and scientific-technical potential with the involvement of foreign investors and subjects of economic activity from the private sector of the economy.

SECTION I. GENERAL PROVISIONS

ARTICLE 1. THE CONCEPT OF A FREE ECONOMIC ZONE

A free economic zone is a particularly separated territory with the fixed administrative borders to be governed by special regimen. A free economic zone occupies the territory the borders of which are established by legislative acts of Turkmenistan.

On the territory of a free economic zone, subjects of economic activity from the private sector of the economy of Turkmenistan and foreign investors are allowed to carry out all kinds of economic, financial and other activity except those prohibited by the legislation of Turkmenistan.

ARTICLE 2. LEGISLATION ON FREE ECONOMIC ZONES

1. Legal relations within free economic zone are regulated by the present Law and other legislative acts of Turkmenistan.

2. If an international agreement with the participation of Turkmenistan contains the provisions different from the provisions of the present Law the former is applied.

ARTICLE 3. SETTING UP A FREE ECONOMIC ZONE

Setting up a free economic zone and regulation of it's operation are decreed by the President of Turkmenistan.

ARTICLE 4. SETTING UP AND LIQUIDATION OF AN ENTERPRISE WITHIN THE FREE ECONOMIC ZONE

1. Enterprises set up within the free economic zone are registered in accordance with the procedure stipulated by the legislation of Turkmenistan. Enterprises with foreign participation are registered by a body authorized by the Cabinet of Ministers.

The enterprise with foreign participation acquires the status of a legal entity from the date of obtaining the certificate of the state registration (re-registration) issued by the holder of the Unified State Register of Enterprises and Organisations of all forms of property and activity.

2. Enterprises operating in a free economic zone irrespective of their legal organizational forms are liquidated in accordance with the legislation of Turkmenistan.

ARTICLE 5. GUARANTEES OF RIGHTS AND INTERESTS OF THE SUBJECTS OF ECONOMIC ACTIVITY

1. Turkmenistan guarantees the observance of the rights and legal interests of economic subjects in a free economic zone.

2. Nationalisation by the state of the property of the subjects of economic activity in a free economic zone is not permitted.

3. Any discrimination against enterprises with foreign investments as compared with other enterprises operating in a free economic zone as well as compulsory withdrawal of foreign investments (nationalisation, requisition, confiscation) or any other steps entailing similar consequences are not permitted in a free economic zone.

It is prohibited to sequester the invested property, except the temporary suspension of the right until the complete liquidation by an investor of his debts.

Compulsory withdrawals can only be carried out by the court verdict on the conditions of the payment of a compensation which is equal to the real (market) value of investments to be withdrawn including the lost profit as estimated at the time of the actual compulsory withdrawal or at the moment of taking the resolution to make such actions.

Compensation is made in the same currency as of the initial investment currency.

4. Foreign investors operating in a free economic zone are guaranteed the right to repatriate the after-tax earned foreign currency proceeds abroad. In a free economic zone foreign investors have the unlimited right to transfer, convey, pawn, export and terminate the investment of hard currency.

5. Central and local government bodies cannot prevent the citizens of Turkmenistan travelling between a free economic zone and other regions of the country.

SECTION II. OPERATION OF A FREE ECONOMIC ZONE

ARTICLE 6. BASIC PRINCIPLES OF THE ACTIVITY OF ECONOMIC SUBJECTS

1. Economic relations between enterprises located in a free economic zone are based on the contracting principles. Enterprises form independently their production programs and sell their products (services). The output of enterprises is left at their complete disposal.

2. A free economic zone is formed and operated on the principles of self-financing including the one of foreign currency.

3. Subjects of economic activity operating in a free economic zone are entitled to raise credits from the foreign banks and attract the services of foreign insurance companies for conclusion of all types of insurance contracts.

4. The consumption funds of enterprises located in a free economic zone are not regulated by the state.

5. The terms of economic activity of foreign investors, related to the prospecting, exploration, exploitation and production of renewable and non-renewable natural resources including those of the off-shore economic zone, are not regulated by the proper legislative acts of Turkmenistan.

ARTICLE 7. PECULIARITIES OF THE EXPORT-IMPORT OPERATIONS IMPLEMENTATION

1. A free economic zone has a simplified procedure for export-import operations, providing for the following:
- the export of goods manufactured in a free economic zone is not subject to quotation and licensing except certain groups of products to be listed by the Cabinet of Ministers;
- goods are considered to have been manufactured in a free economic zone if the amount of the value added as a result of processing exceeds 30 percent of the total value;
- enterprises and organisations are entitled to perform barter and intermediary operations with goods and services produced in a free economic zone;
- the import of goods (services) into a free economic zone is not subject to quotation and licensing except those imported in accordance with the special regulations and inter-governmental agreements.

ARTICLE 8. PECULIARITIES OF CUSTOMS PROCEDURE

1. The following customs procedure shall be used on the territory of a free economic zone:
- goods and other assets imported into the territory of a free economic zone shall be exempt from customs duties;
- goods and other assets exported from a free economic zone to other countries shall be exempt from customs duties except for that part of goods, assets having foreign origin;
- goods and other assets imported to a free economic zone and exported from it shall be subject to mandatory declaration.

2. Transit and resale of commodities that have not been processed in a free economic zone through the territory of a zone to another regions of Turkmenistan, as well as the export of goods from another regions of Turkmenistan through the territory of a free economic zone shall not be granted any customs and taxation privileges.

3. Control over the export from a free economic zone of goods and assets of foreign origin imported into it on a duty-free basis shall be exercised by the Main State Tax Inspectorate of Turkmenistan by checking the corresponding documents.

ARTICLE 9. TAXATION

1. The following taxation procedure shall be used on the territory of a free economic zone:
- enterprises operating in a free economic zone shall be exempt from paying the tax on profit for the first three profit-generating years;
- the profit tax for enterprises with foreign investments, that have a foreign partner's share of more than 30 percent in the statutory fund, shall be decreased by 50 percent for the period of the following three years after the initial profit-generating three years; for the period of the following ten years the profit tax shall be decreased by 30 percent;
- for the enterprises, the term of operation of which has been less than five years, the exemption from profit tax during the initial three profit-generating years shall be considered a form of a tax credit to be paid at the time of an enterprise liquidation by the reasons other than bankruptcy;
- within the initial five years of operation in a free economic zone the property tax shall be decreased by 50 percent of the established rate;
- the profit reinvested in export-oriented and technologically advanced objects as well as in research and experimental-development works and for environmental protection, personnel training and retraining, in infrastructure and social objects of a free economic zone shall be tax exempt.

Export-oriented objects mean enterprises with at least 70 percent of their output being intended for export. Conclusions allowing to classify objects as technologically advanced ones shall be drawn up by the corresponding academies of sciences of Turkmenistan;
- citizens of Turkmenistan, foreign citizens and persons without citizenship shall be taxed on their income at the rates established by the legislation of Turkmenistan and in the currency income has been received in, except for investors of Turkmenistan and other countries who earn their income in the form of dividends, interest, copyright and license royalties, rent, freight, participation, on a share basis, in other enterprises located in a free economic zone and taxed at a rate of 10 percent.

2. Amounts of income generated from freight and paid to foreign subjects of economic activity for the performance of international transportation shall be taxed at a rate of 3 percent.

3. Foreign partners in joint ventures located in a free economic zone shall be exempt from paying tax on the repatriation of their profit outside Turkmenistan.

4. If an international agreement signed by Turkmenistan contains provisions different from those stipulated by the present article the provisions of the international agreement shall prevail.

5. The present article shall not affect taxation privileges established by general provisions of international law and specific agreements of Turkmenistan with other states.

6. Taxation of income and profits of foreign legal entities and physical persons may be terminated or limited on a mutual basis if in a corresponding foreign state the same measures are applied to the subjects of Turkmenistan concerning the similar taxes; this fact must be confirmed by the tax bodies of this state.

A foreign legal entity or physical person entitled by an international agreement to a full or partial exemption from the income tax from the sources of Turkmenistan shall submit an application for reduction or cancellation of the tax in the procedure established in Turkmenistan.

7. When making commercial transactions with foreign partners it is prohibited to include in a contract tax stipulations which provide that a subject of economic activity paying for a transaction and for dividends assumes an obligation to bear the expenses for paying taxes on income and profit of foreign partners.

SECTION III. FOREIGN CURRENCY AND MONETARY MECHANISM OF PRICING

ARTICLE 10. MONETARY AND FOREIGN CURRENCY CIRCULATION

1. Investors operating in a free economic zone may have current and payment accounts (in foreign currency and in the currency of Turkmenistan) in banks of Turkmenistan with the right to spend the corresponding funds on the whole territory of Turkmenistan in accordance with the current legislation. To transfer funds kept in their accounts out of the country, foreign investors may buy foreign currency by the rate established in the currency exchange of Turkmenistan.

2. In cases when foreign investors produce the import-substituting output that is of high importance to the national economy, the translation of a part of the profit belonging to the foreign investor into the currency of Turkmenistan may be done by a mutually agreed rate at the expense of currency funds of the parties concerned.

3. The registration of banks and other financial institutions in a free economic zone including branches of foreign banks and banks with foreign participation as well as the performance of financial operations and circulation of all currencies within the territory of a free economic zone shall be monitored by the Central Bank of Turkmenistan.

4. The Central Bank of Turkmenistan shall be authorised to give a permission for the operations with cash (non-cash) foreign currency and to determine a special procedure of its spending on the territory of a free economic zone and its transfer abroad; the procedure shall be set up with the purpose of stimulating the development of free entrepreneurship in a zone.

5. Banks of a free economic zone shall have the right to open accounts for legal entities and physical persons of Turkmenistan and foreign countries in the currency of Turkmenistan and foreign currency.

ARTICLE 11. PRICING

The procedure of free pricing shall be applied to all goods manufactured and services rendered in a free economic zone.

ARTICLE 12. RENT

1. Legal entities and physical persons of Turkmenistan and other states operating on the territory of a free economic zone shall be exempt for three years from paying rent for land starting from the moment of signing a rent agreement.

Upon expiration of the exemption period the rate of the rent payment for land shall be decreased: for enterprises with a foreign share in the statutory fund not less than 30 percent the rate shall be decreased by 50 percent; for physical persons and legal entities of Turkmenistan the rate shall be decreased by 20 percent.

2. Investors of Turkmenistan and foreign states have the right for a sublease of property and assignment of rights for use by a mutual agreement of the parties which have signed a lease agreement or, their legal successors. The rights for use may be used by an investor as pledge.

3. The terms of agreements on rent of land lots, buildings constructions and other objects may be changed in accordance with the legislation of Turkmenistan by a mutual agreement of the parties or by the decision of Economic court.

ARTICLE 13. FOREIGN ECONOMIC ACTIVITY

All legal entities and citizens operating in a free economic zone shall independently participate in foreign economic activity including commercial intermediary operations.

Participants of foreign economic activity shall be registered by the Committee on foreign economic affairs at the President of Turkmenistan.

ARTICLE 14. LABOUR RELATIONS

1. Labour relations in enterprises located in a free economic zone shall be regulated by collective and individual agreements (contracts) in accordance with the legislation of Turkmenistan. When regulating wages salaries the pay tariff system shall be referred to as recommendation source only.

2. Minimum wages, salaries, student grants, pensions, benefits and other social allowances set in a free economic zone can not be established at rates lower than the amounts of similar payments specified in the legislation of Turkmenistan.

3. Enterprises of a free economic zone are entitled to pay employees' wages and salaries in foreign currency.

4. Labour terms with respect to foreign personnel shall be stipulated in individual contracts. The after-tax foreign currency income of these employees may be freely repatriated abroad.

5. No limitations on signing contacts with the citizens of Turkmenistan on the grounds related to their places of residence shall be permitted in a free economic zone.

ARTICLE 15. PROCEDURE FOR RESOLVING DISPUTES

Disputes of the subjects of economic activity in a free economic zone with the state agencies, other legal entities and citizens of Turkmenistan, as well as disputes of between the subjects of economic activity shall be considered in law courts of Turkmenistan.

Saparmurat Turkmenbashy, President of Turkmenistan
The city of Ashgabat, October 8, 1993
With change and amendments by Medjlis of September 23, 1994

FREE ECONOMIC ZONES IN TURKMENISTAN

ASHGABAT - BUZMEN

The export-oriented industrial zone - it covers the interval of the circuit highway from Ashgabat to Buzmein with the width of 5 km to the north of the railway. The sectors of priority development are: agroindustrial processing, construction industry, research- and energy-consuming industries, as well as manufacture of consumption goods.

MARY - BAIRAMALY

It covers the interval of the highway from Mary to Bairamaly with the width of 5 km along the road. The sectors of priority development are: agroindustrial processing, agricultural machinery construction, energy-consuming production, manufacture of consumption goods.

CHELEKEN - OKAREM

It covers the Cheleken peninsula and the Caspian coast up to Okarem. The sectors of development are: petrochemical industry, fishing industry, tourism and vacation industry.

DASHKHVUZ - AIRPORT

It covers the interval of the highway Dashkhovuz - Airport 5 km wide. The sectors of priority development are: production and processing of agricultural products, labour-consuming industrial production, folk crafts, tourism, manufacture of consumption goods.

CHERDJEV - SEIDI

It covers the interval of the highway from Cherdjev to Seidi 1 km wide. The sectors of priority development: light and food industry, device construction, machinery construction.

BAKHERDEN - GYZYLARBAT

It covers the interval of the highway from Bakherden to Gyzylarbat with the width of 3 km to the north and south along the road. The sectors of priority development are: agroindustrial processing, construction industry, recreation, traditional crafts and manufacture of consumption goods.

ASHGABAT - ANNAU

Industrial zone - it covers the interval of the highway from Ashgabat to Annau with the width of 5 km to the north of the railway. The sectors of priority development are: agroindustrial processing, research and energy-consuming productions and manufacture of consumption goods

LAW OF TURKMENISTAN ON ENTEPRENEURIAL ACTIVITY IN TURKMENISTAN

SECTION 1. GENERAL PROVISIONS

ARTICLE 1. ENTREPRENEURSHIP

Entrepreneurship is initiative, independent activity of citizens aimed at obtaining profit or income and carried out on one's own behalf, at one's own risk and on one's own property liability of legal entity - enterprise. An entrepreneur may carry out any kinds of activities not prohibited by legislative acts of Turkmenistan.

ARTICLE 2. LEGISLATION ON ENTREPRENEURIAL ACTIVITY

Relations connected with entrepreneurial activity irrespect of the property forms, type and sphere of activity are regulated by the present Law and other legislative acts of Turkmenistan.

In relationships where one of the parties is a foreign physical person or legal entity, international treaty rules are applied, if the current legislation of Turkmenistan doesn't stipulate the other rules.

ARTICLE 3. SUBJECTS OF ENTREPRENEURIAL ACTIVITY

The subjects of entrepreneurial activity (entrepreneurs) in Turkmenistan may be:
physical persons and legal entities of Turkmenistan and other states as well as the persons without citizenship.

The status of entrepreneur is obtained after the state registration in the order established by the legislation of Turkmenistan. It is prohibited to carry out entrepreneurial activities without registration.

ARTICLE 4. FORMS OF ENTREPRENEURIAL ACTIVITY

Turkmenistan recognizes any forms of entrepreneurial activity carried out within the legal framework and provides their legal protection and support. Entrepreneurial activity may be carried out in the following forms:
without application of hired labour and formation of a legal entity;
with application of hired labour and formation of a legal entity.

Entrepreneurial activity may be carried out by the hired head of an enterprise, if he is granted all rights and powers by contract with the owner of the enterprise property or a body (person) authorised by him.

ARTICLE 5. IMPERMISSIBILITY OF LIMITATION OF COMPETITION IN ENTERPRENEURIAL ACTIVITY

It is not allowed for entrepreneurs to use actions limiting competition if it is not stipulated by the legislative documents of Turkmenistan, including: actions undermining competitor's reputation, conclusion of collusions on the limitation of production, division of markets, maintenance of monopolic high or low prices;
appropriation of the other's trade (firm) marks, information enabling to copy the goods of other producers as well as the other actions not stipulated in the legislation.

Profit received as the result of limitation of competition and other actions not stipulated in the legislation are subject to penalty in the established order.

SECTION II. RIGHTS OF AN ENTREPRENEUR, GUARANTEES OF ENTREPRENEURIAL ACTIVITY

Article 6. Rights of an entrepreneurIn accordance with the legislation of Turkmenistan an entrepreneur has the right:
to institute any kinds of enterprise for implementation of his activities;
to acquire totally or partially property of enterprises irrespect of the forms of property, other property, property and non-property rights;
to participate with his property in the activities of other economic subjects;
to use by agreement of the parties the property of legal entities and physical persons;
to hire and discharge employees on the contract principles and under other conditions established by the legislation;
to establish independently forms, systems and amounts of wages and other types of income of persons working for hire;
to form independently the program of economic activity, to choose suppliers and customers of his production (works, services), to establish prices and tariffs for it in accordance with the legislation of Turkmenistan and concluded contracts;
to open accounts in banks, to carry out currency and other operations;
to use profit (income) remained at his disposal.

If entrepreneurial activity is carried out on the contract principles, the order of profit distribution is regulated by the contract;
to receive any income in the unlimited amount;
to use the state system of social security and social insurance;
to appeal in the established order the actions of state and other bodies infringing on his rights or legal interests;
to be the participant of foreign economic relations.

ARTICLE 7. OBLIGATIONS OF ENTREPRENEURS

In accordance with the legislation of Turkmenistan and concluded contracts (agreements) an entrepreneur is obliged:
to pay not less than state minimum wage to persons working for hire;
to pay to the State Fund of social insurance for insurance of persons working for hire in the order and amount established by the legislation;
to pay completely to all hired workers irrespect of the financial condition of enterprise;
to carry out measures to ensure ecological safety, protection of labour, safety techniques, industrial hygiene and sanitation, being governed by the regulations and standards in force;
to observe the rights and legal interests of consumers and to ensure the appropriate quality of goods (works, services) produced;
to obtain special permission (licence) for activity in the spheres subjected to licensing;
to present in time all necessary information to the state bodies and tax inspection in the established order;
to announce the bankruptcy of the enterprise in case if it is impossible to fulfil the obligations to creditors.

ARTICLE 8. RESPONSIBILITY OF ENTREPRENEUR

An entrepreneur, carrying out his activity with establishment of a legal entity, is responsible according to the Law of Turkmenistan "On Enterprises". An entrepreneur, carrying out his activity without establishment of a legal entity is liable for all obligations related to this activity with all his property, with the exception of that property which is not subject to the sequestration in accordance with the legislative documents of Turkmenistan. An entrepreneur, carrying out his activity on the contract principles, is responsible to the owner of the property for the obligations of enterprise he manages in the order and under conditions of the contract concluded between them.

ARTICLE 9. STATE REGISTRATION OF ENTREPRENEURIAL ACTIVITY

Registration of entrepreneurial activity with establishment of a legal entity is carried out in the order stipulated by the Law of Turkmenistan "On Enterprises".

Registration of entrepreneurial activity without establishment of a legal entity is carried out by local executive bodies at the place of activity of an entrepreneur in the order determined by the Cabinet of Ministers of Turkmenistan.

Refusal for the state registration of the entrepreneurial activity or breach of the order and terms of registration may be appealed in the court.

ARTICLE 1 0. REGISTRATION OF TRADE (FIRM) MARK

Registration and use of trade (firm) mark is carried out in accordance with the legislation of Turkmenistan.

ARTICLE 1. TERMINATION OF ENTREPRENEURIAL ACTIVITY

Entrepreneurial activity is terminated on the resolution of the owner of the court.

Entrepreneurial activity is terminated by the court in case of:
carrying out entrepreneurial activity prohibited by the legislation of Turkmenistan or without special permission (licence) for this activity; multiple or serious violations of the legislation;
violations of the standards of ecological safety;
declaration that the entrepreneur is bankrupt;
other reasons stipulated by the legislation of Turkmenistan. The court taking resolution about termination of the entrepreneurial activity in cases stipulated in this Article, determines the order and period for termination of entrepreneurial activity in accordance with the legislation or Turkmenistan.

In case of death of an entrepreneur, his rights and obligations related to the entrepreneurial activity shall be transferred to his heirs. Entrepreneurial activity, carried out on the contract principles, may be terminated at the end of the period of expiration of the contract or in case if the contract cancelled by one of the sides in the order stipulated by the contract.

SECTION III. REGULATION OF INTERRELATIONS BETWEEN ENTREPRENEURS AND THE STATE

ARTICLE 12. STATE SUPPORT OF ENTREPRENEURIAL ACTIVITY

Turkmenistan guarantees the observance of the rights and legal interests of entrepreneurs, creates for them conditions for competition, provides support and equal opportunities for entrepreneurs to get material, finance, labour, information, nature and other resources.

ARTICLE 13. PROTECTION OF THE RIGHTS OF ENTREPRENEURS

Turkmenistan guarantees inviolability of property and ensures protection of an entrepreneur's right of ownership.

Interference into the activity of entrepreneurs by the state or other bodies or officials is not allowed, except the reasons established by the legislation of Turkmenistan and within the limits of powers of the bodies mentioned.

Losses caused to entrepreneur by groundless interference of the state or other bodies or officials into entrepreneur's activity, should be compensated by these bodies or officials. Disputes about damage compensation are settled in the court.

ARTICLE 14. STATE REGULATION OF ENTREPRENEURIAL ACTIVITY

Turkmenistan ensures freedom of competition between entrepreneurs, protects consumers against results of unfair competition and monopoly in all spheres of entrepreneurial activity.

Bodies of the state management organize their relations with entrepreneurs using:
tax and finance-credit policy, including establishment of tax rates and interest rates for state credits, tax privileges, prices and rules of pricing, special grants and subsidies, amounts of economic sanctions;
state property and system of reserves, licences, concessions, leasing, social, economic and other standards and norms;
external economic and currency policy;
state orders;
scientific-technical and social state and regional program.

ARTICLE 15. PROFIT (INCOME) TAXATION

Incomes of citizens received from entrepreneurial activity, which carried out without establishment of a legal entity, are taxed in the order stipulated for the taxation of citizens.

Profit received from the entrepreneurial activity, which carried out with establishment of a legal entity, is taxed in the order, determined for the taxation of legal entities. Taxation of the personal income of entrepreneur in this case is carried out in the order stipulated for the taxation of citizens.

ARTICLE 16. ECONOMIC DISPUTES

An entrepreneur or bodies, or persons authorized by him may dispute all actions or claims given to him and sanctions imposed in the order established by the legislative documents of Turkmenistan, except cases when recovery is carried out in the nonappealable order.

The President of Turkmenistan Saparmurat Turkmenbashy

TURKMENISTAN: OVERVIEW OF THE COPYRIGHT AND PATENT SYSTEM

BACKGROUND

3. THE GOTX'S FIRST STEP TOWARD PROTECTION OF THE INTELLECTUAL PROPERTY RIGHTS OF FOREIGN INVESTORS CAME IN SEPTEMBER 1993 WHEN THE GOTX PASSED A LAW PROTECTING SCIENTIFIC RESEARCH. THEN, IN OCTOBER 1993, THE GOTX PASSED A PATENT LAW EGULATING COPYRIGHTS FOR TECHNICAL INVENTIONS, INNOVATIVE PROPOSALS AND INDUSTRIAL TRADEMARKS. ALSO IN OCTOBER 1993, THE GOTX INSERTED INTO ITS LAW CONCERNING FOREIGN INVESTMENT AN ARTICLE PROTECTING THE INTELLECTUAL PROPERTY OF FOREIGN INVESTORS INCLUDING LITERARY, ARTISTIC AND SCIENTIFIC WORKS, SOFTWARE AND DATABASES, PATENTS AND OTHER COPYRIGHTS FOR INVENTIONS AND INDUSTRIAL SAMPLES, TECHNOLOGY, COMMERCIAL SECRETS, AND TRADEMARKS. THEN, IN OCTOBER 1994, THE GOTX PASSED A LAW ON THE LEGAL PROTECTION OF ALGORITHMS AND SOFTWARE FOR COMPUTERS, DATABASES AND TOPOLOGIES OF INTEGRAL MICROSCHEMES.

4. IN ADDITION TO THIS LEGISLATION, IN JANUARY 1995, TURKMENISTAN SIGNED THE WORLD INTELLECTUAL PROPERTY ORGANIZATION'S (WIPO'S) 1883 PARIS CONVENTION ON PROTECTION OF INTELLECTUAL PROPERTY RIGHTS FOR INDUSTRIAL PROPERTY AND SIGNED THE INTERNATIONAL TREATY ON PATENT COOPERATION. THE GOTX HAS ALSO JOINED WIPO'S EURASIAN PATENT ORGANIZATION CREATED FOR CIS COUNTRIES. (NOTE: CURRENTLY NINE CIS STATES BELONG TO THIS ORGANIZATION. END NOTE.)

5. MOREOVER, THE GOTX SIGNED AN AGREEMENT ON TRADE RELATIONS WITH THE UNITED STATES IN 1993 THAT PROVIDES FAVORABLE TREATMENT FOR COPYRIGHTED MATERIALS. THE AGREEMENT ENVISAGES
THAT TURKMENISTAN JOIN THE BERN CONVENTION FOR THE PROTECTION OF LITERARY AND ARTISTIC WORKS (PARIS 1971) AND CREATE A WORKING GROUP ON INTELLECTUAL PROPERTY MATTERS. (NOTE: TO

DATE, THE GOTX HAS NOT JOINED THE BERN CONVENTION OR CREATED A WORKING GROUP. END NOTE.)

6. CURRENTLY A NEW COPYRIGHT LAW IS BEING DEVELOPED AS PART OF TURKMENISTAN'S CIVIL CODE. HOWEVER, IT IS NOT CERTAIN WHEN THE CIVIL CODE FOR TURKMENISTAN WILL BE APPROVED.

PATENT AGENCY

7. THE GOTX ESTABLISHED A PATENT AGENCY IN 1993 TO PROVIDE FOR THE PROTECTION OF RIGHTS ON INDUSTRIAL INTELLECTUAL PROPERTY, ESTABLISH A SINGLE PATENT SYSTEM AND ISSUE PROTECTIVE DOCUMENTS FOR INDUSTRIAL SAMPLES AND TRADEMARKS. WITH A STAFF OF 20 EMPLOYEES, THE PATENT OFFICE CONSIDERS AND APPROVES ALL INDUSTRIAL PATENT APPLICATIONS IN TURKMENISTAN AND PUBLISHES INFORMATION ABOUT THE PATENTS THAT ARE APPROVED. (NOTE: THE FIRST EDITION OF THE TURKMENISTAN PATENT AGENCY BULLETIN WAS ISSUED RECENTLY. IT CONTAINS THE ENTIRE TEXT OF THE PATENT LAW; THE PROVISION ON THE PATENT AGENCY; THE ACT ON ADHERENCE TO THE EURASIAN PATENT CONVENTION; THE LAW ON LEGAL PROTECTION OF ALGORITHMS, SOFTWARE, DATABASES AND TOPOLOGICAL INTEGRAL MICROSCHEMS; AND SOME EXTRACTS FROM THE PROVISION ON DUTIES CHARGED FOR ISSUING PATENTS FOR INVENTIONS AND INDUSTRIAL SAMPLES AND REGISTRATION OF TRADEMARKS. END NOTE.) ACCORDING TO DR. RASHIT AGABAYEV, THE PATENT OFFICE DIRECTOR, THE GOTX PLANS TO DEVELOP FURTHER ITS INDUSTRIAL PATENT LAW TO CONFORM TO WORLD STANDARDS. HOWEVER, THE MEJLIS (PARLIAMENT) IS UNLIKELY TO TAKE UP THIS ISSUE UNTIL THE CIVIL CODE IS PASSED.

8. FOR MORE INFORMATION ABOUT APPLYING FOR A PATENT IN TURKMENISTAN, CONTACT THE CABINET OF MINISTERS OF THE TURKMENISTAN PATENT AGENCY AT THE FOLLOWING ADDRESS:

DR. RASHIT AGABAYEV, DIRECTOR (SPEAKS RUSSIAN)
PATENT AGENCY

13 AITAKOV STREET
ASHGABAT, TURKMENISTAN 744028
TEL: 9 (9312) 41-58-73 OR 78
FAX: 9(9312) 41-58-72

ADVANTAGES OF PATENT REGISTRATION

9. PATENT REGISTRATION IS NOT REQUIRED. HOWEVER, THERE ARE ADVANTAGES TO DOING SO. BESIDES HAVING THE EXCLUSIVE RIGHT TO USE A PARTICULAR INNOVATION, TRADEMARK, OR TECHNOLOGY, ETC.,
A COMPANY HOLDING A PATENT CAN RECEIVE FAVORABLE TAX TREATMENT, PROVIDED THAT:
- AN INNOVATION IS USED IN A COMPANY'S OWN PRODUCTION; - AN INNOVATION LICENSE WAS PURCHASED BY THE PATENT HOLDER; - AN INNOVATION IS USED AFTER A LICENSE HAS BEEN BOUGHT; AND
- A NEW MACHINE OR EQUIPMENT WAS MADE BASED ON A PATENT INVENTION. THE CABINET OF MINISTERS DETERMINES THE FORM AND SIZE OF THE FAVORABLE TAXATION. COMPANIES MAY ALSO SELL PATENT RIGHTS.

PATENT DUTIES

10. THE PATENT AGENCY CHARGES DUTIES FOR ISSUING PATENTS ON INNOVATIONS AND INDUSTRIAL SAMPLES AND FOR THE REGISTRATION OF TRADEMARKS. THESE DUTIES MUST BE PAID TO THE PATENT AGENCY WITHIN TWO MONTHS, BEGINNING THE DAY A DECISION ON ISSUING A PATENT AND/OR REGISTRATION OF A TRADEMARK IS MADE.

FOREIGN ENTITIES NOT REGISTERED IN TURKMENISTAN AND FOREIGN CITIZENS NOT RESIDING IN TURKMENISTAN MUST PAY PATENT DUTIES IN DOLLARS AT THE CURRENT EXCHANGE RATE. BELOW ARE
PATENT DUTIES (IN DOLLARS) FOR SOME SERVICES:

- APPLICATION FOR ONE INNOVATION USD 100

- APPLICATION FOR SEVERAL INNOVATIONS USD 100 FOR THE FIRST AND 25 PER EACH ADDITIONAL INNOVATION

- APPLICATION FOR ONE VARIANT OF AN INDUSTRIAL SAMPLE USD 100

- APPLICATION FOR SEVERAL VARIANTS USD 100 FOR THE
OF AN INDUSTRIAL SAMPLE FIRST AND 25 FOR EACH ADDITIONAL SAMPLE

- APPLICATION FOR A JUDGMENT ABOUT A REFUSAL TO ISSUE A PATENT FOR AN INNOVATION OR INDUSTRIAL SAMPLE USD 500

THE COMPLETE LIST OF DUTIES FOR ISSUING A PATENT AND REGISTRATION OF TRADEMARKS IS AVAILABLE FROM THE U.S. EMBASSY IN ASHGABAT.

COPYRIGHT LAW

11. CURRENTLY, THERE IS NO COPYRIGHT LAW AND NO AGENCY CHARGED WITH IMPLEMENTING COPYRIGHT LEGISLATION--BOTH OF WHICH ARE PREREQUISITES TO JOINING THE BERN CONVENTION.
THEREFORE, SUCH ARTICLES AS VIDEOS, CASSETTE TAPES AND LITERATURE ARE FREELY COPIED AND SOLD IN TURKMENISTAN.

HOWEVER, THE SUPPLY AND DEMAND FOR AMERICAN COPYRIGHTED MATERIALS APPEARS TO BE MINIMAL. A COMPANY THAT PLANS TO ENGAGE IN BUSINESS IN TURKMENISTAN SHOULD WORK WITH THE GOTX TO ENSURE THAT COPYRIGHTED MATERIALS THAT COMPRISE A PART OF THE COMPANY'S INVESTMENT ARE APPROPRIATELY PROTECTED.

SYSTEM AND PROCEDURESFOR CERTIFICATION OF TELECOMMUNICATIONS EQUIPMENT IN TURKMENISTAN

1. INTRODUCTION

Certification of products is an activity designed to attest that a product conforms to established requirements.

Certification is conducted for the following purposes:

- creating conditions for activities of enterprises, entities, organizations and businessmen on the common commodity market of Turkmenistan and for participation in international economic, scientific and technical cooperation and in international trade;
- protecting consumers from negligence of a manufacturer (seller, operator);
- monitoring a product's safety for the environment, and for the life, health and property of people;
- assisting consumers in making competent choices of products;
- confirming products' quality indicators as reported by a manufacturer.

The activity tasks for certification are those procedures used to determine whether or not the given technical device meets certain standards as well as technical and administrative requirements.

The organizations that establish obligatory requirements for the certification of telecommunications equipment are:

The Ministry of Posts and Telecommunications and the General State Inspectorate for Standardization, Metrology, Labor Protection and Safety of Works in the National Economy of Turkmenistan.

2. LEGISLATIVE BASE (LEGAL BASIS) OF CERTIFICATION

A telecommunications equipment certification system is being developed in Turkmenistan.

At present, telecommunications equipment certification is not conducted in Turkmenistan because of the absence of a certification center. In general, the Ministry of Posts and Telecommunications is responsible for wireless and wireline telecommunications equipment.

Certificates or documents attesting to their recognition are produced to the Customs Authorities together with the cargo customs declaration and are necessary for obtaining a permission to import products into Turkmenistan (Law "On Certification of Products and Services," Article 8.2).

There are no documents regulating telecommunications equipment certification in Turkmenistan. There are the Law "On Certification of Products and Services" approved by the President of Turkmenistan on October 8, 1993, No. 897-XII, and other normative documents.

There is no telecommunications equipment certification system in Turkmenistan, which is why certificates of organizations of the countries of the Commonwealth of Independent States within the framework of the Regional Commonwealth in the field of Communications are accepted, but the priority is given to certificates from Russia.

The Ministry of Posts and Telecommunications of Turkmenistan gave its consent to organize a Central Asian certification center in Tashkent, Uzbekistan.

It is planned to organize the certification center on the basis of the metrological laboratory of the Production Association of Backbone Lines and TV (1996-97).

Application of other countries' certificates is allowed if they are recognized by the authorized body (Law "On Certification of Products and Services," Article 7.4).

To ensure recognition of certificates and compliance marks abroad, the certification system is being created in accordance with the existing international norms and rules, and in cooperation with inter-regional national certification systems of other countries in accordance with the following documents: ISO/IEC Guides 2, 7, 16, 23, 25, 27, 39, 40, 43, 45, 48, 49, 53-56 and European standards of the series 45000.

3. MINISTERIAL ACTS DEFINING ATTACHMENT OF TELECOMMUNICATIONS EQUIPMENT TO THE NETWORK

There are no ministerial acts defining certification of telecommunications equipment. Relations in the area of certification are regulated by the Law and legislative documents issued in conformance with it. There is a collection of regulatory and technical documents -- "State Certification System of Turkmenistan," Part 1, 1995.

To attach equipment to the public network, a certificate of one's own country or a recognized certificate granted in other countries, is required.

The terms of contracts (agreements), concluded for equipment to be imported into Turkmenistan, must foresee availability of a certificate and mark of conformity that would confirm the equipment's conformance to the established requirements. These certificates and compliance marks must be granted or recognized by the authorized body of Turkmenistan (Law "On Certification of Products and Services," Article 8).

Certificates and marks of conformity are recognized on the basis of multilateral and bilateral certification agreements to which Turkmenistan is a party.

Failing such agreements, documents granted by foreign certification organizations (centers) and individual firms for the products to be imported can be accepted as valid for one occasion. In this case, equipment may be re-tested completely or some characteristics may be tested to confirm the product's conformity with the established requirements (Gosstandart of Turkmenistan, TDS 1.2-93, Article 5.8).

Radioelectronic equipment (radio telephones, radio in the local loop, satellite communications equipment, personal mobile radio stations) can be imported into Turkmenistan only with the permission of the State Radio Frequency Commission of Turkmenistan for operation in the preliminarily allocated frequencies.

The General State Inspectorate of Turkmenistan arranges publishing of advertisements only for certified types of products (Gosstandart of Turkmenistan, TDS 1.2.01-93, Article 4.7).

A manufacturer or vendor of equipment may obtain information about marketing rules for radio electronic facilities at the General State Inspectorate of Turkmenistan and in the press.

As regards standard network termination points, at present State standards developed under the former Soviet Union for each type of standard network termination point are used, but they are being re-registered.

4. STRUCTURE AND ORGANIZATIONAL SCHEME FOR CERTIFICATION OF COMMUNICATIONS TECHNICAL EQUIPMENT

Currently there is no certification center in Turkmenistan, but it is planned to open in 1996-97, which is why we forward our proposals on its structure and organizational scheme.

The following bodies constitute the organizational structure of the state certification system:

- State Certification Body for products and services (General State Inspectorate of Turkmenistan);
- Certification Body (leadership) for communications products and services (Ministry of Posts and Telecommunications of Turkmenistan);
- testing laboratories (centers).

5. ORDER AND PROCEDURE OF CERTIFICATION

5.1 Are there rules and publications that specify the application and approval procedures? If yes, how can applicants obtain copies of these rules and publications? Describe the procedures for terminating a certificate and reasons for which a certificate would be terminated. Describe the validity period of a certificate (minimum, maximum, and reasons for choosing one or the other).

The procedure for filing and considering the declaration-application, and receiving a certificate are set out in Gosstandart of Turkmenistan TDS 1.2.01-93, "Products Certification Procedure."

When changing the design (composition) of a product or its production technology affects the characteristics tested during certification, an applicant should report the changes to the body that granted the certificate, which makes a decision about the necessity to perform new tests or to estimate the state of production of those products.

If a norm for a certification characteristic that is fixed in a regulatory document is changed and becomes tighter, the certificate is cancelled from the date of introduction of the change (Gosstandart of Turkmenistan TDS 1.2.01-93).

The term of validity of a certificate is established by the Certification Body taking account of the term of validity of regulatory documents for the products as well as the term for which the production or quality system is certified, but not longer than three years.

If products are certified within an international system or agreement, the procedure for granting certification, the form of the certificate, and the term of its validity are determined taking account of the rules of this system or agreement (Gosstandart of Turkmenistan TDS 1.2.01-93).

5.2 What organization must the manufacturer contact to begin the certification process?

To certify a product within the framework of a domestic or foreign system, an applicant has to file a declaration-application with the respective accredited body for certification of homogeneous products.

5.3 What fees are charged for certification and how (on what basis) are they established?

The client pay all of the expenses related to certification irrespective of the results.

When certifying products, the following list of works is payable:

-- FILING AN APPLICATION FOR PRODUCTS CERTIFICATION AND OTHER DOCUMENTS. Payment is made for the work in accordance with tariffs developed taking account of the required time or in accordance with agreements.
-- PERFORMANCE OF TESTS. Paid according to the approved tariffs or agreements between a testing laboratory and the Certification Body.
-- EVALUATION OF QUALITY SYSTEM AND/OR CERTIFICATION OF PRODUCTION. Paid on the basis of agreements depending on the quantities and the required time.
-- EXECUTION AND REGISTRATION OF A COMPLIANCE CERTIFICATE. The amount to be paid includes certification expenses of the attested or accredited laboratory and constitutes 20% of their costs.
-- ISSUANCE OF CERTIFICATION. The amount is 0.5% of the price of the certified products (works, services).

5.4 Is there a standardized form that must accompany a certification request? If yes, please attach a copy of the form.

See Annex 2.

5.5 What other information must be filed, such as a test report, photographs, technical descriptions, and in what language?

A technical description and technical specifications, and a decision of the State Radio Frequency Committee (GKRCh), in the state (Turkmen) or Russian languages.

5.6 Is the applicant required to submit a sample of the equipment for testing?

Yes. A sample of the equipment is submitted to a testing laboratory. The number of samples to be tested and the procedure for their selection are determined by the test program and methods.

5.7 Please describe how applications are processed from submittal to grant of certification. What procedures exist for enforcement of the terms of the certificate? What procedures exist to prolong the certificate's validity?

There is no certification center.

5.8 How long does it normally take for an application to be processed and granted? Describe causes of delays in the certification process.

There is no certification center.

5.9 Who can an applicant contact to find out the status of an application while it is being processed?

The Technical Department of the Ministry of Posts and Telecommunications of Turkmenistan.

Address: Ashgabat, ul. Zhitnikov, 36. Chief of the Technical Department -- Mr. Eemberdy Mamedov.

Tel: 011 7 363 2 35 40 20; fax: 011 7 3632 39 04 20.

5.10 Is there a dispute resolution procedure available to applicants? Can an applicant appeal a denial of an approval or a delay in processing an application?

Disputed questions in the area of certification are considered under the procedure specified by the legislation of Turkmenistan (Law "On Certification of Products and Services," Article 11).

5.12 How can manufacturers obtain copies of the standards, technical requirements, testing programs and methodologies?

They are sold by retail, are available from Gosstandart of Turkmenistan and in many other ways, on a contractual basis.

5.13 Can manufacturers participate in development of the standards? How?

The System provides manufacturers, consumers, public organizations, certification bodies, testing laboratories as well as other concerned enterprises, organizations and departmental people free access to information about activities within the System, including its rules, participants, results of accreditation and certification.

Confidentiality of information that constitutes a commercial secret is ensured (Gosstandart of Turkmenistan TDS 1.2-93, Article 4.8).

5.14 Does a test laboratory need to be recognized or accredited by the certification agency or some other party before its test data can be accepted by the certification agency? If yes, please describe the process for obtaining recognition or accreditation. Describe what agency must register, appoint, or accredit a laboratory.

If different parameters were tested in different accredited (attested) laboratories (centers), a certificate of conformity is granted when all of the necessary test reports are available and when the test results are positive. In this case all of the test reports must be listed in the certificate with indication of the test laboratories (centers) that issued those reports as well as recognized certificates (if present).

After receiving positive results of test reports, a certificate for production or a certificate for a quality system, the Certification Body executes a certificate, registers it in the State Registry of the System and hands it to the applicant (Gosstandart of Turkmenistan TDS 1.2.01-93, Articles 4.4.2, 4.4.3).

5.15 Can the laboratory of a manufacturer be accredited/recognized as operating a valid test laboratory? If so, what is the process for obtaining manufacturer's lab accreditation?

Accreditation of a test laboratory in the System is a formal recognition of the technical competence and independence of the laboratory from the designers, manufacturers (suppliers) and consumers of products (services, works) or only of its technical competence in carrying out tests of specific products in accordance with the requirements of standards or other legal documents.

Any laboratory can be accredited irrespective of its ownership and form of property (Gosstandart of Turkmenistan TDS 1.2.02-93, Article 2.1).

5.16 Are test results accepted from parties outside of your country? From manufacturer laboratories outside of your country?

Test results may be accepted in case of their accreditation in the certification System.

5.17 Is certification based on tests of a single sample? If no, how many samples must be tested?

The number of samples and the procedure for their selection is determined by the test program and methodology.

5.18 Can a prototype of the equipment be tested or does a final production sample have to be tested?

Prototypes of equipment may be tested if their design, composition, and production technology are the same as those of the products delivered to consumers (Gosstandart of Turkmenistan TDS 1.2.01-93, Article 4.2.4).

5.19 Are the methods of testing (such as test specifications, procedures, and setups) published? If yes, indicate how they can be obtained.

No. Certification is conducted under the schemes, classification of which is given by ISO. As the international and national certification process develops and in connection with the peculiarities of a specific product, other schemes may be used.

5.20 Who can an applicant call with questions about testing procedures? Contact telephone, fax, telex, etc.

See point 5.9.

5.21 After equipment is authorized, what modifications can be made to the equipment without seeking a modification to the existing authorization?

No modifications are allowed.

6. LIST OF TELECOMMUNICATIONS EQUIPMENT REQUIRING CERTIFICATION IN THE CERTIFICATION SYSTEM OF THE COMMUNICATIONS ADMINISTRATION

6.1 Which are the main kinds of telecommunications equipment subject to certification requirements?

All kinds of wireline and wireless communications equipment as well as equipment used to organize communications are subject to certification. Radio devices must have a permit from the State Radio Frequency Commission (GKRCh) for use of frequencies.

6.2 Which are the main kinds of telecommunications equipment not subject to certification (outdated, infringing the information safety of state, departmental not connected to public networks, technological communication)?

Technological communications networks and departmental communications network equipment (except parameters for interaction with the public networks), obsolete equipment (for instance, step-by-step exchanges, telephones sets with carbon transmitters, etc.) are not subject to certification.

6.3 Is certification required for telephone network equipment, such as switches? If yes, what is the objective of these requirements?

Certification of switching equipment is required to guarantee compatibility with the existing public switched telephone network, safety, and reliability.

6.4 Is certification required for customer premises equipment that connects to the telephone network? If yes, what is the objective of these requirements?

To guarantee compatibility, reliability and performance.

6.5 Is certification required for wireless telecommunications equipment, whether or not connected to the telephone network? If yes, what types of wireless equipment require certification and what is the objective of these requirements?

Yes, certification is required to guarantee electromagnetic compatibility, monitor implementation of the decisions of the State Radio Frequency Commission (GKRCh), and control harmful interference.

6.6 Is certification required for compliance with electromagnetic compatibility (EMC) standards? If yes, what is the scope of these requirements?

The telecommunications certification system will perform tests only for radio equipment.

6.7 Is certification required to meet other objectives, such as electrical safety, avoidance of radio hazards, etc.? If yes, please describe.

Yes.

7. LIST OF CERTIFICATION LABORATORIES AND CENTERS

In Turkmenistan there are as yet no certification centers and test laboratories for communications equipment. They are being organized.

Annex
(obligatory)

____
name of the Certification Body

____
address

DECLARATION-APPLICATION
for conducting products certification in the Certification System

1. ____
name of manufacturer, vendor (hereinafter referred to as applicant)

____________________ in the person of ______________________________
address, code full name of Director

declares, that ____

____

name of product, code

____

serial production or batch (each unit) under individual production

______________, produced under ______________________________________

name and properties of the document (technical

____complies with the requirements of

specification --TY, standards)

_________________________________ and asks to conduct products certification for

name and numbers of standards

conformity with the requirements of the indicated standards.

2. The applicant undertakes:
-- to fulfill all certification terms;
-- to ensure that certified indicators of a product marked with the compliance mark to do not change;
-- to pay all certification expenses.

3. Additional information ____

____

Director of the enterprise	Signature	Print
Chief accountant	Signature	Print
Stamp	Date	

TRAVELING TO TURKMENISTAN

GETTING THERE

Air

The domestic airline is *Turkmenistan Airlines (T5).* There are international connections to London, Birmingham, Istanbul, Abu Dhabi (UAE), Kyiv (Ukraine), Moscow and Karachi (Pakistan). Ashgabat is also served by *Iranian Airlines* from Tehran, by *Lufthansa* from Frankfurt/M and by *Turkish Airlines* from Istanbul. There are connections within the CIS to Moscow and St Petersburg (Russian Federation), Tashkent (Uzbekistan), and Kyiv (Ukraine). All flight tickets bought by foreigners within Turkmenistan must be paid for in hard currency. The prices tend to be ten times as much as those that locals pay.

Approximate flight times

From *London* to Ashbagat is 6 hours 30 minutes, from *Istanbul* is 2 hours 30 minutes, from *Abu Dhabi* is 2 hours, from *Karachi* is 4 hours 30 minutes, from *Tehran* is 1 hour, from *Moscow* is 3 hours 30 minutes, from *Tashkent* is 2 hours and from *Kyiv* is 2 hours.

International airport

Ashgabat Airport (ASB) is approximately 4km (2.5 miles) north of the city center. A new terminal building has resulted in an increase of capacity. The airport is served by buses and taxis.

Sea

There are ferries to Turkmenbashi (formerly Krasnovodsk) from Baku (Azerbaijan) and an irregular service to Astrakhan (Russian Federation). It is theoretically possible to travel from Moscow to Turkmenbashi via the Volga River and the Caspian Sea without setting foot on dry land.

Train

The *Trans-Caspian Railway* connects Turkmenistan with the rest of the Central Asian republics and thence to Moscow and the rest of the CIS. The terminus is in Turkmenbashi on the Caspian Sea, from where it runs through Ashgabat before it crosses into Uzbekistan near the city of Chardzhou. Approximate rail times from Turkmenbashi to Tashkent is 24 hours, to Dushanbe is 36 hours and to Moscow is 3 days. A rail link to the Iranian network, enabling train travel from Turkmenistan to Turkey (Istanbul), was completed in 1996.

Road

Turkmenistan is connected by road to Kazakhstan, Uzbekistan and to Mashad and Tehran in Iran. The crossing into Iran is only open to nationals of the CIS and Iran. It is possible to obtain special permission to cross the border from the Iranian and Turkmen authorities, but this should be done before departure. There is also a road to Herat in Afghanistan from Mary.

Bus

Services are available to the capitals of the neighbouring republics, and north across the Kara-Kum desert to Kunya-Urgench with connections to Urgench and Khiva in Uzbekistan.

GETTING AROUND

Air

Turkmenistan Airlines runs regular flights between Ashgabat, Mary, Chardzhou and Turkmenbashi. All flight tickets have to be paid for in hard currency.

Approximate flight times

From Ashgabat to *Mary* is 1 hour and to *Chardzhou* is 1 hour 30 minutes.

Train

The *Trans-Caspian Railway* runs from Turkmenbashi (formerly Krasnovodsk) in the west, through Ashgabat and Mary to Chardzhou in the east before continuing to Bukhara in Uzbekistan.

Road

Traffic drives on the right. The main road in Turkmenistan runs along the route of the *Trans-Caspian Railway* (see above). There is also a road that runs north from Ashgabat to Tashauz and Kunya-Urgench before crossing into Uzbekistan. This road crosses 500km (311 miles) of the Kara-Kum desert.

Bus

Services are available to all the major towns, including Kunya-Urgench.

Taxi

Taxis and chauffeur-driven cars for hire can be found in all major towns. Many are unlicensed and travelers are advised to agree the fare in advance. As many of the street names have changed since independence, it is also advisable to ascertain both the old and the new street names when asking directions.

Car rental

Self-drive hire is available from a few large hotels.

Traffic regulations

Drinking and driving is strictly forbidden.

Documentation

An International Driving Permit, or national licence with authorised translation, is required.

ACCOMMODATION

Hotels

There are no restrictions on where foreigners can stay in Turkmenistan. When Turkmenistan gained independence, there was an acute shortage of hotel accommodation, a situation which the Turkmen are working hard to rectify. Feverish hotel construction is underway in Ashgabat. A row of luxury hotels has recently been built on the edge of town along a road known locally as the 'Miracle Mile'. These are small hotels with between 15-40 rooms that are owned and run by various ministries and governmental organisations. Architectural motifs are mosques, palaces and fortresses. Every provincial centre has at least one hotel, but visitors should not expect Western standards of comfort and amenities. The exception is a new hotel which recently opened in Turkmenbashi; however, as it only has 40 rooms, it is advisable to contact a recognised Turkmen tour company for a reservation. Accommodation and services in hotels are payable in hard currency, usually US Dollars.

Rest Houses

Dom Otdykha (literally 'rest houses') were built on the shores of the Caspian Sea by co-operatives and other concerns for fatigued workers. It is sometimes possible for travelers to obtain accommodation in them.

Camping

There are campsites on the shores of the Caspian Sea, and the facilities are in the process of being improved.

MONEY

Currency

1 Manat (TMM) = 100 tenge. Notes are in denominations of TMM1000, 500, 100, 50, 10, 5 and 1. Coins are in denominations of 50, 20, 10, 5 and 1 tenge.

Currency exchange

The preferred hard currency is US Dollars and visitors carrying other currencies may find it hard to change them. It is advisable to take new, clean US Dollar notes in small denominations. Foreign currency can be changed at banks and major hotels. Foreigners are expected to pay all travel and hotel bills in hard currency, and prices bear little relation to what locals are expected to pay. Most packages are all-inclusive and extra payment of accommodation and meals is unnecessary.

Credit cards

Accepted at some of the newer hotels.

Travelers checks

Only travelers checks drawn on banks with reciprocal arrangements with the Turkmen National Bank are accepted.

Exchange rate indicators against the US Dollar

The exchange rate was US$1 = TMM1000 (official) or TMM3000 (commercial) in April 1996, when it was announced that the official rate would be discontinued. From then on, a unified exchange rate was introduced for all transactions, determined by trading on the Turkmen Interbank Currency Exchange, which commenced operations in 1996.

Date	Mar'98	Nov'98	Aug'99
$1.00=	4165.00	5200.00	5200.00

Currency restrictions

The import and export of local currency is prohibited for foreigners. Import of foreign currency is unlimited subject to declaration, and export is limited to the amount declared on import.

BUSINESS TRAVEL

VISAS

No one will be allowed to enter Turkmenistan without a valid visa or an invitation letter stamped by the Turkmenistan Ministry of Foreign Affairs. Airlines have been instructed not to board anyone who does not have a valid visa or invitation letter. Furthermore, travelers who do not have a visa cannot register at hotels and will be required to leave the country immediately via the route by which they entered. Visas for Turkmenistan are issued by the Embassy of Turkmenistan in Washington, D.C.. Turkmen authorities require inviters to take financial responsibility for the invited.

To issue an invitation, the Embassy needs full passport information, date and time of arrival, flight information, purpose of visit, and a fax number to which the approved invitation can be sent. A copy of the approved invitation must be in the traveller's hand to ensure airline boarding.

With an approved invitation, a ten day visa can be obtained upon arrival at the airport. Extensions may be authorized by applying at the Ministry of Foreign Affairs on Mondays, Thursdays and Fridays, though a letter of invitation from the traveller's host should be furnished when applying.(Contact information for the Turkmenistan Embassy and Ministry of Foreign Affairs can be found below.)

DOMESTIC TRAVEL

Travel to or throughout Turkmenistan by rail is not recommended. Travel by air may be disrupted by fuel shortages or other problems.

MEDICAL FACILITIES

Medical care in Turkmenistan is limited. The U.S. Embassy maintains a list of English-speaking physicians in the area. There is a severe shortage of basic medical supplies, including disposable needles, anesthetics, and antibiotics. Elderly travellers and those with existing health problems may be at risk due to inadequate medical facilities. Doctors and hospitals often expect immediate cash payment for health services. U.S. medical insurance is not always valid outside the United States. Travellers have found that in some cases, supplemental medical coverage has proved to be useful.

Further information on health matters can be obtained from the Centers for Disease Control's International Travelers' Hotline, phone: (404) 332-4559. Additional medical information can be found in the Department of State's brochure, "Tips for Travelers to Russia," which includes information on Turkmenistan. This handout can be obtained from the BISNIS Office of the U.S.

Department of Commerce in Washington, D.C. Also see the document "Health Issues in Turkmenistan" on the BISNIS website.

CURRENCY REGULATIONS

Turkmenistan is a cash-only economy. Traveller's checks and credit cards are not commonly accepted; however, several new hotels accept credit cards. Only Vnesheconombank cashes travellers checks or accepts Visa, Mastercard and Eurocards for cash advances. Travellers are advised to take only new, clean dollar bills with them (1990 and newer).

DRUG PENALTIES

U.S. citizens are subject to the laws of the country in which they are travelling. Penalties for possession, use or trafficking in illegal drugs are strict and convicted offenders can expect jail sentences and fines.

Registration: Americans are encouraged to register at the consular section of the U.S. Embassy where they can obtain updated information on travel and security within Turkmenistan. Contact information for the U.S. Embassy is listed below.

ACCOMMODATIONS

Ak Altin Plaza

Magtum Guli Avenue
Pobedy Park
Dzerjinsky Boulevard
Ashgabat
phone: 993 (12) 51-21-81
fax: 993 (12) 51-21-77

Emperyal's Grand Turkmen

Goroglu Street. No. 7
Ashgabat
phone: 993 (12) 51-20-50
Fax: 993 (12) 51-20-48

TURKMEN HOLIDAYS

January 12 Turkmen Memorial Day
February 19 President's Birthday
March 8 International Women's Day
March 21 Novruz Bairam
May 9 Victory Day
May 18 Day of National Unity and Revival
May-June Kurban Bairam (three days to be determined by lunar calendar)
October 27-28 Independence Day

VISA REQUIREMENTS

Procedure for Obtaining a Visa: Please read the following directions below. Questions regarding visas, requests for applications, and completed applications should be directed to the Embassy of Turkmenistan:

The Embassy of Turkmenistan
2207 Massachusetts Ave., NW
Washington, DC 20008

Phone: 202-588-1500; Fax: 202-588-0697

All Applicants: Obtain a visa application from the Embassy of Turkmenistan in Washington D.C., or download the visa application form. Complete the visa application supplying dates in the order of day-month-year. Submit a signed passport valid for **at least 6 months** from the date of departure. **The Embassy must have the original passport to process a visa.**Submit one recent passport size photo.

Submit a check or money order payable to the Embassy of Turkmenistan (for the appropriate fee see ***Visa Cost Schedule***).

Submit a letter of invitation from the person or company to be visited in Turkmenistan **certified** by the Ministry of Foreign Affairs in Ashgabat. If you are traveling as a tourist and will not be meeting anyone in Turkmenistan, you must contact the State Tourism Corporation of Turkmenistan "Turkmen Siyahat" Tel: (993-12) 35-47-77 or 39-86-91; Fax: (993-12) 39-67-40 or 39-00-65. "Turkmen Siyahat" will assist in the planning of your visit and provide the certified letter.

Enclose self-addressed, stamped envelope or pre-paid courier package for the return of the passport, unless you plan to pick it up from the Embassy.
Legal Resident Aliens: In addition to the requirements listed above, legal resident aliens of the United States, Canada, and Mexico must have a valid visa for re-entry into their country of residence and must submit a copy of their resident alien card.
Checklist: 1-Visa application
2-Passport
3-One passport size photo
4-Check or money order
5-Certified letter of invitation
6-Self-addressed, stamped envelope or pre-paid courier package

The processing time for a visa is five business days. It is possible, however, to expedite the process to less than three business days if the application is complete, the paperwork is in order, and an additional 50% of the cost of the visa is included in the payment. Applicants must provide the return fees for any mail service they decide to use.

Please, note that the answers to questions #14-18 on the visa application will be reflected in the issued visa.

FLYING TO TURKMENISTAN

SPECIAL NOTE TO TRAVEL AGENTS: Turkmenistan Airlines' IATA code is T5. International schedules are published in OAG. For fares and availability, bookings, and ticketing instructions, please contact Turkmenistan Airlines' London office listed below.

Several airlines fly to Turkmenistan including Turkmenistan Airlines and Lufthansa. Below is listed the contact numbers for Turkmenistan Airlines offices throughout Europe and Central Asia as well as the specific flight available from Birmingham, and London, England.

Turkmenistan Airlines - the only airline offering non-stop service from Europe to Turkmenistan. Check Birmingham International Airport's Home Page for flight changes

Aircraft types:
733: Boeing 737-300
757: Boeing 757-200

Convenient connections to Delhi, Karachi, Abu-Dhabi, and Central AsiaAll international flights are operated by western-trained pilots using brand new two-class configuration Boeing aircraft
Airport Information Desk: (99312) 51-00-18; 51-00-19International Ticket Office: (99312) 39-42-71

Turkmenistan Airlines Offices

Moscow (7-095) 194-6498; 194-6718London Tel: 44-181 563-0565 - Fax: 44-181 748-9866 Istanbul Tel: 90212 2414601/2340025; 2339306KarachiTel: 92-21 51 39 41Abu DhabiTel: 9712 663100DelhiTel: 9111 3312916/3311593KievTel: 380-044 4164092

Airlines in Turkmenistan

(Note: dial 99312 before the phone numbers)

Aerosweet • 71 Magtymguly St -Tel: 35-01-64; 51-01-06**Iranian Airlines**• 71 Magtymguly St• Tel: 51-06-41; 51-06-42**Lufthansa** • New Airport • Tel:51-06-84; 51-03-31**Pakistani International Airlines**• 71 Magtymguly St• Tel: 51-18-38**Turkish Airlines** • 71 Magtymguly St • 51-16-66; 51-22-19; 51-06-66(94)**Turkmenistan Airlines**• 80 Magtymguly St • 25-48-57

TRAVEL AGENTS IN TURKMENISTAN

Turkmensiyahat Corporation
30 Khudaiberdyeva St
Tel: 99312-39-77-71 Fax: 39-67-40

Turkmenintur Travel Agency
74 Magtymguly St
Tel: 99312-35-69-32 Fax: 39-00-26

Turkmensiyahat Amalgamation
60 A Gorogly St
Tel: 99312-24-73-32 Fax: 34-34-97

Chalt
Oktyabirskaya Hotel
Tel: 99312- 41-03-01

Latif Travel Agency
36A Khudaiberdyev Street
Tel: 99312- 41-50-77; 41-50-87
Fax: (993 12) 41-90-39, 41-50-77
E-mail: latif@cat.glasnet.ru
website: http://www.turkmenistan-travel.com

Ashgabat-Intorg
72 Annadurdyeva St
Tel: 51-21-43; 51-24-10 Fax: 51-24-61

Tokai
140/2 Ata Govshudov St
Tel: 39-77-65; 42-98-77

Timur & K
29 Turkmenbashi Ave
Tel: 35-08-70 Fax: 35-08-70

Esset
56 Azadi St
Tel: 39-01-02

Gezelench
19 Turkmenbashi Ave
Tel: 35-63-51 Fax: 35-63-51

Solnechnei Dom
5a Pomma St
Tel: 51-11-46

Koitendagh
36 Khudaiberdyeva St
Tel: 41-50-80

Rova
95 Magtymguly Ave
Tel: 35-52-69

Gumry
8 Lechebnaya St
Tel: 47-42-64; 44-31-56

Zehin
18 Kerkinskaya St
Tel: 4-01-73

HOTELS IN ASHGABAT

The larger hotels are in the process of establishing systems to accept credit cards. However, at this time, it is recommended that you bring enough American dollars to cover all of your expenses.

Below are the addresses, phone numbers, and facilities of two of Ashgabat's finest five-star hotels:

The Ak Altin Plaza Hotel***

141/1 Magtymguli Avenue

P.O. Box 84

Ashgabat, Turkmenistan744000

tel: (99312) 51-21-81

fax: (99312) 51-21-77, 51-21-79

The Ak Altin Plaza Hotel is an eleven story building with 137 rooms, including 20 suites.All rooms have air-conditioning, minibars, satellite TV, direct telephone lines, and hair dryers.Services include laundry and dry-cleaning, a business center, room service and an on-site doctor's office.Amenities include indoor and outdoor swimming pools, and a health and fitness center with a sauna and Turkish bath.Dining facilities are made up of two restaurants and two private dining rooms.The banquet and conference facilities total an area of 384 square meters and seat 350 people

Grand Turkmen Hotel and Casino***

Georogly Street, No. 7

Ashgabat, Turkmenistan744000

tel: (99312) 51-20-50
fax: (99312) 51-20-48, 51-20-49

The Grand Turkmen Hotel has 120 rooms including 20 suites and 4 presidential suites with private jacuzzis.Rooms feature air-conditioning, direct-line telephones, private baths, hair dryers, shaver outlets and adapters, color TV, international television broadcasting, and minibars.Guest services include translators, secretarial services, an in-house doctor, a drug store, a beauty parlor, and laundry services.The recreation facilities are comprised of the casino, disco, health club, sauna, outdoor swimming pool, sundeck and tennis courts.Restaurants offer international cuisine as well as outside catering.

SUPPLEMENTS

Please note:
Turkmenistan has introduced a new country code numbers;
the number 7 will no longer need to be dialed:
993-12 for Ashgabat
993-522 for Mary
993-422 for Turkmenabat
The old country codes7-3632 for Ashgabat, 7-37022 for Mary and 7-37822 for Turkmenabat are not valid.

SMALL AND MEDIUM ENTERPRISE DEVELOPMENT AGENCY -- SMEDA

Smeda is a joint-venture between the European Union and the Government of Turkmenistan.

Are you looking for someone in Turkmenistan who can:

- Make contacts for your company with local and international businesses;
- Do market research
- Perform business training for your staff
- Develop and initiate promotional activities.

For foreign companies and businessmen, qualified SMEDA staff with strong knowledge in all aspects of small and medium business will serve you on an international level.

- Do you want to obtain a clear picture of the Turkmen economy?
- Do you experience problems with keeping up with changes in the Turkmen legislation?
- Do you want to set up a business in Turkmenistan?
- Are you looking for a Turkmen buyer or supplier?

SMEDA WILL ASSIST YOU AND WILL BE
YOUR ACCESS TO RELIABLE INFORMATION

Laws and regulations and other documents available through SMEDA
Contact:
Dovodov Murad, Business Communication Centre
8 Sokolovskogo St.
744000 Ashgabat Turkmenistan
SMEDA-P.O.-box 3/56
Ashgabat-Crugozor
Tel: +993 12 34 42 59
Tel: +993 12 34 51 49
Fax +993 12 34 51 49
E-mail: smeda@cat.glasnet.ru

WHY SMEDA?

Many overseas and local companies operating or planing to do business in Turkmenistan face difficulties in getting access to trustworthy commercial information. Prompt and verified information on legal, taxation, economic and other business-related matters, is very often the essential factor of success in Turkmenistan. SMEDA (Small and Medium Enterprise Development Agency) is proud to present itself as one of the leaders in the consultancy business in the country since 1995. Our assistance in obtaining reliable information will enable you to avoid mistakes and design a feasible action strategy. We offer quality legal, taxation, business and marketing advice at affordable prices. As part of our service package we also provide business support services such as visa arrangement, hotel reservation, car and interpreter hire. We are extremely flexible about our services and ready to deliver services beyond our regular range.

WHAT DO WE DO?

LEGAL ADVICE

* How to start up a business
* How to register a local or foreign company
* Advice on contracting (correspondence of contracts to the Turkmen legislation, analysis of possible consequences)
* Licensing in Turkmenistan
* Employment procedures
* Preparation of founding documents for a Turkmen company
* Preparation of registration documents for a foreign company
* Preparation of contracts
* Advice on legal claims
* Research on commercial legislation of foreign countries
* List of Turkmen legislation on a subject
* Texts of Turkmen legislative acts (in Russian and English)

TRADE PROMOTION

* Market research (Turkmen and foreign markets)
* Search for suppliers/buyers
* Advice on export/import banking
* Advice on international transportation
* Programme Arranging Service for Business Delegations
* Advice on registration of international contracts at the State Commodity and Raw Materials Exchange of Turkmenistan

BUSINESS ADVICE

* Feasibility study
* Business plan
* Financial plan
* Loan application

ADVICE ON TAXATION, ACCOUNTING AND CUSTOMS PROCEDURES

BUSINESS SUPPORT SERVICES

* Interpreter hire * Certification of translations into and from English * Telecommunication * Access to computer facilities * Photo copying, Printing, Scanning, Binding * Car hire * Organisation of business trips

BROCHURES

* Turkmen Commercial Legislation (2 Volumes, English)
* Turkmen Taxation Legislation (English)

BUSINESS COURSES

* Financial Management
* Marketing
* Business Planning

Table of Contents of laws, regulations and other documents available through SMEDA:

- The constitution of Turkmenistan
- Law of Turkmenistan on entrepreneurial activity in Turkmenistan
- Law of Turkmenistan on enterprises
- The law of Turkmenistan on investment activities in Turkmenistan
- Law of Turkmenistan on the central bank of Turkmenistan
- Law of Turkmenistan on commercial banks and bank activities
- Law of Turkmenistan on the foreign currency control
- Law of Turkmenistan on commodity and raw material exchange
- Law of Turkmenistan on chamber of commerce
- Statute on the ministry for foreign economic relations of Turkmenistan
- The law of Turkmenistan on free economic zones
- List of free economic zones in Turkmenistan
- The law of Turkmenistan on foreign investments in Turkmenistan
- Law of Turkmenistan on foreign economic activities in Turkmenistan
- The law of Turkmenistan on foreign concessions
- Resolution of president of Turkmenistan 12 1603 on the guarantees of protection of foreign investments and capitals
- Statute on the procedure of the state registration of enterprises (institutions, organisations) with foreign investments and registration of branches and representations of foreign firms
- Decree of the president of Turkmenistan on the transition to the international principles of cargo transportation settlements
- Taxes

Instructions, Laws and Provisions available in English

- Overview of the taxes and charges in Turkmenistan on 1st of April 2002
- Provision on non-cash payments in Turkmenistan
- Letter on clarification of tax privileges for foreign investors
- Instruction on calculation of wage fund exceed levy.
- Law On Profit Tax
- Law on VAT
- Instruction on payment and calculation of VAT
- Provision on Annual Bookkeeping Reporting in Turkmenistan
- Instruction on calculation of Expenses are to be included in Prime Cost
- Instruction on taking stock and financial obligations
- Instruction on payment and calculation of tax on owners of transport facilities
- Regulations on Stock Exchange deal registration
- Reporting of foreign entities in Turkmenistan
- Audit activity act of Turkmenistan

- Regulations on opening and maintenance of hard-currency accounts by banks in Turkmenistan
- Law on property
- Provision on accountancy in Turkmenistan
- Law on accountancy in Turkmenistan
- Instruction on payment and calculation of Excise charges on goods produced in Turkmenistan and exporting product out of the country
- Instruction on payment and calculation of Excise charges on importing goods
- Instruction on payment and calculation of Social Securities and Pension charges
- Instruction on payment and calculation of Property Tax
- Instruction on payment and calculation of Profit Tax by foreign entities (Instruction No 9)
- Local taxes
- Instruction on payment of Health insurance
- Instruction on calculation of Personal Income Tax
- Instruction on payment and calculation of Profit Tax

THE CHAMBER OF COMMERCE

According to the Chamber, technical know-how and up-to-date equipment for small and medium production facilities are required. Some of the areas of food production where assistance is particularly needed include:

i. dairy processing
ii. meat processing
iii. cheese production
iv. beer production
v. canned products production
vi. fruit and vegetable processing
vii. agricultural waste processing

The Chamber would also like to exhibit equipment and technology for food packaging, including technology for glass, brick, plastic, and iron production facilities. With such technology, the Chamber believes Turkmenistan could develop the entire food production process from harvesting to packaging.

The Chamber is also very interested in attracting American food processing exhibitors to the trade show and is therefore interested in contracting with an American trade show organizer. Trade show organizers interested in this opportunity can contact the Chamber of Commerce of Turkmenistan directly at the following address:

Mr. Agamamed Sakhatov, Deputy Chairman (speaks Russian and Turkmen)
92 Kemine Street
Ashgabat, Turkmenistan 744000
Tel: (99312) 25-64-03 or 47-44-19
Fax: (99312) 47-69-79

U.S. COMPANIES IN TURKMENISTAN

(1) ACC (American Communications Consultants, Inc.)

Operation of laundry bar soap production plant in Chardjou.

Besim Uysal 335 Stanley Plaza Blvd.
President Newark, DE 19713
25 Makhtumkuli Street Tel:(302)455-1040
Ashgabat, Turkmenistan 744000 Fax:(302)455-1047
Tel: (993)(12)47-31-47; 47-31-48 E-mail: acc1us@aol.com
Fax: (993)(12)47-31-49

(2) Alma Industrial Inc.

Construction of a glass plant and a pharmaceutical plant and sale of turnkey dairy and meat processing plants.

Batyr Yapaev Vladimir Karlinskiy
Director President
Akrap Holding Firm 1265 Firwood Drive
57 Azadi Street Pittsburgh, PA 15243
Ashgabat, Turkmenistan 744000 Tel:(412)276-5969
Tel:(993)(12)51-14-17; 25-55-24 Fax:(818)996-4507
Fax:(993)(12)51-14-17

(3) Arthur Andersen

Auditing and business, tax, and outsourcing consulting services.

Donald J. Leland Arthur Andersen LLP
Country Manager 33w Monroe Street
Transport center Chicago, IL 60603-5385
2nd floor Tel:(312)580-0033
95 Azadi Street Fax:(312)507-6748
Ashgabat, Turkmenistan 744000
Tel:(993)(12)51-24-05
Fax:(993)(12)51-24-03
Mobile phone: 30-23-60
E-mail: aaashgb@cat.glasnet.ru or Tatyana.ziza@tm.arthurandersen.com

(4) Barash Communication Technologies, Inc.

Cellular communication and paging services.

Oraz Gurbanov Mikhail Barrash
Executive Director President
56 Khudaiberdiev Street P.O. Box 330579
Ashgabat, Turkmenistan 744000 Fort Worth, TX 76163
Tel:(993)(12)41-94-92; 41-94-97 Tel:(817)292-2842
Fax:(993)(12)39-90-80 ;41-94-98 Fax:(817)370-94-96

(5) Belcom, Inc.

Telecommunications services via satellites.

Vladislav Gurin 6560 Rock Spring Drive
Sales Manager Bethesda, MD 20817
4-25 Ostrovsky Street Tel:(301)214-3355
Ashgabat, Turkmenistan 744000 Fax:(301)214-7100
Tel/Fax:(993)(12)44-51-47

(6) Boeing Commercial Airplane Group

Aircraft sales, training, and maintenance.

Jeff Mcbroom Aldo Basile
Customer Services International Sales
Representative Director
International Airport P.O. Box 3707, ms 2h-96
Ashgabat, Turkmenistan 744000 Seattle, WA 98124-2207
Tel/Fax:(993)(12)37-81-38 Tel:(425)237-2684
Fax:(206)237-1706 Fax: (425) 237-8067
Tel:(993)(12)51-24-48

(7) Brown and Williamson (represents British American Tobacco)

Marketing tobacco products.

Murad Berdiyev Erfan Naser
Office Manager Regional Manager
Rasul Nazarov Ila Bekhozin Street
Area Manager Almaty, Kazakstan 480023
18/2 Krasnovodskaya Street Tel:7(3272)61-96-88
Ashgabat, Turkmenistan 744000 Fax:7(3272)61-87-14
Tel:(993)(12)36-17-35
Fax:(993)(12)36-13-92
Mobil phone:(993)(12)30-03-37

(8) Catermar USA, Inc.

Food shipment and catering services.

Osvaldo Gomes Jeff Roberts
Director Corporate Controller
Mizan Business Center 7324 SW Freeway
Office 409 Suite 1790 .
Berzengi, Ashgabat Houston, TX 77074
Turkmenistan 744000 Tel:(713)271-2333
Tel:(993)(12)51-86-51 Fax:(713)271-2444
Fax:(993)(12)51-86-52 E-mail: jarcar@aol.com
E-mail:catashg@cat.glasnet.ru www.catermar.com

(9) J. I. Case Corporation (represented by IP Consult)

Sales and training in the use of agricultural equipment, combines and cotton pickers.

John Machin Jean-Pierre Rosso
General Manager President
IP Consult 700 State Street
Mersedes Bens office Racine, WI 53404
7 Aytakov Street Tel:(414)636-6011
Ashgabat, Turkmenistan 744000
Tel:(993)(12)51-18-58 ;51-18-59; 51-18-61
Fax:(993)(12)51-18-60

(10) Caterpillar

Distributing and maintaining earthmoving equipment, generators, lifttrucks, agricultural equipment and spare parts.

Bulent Yamach 100 N.E.. Adams Street
Country Director Peoria, IL 61629
Borusan Makina Company Tel:(309)675-1000
International Business Center www.cat.com
A Block Office: 16
Mir 2/1 district
1, Yunus Emre Street
Ashgabat, Turkmenistan 744000
Tel:(993)(12)51-90-01/02/03
Fax:(993)(12)51-90-03

(11) Central-Asian American Enterprise Fund

Three principal activities: direct investments, joint ventures, and small business loans.

Paul Hamlin Oon Nicholson
Acting Vice President President
2 Pushkin Street 1 Turab Tulla Street
Ashgabat, Turkmenistan 744000 Tashkent, Uzbekistan 700066
Tel:(993)(12)39-24-93 Tel:(3712)89-11-34,35 or 36
Fax:(993)(12)39-01-52 Fax:(3712)89-11-38
E-mail: caaef@online.tm

(12) Coca Cola

Joint venture with the state association on food production to develop production of Coca Cola.

Nabi Suray James T. Hill
General Manager Managing Director
165 Khuoayberdiev Street Fahrettin Kerim Gokay Cad.
9th District, Ashgabat 35 Altunizade
Turkmenistan 744000 81020 Istanbul, Turkey
Tel:(993)(12)35-02-17; 41-82-69 Tel:90(216)327-0000
Fax:(993)(12)41-82-98; 33-11-23 Fax:90(216)326-3232

(13) Colgate-Palmolive Co.

Distribution of Colgate products.

Zeki Apak Reuben Mark
General Coordinator Chairman & CEO
Barakat Turkman Ltd. 300 Park Avenue
42 Anoaliba Street New York, NY 10022
Ashgabat, Turkmenistan 744000 tel:(212)310-2000
Tel:(993)(12)41-96-15/16
Fax:(993)(12)41-89-03

(14) Compressor Controls Corporation

Distribution of turbomachinery control systems in the Central Asian region

Batyr Orazov 11359 Aurora Avenue
Regional Sales Rep. Des Moines, IA 50322
Apartment 24 Tel:(515)270-0857
114, Khudayberoiev Street Fax:(515)254-2466
Ashgabat, Turkmenistan 744000
Tel/Fax:(993)(12)39-22-10; 41-30-90

(15) Culligan (subsidiary of U.S. Filter)

Construction of water purification plant in Ashgabat and water desalination plants in Balkan Yelayat

Beyhan Nakiboglu Evan M. Lovell
President (Nema Kimya) Director
Rejep Rejepov Int'l Development Group
Culligan Representative Culligan Int'l Company
Devyanosty Razyezd One Culligan Parkway
construction site of Northbrook, IL 60062-6209
water plant near Ashgabat Tel:(847)205-6105
Turkmenistan 744000 Fax:(847)205-6040
Tel/Fax:(993)(12)35-50-35; 51-13-51
Mobil phone:(993)(12)30-06-76

(16) Ernst & Young

Auditing, accounting, tax and business consulting services.

Jody Campbell 787 Seventh Street
Director New York, NY 10019
Mizan Business Center Tel:(212)773-2848
Berzengi, Ashgabat Fax:(212)773-6350
Turkmenistan 744000
Tel/Fax:(993)(12)51-86-47

(17) Ford Motor Corporation

Distributorship of cars and spare parts.

Ender Kiy Robert L. Rewey
General Manager Vice President
Ram Auto Ltd., a Division 300 Renaissance Ctr.
Of Koc International Box 437703
30 Ostrovsky Street Detroit, MI 48243
Ashgabat, Turkmenistan 744000 Tel:(313)322-3000
Tel:(993)(12)30-41-02
Fax:(993)(12)35-06-39

(18) General Electric

Sale of compressor stations.

Mithat Aksoy One River Road
Country Manager Schenectady, NY 12345
6 Nurberdy Pomma Street Tel:(518)385-1013
Ashgabat, Turkmenistan 744000 Fax:(518)385-3649
Tel/Fax:(993)(12)51-23-43

(19) Genwest Systems, Inc.

Oil spill response, incident command system training, mapping/gis, environmental database programming services.

Daniel Rutz John Murphy
Systems Engineer President
23 Ostrovsky Street P.O. Box 397
2-nd floor Edmonds, WA 98020-0397
Ashgabat, Turkmenistan 744000 Tel:(425) 771-2700
Tel:(993)(12)34-49-92 Fax:(425)672-8471
Fax:(993)(12)34-75-97
E-mail: danr@genwest.com

(20) Halliburton International Inc.

Oil field service contractor involved in Dragonoil (Ireland), Monument (Great Britain), and Petronas (Malaysia) operations in Turkmenistan.

Cecil Davidson Roger Rion, CEO
Country Manager P.O. Box 819052
Mizan Business Center Dallas, TX 75381-9052

Berzengi, Ashgabat, Tel:(214)418-3200
Turkmenistan 744000 Fax:(214)418-3211
Tel:(993)(12)51-80-95; 51-80-50
Fax:(993)(12)51-80-33
Mobil phone:(993)(12)30-25-87

(21) Hewlett Packard (represented by Intec, Ltd., an authorized service provider and reseller)

Sale and repair of computers and Xerox equipment.

Arthur Ovezmuradov Hewlett Packard Ges.m.b.h.
Director Liebglasse 1
25/22 Turkmenbashi Street a-1222 Wien
Ashgabat, Turkmenistan 744000 Tel:01/25 000-0
Tel:(993)(12)35-02-41/42/43 Fax:01/25 000-444
Fax:(993)(12)35-02-39
E-mail: info@int.ashgabad.su

(22) International Business Services

Establishing entrepreneurial training centers for local businesses to teach business English, computer skills, business market research, business operations and other topics.

Johnny Yernon
Director
P.O. box 2/52
Ashgabat, Turkmenistan 744000
Tel/Fax:(993)(12)35-42-34
E-mail: vernonjba@aol.com

(23) International Executive Service Corps

Business consulting services by retired American experts.

Jeren Niyazberdieva Brian Quigley
Batyr Niyazberdiev Regional Director
Representatives 20, 2nd Sapyornaya Street
2 Pushkin Street Tashkent, Uzbekistan 700015
Ashgabat, Turkmenistan 744000 Tel/Fax:(3712)554-008; 406-466
Tel/Fax:(993)(12)39-58-17 E-mail: iesc@nyatov.com
E-mail: iesc@online.tm

(24) John Deere Int'l (represented by AIA Limited)

Distribution and servicing of John Deere equipment.

Hasan Besneli Hans W. Becherer
International Vice Chairman
President Deere & Company
Noel Pearce John Deere Road
Country Manager Moline, IL 61265
Aia Limited Tel:(309)765-8000; 765-7141
101-a, Trud Street Fax:(309)765-7119
Ashgabat, Turkmenistan 744022 E-mail: nl28382@deere.com
Tel:(993)(12)32-72-11; 32-72-13; 32-72-14; 32-72-15
Fax:(993)(12)32-72-12
E-mail: thsrw@cat.glasnet.ru

(25) Mayer, Brown & Platt

Consulting with the oil and gas ministry of Turkmenistan.

Ashir Abdullayev Nabil L. Khodadad
Attorney Partner
Oil and Gas Ministry Bucklersbury House
27, Bitarap 3, Queen Victoria Street
Turkmenistan Street London, ec4n 8el, England
Ashgabat, Turkmenistan Tel:(0171)246-6211
744000 Fax:(0171)329-4465
Tel:(993)(12)35-52-47 www.mayerbrown.com
Fax:(993)(12)51-00-74

(26) Motorola GMBH

Distribution of radio and telecommunications equipment.

Vladislav Sorokin John N. Palle
Representative Vice President
Private Residence Hagenauer Street, 55
Ashgabat, Turkmenistan 744000 65203 Wiesbaden, Germany
Tel/Fax:(993)(12)43-60-08 Tel:(49-0)611/3611-685
Fax:(49-0)611/3611-483 Email: johnjnp@euro.csg.mot.com
E-mail: vlad@cat.glasnet.ru

(27) Mobil New Exploration and Producing Ventures Turkmenistan

Oil field exploration and development. Distribution of engine and transmission oil.

Larry Salz Lee High
Country Manager Geological Consultant
Room 116 3000 Pegasus Ark Drive
Mizan Business Center Dallas, TX 75247
Berzengi, Ashgabat, Tel:(214)951-2459
Turkmenistan 744000 Fax:(214)905-7282; (214)905-7790

Mobil phone: 30-21-36
Tel:(993)(12)51-85-23
Fax:(993)(12)51-85-24

(28) Pipeline Solution Group International Ltd. (PSG)

Psg was chosen to lead the trans-caspian pipeline consortium to implement Turkmenistan - Azerbaijan-Georgia- Turkey gas pipeline construction project.

Gulnara Bekieva Edward Smith
Office Manager President & CEO
Transport Center 49 Park Lane
95 Azadi Street London wly 4eq
Ashgabat, Turkmenistan 744000 United Kingdom
Tel:(993)(12)39-87-77 Fax:(44-0171)535-8510
Tel/Fax:(993)(12)51-07-77 Fax:(44-0171)535-8600
E-mail: smithem@psgint.com

(29) Procter & Gamble

Distribution of products made by Procter & Gamble.

Khikmet Salkyn Hans-Peter Heissen
Representative Manager General Manager
Asia Trading & Procter & Gamble Caucasian
Shipping Ltd. Co. & Central Asian Republics
1 Tretya Pyatiletka Street Eski Uskudar Cad.
Ashgabat, Turkmenistan 744000 Nora center, 81090
Tel:(993)(12)32-03-07/08 Iserenkoy, Istanbul, Turkey
Fax:(993) (12)32-03-40 Fax:(90-216)463-8299
Fax:(90-216)463-8353

(29) Steelcase Inc.

Sale of office furniture in the region.

Dmitry Golovin James P. Hackett
Representative President & CEO
Ashgabat, Turkmenistan 744000 901 Fourty Fourth Street
Tel/Fax:(993)(12)41-28-42 Grand Rapids, MI 49508-7594
Tel:(616)247-2710
Fax:(616)247-2295

(31) United Parcel Service (UPS)

Provides both incoming and outgoing mail services.

Serdar Yagdyev James P. Kelly
Director President
Individual Firm "Serdar" 55 Glenlake Pkwy
House 4, District Mir 2/2 N.E., Atlanta, GA 30328
Ashgabat, Turkmenistan 744000 Fax:(404)828-6000
Tel:(993)(12)44-82-16
Fax:(993)(12)44-89-81

(32) USA International

Authorized representative for Telenor satellite services.

Hunter Debutts Residential Office
Vice President 6166 Leesburg Pike #A302
16/5, Gorogly Street Falls Church, VA 22044
Ashgabat, Turkmenistan 744000 Fax:(703)534-8299
Tel/Fax:(993)(12)39-55-56 Fax:(703)534-9386
E-mail: h.debutts@worldnet.att.net

(33) Western Atlas International (represented by Petro Alliance)

Petro Alliance, a joint venture of Western Atlas International, Inc. and M.D. Seis Ltd. (Russia), conducts seismic surveys in the Balkan Yelayat.

James R. Ashland Gary M. Bennett
Resident Manager CIS Manager
112, Ata Goushudov Street 10001 Richmond Avenue
Ashgabat, Turkmenistan Houston, TX 77042-4299
744000 Fax:(713)972-5484
Tel:(993)(12)39-44-13; 51-05-90; 35-47-18 Fax:(713)789-0172
Fax:(993)(12)35-43-64

U.S. COMPANIES ACTIVE IN TURKMENISTAN

(1) Bertling Logistics, Inc.

Shipping services in the Central Asian region.

Simon Harris
Manager, Business Development
In the Caspian region
15500 Vickery Drive
Houston, TX 77032
Tel:(281)774-2300
Fax:(281)449-7667
E-mail: simon harris@bertlingusa.com

(2) Exxon Exploration Company

Implemented a feasibility study of the Turkmenistan- China-Japan oil and gas pipeline construction project and geological study of hydrocarbon resources.

800 Gessner
Houston, TX 77024
Tel:(281)423-5065
Fax:(713)935-6041

(3) Mafco Worldwide Corporation

Purchase of licorice root and extract and negotiation with the Health Ministry on manufacturing licorice extract in Turkmenistan.

Stephen G. Taub
President
3rd Street & Jefferson Avenue
Camden, NJ 08104
Tel:(609)968-4071
Fax:(609)964-6029

(4) Murphy Shipping & Commercial Services Ltd.

Shipping services in the Caspian region.

Ron Johns
President
8960 Spring Branch Dr.
Houston, Texas 77080
Tel:(713)722-8088
Fax:(713)722-0105

(5) Sikorsky Aircraft United Technologies

Helicopter sales.

Deniz Dalay
Commercial Marketing Manager
6900 Main Street
P.O. Box 9729
Stratford, CT 06497-9129
Tel:(203)386-4263
Fax:(203)386-7189

SELECTED GOVERNMENT CONTACTS

President Saparmurad A. Niyazov

Tel: 993 (12) 25-45-34
Head of President's Office
Tel: 993 (12) 25-79-46
Deputy Director of President's Office
Tel: 993 (12) 25-37-51
Press Coordinator
Tel: 993 (12) 25-46-92

Deputy Chairman of the Cabinet of Ministers, Chief of Staff, and Minister of Social Welfare

Ilaman Shikhyev

Ministry of Economics and Finance
Minister Matkarim Rajapov
Borodinskaya Street, no. 2
744000 Ashgabat, Turkmenistan
Tel: 993 (12) 25-16-53
Fax: 993 (12) 25-65-11 or 29-31-49

Ministry of Foreign Affairs
Foreign Minister Boris Shikmuradov
Prospekt Lenina, no. 11
Ashgabat, Turkmenistan
Tel: 993 (12) 25-14-63

Ministry of Oil and Gas Industry and Mineral Resources
Minister Batyr Sarjayev
28 Gogolia St.
Ashgabat, Turkmenistan
Tel: 993 (12) 29-38-27
Fax: 993 (12) 51-04-43

Ministry of Commerce and Foreign Economic Relations
Minister Dortguly Aidogdyev
Kemine Street, no. 92
Ashgabat, Turkmenistan
Tel: 993 (12) 29-75-11
Fax: 993 (12) 29-75-24

State Agency for Foreign Investment
Mr. Yolly Gurbanmuradov
Director
53 Azadi Street
Ashgabat, Turkmenistan 74400

Tel: 993 (12) 35-02-31 or 35-03-18
Fax: 993 (12) 35-04-15

Ministry of Trade
Minister Khalnazar Agakhanov
Pervomayskovo Street, no. 1
744000 Ashgabat, Turkmenistan
Tel: 993 (12) 25-10-47
Fax: 993 (12) 29-51-08

State Commodity and Raw Materials Exchange
Chairman Berdimurad Rejepov
Magtumguly Street #111
Ashgabat, Turkmenistan
Tel: 993 (12) 25-43-21; fax: 993 (12) 51-03-04

State Customs Office
7 Stepan Razin
7440225 Ashgabat
Tel: 993 (12) 47-04-55; fax: 993 (12) 47-02-21

American Business Liaison
Deputy Chairman of the Cabinet of Ministers: N.T. Suyunov
Gogol Street, no. 17
74000 Ashgabat, Turkmenistan
Tel: 993 (12) 25-33-86

Turkmenistan National Bank
Chairman Khudajberdy Orazov
Gogol Street, no. 22
744000 Ashgabat, Turkmenistan
Tel: 993 (12) 25-61-31; fax: 993 (12) 51-03-10 or 51-08-12

Vnesheconombank
Chairman Yolly Gurbanmuradov
Zhitnikova Street, no. 22
Ashgabat, Turkmenistan 744000
Tel: 993 (12) 51-03-70, 35-00-30
Fax: 993 (12) 51-00-70, 39-79-82
Hours: 9:30 am - 1:00 pm.

Turkmenbank
Chairman Seitbay Kandymov
Loa Gerogly Street
Ashgabat, Turkmenistan 744000
Tel:(993)(12)51-07-21, 51-07-05
Fax:(993)(12)51-02-46

SELECTED BUSINESS AND INTERNATIONAL CONTACTS

The Embassy of Turkmenistan
The Honorable Halil Ugur
Ambassador
2207 Massachusetts Avenue, N.W.
Washington, D.C. 20008
Tel: (202) 588-1500
Fax: (202) 588-0697
Website: www.infi.net/~embassy

U.S. Embassy in Turkmenistan
The Honorable Steven Mann
American Embassy Ashgabat
U.S. Department of State
Washington, DC 20521-7070
local address:
9 Pushkin Street
Ashgabat 744000
Tel: 993 (12) 51-13-06; 35-00-45; 35-00-46
Fax: 993 (12) 51-13-05
Website: www.usemb-ashgabat.usia.co.at/

Deputy Chief of Mission: Dianne E. Markowitz
Political/Economic Officer: David Whiddon
U.S. and Foreign Commercial Service Representative: Irina Begjanova
E-mail: begjanovai#ashgawpoa.us- state.gov

Emergency Services Telephone Numbers for Americans:
Consular Affairs
American Embassy Ashgabat
Tel: 993 (12) 24-49-25

Hospital of Medical and Sanitation Amalgamation
21 Turkmenbashi Street
Tel: 993 (12) 29-08-77 or 25-57-16 (after 7pm)

Local Police
Dial (02) (not English speaking)

Ministry of Foreign Affairs
Tel: 993 (12) 29-19-22

Turkmenistan Chamber of Commerce
Ms. Khodjanazarova Jennet Khakberdiyevna (English speaker)
B. Karriev St. 17
Ashgabat, Turkmenistan
Tel: 993 (12) 25-57-56 or 25-30-29
Fax: 993 (12) 25-30-29 or 47-44-19

U.S. - Turkmenistan Business Council
805 15th Street, N.W. Suite 500
Washington, D.C. 20005
Tel: (202) 682-0534
Fax: (202) 371-6601

SELECTED U.S. GOVERNMENT GRANTEES AND CONTRACTORS

Caspian Finance Center
Ankara, Turkey
Deborah Forhan (TDA)
Peter Ballinger (OPIC)
Tel: 90-312-468-6110 ext. 2075
Fax: 90-312-466-6082
Email: info@tda.gov

Hagler Bailly Consulting Firm
Ministry of Oil and Gas
11 Neutral Turkmenistan Street
Ashgabat, Turkmenistan 744000
Tel/Fax: [9](9312) 35-43-05, 39-30-85

Booz Allen and Hamilton
Ministry of Economics and Finance Room 118
4 Nurberdy Pomma Street
Ashgabat, Turkmenistan 744000
Tel: [9](9312) 51-17-47, 51-19-31
Fax: [9](9312) 51-04-97, 51-11-62

Counterpart Consortium
Roselie Vasquez
26 Akademik Petrov Street
Ashgabat, Turkmenistan 744000
Tel: [9](9312) 35-71-20
Fax: [9](9312) 35-71-25

Eurasia Foundation
Dmitry Shevkun
20A Komsomolskaya Street
Ashgabat, Turkmenistan 744000
Tel: [9](9312) 39-36-95
Fax: [9](9312) 39-06-13

Winrock International
Joe Dale
16 Kurban Durdy Street
Ashgabat, Turkmenistan 744000
Tel/Fax: [9](9312) 51-04-22

Central Asian-American Enterprise Fund
Office Head: Paul Hamlin, Vice President
Arun Hsu
2 Pushkin Street
Ashgabat, Turkmenistan 744000
Tel: +9 93-12-35-74-45; 35-28-75
Fax: +993-12-39-01-52
Email: caaef@online.tm
Website: www.caaef.com/

INTERNATIONAL ORGANIZATIONS

EBRD
Jaap Sprey
95 Azadi Street
Ashgabat, Turkmenistan 744000
Tel/Fax: [9](9312) 35-47-00 or 51-22-63

World Bank
Guljakhan Kurbanova
40 Atabaev Street
Ashgabat, Turkmenistan 744000
Tel: [9](9312) 41-97-35, 35-04-77
Fax: [9](9312) 41-31-56

TICA (Turkish International Cooperation Agency)
Ferhat Kuchuk Oglu
17 Neutral Turkmenistan Street
Ashgabat, Turkmenistan 744000
Tel: [9](9312) 51-03-64, 51-12-36
Fax: [9](9312) 51-16-39

IMF
Jon Craig
17 Neutral Turkmenistan Street
Ashgabat, Turkmenistan 744000
Tel/Fax: [9](9312) 35-16-61

EU-TACIS
Boris Smolin
97 Kemine Street
Ashgabat, Turkmenistan 744000
Tel: [9](9312) 51-21-17
Fax: [9](9312) 51-17-21

FOREIGN EMBASSIES AND MISSIONS

(1) ARMENIA

MR. ARAM GRIGORIAN TEL:(993)(12) 39-55-42
AMBASSADOR FAX:(993)(12) 39-55-38
ADDRESS: 14 GEROGLY STREET,
ASHGABAT, **TURKMENISTAN** 744000

(2) AFGHANISTAN

MR. SHAKHMARDANKUL TEL:(993)(12) 39-58-20
CHARGE D'AFFAIRES FAX:(993)(12) 39-58-21
ADDRESS: 14 GEROGLY STREET
ASHGABAT, **TURKMENISTAN** 744000

(3) CHINA

MR. YIN SONG LYN TEL:(993)(12) 47-36-83
AMBASSADOR FAX:(993)(12) 51-14-50
ADDRESS: 2 STEPAN RAZIN STREET,
ASHGABAT, **TURKMENISTAN** 744000

(4) EUROPEAN BANK FOR RECONSTRUCTION AND DEVELOPMENT (EBRD)

MR. JAAP SPREY TEL/FAX:(993)(12) 35-47-00
HEAD OF MISSION ADDRESS: 54A TELLIA STREET,
ASHGABAT, **TURKMENISTAN** 744000

(5) EUROPEAN UNION TECHNICAL ASSISTANCE FOR CIS (EU-TACIS)

MR. BORIS SMOLIN TEL/FAX:(993)(12) 51-21-17
ADVISER ADDRESS: 92 KEMINE STREET,
ASHGABAT, **TURKMENISTAN** 744000

(6) FRANCE

MR. YVES BARGAIN TEL:(993)(12) 51-06-23
AMBASSADOR FAX:(993)(12) 51-06-99
ADDRESS: OFFICE BUILDING, AK
ALTYN PLAZA HOTEL, 141/1
MAKHTUMKULI STREET, ASHGABAT,
TURKMENISTAN 744000

(7) GEORGIA

MR. HENRY PATARAYA TEL:(993)(12) 39-57-21
EXTRAORDINARY FAX: N/A
REPRESENTATIVE ADDRESS: 14
GEROGLY STREET,
ASHGABAT, **TURKMENISTAN** 744000

(8) GERMANY

MR. HANS JURGEN TEL:(993)(12) 51-21-44, 45, 46
KEILHOLZ FAX:(993)912) 51-09-23
AMBASSADOR ADDRESS: OFFICE BUILDING, AK
ALTYN PLAZA HOTEL, 141/1
MAKHTUMKULI STREET, ASHGABAT,
TURKMENISTAN 744000

(9) INDIA

DR. GEORGE JOSEPH TEL:(993)(12) 41-89-23
AMBASSADOR FAX:(993)(12) 46-90-30
ADDRESS: 11 JAPPAROV STREET,
ASHGABAT, **TURKMENISTAN** 744000

(10) INTERNATIONAL MONETARY FUND (IMF)

MR. JON CRAIG TEL:(993)(12) 35-16-61
REPRESENTATIVE FAX:(993)(12) 39-24-76
ADDRESS: 17 NEUTRAL
TURKMENISTAN STREET, ASHGABAT,
TURKMENISTAN 744000

(11) INTERNATIONAL OFFICE FOR MIGRATION

MR. ZLATKO ZHIGOVICH TEL:(993)(12) 41-07-21
REPRESENTATIVE FAX:(993)(12) 35-22-20
ADDRESS: 40 ATABAYEVA STREET,
ASHGABAT, **TURKMENISTAN** 744013

(12) IRAN

MR. SEID MEHTI MIR TEL:(993)(12) 24-46-11
ABU TALIBI ADDRESS: 3 TEHERAN
STREET,
AMBASSADOR ASHGABAT,
TURKMENISTAN 744000

(13) KAZAKHSTAN

MR. VALERIY TEMIRBAYEV TEL:(993)(12) 35-51-11
AMBASSADOR FAX: (993)(12) 39-59-32
ADDRESS: 14 GEROGLY STREET,
ASHGABAT, **TURKMENISTAN** 744000

(14) KYRGYZSTAN

MR. MARKIL IBRAYEV TEL/FAX:(993)(12) 35-55-06
AMBASSADOR TEL:(993)(12) 35-34-94
ADDRESS: 14 GEROGLY STREET,
ASHGABAT, **TURKMENISTAN** 744000

(15) PAKISTAN

MR. TARIQ OSMAN HYDER TEL:(993)(12) 51-22-87
AMBASSADOR FAX: (993)(12) 51-23-04
ADDRESS: 92 KEMINE STREET,
ASHGABAT, **TURKMENISTAN** 744000

(16) POLAND

MR. VLADIMIR TEL:(993)(12) 29-87-20
PAVLOTSKIY ADDRESS: 64 KARRIYEV
STREET,
HONORARY CONSUL ASHGABAT,
TURKMENISTAN 744000

(17) ROMANIA

MR. ION POROJAN TEL:(993)(12) 46-88-04
CHARGE D'AFFAIRES ADDRESS: 11
JAPPAROV STREET,
ASHGABAT, **TURKMENISTAN** 744000

(18) RUSSIA

MR. VADIM CHEREPOV TEL:(993)(12) 35-39-57
AMBASSADOR FAX:(993)(12) 39-84-66
ADDRESS: 11 TURKMENBASHI
STREET, ASHGABAT, **TURKMENISTAN**
744000

(19) TAJIKISTAN

MR. AKBARSHO TEL:(993)(12) 35-56-96
ISKANDEROV FAX:(993)(12) 39-31-74
AMBASSADOR ADDRESS: 14 GEROGLY
STREET,
ASHGABAT, **TURKMENISTAN** 744000

(20) TURKEY

MR. YIGIT ALPOGAN TEL:(993)(12) 51-00-11
AMBASSADOR FAX:(993)(12) 51-08-94
ADDRESS: 9 SHEVCHENKO STREET,
ASHGABAT, **TURKMENISTAN** 744000
(21) TURKISH AGENCY FOR
INTERNATIONAL COOPERATION
(TICA)

MS. YESHIM ORHAN TEL:(993)(12) 51-03-64
REPRESENTATIVE FAX:(993)(12) 51-16-39
ADDRESS: 17 BITARAP
TURKMENISTAN STREET, ASHGABAT,
TURKMENISTAN 744000

(22) UKRAINE

MR. VADIM CHUPRUN TEL:(993)(12) 39-13-73
AMBASSADOR FAX:(993)(12) 39-10-28
ADDRESS: 11 JAPPAROV STREET,
ASHGABAT, **TURKMENISTAN** 744000

(23) UNITED ARAB EMIRATES

MR. IBRAGIM MUHAMED TEL:(993)(12) 51-85-71
OMAR FAX:(993)(12) 51-85-74
FIRST SECRETARY ADDRESS: EMPERYAL INTERNATIONAL
BUSINESS CENTER, TURKMENBASHI STREET, ASHGABAT, **TURKMENISTAN** 744000

(24) UNITED KINGDOM

MR. NEIL KENNETH HOOK TEL:(993)(12) 51-08-61
AMBASSADOR FAX:(993)(12) 51-08-68
ADDRESS: OFFICE BUILDING,
AK ALTYN PLAZA HOTEL, 141/1 MAKHTUMKULI STREET, ASHGABAT, **TURKMENISTAN** 744000

(25) UNITED NATIONS CHILDREN'S FUND (UNICEF)

MS. SERAP MAKTAV TEL:(993)(12) 35-08-31
REPRESENTATIVE FAX:(993)(12) 35-08-30
ADDRESS: 40 ATABAYEV STREET,
ASHGABAT, **TURKMENISTAN** 744013

(26) UNITED NATIONS DEVELOPMENT PROGRAM (UNDP)

MR. OMER ERTUR TEL:(993)(12) 41-01-77
UN PROGRAM COORDINATOR FAX:(993)(12) 41-31-56
ADDRESS: 40 ATABAYEV STREET,
ASHGABAT, **TURKMENISTAN** 744013

(27) UNITED NATIONS EDUCATIONAL, SCIENTIFIC AND
CULTURAL ORGANIZATION (UNESCO)

MR. GUVANDYK POLATOV TEL/FAX:(993)(12) 35-53-67
REPRESENTATIVE ADDRESS: 15 GOGOLYA STREET,
ASHGABAT, **TURKMENISTAN** 744000

(28) UNITED NATIONS HIGH COMMISSION ON REFUGEES (UNHCR)

MS. FRANCOISE MULLER TEL:(993)(12) 35-06-01
SENIOR LIASON OFFICER FAX:(993)(12) 51-24-07
ADDRESS: 40 ATABAYEVA STREET,
ASHGABAT, **TURKMENISTAN** 744013

(29) UNITED NATIONS POPULATION FUND (UNPF)

MS. JAMAL TEL:(993)(12) 41-97-76
ORAZVALIYEVA FAX:(993)(12) 35-26-75
PROJECT OFFICER ADDRESS: 40 ATABAYEVA STREET,
ASHGABAT, **TURKMENISTAN** 744013

(30) UNITED STATES OF AMERICA

MR. MICHAEL COTTER TEL:(993)(12) 51-13-06
AMBASSADOR FAX:(993)(12) 51-13-05
ADDRESS: 9 PUSHKIN STREET,
ASHGABAT, **TURKMENISTAN** 744000

(31) UZBEKISTAN

MR. ABDUAHAD JALILOV TEL:(993)(12) 35-06-79
AMBASSADOR FAX:(993)(12) 36-23-85
ADDRESS: 50-A GEROGLY STREET,
ASHGABAT, **TURKMENISTAN** 744000

(32) WORLD BANK

MS. GULJAHAN TEL:(993)(12) 41-97-35
KURBANOVA FAX:(993)(12) 41-31-56 OR 57
LIASON OFFICER ADDRESS: 40 ATABAYEV STREET,
ASHGABAT, **TURKMENISTAN** 744013

(33) WORLD HEALTH ORGANIZATION

MS. ZAHIDE KOCADAG TEL:(993)(12) 35-01-31
REPRESENTATIVE FAX:(993)(12) 35-01-30
ADDRESS: 90 MAKHTUMKULI STREET,
ASHGABAT, **TURKMENISTAN** 744000

MAJOR MASS MEDIA

There are a number of publications in Turkmenistan. The major newspaper and tv/radio medium is government owned.

The periodicals include 23 state editions. Fourteen newspapers and 10 magazines are published in the capital, including one magazine and 2 newspapers in Russian, and 1 newspaper (Zaman) in Turkish. The main government dailies are "Turkmenistan" in Turkmen, and Neytralni Turkmenistan (Neutral Turkmenistan) in Russian. "Vecherny Ashgabat" is issued three times a week. Almost all the publishers of newspapers and magazines are located in the Ashgabat Press House.

Turkmen Press is the only informational agency in the country. Besides distribution of breaking news in Turkmenistan within the country and abroad, it publishes the newsletter "Turkmenistan News" weekly in Turkmen, Russian and English.

To subscribe to "Turkmenistan News" in Turkmen, Russian or English, call 7(3632) 25-30-87 or 29-27-42 or 29-51-65

Broadcasting of the National TV and Radio Comapny of Turkmenistan is in Turkmen and Russian and has three channels. The first channel broadcasts the Public Russian Television. Programs of Turkish Television are broadcast between 17:00h and 21:00h. Radio broadcasting is carried out by the local channel and Russian "Mayak."

The following is a list of media contacts provided by the American Embassy in Ashgabat. Note, all offices reside in Ashgabat, Turkmenistan 744004, and can be reached by phone or fax using the 7(3632) code unless otherwise noted.

Turkmen Press Agency
Lyudmila Glazovskaya, Director
Gogal Street, 24
Tel: (993-12)35-12-21; Fax: 51-09-18

NEWSPAPERS:

"Neutral Turkmenistan"
Russian language, circulation 40,000
Editor: Balkan Gafour
Atabaev Street, 24
Tel: 39-42-76 or 35-22-14 or 39-42-76
fax: 35-40-10

"Nesil"
Turkmen Language, circulation 52,700
Editor: Annamurad Poladov
Atabaev Street, 24
Tel: 35-22-54 or 46-70-91

"Ashgabat"
Russian Language, circulation 29,700
Editor: Annageldy Nurmuradov

Atabaev Street, 24
Tel: 46-84-44

"Ashgabat Ashgamy"
Turkmen language, circulation 70,000
Editor: Oraz Akgaev
Atabaev Street, 20
Tel: 46-68-95

"Turkmenistan"
Turkmen language, circulation 70,000
Editor: Kakabay Yliasov
Atabaev Street, #20
Ashgabat, Turkmenistan 744000
tel: 35-51-24

"Vatan"
Turkmen language, circulation 95,400
Editor: Annageldy Nurgeldyev
Atabaev Street, 20
Tel: 35-43-10 or 46-87-31

MAGAZINES

"Financial News"
Russian and English Language
Editor: Balkan Gafurov
Atabaev Street, 20 Tel: 39-42-76 or 35-25-47 or 39-14-84

Regional Newspapers

"Balkanskiye Vesti"
Russian and Turkmen languages, circulation 7,000
Editor: M. Mamedov
Pl. Pobeda #2, Turkmenbashi, Turkmenistan
Tel: 7(37022) 7-54-43

"Maryiskaya Pravda"
Russian and Turkmen languages, circulation 25,500
Editor: N. Dudko
Magtumguli Street, 35
Mary, Turkmenistan 754000
Tel: 7(37822) 5-74-18

"Lebapskaya Pravda"
Russian and Turkmen language, circulation 26,430
Editor:
Prospect Niyazov #44, Charjou, Turkmenistan 746100
Tel: 7(36022) 2-48-96

"Dashowuzskaya Pravda"
Russian and Turkmen language, circulation 15,000

Editor: K. Kurovski
Karl Marx St., 8
Dashowuz, Turkmenistan 746300
Tel: 7(36022) 2-48-96

TV AND RADIO ADVERTISING:

MR. Isa Arazmedov, Chairman (speaks Russian and Turkmen)
National Tevevision and Radio Company
Molla Nepesa Street, 3
Ashgabat, Turkmenistan, 744000
Tel: 7-3632-35-15-15 Fax: 7-3632-39-48-21
Working hours are from 9 a.m. till 6 p.m.; lunch break from 1 p.m. till 2 p.m. every day
Except Saturday and Sunday.

CUSTOMS GLOSSARY

"Buy National" Bias Refer to: Government Procurement Policies and Practices,

Access Market Refer to: Market Access,

Access to Supplies Refer to: Supply Access,

Accession The process of adhering to a legal instrument. In the case of GATT, the prospective Contracting Party enters into accession negotiations with the Contracting Parties to determine the concessions (trade liberalization) or other specific obligations it must undertake before accession is concluded. Prospective members may be accorded "provisional accession," which obligates them to apply GATT rules in their commercial relationships with other Contracting Parties, but not to make tariff concessions. Accession to GATT does not automatically involve adherence to the Codes of Conduct negotiated during the Tokyo Round.
See also: Concession, Contracting Party, General Agreement on Tariffs and Trade, Grandfather Clause, Protocol of Accession, Protocol of Provisional Application, dd, http://www.asycuda.org,

ACP Countries African, Caribbean and Pacific countries associated with the European Community under the Lomé Convention
See also: Lomé Convention, http://www.asycuda.org,

Across the Board (Linear) Tariff Reduction Refer to: Linear Reduction of Tariffs,

ACTN Refer to: Advisory Committee for Trade Negotiations,

Ad Valorem Equivelant The duty collected under a specific tariff or a compound tariff expressed as a percentage of the value of the imported item. Since a specific tariff is calculated on the basis of units (of volume or weight), rather than value, and prices can change over time, the ad valorem equivalent could differ when calculated for different time periods
See also: Ad Valorem Tariff, Compound Tariff, Specific Tariff,

Ad Volorem Tariff A tariff calculated "according to value," or as a percentage of the value of goods cleared through customs, e.g., 15 percent ad valorem means 15 percent of the value
See also: Specific Tariff, Tariff, Valuation,

Added Value Tax Refer to: Value Added Tax.,

Additionality A measure of the net increase in capital inflows into assisted developing countries as contrasted with a diversion from one form or target of development assistance to another.
See also: Bilateral Aid, Multilateral Aid, Official Development Assistance, Transfer Payments,

Adjustment Assistance Financial, technical or other assistance to firms, workers and communities to help them cope with adjustment difficulties arising from increased import competition or other changes in the economic environment. The objective of the assistance is usually to help an industry to become more competitive in the same line of production, or to move into other economic activities. The aid to workers can take the form of training (to qualify the affected individuals for employment in new or expanding industries), relocation allowances(to help them move from areas characterized by high unemployment to areas where employment may be available), or unemployment compensation (to tide them over while they are searching for new jobs). The aid to firms can take the form of loans or guarantees of loans, tax benefits or other assistance. The benefits of increased trade to an importing country generally exceed the costs of adjustment, but the benefits are widely shared and the adjustment costs are sometimes narrowly--and some would say unfairly--concentrated on a few domestic producers and communities. Both import restraints and adjustment assistance can be designed to reduce these hardships, but adjustment assistance--unlike import restraints--allows the economy to enjoy the full benefits of lower-cost imported goods. Adjustment assistance can also be designed to facilitate structural shifts of resources from less productive to more productive industries, contributing further to greater economic efficiency and improved standards of living.
See also: Adjustment, Escape Clause, Structural Change, Trade Act of 1974,

Adjustments The process of adaptation in an economy triggered, for example, by technological developments, changes in demand or shifting external trade patterns. The changes may involve a reallocation of labor and capital away from uncompetitive products or sectors and into new or other lines of production in which the economy is competitive. In the specific sense used by the International Monetary Fund, adjustment means the adoption of macroeconomic policies, including monetary, fiscal and exchange rate policies, to adjust the level of domestic economic activity to conditions prevailing in the world economy, with the objective of correcting balance of payments disequilibria and pursuing domestic objectives such as lower inflation.
See also: Adjustment Assistance, Balance of Payments, Competitive, Conditionality, Devaluation, International Monetary Fund, Macroeconomics, Safeguards, Structural Change, Technology, Fair Market Value,

Adjustments In calculating the margin in an anti-dumping determination, various adjustments are made to both United States price and foreign market value to ensure that price comparisons between the two are not distorted by factors extraneous to the central issue of price discrimination between markets. Differences in price for which adjustments are made include differences in physical characteristics, quantities sold, packing and delivery costs, circumstances of sale, and applicable indirect taxes and duties.
See also: Adjustment Assistance, Balance of Payments, Competitive, Conditionality, Devaluation, International Monetary Fund, Macroeconomics, Safeguards, Structural Change, Technology, Fair Market Value,

Advanced Developing Countries Refer to: Developing Countries, Newly Industrializing Countries,

Advertising Refer to: Services,

Advisory Committee For Trade Negotiations (ACTN) A group of eminent individuals appointed by the U.S. president to advise him on trade agreements and trade policy.
See also: United States Trade Representative,

Agency For International Development (AID) The unit within the U. S. government responsible for

the administration of U.S. bilateral development assistance programs. AID also participates actively in the development of other U.S. policies and programs related to Third World economic development.
See also: Bilateral Aid, Developing Countries, Official Development Assistance,

Agreement On Subsidies And Countervailing Duties Refer to: Countervailing Duties, Export Subsidies,

Agricultural Adjustment Act Of 1933 Refer to: Section 22,

Agricultural Trade Development And Assistance Act of 1954 Refer to: Public Law 480,

AID Refer to: Agency for International Development,

Aircraft Agreement The "Agreement on Trade in Civil Aircraft," sometimes also referred to as the "Aircraft Code," was signed in Geneva in December 1979 and entered into force on January 1, 1980. This was the only multilateral sectoral agreement designed to expand trade in manufactured products that was negotiated during the 1973-79 Tokyo Round of GATT negotiations, and it was intended to provide a new international framework for free trade in civil aircraft. It uniquely addressed tariff and non-tariff issues in a single sectoral context. Tariffs on civil aircraft, engines, most components and ground flight simulators were eliminated. On non-tariff issues, the agreement established new international commitments concerning government intervention in aircraft, aircraft component and simulator procurement, including disciplines on: technical or standards barriers with respect to certification requirements and specifications on operations and maintenance procedures; government-directed procurement actions and mandatory subcontracts, sales-related inducements, quantitative trade restrictions and government supports. Subsequent negotiations have resulted in modifications to the agreement and additions to its annex of duty-free items in 1982, 1983, 1985 and 1986. The original signatories to the agreement were Austria, Canada, the member states of the European Economic Community, the European Community, Japan, Norway, Sweden, Switzerland and the United States. Rumania and Egypt acceded to the agreement later, as did Greece, Portugal and Spain when they joined the EC. Currently there are 22 signatories to the agreement.
See also: Free Trade, Non-Tariff Measures, Tariff,

Aircraft Code Refer to: Aircraft Agreement,

Andean Pact An arrangement between Bolivia, Colombia, Ecuador, Peru and Venezuela for the coordination of economic policies, including the formation of a free trade zone in the Andean region.
See also: Free Trade Zone,

Antiboycott Legislation The Export Administration Act was promulgated in 1969, amended in 1977 and 1979, and expired in 1990 but was continued by Executive Order 12730 under the International Emergency Economic Powers Act. It declares the policy of the United States to oppose restrictive trade practices or boycotts by foreign countries against countries friendly to the United States. The U.S. Department of Commerce, Bureau of Export Administration, Office of Antiboycott Compliance enforces regulations prohibiting U.S. citizens from engaging in a wide variety of activities that comply with, further, or support unsanctioned foreign boycotts. Prohibited activities include refusing and agreeing to refuse to do business for boycott reasons, taking discriminatory actions that are boycott based, furnishing of information about business relationships with or in a boycotted country or with blacklisted persons, and engaging in evasion activities, such as devices or schemes intended to place a blacklisted person at a commercial disadvantage. The principle focus of the regulatory activities of the Office of Antiboycott Compliance relate to the Arab boycott of Israel. In addition, the U.S. Treasury Department

enforces the antiboycott provisions of the Tax Reform Act of 1976 which prohibit certain tax benefits to those who agree to "participate in or cooperate with an international boycott."
See also: Boycott and Export Administration Act of 1979,

Anti-Dumping Code A code of conduct negotiated under the auspices of GATT during the Tokyo Round (replacing an earlier code negotiated during the Kennedy Round) that established both substantive and procedural standards for anti-dumping proceedings in signatory countries. The Anti-Dumping Code was implemented in the United States through the U.S. Trade Agreements Act of 1979, which repealed the Anti-Dumping Law of 1921 and inserted new anti-dumping provisions in the Tariff Act of 1930, providing for the imposition of special duties equivalent to the margin of "dumping" of imported merchandise. Goods imported into the United States are considered "dumped" when they are found to have been sold at less than fair value and to have caused or threaten to cause material injury to a U.S. industry.
See also: Codes of Conduct, Dumping, Kennedy Round, Trade Agreements Act of 1979,

Anti-Dumping Duties Refer to: Dumping,

Anti-Trust A term used to describe a policy or action that seeks to curtail monopolistic power within a market.
See also: Export Trading Company, Market, Monopoly, Restrictive Business Practices, Webb-Pomerene Act,

APEC Refer to: Asia-Pacific Economic Cooperation,

Apparel Refer to: Multi-Fiber Arrangement Regarding International Trade in Textiles, Textiles,

Appraisal Refer to: Valuation,

Arbitration An arrangement through which two parties to a dispute agree to the appointment of an impartial chairman or group of competent persons to decide the issue, the disputants agreeing in advance to abide by the decision rendered.
See also: Dispute Settlement, Panel of Experts,

Article 11 (GATT Article XI). GATT provision that prohibits the use of quantitative restrictions (e.g., embargoes, bans, quotas, restrictive licenses) to regulate imports and exports, except under certain specific conditions, or unless provided for in some other GATT Article
See also: Quantitative Restrictions, Section 22,

Article 19 (GATT Article XIX). GATT provision that prescribes when emergency action (e.g., restrictive measures other than normal tariffs) can be taken against imports that are injuring domestic producers.
See also: Escape Clause, Safeguards,

Article 23 (GATT Article XXIII). Along with Article XXII, the provision of the GATT that requires GATT members to consult with each other concerning disputes that arise under GATT rules. Article XXIII also sets the basic provisions for resolving disputes that cannot be settled through bilateral consultations.
See also: Consultation, Dispute Settlement, Quantitative Restrictions,

Article 24 (GATT Article XXIV). Regulates how customs unions and free trade areas may be formed as exceptions to the most-favored-nation (MFN) provisions of Article I. Provides for notification to the GATT Contracting Parties, review in a Working Party, and the application of substantive criteria to the formation of such regional trade associations.
See also: Customs Union, Free Trade,

Article of GATTS : Article of XXI Refer to: Quantitative Restrictions,

Article of GATTS : Article XXIV Refer to: Article 24, Customs Union,

Articles of GATT : Article ARTICLE XVI. See Border Tax Adjustments; Export Subsidies.

Articles of GATT : Article XI
See also: Article 11, Quantitative Restrictions, Section 22,

Articles of GATT : Article XII Refer to: Quantitative Restrictions,

Articles of GATT : Article XIII Refer to: Quantitative Restrictions,

Articles of GATT : Article XIX Refer to: Article 19, Escape Clause, SafeguardsArticle ,

Articles of GATT : Article XV Refer to: Balance of Payments Consultations,

Articles of GATT : Article XVI Refer to: Border Tax Adjustments, Export Subsidies,

Articles of GATT : Article XVIII Refer to: Quantitative Restrictions,

Articles of GATT : Article XX Refer to: Quantitative Restrictions,

Articles of GATT : Articles XXII, XXIII

Articles of GATT : Articles XXXVI, XXXVII, XXXVIII Refer to: General Agreement on Tariffs and Trade, Part IV of the GATT,

Articles of GATT: Article I Refer to: Enabling Clause, Most-Favored-Nation Treatment,

Articles of GATT: Article II Refer to: Concession,

Articles of GATT: Article III through XXIII Refer to: Codes of Conduct,

Articles of GATT: Article IV Refer to: Border Tax Adjustments, Countervailing Duties, Dumping,

Asia-Pacific Economic Cooperation (APEC) A forum established as a vehicle for multilateral cooperation among the market-oriented economies of the region to better manage their growing interdependence and sustain economic growth. Begun in 1989 as an informal grouping of 12 Asia-Pacific economies (Australia, Brunei, Canada, Indonesia, Japan, South Korea, Malaysia, New Zealand, Phillippines, Singapore, Thailand and the United States), APEC admitted the People's Republic of China, Chinese Taipei and Hong Kong in November 1991, and Mexico and Papua/New Guinea in November 1993, bringing membership to 17. Annual meetings of foreign and economic ministers have been held, with the first in Canberra, Australia, in November 1989. The United States hosted a ministerial in November 1993 in Seattle, Washington.

Associated States Refer to: ACP Countries, European Community, Lomé Convention,

Association Agreement Refer to: European Community,

ATA Carnet An international customs document that is recognized as an internationally valid guarantee and may be used in lieu of national customs documents and as security for import duties and taxes to cover the temporary admission of goods and sometimes the transit of goods.

The ATA ("Admission Temporaire-Temporary Admission") Convention of 1961 authorized the ATA Carnet to replace the ECS ("Echantillons Commerciaux-Commercial Samples") Carnet that was created by a 1956 convention sponsored by the Customs Cooperation Council. ATA Carnets are issued by National Chambers of Commerce affiliated with the International Chamber of Commerce, which also guarantees payment of duties in the event of failure to re-export.
See also: Customs Cooperation Council,

Australia-New Zealand Closer Economic Relations Agreement (CER) An agreement aimed at increasing trade links by liberalizing trans-Tasman trade, therefore allowing for more efficient use of each country's resources. Implemented on January 1, 1983, the CER has the ultimate goal of eliminating import quotas and tariffs by 1995 and eliminating import licensing requirements by 1999. The CER contains provisions to gradually reduce duties, quotas and licensing requirements. It also provides for the elimination of domestic export incentive schemes in Australia-New Zealand transactions, extension of government purchases between the two countries and harmonization of customs policies.
See also: Bilateral Trade Agreement, Binding Concessions, Trade Agreement, Export Quotas,

Balance Of Concessions Refer to: Concession, Reciprocity,

Balance Of Payments A tabulation of a country's credit and debit transactions with other countries and international institutions. These transactions are divided into two broad groups: current account and capital account. The main items included are exports and imports of goods and services (the balance of trade), foreign direct investments, intergovernmental loans, transfer payments, capital inflows and outflows, and changes in official gold holdings and foreign exchange reserves.
See also: Adjustment, Capital Account, Current Account, International Monetary Fund, Invisible Trade, Macroeconomics, Quantitative Restrictions, Transfer Payments, Visible Trade,

Balance Of Payments Consultations Article XV of GATT requires coordination between the General Agreement on Tariffs and Trade and the International Monetary Fund to ensure that the trade and payments implications of any quantitative restrictions imposed for balance of payments reasons are fully analyzed within the respective jurisdictions of both organizations. Any Contracting Party that imposes such quantitative restrictions for balance of payments reasons is expected to hold consultations with other interested Contracting Parties. The Framework Agreement concluded during the Tokyo Round provided that any other trade restrictive measures imposed for balance of payments reasons should also be discussed in such consultations.
See also: Consultations, Exchange Controls, Framework Agreement, General Agreement on Tariffs and Trade, International Monetary Fund, Prior Deposits, Quantitative Restrictions,

Balance Of Trade A component of the balance of payments, or the surplus or deficit that results from comparing a country's expenditures on merchandise imports and receipts derived from its merchandise exports.
See also: Credit, Mercantilism,

Banking Refer to: Credit, Interest, Loan, Services,

Barter The direct exchange of goods for other goods, without the use of money as a medium of exchange and without the involvement of a third party.
See also: Countertrade, Money,

Basket Of Currencies Refer to: Par Value, Special Drawing Rights,

BDV Refer to: Customs Valuation Code,

Beggar-Thy-Neighbor Policy A course of action through which a country tries to reduce unemployment and increase domestic output by raising tariffs and instituting non-tariff barriers that impede imports, or by accomplishing the same objective through competitive devaluation. Countries that pursued such policies in the early 1930s found that other countries retaliated by raising their own barriers against imports, which, by reducing export markets, tended to worsen the economic difficulties that precipitated the initial protectionist action. The Smoot-Hawley Tariff Act of 1930 is often cited as a conspicuous example of this approach.
See also: Column 2 Rates, Devaluation, Protectionism, Retaliation, Tariff Act of 1930,

Bern Convention The International Union for the Protection of Literary and Artistic Works, signed at Bern, Switzerland, on September 9, 1886, with additional protocols and revisions signed in 1914, 1928, 1948, 1967, and 1971, is a major multinational treaty concerning the scope of copyright protection to be afforded works prepared by foreign persons whose countries are signatories. It provides copyright protection in the form of national treatment and also requires member countries to provide certain minimum protections for specified types of works. For instance, it requires that literary works be protected for the life of the author plus 50 years and forbids imposition of formalities (e.g., a copyright notice) as a condition of protection. The other major copyright treaty, the Universal Copyright Convention, is somewhat less protective of the rights of authors. After decades of refusing to join, the United States became a signatory of the Bern Convention in 1989. It is now pressing other nonmembers to enhance their respective copyright laws and join Bern.
See also: Copyright, Intellectual Property, Trademark,

Bern Union Refer to: World Intellectual Property Organization,

Bilateral Agreement or arrangement involving two sides.
See also: Multilateral, Unilateral,

Bilateral Aid Development assistance provided directly by a donor country to a recipient country (as opposed to aid channeled through multilateral institutions).
See also: Agency for International Development, Multilateral Aid,

Bilateral Investment Treaty (BIT) An agreement establishing the terms and conditions for private investment by nationals and companies of one country in the country of the other.

Bilateral Trade Agreement A formal or informal agreement involving commerce between two countries.
See also: Consultations, Multi-Fiber Arrangement Regarding International Trade in Textiles, Trade Agreement,

Bill A document giving evidence of indebtedness of one party to another, as, for example, a written order for goods that can be used as security for a loan to the supplier of the goods from a bank, or a security such as a Treasury bill.
See also: Euro-Dollars, Medium of Exchange, Security, Trade Agreements Act of 1934,

Binational Panel In the context of the U.S.-Canada Free Trade Agreement, binational panels were established to assist in the resolution of trade disputes which have been referred by the U.S.-Canada Trade Commission for panel consideration. The composition of panels under the CFTA is spelled out in Chapter 5, 18 and 19 of the agreement. Rosters of eligible candidates were maintained by both countries.
See also: Bilateral Trade Agreement, U.S.-Canada Free Trade Agreement, U.S.-Canada Trade Commission,

Binding A provision in a trade agreement that no tariff rate higher than the rate specified in the

agreement will be imposed during the life of the agreement.
See also: Bound Rates, Compensation, Concessions, Tariff,

BIT Refer to: Bilateral Investment Treaty,

Bogus Goods Refer to: Commercial Counterfeiting,

Bond An interest-bearing certificate issued by a government or a business promising to pay the holder a specified sum on a specified date. A bond is a common means of raising capital.
See also: Capital Market, Credit,

Bonded Goods Imported goods stored in a bonded warehouse, usually after the owners of the goods have deposited a bond guaranteeing that the duty will be paid when and if the goods are withdrawn for domestic sale.
See also: Bond, Bonded Warehouse,

Bonded Warehouse A secure storage area in which goods, subject to excise taxes or customs duties, are stored pending payment of taxes or duties.
See also: Free Zone,

Border Tax Adjustments The remission of indirect taxes on exported goods, including sales taxes and value added taxes, designed to ensure that national tax systems do not impede exports, and the imposition of domestic taxes on imported goods, to ensure that they do not receive preferential treatment, as compared with domestically produced goods. Frontier adjustments on exports are permitted for indirect taxes under Articles VI and XVI of GATT, but not for direct taxes (such as income taxes assessed on producing firms). The U.S. government makes little use of border tax adjustments, since it relies more heavily on income (or direct) taxes than do most other governments, and since most goods exported from the United States are not subject to indirect taxes.
See also: Direct Tax, Indirect Tax, Tax, Value Added Tax,

Bound Rates Tariff rates resulting from GATT negotiations that are incorporated in a country's schedule of concessions and are thus enforceable as an integral element of GATT. If a Contracting Party raises a tariff to a higher level than its bound rate, the major beneficiaries of the earlier binding have a right under the GATT to receive compensation, usually in the form of reduced tariffs on other products they export to the country. If the beneficiaries do not receive such compensation they may retaliate by raising their own tariffs against an equivalent value of the original country's exports.
See also: Binding, Compensation, Concession, Contracting Party, Retaliation, Tariff,

Bounties Payments by governments to producers of goods, often to strengthen their competitive position.
See also: Countervailing Duties,

Boycott A refusal to deal commercially or otherwise with a person, firm or country.
See also: Coordinating Committee on Export Controls, Embargo, Export Administration Act of 1979,

Bretton Woods Conference A meeting of Central Bank economists and other government officials, formally known as the United Nations Monetary and Financial Conference, that took place in Bretton Woods, New Hampshire, in July 1944. The conference was convened to consider alternative proposals put forward by British and American financial experts relating to international payments problems, the economic reconstruction needs of Europe upon the conclusion of World War II, and the need to ensure stable exchange rates and free convertibility

of currencies. The compromise solution negotiated at Bretton Woods envisaged the establishment of an International Monetary Fund and an International Bank for Reconstruction and Development (the World Bank). The presumed need for an International Trade Organization was also informally considered at Bretton Woods.
See also: General Agreement on Tariffs and Trade, International Monetary Fund, World Bank,

Bridging Credit Borrowing ahead of receiving payment for a sale, or short term credit to a customer pending his receipt of funds from another source.
See also: Credit,

Broker An intermediary between a buyer and a seller in a highly organized market, as in the case of a stockbroker.
See also: Capital Market, Market, Security,

Brussels Definition Of Value Refer to: Customs Valuation Code,

Brussels Ministerial The Uruguay Round of Multilateral Trade Negotiations was scheduled to conclude at an EC-hosted ministerial meeting in Brussels, December 3-7, 1990; however, discussions broke down and the conclusion of the Round was postponed.
See also: Uruguay Round,

Brussels Tariff Nomenclature Refer to: Customs Classification,

BTN Refer to: Customs Cooperation Council Nomenclature,

Buffer Stocks Commodity stockpiles managed in such a way as to moderate price fluctuations. Goods may be sold from a stockpile when prices reach or approach predetermined ceiling prices, and purchased for the stockpile when prices reach or approach predetermined floor levels. Rubber and cocoa are among the commodities considered most likely to benefit from buffer stocks, and international commodity agreements exist for both of these products.
See also: Commodity, Common Fund, Integrated Program for Commodities, International Commodity Agreement, Strategic Stockpiles,

Bulk Carrier A transporter (usually an ocean-going vessel) of large, heavy cargoes on unscheduled services. "Dry" cargoes are usually mineral ores (such as phosphates or manganese), as opposed to "liquid hydrocarbons," a phrase that usually refers to petroleum.

Buy American Act U.S. legislation passed in 1933 which mandates preference for the purchase of domestically produced goods over foreign goods in U.S. government procurement. The president has the authority to waive the Buy American Act within the terms of a reciprocal agreement or otherwise in response to the provision of reciprocal treatment to U.S. producers. Under the 1979 GATT Government Procurement Code, the U.S.-Israel FTA, and the U.S.-Canada FTA, the United States provides access to the government procurement of certain U.S. agencies for goods from the other parties to those agreements. Other "buy-national" legislative provisions also exist separately from the Buy American Act requirements.
See also: Government Procurement Policies and Practices, U.S.-Israel Free Trade Agreement, U.S.-Canada Free Trade Agreement,

Buy-Back Refer to: Countertrade,

C and F An abbreviation used in some international sales contracts when the selling price includes the cost of the goods and freight but not the cost of insurance. The formula is often used when the government in the importing country requires that insurance must be supplied from a company subject to its jurisdiction.

See also: CIF, FAS, FOB,

Cairns Group A group of agricultural-exporting nations comprising Australia, Argentina, Brazil, Canada, Chile, Colombia, Fiji, Hungary, Indonesia, Malaysia, New Zealand, the Philippines, Thailand and Uruguay, established to develop a common negotiating position for the Uruguay Round.
See also: Codes of Conduct, Multilateral Agreement, Uruguay Round,

CAP Refer to: Common Agricultural Policy,

Capital Property or wealth that yields income expressed in terms of money, or the accumulated stock of tools, machinery, equipment, buildings and other goods employed, in turn, to produce other goods and services.
See also: Capital Goods, Infrastructure, Interest, Money, Profit, Risk,

Capital Account That portion of a country's balance of payments that includes the inward and outward flow of money for investment and international grants and loans (public and private).
See also: Balance of Payments, Current Account,

Capital Goods Industrial products or other goods that are used in the creation of additional wealth, such as machine tools. Capital goods are sometimes called intermediate goods because they only indirectly satisfy human wants, and sometimes producer goods, because they are used to produce other goods.
See also: Capital, Consumer Goods, Production,

Capital Market The market for longer-term loanable funds. The capital market in a country is not one institution; rather it includes securities exchanges, underwriters, investment banks and insurance companies that canalize supply and demand for long-term capital and claims on capital, especially when concentrated in such major financial centers as New York City or London. The marketing of securities is an important element in the efficient working of a capital market.
See also: Capital, Developing Countries, Insurance, International Finance Corporation, Market, Security, Underwriter, World Bank,

Cargo Sharing The reservation and division of maritime traffic between designated trading partners who agree that vessels owned or controlled by either will carry a specified percentage of the cargo moving between them.

Caribbean Basin Initiative (CBI) A broad program to promote economic development through private-sector initiative in Central America and the Caribbean islands. The goal is to expand foreign and domestic investment in nontraditional sectors, diversifying CBI country economies and expanding their exports. The major elements of the program are: duty-free entry to the United States in perpetuity for a wide-ranging group of products; U.S. economic assistance to the region; continuing self-help efforts to improve investment climate and trade; a deduction on U.S. taxes for countries that hold conventions in qualifying CBI countries to increase tourism; U.S. government, state government and private-sector promotion programs; and support from other trading partners and multinational development institutions.
See also: Developing Countries, Economic Development, Liberalization, Tariff Quota,

Carnet Refer to: ATA Carnet,

Cartel An alliance or arrangement among industrial, commercial or state-controlled enterprises producing the same commodity, aimed at regulating the purchase, production or marketing of the commodity. A cartel agreement is often accompanied by output and investment quotas. When a

cartel gains monopoly power, it will normally seek to maximize profits by raising prices and limiting supply.
See also: Commodity, Monopoly, Organization of Petroleum Exporting Countries,

Case Law The codes of conduct negotiated in the Tokyo Round are expected to evolve according to decisions made with respect to specific "cases" resulting from allegations of violation brought before the committees responsible for monitoring the codes. The decisions made in these cases serve as precedents that are taken as interpretations of the relevant provisions applicable to future cases
See also: Codes of Conduct, Dispute Settlement, Tokyo Round,

CBI Refer to: Caribbean Basin Initiative,

CCC Refer to: Commodity Credit Corporation, Customs Cooperation Council,

CCCN Refer to: Customs Classification,

Ceiling Prices Refer to: Buffer Stocks,

Central Planning Refer to: Non-Market Economy,

CER Refer to: Australia-New Zealand Closer Economic Relations Agreement,

Certificate Of Origin Refer to: Customs and Administrative Entry Procedures,

CET Refer to: Common External Tariff,

CFTA Refer to: Binational Panel , U.S.-Canada Free Trade Agreement,

CIF An abbreviation used in some international sales contracts, when the selling price includes all "costs, insurance and freight" for the goods sold ("charge in full"), meaning that the seller arranges and pays for all relevant expenses involved in shipping goods from their point of exportation to a given point of importation. In trade statistics, "CIF value" means that all figures for imports or exports are calculated on this basis, regardless of the nature of individual transactions.
See also: C and F, FAS, FOB,

CIT Refer to: Court of International Trade,

Clearing Agreements Refer to: Countertrade,

COCOM
See also: Coordinating Committee on Export Controls,

Codes of Conduct International instruments that indicate standards of behavior by nation states or multinational corporations deemed desirable by the international community. Several codes of conduct were negotiated during the Tokyo Round that liberalized and harmonized domestic measures that might impede trade, and these are considered legally binding for the countries that choose to adhere to them. Each of these codes is monitored by a special committee that meets under the auspices of GATT and encourages consultations and the settlement of disputes arising under the code. Countries that are not Contracting Parties to GATT may adhere to these codes. GATT Articles III through XXIII also contain commercial policy provisions that have been described as GATT's code of good conduct in trade matters. The United Nations has also encouraged the negotiation of several "voluntary" codes of conduct (meaning that they are not legally binding), including one that seeks to specify the rights and obligations of transnational

corporations.
See also: Aircraft Agreement, Anti-Dumping Code, Articles of GATT, Case Law, Countervailing Duties, Customs Valuation Code, Dispute Settlement, Export Subsidies, Government Procurement Policies and Practices, Liberalization,

Collateral Refer to: Security,

Column 1 Rates U.S. tariff rates (nearly all of which are "bound" rates) established through trade negotiations. They are usually substantially lower than column 2 rates and apply to all countries to which the United States grants most-favored-nation treatment.
See also: Bound Rates, Column 2 Rates, Most-Favored-Nation Treatment,

Column 2 Rates U.S. statutory thrift rates, generally set by the Smoot-Hawley Tariff Act of 1930, as amended. These rates are substantially higher than column 1 rates. For countries receiving most-favored-nation treatment, they have been supplanted by lower tariffs established through concessions, which are set out in column 1 of the tariff schedule. Column 2 rates are currently assessed only on imports from countries that do not receive most-favored-nation treatment from the United States, all of which are state trading nations.
See also: Column 1 Rates, Concession, Most-Favored-Nation Treatment, State Trading Nations, Tariff Act of 1930. ,

COMECON Refer to: Council for Mutual Economic Assistance,

Commercial Counterfeiting The production or marketing of goods with the intent of defrauding the purchaser by falsely implying, directly or indirectly, that the goods are produced by a known and reputable manufacturer. Counterfeit goods are usually distinguished from bogus goods in that in addition to replicating the legitimate good, they bear a forged trademark. The Uruguay Round accord includes TRIPS provisions to discourage counterfeiting.
See also: Intellectual Property, Trademark, Trade-Related Aspects of Intellectual Property Rights (TRIPS),

Commercial Paper Short-term financial instruments that can be bought and sold, particularly promissory notes that call for the payment of specified amounts of money at a given time.
See also: Bond, Capital Market, Loan, Security,

Commission Of The European Community Refer to: European Community,

Commodity Broadly defined, any article exchanged in trade, but most commonly used to refer to raw materials, including such minerals as tin, copper and manganese, and bulk-produced agricultural products such as coffee, tea and rubber.
See also: Buffer Stocks, Common Fund, Forward Market, Integrated Program for Commodities, Primary Commodity, Tropical Products,

Commodity Agreement Refer to: International Commodity Agreement,

Commodity Credit Corporation (CCC) A public corporation attached to the U.S. Department of Agriculture that provides financial and other services associated with public price-support activities for certain agricultural commodities, including loans, guarantees, purchases, sales, storage, transport and export programs.
See also: Export Enhancement Program,

Commodity Exchange Refer to: Forward Market,

Commodity Stockpiles Refer to: Buffer Stocks,

Common Agricultural Policy (CAP) A comprehensive system of production targets and market regulations adopted by the European Community covering most agricultural goods produced within the Community. Its purposes are to achieve fair and rising standards of living for the farm populations of member states, stable agricultural markets, increased farm productivity and food security within the Community. To achieve these objectives, the CAP relies on uniform prices and the free circulation of agricultural goods among member states; preferences for agricultural products produced within the Community; the imposition of variable levies on imported goods to bring their prices to the level of Community prices; and subsidization of exports to countries outside the Community. (In practice, agricultural prices sometimes vary from one member country to another, principally because exchange rates applied to goods moving from one country to another within the Community do not always reflect market exchange rates.) The European Community finances the CAP through receipts from customs duties, including variable levies, and the value added tax.
See also: Conversion Product, Deficiency Payments, European Community, Export Subsidies, Restitutions, Threshold Price, Value Added Tax, Variable Levy,

Common External Tariff (CET or sometimes CXT). A tariff rate uniformly applied by a common market or customs union, such as the European Community, to imports from countries outside the union. For example, the European Common Market is based on the principle of a free internal trade area with a common external tariff (sometimes referred to in French as the Tariff Exterieur Commun (TEC) applied to products imported from non-member countries. "Free trade areas" do not necessarily have common external tariffs and free trade agreements seldom have common external tariffs.
See also: Customs Union, European Community, Free Trade Area. ,

Common Fund An international institution designed as the centerpiece of the UNCTAD Integrated Program for Commodities (IPC). Its first account (sometimes called its first "window," and financed from mandatory contributions of member governments) provides funds to help finance buffer stocks operated under International Commodity Agreements to stabilize commodity prices. Its second account (sometimes called its second "window," and largely financed by voluntary contributions) supports research and development and export promotion for selected commodities.
See also: Buffer Stocks, Integrated Program for Commodities, International Commodity Agreement,

Common Market Refer to: Customs Union, European Coal and Steel Community, European Community,

Comparative Advantage A central concept in international trade theory which holds that a country or a region should specialize in the production and export of those goods and services that it can produce relatively more efficiently than other goods and services, and import those goods and services in which it has a comparative disadvantage. This theory was first propounded by David Ricardo in 1817 as a basis for increasing the economic welfare of a population through international trade. The comparative advantage theory normally favors specialized production in a country based on intensive utilization of those factors of production in which the country is relatively well endowed (such as raw materials, fertile land or skilled labor), and perhaps also the accumulation of physical capital and the pace of research.
See also: Competitive, Efficiency; Exports, Imports, Structural Change, Welfare,

Compensation The principle, central to GATT, that any country that raises a tariff above its bound rate, withdraws a binding on a tariff, or otherwise impairs a trade concession must lower other tariffs or make other trade concessions to offset the disadvantage suffered by countries whose exports are affected.

See also: Binding, Bound Rates, Concession, Consultations, General Agreement on Tariffs and Trade,

Compensation Trade Refer to: Countertrade,

Compensatory Finance A loan or transfer of financial resources on concessional terms to a country when its export receipts--either total receipts from merchandise exports or receipts from a component of total exports, such as an individual commodity or a stated group of commodities--fall below a predetermined level. The loan, to be repaid according to a previously agreed formula, is intended to stabilize the country's export receipts over an indicated period. Compensatory arrangements exist under the International Monetary Fund and the Lomé Convention.
See also: Commodity, International Monetary Fund, Lomé Convention,

Compensatory Tariff Reductions Refer to: Special and Differential Treatment,

Competitive A competitive product is one that can be sold in an appropriate quantity within a specific market because buyers consider its price and quality acceptable, taking account of support services, credit, delivery terms, guaranteed repairs and promotion, or a combination of such considerations, in comparison with other available goods.
See also: Comparative Advantage, Efficiency, Export Promotion, Market, Monopoly, Safeguards, Structural Change, Tariff,

Competitive Devaluation Refer to: Beggar-Thy-Neighbor Policy,

Competitive Need Refer to: Generalized System of Preferences,

Compound Tariff A combination of an ad valorem tariff plus a specific tariff. Also called a "mixed tariff."
See also: Ad Valorem Equivalent, Ad Valorem Tariff, Specific Tariff, Tariff,

Concession A grant of a position, privilege or right by a negotiator to induce the other party to yield an equivalent position, privilege or right. In GATT trade negotiations, a country normally makes concessions in the form of reductions or bindings in its tariff and non-tariff import barriers in exchange for reductions in the barriers of other countries to its exports. A country's "schedule of concessions," accepted as part of its obligations to other Contracting Parties, becomes an integral part of GATT under Article II of the General Agreement
See also: Binding, Bound Rates, Compensation, Escape Clause, Most-Favored-Nation Treatment, Negotiations, Offer List, Principal Supplier, Reciprocity, Safeguards,

Concessional Aid Refer to: Official Development Assistance,

Conditional Most-Favored-Nation Treatment The extension of concessions by an importing country to other countries that provide equivalent benefits for its exports. The United States applied conditional most-favored-nation treatment in its trade relations with other countries from 1789 to 1923, when it first applied unconditional most-favored-nation treatment in a commercial treaty with Germany. More recently, signatories to the Agreement on Government Procurement, including the United States, have applied conditional most-favored-nation treatment to their trade with each other, in the sense that benefits foreseen in the agreement are extended only to countries that sign it.
See also: Government Procurement Policies and Practices, Most-Favored-Nation Treatment,

Conditionality The set of conditions attached to the use of its resources by the International Monetary Fund, involving undertakings and adjustment policies that will restore a sustainable balance of payments position within a one- to three-year period.

See also: Adjustment, International Monetary Fund,

Constructed Value Refer to: Dumping,

Consular Formalities and Documentation Certain documents or procedures required by some countries before their customs authorities will permit goods produced in other countries to enter their markets, such as special invoices approved by a consul or other official of the importing country. These procedures impede trade, particularly when fees are charged for the authorizations. The number of countries that apply consular formalities has declined in recent years and most countries that still apply them are developing countries.
See also: Non-Tariff Barriers, Tokyo Round,

Consular Invoice Refer to: Consular Formalities and Documentation, Customs and Administrative Entry Procedures,

Consultations Formal discussions between two or more parties to an agreement, particularly with respect to their rights under the agreement. GATT Article XXII obligates a Contracting Party to consult on any GATT-related matter whenever any other Contracting Party requests it to do so. GATT Article XXIII provides that any country that believes its trade interests have been adversely affected--"nullified" or "impaired"--by changes in the trade regime of another country or by another country's failure to carry out its GATT obligations may request bilateral consultations with the concerned party. If such government-to-government consultations do not yield results satisfactory to the concerned parties, the complaining country may seek the establishment of a special panel under the aegis of GATT to review the facts and recommend compensation or other appropriate action. A GATT Contracting Party is also expected to hold consultations with other interested Contracting Parties to discuss any trade restrictive measures it imposes for balance of payments reasons. Bilateral agreements may also provide for consultations under specified circumstances.
See also: Balance of Payments Consultations, Compensation, Dispute Settlement, Panel of Experts,

Consulting Services Refer to: Services,

Consumer Goods Goods that directly satisfy human desires (as opposed to capital goods). An automobile used for pleasure is considered a consumer good. An automobile used by a businessperson to deliver wares is considered a capital good.
See also: Capital Goods, Consumers, Goods,

Consumer Preference Refer to: Demand, Structural Change,

Consumers Individuals or groups who consume or use economic goods, thus deriving utility from them.
See also: Consumer Goods, Microeconomics, Utility,

Consumption The purchase and utilization of goods or services for the gratification of human desires or in the production of other goods or services. The consumer may be an individual, a business firm, a public body or other entity.
See also: Production, Utility,

Consumption Tax Refer to: Excise Tax,

Contracting Party A country or economic entity (e.g., Hong Kong) that has adhered to the General Agreement on Tariffs and Trade (GATT), thereby accepting the body of specified obligations and benefits contained therein. The signatories of GATT are referred to in GATT documents as the

CONTRACTING PARTIES, in capital letters, when they act collectively within the framework of the General Agreement.
See also: General Agreement on Tariffs and Trade, Protocol of Provisional Application,

Conventional Tariff A tariff established through a "convention" (or international agreement) resulting from tariff negotiations and hence not subject to modifications by national action.
See also: General Tariff,

Conversion Product A product whose price is affected under the Common Agricultural Policy of the European Community by the price of feed grains, such as pork, eggs and poultry. Its value is determined by the feed cost per unit produced.
See also: Common Agricultural Policy,

Convertibility A characteristic of a currency when it may be legally exchanged by its holder for other currencies through banks in the issuing country.
See also: Currency, International Monetary Fund,

Coordinating Committee For Multilateral Export Controls (COCOM) A committee consisting of representatives from all NATO countries (except Iceland) for coordinating policies restricting exports of products of potential strategic value to the former Soviet Union and certain other countries. Created in 1949, the committee not only reviewed military technology transfer for potential embargo, but also tried to anticipate the "end use" of products manufactured for civilian purposes, such as computers and transistors. For reasons including the disintegration of the Soviet Union, and the goal of assisting economic and political reform in Russia and the New Independent States, the United States and its COCOM partners agreed in 1993 to end the Cold War regime effective March 31, 1994, and to work toward a new arrangement to enhance transparency and restraint in conventional weapons and sophisticated technologies to countries whose behavior is cause for serious concern and to regions of potential instability. COCOM members agreed to maintain the existing lists as the basis for national export controls after March 31 while new control lists and arrangements were being finalized.
See also: Boycott, Export Administration Act of 1979,

Copyright An exclusive right conferred by a government for a specified period to the creator of literary or artistic works such as books, maps, articles, drawings, charts, photographs, musical compositions, motion pictures, recordings or computer programs. The Uruguay Round accord on trade-related aspects of intellectual property (TRIPS) incorporates all substantive trade-related protection afforded under the Bern Convention for the Protection of Literary and Artistic Works, clarifying that computer programs are protected as literary works and compilation of databases as intellectual creation. Protection extends for the duration of the life of the author plus 50 years, and includes rights of translation, reproduction, public performance, broadcasting, adaptation and arrangement, and rental.
See also: Intellectual Property, Trade-Related Aspects of Intellectual Property Rights, World Intellectual Property Organization,

Core Commodities Refer to: Integrated Program for Commodities,

Cost and Freight Refer to: C and F,

Cost, Insurance and Freight Refer to: CIF,

Cotton Textiles Refer to: Multi-Fiber Arrangement Regarding International Trade in Textiles, Textiles,

Council For Mutual Economic Assistance (COMECON) An intergovernmental organization

established in 1949 to coordinate the economies of member states, consisting of the Soviet Union, Bulgaria, Czechoslovakia, the German Democratic Republic ("East Germany"), Hungary, Mongolia, Poland, Romania, Cuba and Vietnam. The purpose of the council, according to its charter, was to improve economic cooperation among participating countries and to accelerate their economic and technological progress. This organization was formally disbanded in June 1991.
See also: Group D,

Council Of The European Community Refer to: European Community,

Counter Purchase Contracts Refer to: Countertrade,

Countertrade Arrangements under which the sale of goods or services from one country to another are linked to sales in the opposite direction. Countertrade arrangements frequently characterize East-West trade. Such transactions include: Counter purchase contracts that expressly stipulate that the vendor must purchase goods from the importer equivalent in value to a specified percentage of the value of the exported goods; Reverse countertrade contracts require the importer (a U.S. buyer of machine tools from Eastern Europe, for example) to export goods equivalent in value to a specified percentage of the value of the imported goods--an obligation that can be sold to an exporter in a third country; Buy-back (or compensation) arrangements, through which a company selling equipment, licenses, technology or a turnkey plant agrees to accept in full or partial payment products manufactured with such equipment, licenses, technology or plant; Clearing agreements between two countries that agree to purchase specific amounts of each other's products over a specified period of time, using a designated "clearing currency" in the transactions; "Switch" arrangements that permit the sale of unpaid balances in a clearing account to be sold to a third party, usually at a discount, that may be used for producing goods in the country holding the balance; Swap schemes through which products from different locations are traded to save transportation costs (e.g., Russian oil may be "swapped" for oil from a Latin American producer, so the Russian oil is shipped to a country in South Asia, while the Latin American oil is shipped to Cuba); and Barter arrangements through which two parties directly exchange goods deemed to be of approximately equivalent value without any flow of money taking place.
See also: Barter, Offset Requirements, Tied Loan,

Countervailing Duties Specific duties imposed on imports to offset the benefits of subsidies to producers or exporters in the exporting country. GATT Article VI permits the use of such duties. The Executive Branch of the U.S. government has been legally empowered since the 1890s to impose countervailing duties in amounts equal to any "bounties"or "grants" reflected in products imported into the United States. Under U.S. law and the Tokyo Round Agreement on Subsidies and Countervailing Duties (the GATT Subsidies Code), a wide range of practices are recognized as constituting subsidies that may be offset through the imposition of countervailing duties. The Trade Agreements Act of 1979, through amendments to the Tariff Act of 1930, established rigorous procedures and deadlines for determining the existence of subsidies in response to petitions filed by interested parties such as domestic producers of competitive products and their workers. In all cases involving subsidized products, whether dutiable or duty-free, from countries recognized by the United States as signatories to the Code on Subsidies and Countervailing Duties, or from countries which have negotiated substantially equivalent obligations in a bilateral agreement with the United States, U.S. law requires that countervailing duties may be imposed only after the U.S. International Trade Commission (USITC) determines that the imports are causing or threatening to cause material injury to an industry in the United States. A USITC injury determination is also required if the merchandise under investigation is a duty-free import from a GATT signatory. Otherwise, where evidence of subsidization is found, countervailing duties may be imposed without the necessity for a material injury investigation by the USITC.
See also: Bounties or Grants, Codes of Conduct, Export Subsidies, Subsidy, Trade Act of 1974,

U.S. International Trade Commission,

Country Of Origin Certificate Refer to: Customs and Administrative Entry Procedures,

Court Of International Trade (CIT) The United States Court of International Trade (formerly the U.S. Customs Court) is a court developed under Article III of the U.S. Constitution to provide a single forum with expertise in international trade law for the judicial review of administrative actions of government agencies arising from import transactions. The Court reviews decisions of the United States Customs Service, the International Trade Administration of the U.S. Department of Commerce and the U.S. International Trade Commission. Such cases include, inter alia, challenges to classification rates and duties charged, anti-dumping and countervailing duty determinations and embargoes or other quantitative restrictions. Generally, in the review of administrative determinations of record, the court will uphold an agency decision unless it is found to be unsupported by substantial evidence, or otherwise not in accordance with law. A party can appeal a decision by the CIT to the Court of Appeals for the Federal Circuit which will apply the same standard of review. Finally, a party can appeal a decision of the Federal Circuit court by filing a writ of certiorari with the United States Supreme Court.

Credit A promise of future payment given in exchange for present delivery of money, goods or services, usually with interest, at a rate that varies with the risk involved and the reputation as a risk that a particular borrower enjoys with an actual or potential lender.
See also: Bond, Bridging Credit, Demand, Interest, Mixed Credits, Purchasing Power, Risk,

Creditor Clubs Refer to: Paris Club,

Currency The circulating media of exchange in a country. Prior to World War I, "currency" generally meant coins and paper money, but with the expanding use of credit instruments, it has come to include checks drawn on bank accounts, postal money orders and prepaid travelers checks which usually require identification of maker or endorser. Most business transactions are carried out by means of bank checks.
See also: Convertibility, Devaluation, Mercantilism, Money, Par Value, Reserve Currency,

Current Account That portion of a country's balance of payments that records current (as opposed to capital) transactions, including visible trade (exports and imports), invisible trade (income and expenditures for services), profits earned from foreign operations, interest and transfer payments.
See also: Balance of Payments, Capital Account, Invisible Trade, Transfer Payments, Visible Trade,

Customs The government service responsible for the assessment and collection of import and export duties and taxes and the administration of other laws and regulations that apply to the importation, transit and exportation of goods.
See also: Customs and Administrative Entry Procedures, Kyoto Convention, Port of Entry, Tariff, Tariff Schedules of the United States, Transit Zone, Valuation,

Customs and Administrative Entry Procedures Clearance formalities at national ports of entry may be considered non-tariff barriers if they result in undue procedural delays that raise import costs. Such formalities may include licensing procedures, health and sanitary controls designed to protect consumers, certificates indicating the country of origin, and consular invoices confirming that the shipment is what it appears to be.
See also: Consular Formalities and Documentation, Kyoto Convention, Licensing, Non-Tariff Barriers, Port of Entry, Quarantine, Sanitary and Health Laws and Regulations,

Customs Area A geographic area, usually but not necessarily identical with one or several

contiguous national political jurisdictions, applying a particular tariff schedule on goods entering or leaving the area.
See also: Customs, Tariffs, Tariff Schedules. ,

Customs Classification The particular category in a tariff nomenclature in which a product is classified for tariff purposes, or the procedure for determining the appropriate tariff category in a country's nomenclature system used for the classification, coding and description of internationally traded goods. Most major trading nations classify imported goods in conformity with the Harmonized Commodity Description and Coding System, also called the Harmonized System. The United States adopted the Harmonized System on January 1, 1989.
See also: Customs Harmonization, Harmonized System, Tariff, Valuation,

Customs Cooperation Council (CCC) Refer to: Customs Harmonization,

Customs Cooperation Council Nomenclature (CCCN) A system for classifying goods for customs purposes, formerly known as the Brussels Tariff Nomenclature (BTN).
See also: Customs Classification,

Customs Duty Refer to: Tariff,

Customs Harmonization International efforts to increase the uniformity of customs nomenclatures and procedures in cooperating countries. Discussions and action to further these efforts are normally coordinated by the Customs Cooperation Council (CCC), an international organization with its secretariat headquartered in Brussels, Belgium. The Harmonized System, a uniform system of tariff classification adopted by most major trading countries in recent years, was one such effort, begun in 1970. The CCC is also involved in developing international standards for the exchange of trade data, determining international rules of origin, and related international customs technical questions.
See also: Customs Classification, Harmonization, Harmonized System, Kyoto Convention,

Customs Union A group of nations that have eliminated tariffs and sometimes other barriers that impede trade with each other, while maintaining a common external tariff on goods imported from outside the union. The Common Market of the European Community is the best known example. GATT Article XXIV defines the meaning of a customs union in GATT and the application of other GATT provisions to customs unions.
See also: Common External Tariff, European Community, Free Trade Area, Kyoto Convention, Trade Diversion, Welfare,

Customs Valuation Code A code of conduct negotiated during the Tokyo Round to establish a uniform, fair and predictable international system for the valuation of goods for customs purposes, and to preclude the use of arbitrary national valuation systems as non-tariff barriers to trade. Also known as the GATT Valuation Code. The code establishes the"transaction value"--or the price actually paid or payable for imported goods plus certain permitted additional costs--as the primary method of valuation by customs officials and specifies a hierarchy of other methods to be employed when the transaction value cannot be used. The code also contains technical provisions intended to ensure equitable currency conversion, rapid clearance of goods when there are delays in determining the value of imported goods, domestic appeal rights, and publication of laws and regulations affecting customs valuation.
See also: Codes of Conduct, Customs, Tokyo Round, Trade Agreements Act of 1979, Valuation,

Customs Warehouse Refer to: Bonded Warehouse,

CXT Refer to: Common External Tariff,

DAC Refer to: Development Assistance Committee,

Data Processing Refer to: Services,

De Facto As it exists in practice.

De Jure According to legal requirements.

Deficiency Payments Government payments to compensate farmers for all or part of the difference between producer prices actually paid for a specific commodity and higher guaranteed target prices.
See also: Common Agricultural Policy, Variable Levy,

Demand The quantity of an economic good that will be bought at a given price at a particular time in a specific market. A demand schedule indicates the quantity of an economic good that will be bought at all possible prices at a particular time in the market. Demand in a market economy is strongly influenced by consumer preference or the individual choices of many independent buyers, based upon their perceptions of value for price.
See also: Goods, Market, Market Economy, Price, Purchasing Power, Supply, Trade Diversion, Utility, Value,

Demand Schedule Refer to: Demand,

Devaluation The lowering of the value of a national currency in terms of the currencies of other nations. Devaluation tends to reduce domestic demand for imports in a country by raising their prices in terms of the devalued currency and to raise foreign demand for the country's exports by reducing their prices in terms of foreign currencies. Devaluation can therefore help to correct a balance of payments deficit and sometimes provide a short-term basis for economic adjustment of a national economy.
See also: Adjustment, Beggar-Thy-Neighbor Policy, Currency,

Developed Countries A term used to distinguish the more industrialized nations--including most OECD member countries--from "developing" or less developed countries. The developed countries are sometimes collectively designated as the Group B countries or the "North" because most of them are in the Northern Hemisphere.
See also: Developing Countries, Group B, Industrial Revolution, Organization for Economic Cooperation and Development,

Developing Countries A broad range of countries that generally lack a high degree of industrialization, infrastructure and other capital investment, sophisticated technology, widespread literacy and advanced living standards among their populations as a whole. The developing countries are sometimes collectively designated as the "South," because a large number of them are in the Southern Hemisphere. All of the countries of Africa (except South Africa), Asia (except Hong Kong, Singapore, South Korea, and Taiwan) and Oceania (except Australia, Japan and New Zealand), Latin America, and the Middle East are generally considered "developing countries," as are a few European countries (Cyprus, Malta, Turkey, Poland, Hungary, the Czech Republic and Slovakia, for example). Some experts have identified four sub-categories of developing countries as having different economic needs and interests: A few relatively wealthy OPEC countries--sometimes referred to as oil-exporting developing countries--share a particular interest in a financially sound international economy and open capital markets. Newly Industrializing Economies (NIEs) have a growing stake in an open international trading system; A number of middle income countries--principally commodity exporters--have shown a particular interest in commodity stabilization schemes. Some 36 very poor countries ("least developed countries") are predominantly agricultural, have sharply limited development prospects

during the near future, and tend to be heavily dependent on official development assistance.
See also: ACP Countries, Economic Development, Graduation, Group of 77, Infrastructure, Least Developed Countries, Newly Industrializing Economies, Official Development Assistance, Organization of Petroleum Exporting Countries, Reciprocity,

Development Assistance Committee (DAC) The OECD body that reviews and assesses resource transfers from developed to developing countries. See also ; .
See also: Official Development Assistance, Organization for Economic Cooperation and Development,

Differential Export Tax A multi-tier export tax usually structured so that the tax on exports of a raw material exceeds the tax (if any) on exports of processed goods made from the raw material, thereby creating an incentive to process the raw material domestically.
See also: Boycott, Embargo, Supply Access,

Differential Treatment (For Developing Country Exports) Refer to: Framework Agreement, Special and Differential Treatment,

Dillon Round Trade negotiations that took place under the aegis of GATT from 1960 to 1962, named after Douglas Dillon, then the U.S. under secretary of state, who publicly proposed the negotiations.
See also: Item-by-Item Negotiations, Round,

Direct Tax A tax that is levied on the wealth or income of individuals. Income, wealth, and inheritance taxes and social security charges are examples of direct taxes.
See also: Equity, Indirect Tax, Tax,

DISC Refer to: Foreign Sales Corporation,

Discrimination Inequality of treatment accorded imports from different trading partners, as through preferential tariff rates for imports from particular countries or trade restrictions that apply to the exports of certain countries but not to similar goods from other countries.
See also: Government Procurement Policies and Practices, Most-Favored-Nation Treatment, Preferences, Quarantine, Sanitary, and Health Laws and Regulations,

Dispute Settlement In the trade context, dispute settlement usually refers to procedures for consultation, conciliation and possible referral to a neutral third party of a dispute between parties to a trade agreement. Under the General Agreement on Tariffs and Trade (GATT), provisions for consultations, and for the GATT Contracting Parties to make recommendations and rulings in particular disputes, are contained in Articles XXII and XXIII. Procedures to implement those provisions were adopted by the Contracting Parties in 1966, 1979, 1982, 1984, 1989 (procedures adopted on an interim basis), and most recently in 1993. Under the 1993 Uruguay Round agreement, countries agreed to change the previous GATT structure for dispute resolution between Contracting Parties as part of the larger effort to create a strong WTO. Most significantly, it is no longer possible for one country to block adoption of the findings of expert GATT panels formed to review complaints. Under the new system, all members must disagree with the panel's findings for them to be blocked. The new dispute settlement process within the WTO follows several stages: consultation and conciliation, establishment of dispute panels, adoption of panel decisions and follow-up surveillance. In addition, the U.S.-Canada Free Trade Agreement contains very detailed procedures for the settlement of disputes arising under that agreement.
See also: Arbitration, Case Law, Codes of Conduct, Consultations, Framework Agreement, Government Policies and Procedures, Panel of Experts, Tokyo Round, Uruguay Round,

Disruption Refer to: Market Disruption,

Distribution The dissemination of goods and services in a market through the ordinary channels of trade.
See also: Export Promotion, Market, Sales Tax, Technology, Trade Fair,

Domestic International Sales Corporation (DISC)
See also: Foreign Sales Corporation,

Domestic Subsidy Any act, practice or measure other than an export subsidy by which a government confers a benefit upon a product and/or enterprise. For purposes of U.S. countervailing duty law, a domestic subsidy is considered countervailable if benefits under a program are provided, or are required to be provided by government action, in law or in fact, to a specific enterprise or industry, or group of enterprises or industries.
See also: Countervailing Duties,

Domestic System Of Production The system of economic production that prevailed in Europe in the 16th and 17th centuries, prior to the Industrial Revolution, under which merchants supplied materials and sometimes tools and machines to workers who produced finished goods in their homes and turned them over to the merchants.
See also: Industrial Revolution, Production,

Double-Column Tariff A tariff schedule listing two duty rates for some or all commodities. Under such arrangements, imports may be taxed at a higher or lower rate, depending upon the importing country's trade and other relationships with the exporting country. Some British Commonwealth countries maintain a double-column tariff that provides preferential tariff treatment to other members of the Commonwealth. The United States and other countries also have lower tariffs for countries to which they grant most-favored-nation treatment.
See also: Column 1 Rates, Column 2 Rates, Most-Favored-Nation Treatment, Preferences, Single-Column Tariff, Tariff,

Downstream Dumping Downstream dumping, also known as "input dumping," is the practice of exporting an end-product containing an input that has been purchased at less than normal value. U.S. anti-dumping law contains provisions for monitoring downstream dumping where the input is already the subject of an anti-dumping duty order. If monitoring reveals that imports of the end-product increase as a result of the diversion of the input product into the end-product, an anti-dumping investigation of the end-product may be initiated.
See also: Anti-Dumping Code, Dumping,

Drawback Import duties or taxes repaid by a government, in whole or in part, when the imported goods are re-exported or used in the manufacture of exported goods.

Dry Cargoes Refer to: Bulk Carrier,

Dual Pricing Selling identical products for different prices in different markets. Dual pricing often reflects export subsidy and dumping practices.
See also: Dumping, Export Subsidies, Restitutions,

Dumping Under U.S. law, dumping consists of sales of merchandise exported to the United States at "less than fair value," when such sales materially injure or threaten material injury to producers of like merchandise in the United States. "Fair value" is usually considered to be a price at which the merchandise is sold within the exporting country or to third countries. "Fair value" can also be the "constructed value" of the merchandise sold in the U.S. market, which is the cost of materials, labor and factory overhead, a minimum of 10 percent for general and administrative costs, a minimum eight-percent profit margin, and packing costs. A "cost of

production" provision requires that dumping determinations ignore sales in the home market of the exporting country or in third-country markets at prices that are too low to "permit recovery of all costs within a reasonable period of time in the normal course of trade." Economists disagree as to the harmful effects of dumping. Some consider dumping to establish a "toehold" in a new market to be a normal commercial practice. Dumping is recognized by GATT rules as a potentially unfair trade practice that can disrupt markets and injure producers of competitive products in the importing country. Dumping is, however, technically legal under GATT rules unless injury is found. In 1993, as part of the Uruguay Round accord, GATT member countries created more detailed rules governing their ability to take action against imports sold at an unfairly discounted export price. Countries agree to terminate all anti-dumping duties after five years (which will require a change in U.S. law) and to raise the "de minimis" rule (the lowest rate at which a dumping margin can be determined) to two percent (U.S. law defines it at 0.5 percent.) The accord also establishes a new Committee on Anti-Dumping Practices, which countries must promptly notify of all dumping actions.
See also: Anti-Dumping Code, Dual Pricing, Market Disruption, Trigger Price Mechanism, U.S. International Trade Commission,

Duty Refer to: Tariff,

Duty Suspension A unilateral non-application of a customs duty, or its application at a reduced level, usually on a temporary basis.
See also: Tariff, Unilateral,

EAEC Refer to: East Asian Economic Caucus,

EAI Refer to: Enterprise for the Americas Initiative,

Earnings Refer to: Foreign Exchange Earnings, Profit,

East Asian Economic Caucus (EAEC) A grouping of East Asian countries, proposed by Malaysia, to coordinate positions on economic issues of interest to the region. ASEAN would be at the core of the EAEC with other members not yet specified, although it is unlikely the United States would be included.
See also: Asia-Pacific Economic Cooperation, Multilateral Agreement,

East-West Trade Referred to trade between the former Soviet Union and the socialist countries of Eastern Europe ("East") on the one hand, and the developed market-economy countries of Western Europe, North America and Japan on the other ("West").
See also: Countertrade, Non-Market Economy, State Trading Nations,

EBRD Refer to: European Bank,

EC Refer to: European Community,

EC 1992 A term used to describe the process within the European Community (EC) to conclude by December 31, 1992 all legal measures necessary to complete the opening of its internal market to the free flow of capital, goods, services and people as foreseen in the 1987 Single Act.
See also: European Community,

ECDC
See also: Economic Cooperation Among Developing Countries,

ECGF
See also: Export Credit Guarantee Facility,

Economic Cooperation AMong Developing Countries (ECDC) Attempts by developing countries, especially the Group of 77, to increase South-South trade and other economic relationships among themselves.
See also: Global System of Trade Preferences, Group of 77, South-South Trade, United Nations Conference on Trade and Development,

Economic Development The process of growth in total and per capita income, especially in developing countries, accompanied by increased infrastructure, more industrial activity, improved agricultural practices, migration of labor from rural to urban industrial areas, rising literacy, broadened employment opportunities and gradually diminishing reliance on official development assistance.
See also: Developing Countries, Infrastructure, Progress, Structural Change, United Nations Development Program,

ECS Carnet Refer to: ATA Carnet,

ECSC
See also: European Coal and Steel Community,

EEC Refer to: European, European Community,

EEC Refer to: European, European Community,

EEP Refer to: Export Enhancement Program,

Effective Tariff Rate The concept that "effective" protection reflected in a tariff rate is the sum of the protection for the component parts of the final manufactured unit. This concept implies that the "nominal" tariff rate of the finished good significantly understates the de facto protection for the value added in the production process. Several academic studies in the late 1960s and early 1970s established the theoretical basis for the effective tariff rate concept, but most trade policy experts see little practical utility in the theory, since the many different circumstances affecting the component parts comprising most industrial products make it difficult to establish their actual "effective" rates.
See also: Nominal Tariff Rate, Tariff, Tariff Escalation,

Efficiency Narrowly, economic efficiency suggests the technical input-output relationship between the quantity of materials used and the quantity of goods produced. More broadly, it implies the best result (taking quality as well as quantity into account) in the production or distribution of goods and services at the least cost. Most economists believe the reduction of barriers to trade contributes to international economic efficiency by encouraging countries to specialize in the production of those goods and services in which they have a comparative advantage, thus making the world's most competitive goods and services available to consumers outside the area that produces them.
See also: Comparative Advantage, Competitive, Entrepreneur, Textiles, Trade Diversion , Welfare,

EFTA Refer to: European Free Trade Association,

Elasticity Refer to: Price Elasticity of Demand, Price Elasticity of Supply,

Embargo In international trade, an embargo refers to government actions limiting or prohibiting imports and/or exports of goods and/or services from or to a country. Such limitations may be applied by the embargoing country against its own nationals, such as the United States embargo

against trade from Cuba, or in concert with other countries against a third country, such as the 1990 United Nations embargo against trade in any form with Iraq or the earlier U.N. embargo against trade with South Africa. Embargoes may also be applied just against trade in certain products regardless of origin, such as the ban on trade in ivory.
See also: Boycott, Supply Access,

Enabling Clause Formally, the "Decision on Differential and More Favorable Treatment, Reciprocity, and Fuller Participation of Developing Countries" that was negotiated during the Tokyo Round as Part I of a new "Framework Agreement" on International Trade. The "Enabling Clause" legalized the extension by developed Contracting Parties of GATT of preferences to developing countries, notwithstanding the most-favored-nation treatment required under GATT Article 1.
See also: Framework Agreement, Generalized System of Preferences, Most-Favored-Nation Treatment, Preferences,

Enterprise For The Americas Initiative (EAI) The Enterprise for the Americas Initiative is a United States program designed to strengthen the economies of countries in Latin America and the Caribbean through debt reduction and increased trade and investment. The investment component is intended to help countries make reforms necessary to attract increased capital flows. The debt component seeks to reward broad economic reforms undertaken by countries in Latin America and the Caribbean by reducing official debt owed to the United States. The trade component is designed to promote a liberalized trading system and is based on the ultimate goal of hemispheric free trade.

Entrepreneur A person who assumes responsibility for organization, management and risk in the production of goods and services. In theory, his enterprise should make a profit if it is economically efficient and incur losses if it is not.
See also: Efficiency, Management, Microeconomics, Profit, Risk,

Equal Percentage Reduction Of Tariffs
See also: Linear Reduction of Tariffs,

Equilibrium A state in which economic forces, likely to cause change in opposing directions are in perfect balance, so that change is unlikely. A market is in equilibrium if the quantities of a product that consumers will buy at the prevailing price exactly match the amount suppliers will sell at that price.
See also: Market, Price,

Equity Fairness, justice. Also the value of property beyond the total amount owed on it.
See also: Direct Tax,

Equity Joint Venture Refer to: Joint Venture,

Equivalence Of Advantages Refer to: Reciprocity,

ERs
See also: Export Restraints,

Escalation
See also: Tariff Escalation,

Escape Clause A provision in a bilateral or multilateral commercial agreement permitting a signatory nation to suspend tariff or other concessions when increased imports cause or threaten to cause serious injury to the producers of competitive domestic goods. GATT Article XIX

sanctions such "safeguard" provisions to help firms and workers injured by increased imports adjust to the rising level of import competition. Section 201 of the U.S. Trade Act of 1974 requires the U.S. International Trade Commission (USITC) to investigate complaints formally known as "petitions" filed by domestic industries or workers claiming that they have been injured or are threatened with injury as a consequence of rising imports and to complete any such investigation within six months. The act provides that if the USITC finds that a domestic industry has been seriously injured or threatened with serious injury, it shall recommend to the president relief to the industry in the form of temporary import restrictions (tariffs, quotas, or tariff-rate quotas) or trade adjustment assistance. The president has discretion to follow the USITC's recommendations on relief, which normally takes the form of increased duties or quantitative restrictions. Such import relief cannot exceed eight years, including extensions.
See also: Adjustment Assistance, Concession, Import Relief, Protectionism, Safeguards, Trade Act of 1974, U.S. International Trade Commission,

ESP Refer to: Exporter's Sales Price,

Euratom
See also: European Community,

Euro-Bonds Refer to: Euro-Dollars,

Euro-Currency
See also: Euro-Dollars,

Euro-Dollars Claims for U.S. dollars held against banking institutions outside the United States. The claims arise when, through the purchase of bills of exchange or similar transactions, a foreign bank credits a dollar deposit account. Such deposit accounts (Euro-dollars) are extensively used outside the United States for financial transactions such as short-term loans or the purchase of dollar bonds called Euro-Bonds that are sometimes issued by U.S. companies to finance their operations, especially those outside the United States.
See also: Bill, Multinational Corporation,

European Bank (EBRD) The European Bank for Reconstruction and Development (EBRD) is a regional development bank with the purpose of supporting market-oriented economic reforms in Central and Eastern Europe (including the former Soviet Union). The EBRD began operating in April 1991.

European Bank For Reconstruction And Development (EBRD) Refer to: European Bank,

European Coal And Steel Community (ECSC) A common market in coal and steel, established by the 1951 Schuman Plan (named after Robert Schuman, French foreign minister), through which France, Italy, the Federal Republic of Germany, Belgium, the Netherlands and Luxembourg abolished tariffs, quotas and currency restrictions affecting intracommunity trade in coal, iron ore and scrap metal. The ECSC subsequently served as a model for the institutions of the European Community.
See also: Customs Union, European Community,

European Community (EC) The European Economic Community (EEC) came into being on January 1, 1958, based on the Treaty of Rome, with six participating member states (France, Italy, the Federal Republic of Germany, Belgium, the Netherlands and Luxembourg). From the beginning, a principal objective of the Community was the establishment of a customs union, other forms of economic integration, and political cooperation among member countries. The Treaty of Rome provided for the gradual elimination of customs duties and other internal trade barriers, the establishment of a common external tariff, and guarantees of free movement of labor

and capital within the Community. The United Kingdom, Denmark and Ireland joined the Community in 1973, and Greece in 1981. Spain and Portugal became members in 1986. A number of other European countries have already, or are expected to apply for membership in the 1990s. Norway, Sweden, Finland and Austria are expected to join the Community in November 1995. Turkey's "Association Agreement" with the Community also calls for its eventual membership. In recent years, the Community made major efforts to "deepen" its integration by attempting to remove remaining barriers to the free movement of goods, people, capital and services within the EC via what became known as the "single market" or "1992" program. Part 1, Article 1 of the Maastricht Treaty on European Union formalized the use of "EC" as a reference to "European Community." The treaty also introduced the term "European Union" as a broader legal entity than the EC. The Community is headquartered in Brussels. The member states, acting through various Councils, set overall EC policy, which is executed by the Commission, the Community's permanent staff. Technical experts from Community capitals meet regularly to deal with specialized issues in such areas as agriculture, transportation, or trade policy.
See also: Common Agricultural Policy, Common External Tariff, Customs Union, European Coal and Steel Community, Lomé Convention, Variable Levy,

European Economic Area Refer to: European Free Trade Association,

European Economic Community
See also: European Community,

European Free Trade Association (EFTA) A regional grouping established in 1960 by the Stockholm Convention, headquartered in Geneva, now comprising Austria, Iceland, Norway, Portugal, Sweden and Switzerland. Finland is an Associate Member. Denmark and the United Kingdom were formerly members, but they withdrew from EFTA when they joined the European Community in 1973. EFTA member countries have gradually eliminated tariffs on manufactured goods originating and traded within EFTA and between EFTA and the EC. Agricultural products, for the most part, are not included on the EFTA schedule for internal tariff reductions. Each member country maintains its own external tariff schedule, and each has concluded a trade agreement with the European Community that provides for the mutual elimination of tariffs for most manufactured goods except for a few sensitive products. As a result, the European Community and EFTA form a de facto free trade area. The EC and EFTA countries have recently agreed to deepen their economic integration via a new treaty creating what is referred to as the European Economic Area (EEA). This treaty provides for the adoption by the EFTA countries of numerous EC laws and regulations with a view towards ensuring the freedom of movement of people, goods, services and capital within Europe.
See also: European Community, Free Trade Area,

European Recovery Program (ERP) Better known as the "Marshall Plan," after U.S. Secretary of State George C. Marshall, who proposed a broad range of trade reform and aid measures to hasten the rehabilitation of European economies after World War II in a speech at Harvard University in Cambridge, Massachusetts on June 5, 1947. The aid program was first administered by the Economic Cooperation Administration (ECA) in Paris, while the program of economic cooperation among the 17 participating European countries was implemented by the Organization for European Economic Cooperation (OEEC). (The original 16 participating European countries were joined by the Federal Republic of Germany in 1949.) Between 1948 and 1951, when the program was terminated, the 17 European countries received more than $12,000 million from the United States.
See also: Organization for European Economic Cooperation ,

European Union The EU is an umbrella reference to the European Community (EC) and to two European integration efforts introduced by the Maastricht Treaty: Common Foreign and Security Policy (including defense) and Justice and Home Affairs (principally cooperation between police and other authorities on crime, terrorism, and immigration issues). The term "European Union" was introduced in November 1993 (when the Maastricht Treaty on European Union entered into force). The term "European Community" (EC) continues to exist as a legal entity within the broader framework of the EU.

Exceptions
See also: Generalized System of Preferences, Linear Reduction of Tariffs,

Exchange Controls The rationing of foreign currencies, bank drafts and other instruments for settling international financial obligations by countries seeking to ameliorate acute balance of payments difficulties. When such measures are imposed, importers must apply for prior authorization from the government to obtain the foreign currency required to bring in designated amounts and types of goods. Since such measures have the effect of restricting imports, they are considered non-tariff barriers to trade.
See also: Balance of Payments Consultations, Currency, Non-Tariff Barriers, Specific Limitations on Trade,

Exchange Rate The price (or rate) at which one currency is exchanged for another currency, for gold or for Special Drawing Rights (SDR's).
See also: Currency, International Monetary Fund, Par Value, Special Drawing Rights,

Excise Tax A selective tax--sometimes called a consumption tax--on certain goods produced within or imported into a country.
See also: Border Tax Adjustments, Indirect Tax, Road Tax, Tax,

Executing Agency Refer to: United Nations Development Program,

Eximbank Refer to: Export-Import Bank of the United States,

Export Administration Act Of 1979 This statute authorizes the U.S. president to control exports to specific foreign destinations of U.S. commodities and technical data, especially high technology products, to protect the national security, to ensure against an excessive drain of scarce goods, or to further foreign policy objectives. It also prohibits compliance with foreign boycotts.
See also: Antiboycott Legislation, Boycott, Coordinating Committee on Export Controls,

Export Credit Guarantee Facility (ECGF) A scheme developed in UNCTAD that would enable developing-country exporters to refinance their export credits extended to importers in other countries under an international guarantee.

Export Credit Insurance Insurance designed to guarantee that the exporter will be paid for his goods after delivery. If the exporter has such insurance, responsibility for collecting payment from the company that imports the goods in another country, or the company's agent, rests with the underwriter of the export credit insurance.
See also: Insurance, Underwriter,

Export Credits Refer to: International Arrangement on Export Credits, Mixed Credits, Subsidy,

Export Embargo Refer to: Embargo, Supply Access,

Export Enhancement Program (EEP) The Export Enhancement Program provides direct U.S. response to export subsidies of other countries by subsidizing U.S.-produced agricultural products into the world market. The EEP was initiated in May 1985 under provisions of the Commodity Credit Corporation (CCC) Charter Act and mandated by provisions of the Food Security Act of 1985; and the Food, Agricultural, Conservation and Trade Act of 1990. Subsidies

are paid to exporting operations in the form of either commodity certificates redeemable for stocks held by the CCC or cash payments.
See also: Export Subsidy, Subsidy,

Export Licensing Refer to: Licensing,

Export Promotion Public- or private-sector support for foreign sales through such activities as trade missions and trade fairs, based on available market information and analysis.
See also: Common Fund, Competitive, Distribution, International Commodity Agreement, International Trade Center UNCTAD/GATT, Market, MITI, Supply, Trade Fair, Trade Mission,

Export Quotas Specific restrictions or ceilings imposed by an exporting country on the value or volume of certain exports imposed to protect domestic producers and consumers from temporary shortages of the goods affected or to bolster their prices in world markets. Some international commodity agreements explicitly indicate when producers should apply such restraints. Export quotas are also often applied in orderly marketing agreements and voluntary restraint agreements, and to promote domestic processing of raw materials in countries that produce them.
See also: International Commodity Agreement, Orderly Marketing Agreements, Voluntary Restraint Agreements,

Export Restraint Agreements
See also: Voluntary Restraint Agreements,

Export Restraints Quantitative restrictions imposed by exporting countries to limit exports to specified foreign markets, usually pursuant to a formal or informal agreement concluded at the request of the importing countries.
See also: Orderly Marketing Agreements, Quantitative Restrictions, Voluntary Restraint Agreements,

Export Subsidy A subsidy such as those described in the Illustrative List of Export Subsidies of the GATT Subsidies Code. For purposes of U.S. countervailing duty law, an export subsidy is considered countervailable when the eligibility for, or the amount of, benefits under a program is tied to the actual or anticipated exportation of merchandise or export earnings.
See also: Countervailing Duty, Illustrative List, Market Access,

Export Trading Company A corporation or other business unit organized and operated principally for the purpose of exporting goods and services, or of providing export-related services to other companies. The Export Trading Company Act of 1982 exempts authorized trading companies from certain provisions of U.S. anti-trust laws.
See also: Anti-Trust, Webb-Pomerene Act,

Exporter's Sales Price (ESP) A statutory term used to refer to the U.S. sales price of merchandise which is sold or likely to be sold in the United States, before or after the time of importation, by or for the account of the exporter. Certain statutory adjustments are made to permit a meaningful comparison with the foreign market value of such or similar merchandise, e.g., import duties, U.S. selling and administrative expenses, and freight are deducted from the U.S. price.
See also: United States Price,

Export-Import Bank Of The United States (EXIMBANK) A public corporation created by executive order of the president in 1934 and given a statutory basis in 1945. The Eximbank makes guarantees and insures loans to help finance U.S. exports, particularly for equipment to be used in capital improvement projects. It also provides short-term, political risk guarantees, either directly or in cooperation with U.S. commercial banks.

See also: Foreign Credit Insurance Association,

Exports Goods and services produced in one country and sold in other countries in exchange for goods and services, gold, foreign exchange or settlement of debt. Countries devote their domestic resources to exports because they can obtain more goods and services with the international exchange they earn from the exports than they would from devoting the same resources to the domestic production of goods and services.
See also: Comparative Advantage, Export Promotion, Macroeconomics, MITI,

Exposure
See also: Reinsurance,

Factory System Of Production
See also: Industrial Revolution,

Fair Refer to: Trade Fair,

Fair Value Refer to: Dumping,

FARA Refer to: Foreign Agents Registration Act,

FAS The term "Free Alongside Ship," in international trade, refers to the point of embarkation from which the vessel or plane selected by the buyer will transport the goods. Under this system, the seller is obligated to pay the costs and assume all risks for transporting the goods from his place of business to the FAS point. In trade statistics,"FAS value" means that the import or export figures are calculated on this basis, regardless of the nature of individual transactions reflected in the statistics.
See also: CIF, FOB,

FCIA Refer to: Foreign Credit Insurance Association,

FCN Refer to: Freedom, Commerce and Navigation Treaty,

Final Act Term used in describing the bringing together of the results of the Uruguay Round Group of Negotiations on Goods (GNG) and Group on Negotiations on Services (GNS) through the Trade Negotiating Committee (TNC). The Final Act provides a framework for the implementation of the results of the Uruguay Round negotiations.
See also: Uruguay Round,

Floor Prices Refer to: Buffer Stocks,

Florence Agreement Officially known as the Agreement on the Importation of Educational, Scientific and Cultural Materials, entered into force in 1952. The agreement is sponsored by the United Nations Educational, Scientific, and Cultural Organization (UNESCO), which has a mandate under its charter to facilitate the exchange of publications, objects of artistic and scientific interest and other materials of information, and to recommend international agreements which will promote the free flow of ideas. The agreement provides for the duty-free entry, under specified conditions, of various categories of materials for educational, scientific and cultural use.

FMV Refer to: Foreign Market Value,

FOB An abbreviation used in some international sales contracts, when imports are valued at a designated point, as agreed between buyer and seller, that is considered "Free on Board." In such contracts, the seller is obligated to have the goods packaged and ready for shipment from

the agreed point, whether his own place of business or some intermediate point, and the buyer normally assumes the burden of all inland transportation costs and risks in the exporting country, as well as all subsequent transportation costs, including the costs of loading the merchandise on the vessel. However, if the contract stipulates "FOB vessel," the seller bears all transportation costs to the vessel named by the buyer, as well as the costs of loading the goods on to that vessel. The same principle applies to the abbreviations "FOR" ("Free on Rail") and "FOT" ("Free on Truck").
See also: C and F, CIF, FAS,

FOR Refer to: FOB,

Foreign Agents Registration Act (FARA) The Foreign Agents Registration Act was designed to guard against undue foreign influence on U.S. policy. FARA mandates public disclosure, through various reports to the Department of Justice, of certain relationships between individuals and entities in the United States and foreign interests. Subject to certain limited exemptions, there are four types of activities which require registration with the Justice Department when performed for a foreign interest by a person or firm in the United States (whether or not U.S. citizens or incorporated in the United States). First, registration is required when engaging in certain political activities, including all attempts to influence U.S. policy or public opinion on behalf of, or even at the request of, a foreign individual or entity. Second, those acting as public relations agents or political consultants in the interests of a foreigner must register. Third, those soliciting or disbursing funds or contributions in the interest of a foreigner must register. Finally, registration is required when representing the interests of a foreigner before the U.S. government.

Foreign Credit Insurance Association An association formed in 1961 to offer export credit insurance backed by the Export-Import Bank of the United States (Eximbank) for U.S. exporters. The association acted as agent for Eximbank offering short-and medium-term insurance coverage. In the fall of 1991, FICA Management Company, Inc. was formed, employing the staff of the association, to act as the servicing company for Eximbank under a two-year contract. FICA Management Company, Inc. will issue Eximbank export credit insurance policies--representing the full faith and credit of the U.S. government--and privately backed association policies.
See also: Export-Import Bank of the United States, Insurance,

Foreign Exchange Claims on a foreign country held in the form of the currency of that country or interest-bearing bonds.
See also: Currency, Money,

Foreign Exchange Controls Refer to: Exchange Controls,

Foreign Exchange Earnings The proceeds from a country's exports of goods, services and capital, normally denominated in convertible currencies.
See also: Currency, Foreign Exchange, Money,

Foreign Market Value (FMV) The price, as defined in the Tariff Act of 1930, as amended, at which merchandise is sold, or offered for sale, in the principal markets of the country from which it is exported. If foreign home market sales are not usable, the foreign market value is based on prices to third countries or constructed value. A number of adjustments must be made to those prices to insure a proper comparison with U.S. prices.
See also: Adjustment,

Foreign Sales Corporation (FSC) An offshore corporation, authorized by the Deficit Reduction Act of 1984, that is eligible for an exemption from federal income taxes on part of its related income. An FSC earns export-related trade income by selling or leasing export property, or by supplying export-related services. The exempt portion of the FSC's foreign trade income is also not taxed when it is distributed to the U.S. corporate shareholders. An FSC must be organized under the laws of a country that has an exchange of information agreement with the United States, or in a qualifying U.S. possession. The FSC is the successor to the Domestic International Sales Corporation (DISC), which was authorized by the U.S. Revenue Act of 1971.

Foreign Trade Zone Refer to: Free Zone,

Forward Market A market in which contracts for future deliveries of goods and securities on a specified date are entered into at fixed prices. The contracts themselves are popularly known as "futures." Many commodity exchanges--wool, cotton and wheat, for example--have established forward markets that permit interested parties to hedge against changes in the prices of the raw materials they use or deal in.
See also: Commodity, Hedge, Market, Spot Market,

FOT Refer to: FOB,

Framework Agreement (Bilateral) A bilateral framework agreement is an agreement between the United States and a trading partner(s) that establishes certain principles which apply to that trade and investment relationship and that also establishes a consultative mechanism which can be used to clarify respective trade policies, resolve specific disputes, or negotiate the reduction or removal of trade or investment barriers. The first such agreement was signed with Mexico in November 1987, with similar agreements subsequently signed with the Philippines and numerous countries in South America, Central America and the Caribbean.
See also: Bilateral, Bilateral Trade Agreement,

Framework Agreement (GATT) With reference to the GATT, the "Framework Agreement" refers collectively to four separate decisions concluded during the Tokyo Round and intended to improve the working of some fundamental provisions of the General Agreement. The four decisions are: "Differential and More Favorable Treatment, Reciprocity and Fuller Participation of Developing Countries." Expands on the concept of special and beneficial treatment for developing countries (LDCs) in the international trading system first established in Part IV of the GATT, reiterating the commitment that concessions should not be expected of LDCs that would be inconsistent with their economic development. It also provided guidelines for trade preferences among LDCs and for the generalized system of preferences granted by developed countries for LDC imports. Developing countries recognized that, as their economies grow stronger, it was expected that they would participate more fully in the framework of GATT rights and obligations. "Declaration on Trade Measures Taken for Balance of Payments Purposes." States principles and codifies practices and procedures regarding the use of trade measures and restrictions applied by governments under Articles XII and XVIII to defend the balance of payments. "Safeguard Action for Development Purposes." Elaborates on provisions in Article XVIII, allowing for protection of LDC "infant industries," and gives LDCs more flexibility in applying trade measures to meet their essential development needs. "Understanding Regarding Notification, Consultation Dispute Settlement and Surveillance." Provides for improvements in the existing mechanisms concerning notification of trade measures, consultations, dispute settlement and surveillance of developments in the international trading system.
See also: Balance of Payments Consultations, Dispute Settlement, Enabling Clause, General Agreement on Tariffs and Trade, Preferences, Reciprocity, Safeguards, Special and Differential Treatment, Tokyo Declaration, Tokyo Round,

Free Alongside Ship Refer to: FAS,

Free List A list of goods not subject to import duties or import-licensing requirements in a particular country.
See also: Licensing,

Free On Board Refer to: FOB,

Free Port Refer to: Free Zone,

Free Trade A theoretical concept that assumes international trade unhampered by government measures such as tariffs or non-tariff barriers. The objective of trade liberalization is to achieve "freer trade" rather than "free trade," it being generally recognized among trade policy officials that some restrictions on trade are likely to remain in effect for the foreseeable future.
See also: Liberalization, Non-Tariff Barriers, Protectionism, Tariff,

Free Trade Area Agreement Agreement between two or more countries to eliminate tariff and non-tariff barriers affecting trade among themselves, while each participating country applies its own independent schedule of tariffs to imports from countries that are not members. Examples are the European Community, the European Free Trade Association, the U.S.-Israel Free Trade Area Agreement, and the U.S.-Canada Free Trade Agreement. The United States, Canada and Mexico completed negotiations on a proposed North American Free Trade Agreement (NAFTA) in August 1992. GATT Article XXIV spells out the meaning of a free trade area in GATT and specifies the applicability of the other GATT provisions to free trade areas.
See also: Common External Tariff, Customs Union, European Free Trade Association, General Agreement on Tariffs and Trade, North American Free Trade Agreement, U.S.-Canada Free Trade Agreement,

Free Trade Zone Refer to: Free Zone,

Free Warehouse Refer to: Free Zone,

Free Zone An area within a country (a seaport, airport, warehouse or any designated area) regarded as being outside its customs territory. Importers may therefore bring goods of foreign origin into such an area without paying customs duties and taxes, pending their eventual processing, transshipment or re-exportation. Free zones were numerous and prosperous during an earlier period when tariffs were high. Some still exist in capital cities, transport junctions and major seaports, but their number and prominence have declined as tariffs have fallen in recent years. Free zones may also be known as "free ports," "free warehouses," "free trade zones" and "foreign trade zones."
See also: Customs,

Freedom, Commerce And Navigation Treaty (FCN) A bilateral establishment treaty defining the legal and commercial rights of the citizens of each country under the laws of the other.

Fusion, Treaty Of Refer to: European Community,

Futures Refer to: Forward Market,

G-5 Refer to: Group of 7,

G-7 Refer to: Group of 7,

G-77 Refer to: Group of 77,

Gate Price Refer to: Variable Levy,

GATT Refer to: General Agreement on Tariffs and Trade,

GATT Ministerial Meeting Of 1982 The first meeting of the GATT Contracting Parties at the ministerial level since the Tokyo Round. The 1982 meeting approved a GATT Work Program for the 1980s looking toward continued liberalization of world trade, with particular attention to trade policy issues that previously received relatively little attention in GATT, such as barriers to agricultural trade, services and obstacles to developing-country exports.
See also: General Agreement on Tariffs and Trade, Liberalization, Services, Tokyo Round, Williamsburg Summit,

GATT Panel A group of trade experts convened by the GATT Contracting Parties to investigate any trade measures in dispute, make findings about the consistency of the measures under the GATT, and provide recommendations as to what the Contracting Parties should request the disputing parties to do, if anything, to meet their obligations under the GATT. Generally, the Contracting Parties select three officials of contracting parties that are not participants in the dispute; while they serve on the panel, these officials are expected to act independently of their governments' interests.
See also: Arbitration, General Agreement on Tariffs and Trade, Dispute Settlement, Panel of Experts,

GATT Work Program For The 1980s. Refer to: GATT Ministerial Meeting of 1982,

General Agreement On Tariffs And Trade (GATT) A multilateral trade agreement among autonomous economic entities (not necessarily countries) aimed at expanding international trade as a means of raising world welfare. The GATT was signed in 1947, as an interim agreement. It has been recognized worldwide as the key international institution concerned with multinational trade negotiations since it became clear that the U.S. Senate would not ratify the Havana Charter of 1948, which would have created an International Trade Organization (ITO) as a Specialized Agency of the United Nations System, similar to the International Monetary Fund and the World Bank. The Interim Commission of the ITO (ICITO), which was established to facilitate the creation of the ITO, subsequently became the GATT Secretariat. Provisions of the General Agreement are applied reciprocally among its Contracting Parties to reduce uncertainty in connection with commercial transactions across national borders. The cornerstone of the GATT has been traditionally the most-favored-nation clause (Article 1 of the General Agreement), but in the 1970s and 1980s, regional and other trade preference systems became pervasive, weakening the role of GATT in ensuring equal market access among GATT members. The designation "GATT" also refers to the organization headquartered at Geneva through which the Contracting Parties consult on a day-to-day basis regarding the application of GATT provisions. The organization also provides a framework for negotiations--called "Rounds"--within which Contracting Parties negotiate to lower tariffs and other barriers to trade and a consultative mechanism that may be invoked by governments seeking to protect their trade interests. With the Tokyo and Uruguay Rounds, the focus of trade liberalization shifted from lowering tariffs to the elimination of non-tariff barriers to trade. Currently, there are 103 GATT Contracting Parties (CPs), accounting for approximately 85 percent of world trade, and some 30 additional countries and dependencies apply GATT provisions on a "de facto" basis and may someday assume full status as Contracting Parties. A number of other countries and customs territories are also seeking membership, including China, Mongolia, Taiwan, Bulgaria, Panama, Paraguay and Honduras. The GATT is the principal point of reference for the conduct of U.S. trade policy. U.S. association with the GATT is implemented through or by an executive order, and is not a treaty obligation. U.S. observance of GATT provisions depends on congressional approval of implementing legislation as well as the policy orientation of the president.
See also: Articles of GATT, Bretton Woods Conference, Codes of Conduct, Compensation, Consultations, Contracting Party, GATT Panel, Grandfather Clause, International Trade Center UNCTAD/GATT, Liberalization,

General Tariff A tariff that applies to imports from countries that do not enjoy either preferential or

most-favored-nation tariff treatment. Where the general tariff rate differs from the most-favored-nation rate, the general tariff is usually an older and higher rate.
See also: Conventional Tariff, Most-Favored-Nation Treatment, Preferences, Tariff,

Generalized System Of Preferences (GSP) A concept developed within UNCTAD to encourage the expansion of manufactured and semi-manufactured exports from developing countries by making such goods more competitive in developed-country markets through tariff preferences. The GSP reflects international agreement, negotiated at UNCTAD-II (New Delhi, 1968), that a temporary and non-reciprocal grant of preferences by developed countries to developing countries would be equitable and, in the long term, mutually beneficial. To meet its GSP commitment, each industrialized nation determined its own system of preferences, specifying the goods, the margins of preference, and in some cases, the value or volume of goods that would benefit from preferential treatment. Twenty-seven industrialized countries, including the United States now maintain GSP programs. The U.S. Trade Act of 1974 authorized the first U.S. GSP arrangement for the period of January 1, 1976 until January 4, 1985. The U.S. program was extended through July 4, 1993, by the Trade and Tariff Act of 1984. An extension of the GSP program in its existing form through September 30, 1994, was secured under a budget legislation package. The Clinton administration is expected to introduce legislation to authorize long-term renewal GSP program in 1994. Approximately 4,100 categories of articles in the tariff schedule have been designated as eligible for duty free entry into the United States under GSP. But the 1974 legislation explicitly indicated a number of "exceptions," including textiles, clothing, watches, steel, footwear, glass, some electronic articles and other sensitive products that could not enter the United States duty free under the GSP authority. The Trade Act of 1974 also stated that any country supplying more than 50 percent of total U.S. imports of a particular item in one year, or exceeding a specified dollar amount for that item, would be ineligible for GSP benefits for that product during the following year because it had no "competitive need" for such benefits. The U.S. Trade Agreements Act of 1979 provided that the 50-percent limit may be waived for a product falling below a certain dollar amount that was to be adjusted annually to reflect changes in the U.S. gross national product. Some developing countries are ineligible to receive U.S. GSP benefits: those that participate in OPEC or "other cartel-like arrangements," those that nationalize property of U.S. citizens without providing satisfactory compensation; those that fail to cooperate in international drug control efforts; most communist states; those that exceed a certain per capita GNP; those that fail to maintain reasonable and equitable market access or adequate intellectual property protection for U.S. goods, services and investment; and those that fail to ensure internationally recognized worker rights. The Enabling Clause, adopted as a consequence of the Tokyo Round, established a legal basis within GATT for extending GSP benefits, notwithstanding GATT's most-favored-nation clause.
See also: Competitive, Enabling Clause, Infant Industry Argument, Lomé Convention, Margin of Preference, North-South Trade, Preferences, Sensitive Products, Special and Differential Treatment, Trade Act of 1974,

Global Quotas Refer to: Quantitative Restrictions, Quantitative Restrictions,

Global Quotas Refer to: Quantitative Restrictions, Quantitative Restrictions,

Global System Of Trade Preferences (GSTP) An objective developed by the Group of 77 within the UNCTAD ECDC (Economic Cooperation Among Developing Countries) program looking toward the negotiation of special intra-developing country preferences and the reduction of non-tariff barriers impeding South-South trade.
See also: Economic Cooperation Among Developing Countries, Group of 77, Non-Tariff Barriers, Preferences, South-South Trade, United Nations Conference on Trade and Development,

GNG Refer to: Final Act,

GNS Refer to: Final Act,

Goods Inherently useful and relatively scarce articles or commodities--distinct from services--produced by the manufacturing, mining, construction and agricultural sectors of the economy. Goods are important economically because they may be exchanged for money or other goods and services.
See also: Capital Goods, Commodity, Consumer Goods, Money, Price, Production, Services, Utility,

Government Procurement Policies And Practices The means and mechanisms through which official government agencies purchase goods and services. Government procurement policies and practices are non-tariff barriers to trade, according to GATT, if they discriminate in favor of domestic suppliers when competitive imported goods are cheaper or of better quality. The United States pressed for an international agreement during the Tokyo Round to ensure that government purchases of goods entering into international trade should be based on specific, published regulations that prescribe open procedures for submitting bids, as had been the traditional practice in the United States. Most governments had traditionally awarded such contracts on the basis of bids solicited from selected domestic suppliers, or through private negotiations with suppliers that involved little, if any, competition. Other countries, including the United States, gave domestic suppliers a specified preferential margin, as compared with foreign suppliers. The Government Procurement Code negotiated during the Tokyo Round sought to reduce, if not eliminate, the "Buy National" bias underlying such practices by improving transparency and equity in national procurement practices and by ensuring effective recourse to dispute settlement procedures. The code became effective January 1, 1981.
See also: Codes of Conduct, Conditional Most-Favored-Nation Treatment, Discrimination, Dispute Settlement, Non-Tariff Barriers, Tokyo Round, Trade Agreements Act of 1979, Transparency,

Graduation The presumption that individual developing countries are capable of assuming greater responsibilities and obligations in the international community--within GATT or the World Bank, for example--as their economies advance, as through industrialization, export development and rising living standards. In this sense, graduation implies that donor countries may remove the more advanced developing countries from eligibility for all or some products under the Generalized System of Preferences. Within the World Bank, graduation moves a country from dependence on concessional grants to non-concessional loans from international financial institutions and private banks.
See also: Developing Countries, Generalized System of Preferences, Loan, Newly Industrializing Countries, Official Development Assistance, World Bank,

Grandfather Clause A provision in a legal instrument, such as GATT, that allows countries that accede to it to maintain preexisting domestic legislation inconsistent with provisions of that instrument.
See also: Accession, General Agreement on Tariffs and Trade, Protocol of Provisional Application, Residual Restrictions,

Grants Refer to: Bounties,

Group A Refer to: Group of 77,

Group B Originally a designation for the developed market-economy countries participating in UNCTAD. In recent years the term has also been used to refer to these same countries when they meet in OECD and other international organizations to develop positions relevant to North-South economic issues.
See also: Market Economy, North-South Trade, Organization for Economic Cooperation and

Development, United Nations Conference on Trade and Development,

Group C Refer to: Group of 77,

Group D Prior to their 1989-1991 conversion to market-oriented policies, Group D consisted of the socialist countries of Eastern Europe participating in UNCTAD, excluding Romania and Yugoslavia (which were considered members of the Group of 77) and Albania (which did not actively participate in UNCTAD and other elements of the United Nations system). Group D countries showed a particular interest in the division of the UNCTAD Secretariat concerned with "Trade Between Countries with Different Economic Systems."
See also: State Trading Nations, United Nations Conference on Trade and Development,

Group of 7 (G-7) The Group of Seven is comprised of the United States, Japan, Germany, France, Italy, the United Kingdom and Canada. It consults regularly for the purpose of coordinating economic policies to achieve sustained economic growth with price stability, foster stability in exchange markets, and promote adjustment in external imbalances. The group also addresses other pressing international economic issues that affect global economic performance. Finance ministers and central bank governors represent their countries at G-7 meetings; additional meetings are held by the deputies of finance ministers. The G-7 is the successor to the Group of 5 (G-5), which was composed of the same countries less Canada and Italy.
See also: Plaza Accord,

Group of 77 Originally, the 77 developing countries represented at UNCTAD-1 in 1964. The delegates established the precedent of meeting together to attempt to develop common positions on major conference agenda items in advance of plenary UNCTAD meetings. The Group of 77 comprises UNCTAD Groups "A" (the African and Asian Groups, with the notable exceptions of Israel and South Africa) and "C" (the Latin American Group). More than 120 developing countries are now members of the "Group of 77" and are represented at its meetings in Geneva, New York, Vienna and Rome, where they seek to develop common positions on trade and development issues under consideration in UNCTAD and other U.N. bodies.
See also: Developing Countries, Economic Cooperation Among Developing Countries, Non-Aligned Movement, North-South Trade, United Nations Conference on Trade and Development,

Grundy Tariff Refer to: Tariff Act of 1930,

GSP Refer to: Generalized System of Preferences,

GSTP Refer to: Global System of Trade Preferences,

Hard Fibers Sisal, abaca and coir.
See also: Integrated Program for Commodities,

Harmonization The process of making procedures or measures applied by different countries--especially those affecting international trade--more compatible, as by effecting simultaneous tariff cuts applied by different countries so as to make their tariff structures more uniform. Most proposals for "harmonizing" tariffs envisage relatively large cuts in high tariffs and smaller cuts in lower tariffs, as contrasted with the "linear reduction" formula used in the Kennedy Round, which called for identical percentage cuts for all applicable tariffs. Tokyo Round tariff cuts increased tariff harmonization among the developed countries.
See also: Customs Harmonization, Kennedy Round, Kyoto Convention, Linear Reduction of Tariffs, Tariff, Tokyo Round,

Harmonized Commodity Description And Coding System Refer to: Customs Harmonization, Harmonized System,

Harmonized System (HS) Formally known as the Harmonized Commodity Description and Coding System, the Harmonized System is a complete product classification system which is organized in a particular framework and which employs a numbering or coding system consistent with its organizational arrangement. At the international level, the HS comprises approximately 5,000 article descriptions which appear as headings and subheadings, arranged in 97 chapters grouped in 21 sections. Sections of the HS group together articles from branches of industry and commerce (e.g., animals and animal products, or textiles and textile articles) or by their functions or use (e.g., footwear, arms and ammunition). The Harmonized System was developed by the Customs Cooperating Council and has been adopted by most major trading nations.
See also: Customs Classification, Customs Harmonization, Harmonized Tariff Schedule of the United States,

Harmonized Tariff Schedule Of The United States (HTSUS) A comprehensive classification of goods specifying the duty that U.S. Customs authorities assess against each imported item. On January 1, 1989, the United States converted its tariff nomenclature structure, known as the Tariff Schedules of the United States, to conform with the Harmonized Commodity Description and Coding System, better known as the Harmonized System, developed by the Customs Cooperation Council.
See also: Bound Rates, Customs, Customs Classification, Customs Harmonization, Harmonized System, Tariff,

Havana Charter Refer to: General Agreement on Tariffs and Trade,

Hawley-Smoot Tariff Act Of 1930 Refer to: Tariff Act of 1930,

Health And Sanitary Controls Refer to: Customs and Administrative Entry Procedures, Quarantine, Sanitary, and Health Laws and Regulations, Standards,

Hedge Action taken by a buyer or seller to protect his business or assets against a change in prices. A miller, for example, might buy a quantity of wheat to convert into flour at a given point in time and agree at the same time to sell a similar quantity of wheat that he does not own, at the same price, for delivery at a designated future point in time. If the price of wheat falls, he will lose on the flour while making a profit on the wheat he can later buy at the lower price; whereas if the price of wheat rises, he will make an extra profit on his flour, which he will have to sacrifice by purchasing wheat at the current high price. In either case, his production profits are protected.
See also: Forward Market,

Horizontal Reduction Of Tariffs Refer to: Linear Reduction of Tariffs,

HS
See also: Harmonized System,

HTSUS Refer to: Harmonized Tariff Schedule of the United States,

IBRD Refer to: World Bank,

ICA Refer to: International Commodity Agreement,

ICITO Refer to: General Agreement on Tariffs and Trade,

IDA Refer to: International Development Association,

IEEPA Refer to: International Emergency Economic Powers Act,

IFC Refer to: International Finance Corporation,

Illustrative List ILLUSTRATIVE LIST. Contained in the Annex to the GATT Subsidies Code, the Illustrative List of Export Subsidies enumerates certain practices that constitute countervailable export subsidies, within the terms of the code, when provided or mandated by a government with respect to goods produced for export. These include direct subsidies to a firm or industry contingent upon export performance, currency retention schemes or other practices that involve a bonus, preferential internal transport and freight charges, remission of direct taxes, provision of services or goods on preferential terms, export credit guarantees, etc.
See also: Countervailing Duties, Subsidy,

IMF Refer to: International Monetary Fund,

Impairment (Of Trade Interests) Refer to: Consultations, Dispute Settlement,

Import Licensing Refer to: Licensing,

Import Quotas Refer to: Quantitative Restrictions,

Import Relief Alleviation of competitive pressures on a domestic industry and its employees through restrictions on the inflow of goods into the relevant market from other countries, as through the imposition of tariffs or quantitative restrictions on imports.
See also: Competitive, Escape Clause, Market, Protection,

Import Restrictions Refer to: Non-Tariff Barriers, Protection, Tariff,

Import -Sensitive Products Refer to: Sensitive Products,

Import Substitution An attempt by a country to reduce imports (and hence foreign exchange expenditures) by encouraging the development of domestic industries regardless of domestic inefficiencies.
See also: Industrial Policy, Infant Industry Argument, Mercantilism,

Imports The inflow of goods and services into a country's market for consumption. A country enhances its welfare by importing a broader range of higher quality goods and services at lower cost than it could produce domestically. The expansion of world trade since the end of World War II has therefore been a principal factor underlying a general rise in living standards in most countries.
See also: Comparative Advantage, Consumption, Customs, Levy, Macroeconomics, Market, Price Elasticity of Demand, Protectionism, U.S. International Trade Commission, Welfare,

Incoterms Model terms promulgated by the International Chamber of Commerce in Paris to govern international sales contracts. The paradigm Incoterms contract is a CIF contract.

Indirect Tax A tax that is levied on expenditure, such as a sales tax imposed at the retail level, excise tax, or value added tax. Some economists say indirect taxes are regressive (in that taxes on commodities burden the poor more than the rich), and inflationary (since they raise prices).
See also: Border Tax Adjustments, Direct Tax, Excise Tax, Inflation, Tax, Value Added Tax,

Industrial Policy Encompasses traditional government policies intended to provide a favorable economic climate for the development of industry in general or specific industrial sectors. Instruments of industrial policy may include tax incentives to promote investments or exports, direct or indirect subsidies, special financing arrangements, protection against foreign

competition, worker training programs, regional development programs, assistance for research and development, and measures to help small business firms. Historically the term industrial policy has been associated with at least some degree of centralized economic planning or indicative planning, but this connotation is not always intended by its contemporary advocates.
See also: Infant Industry Argument, Investment Performance Requirements, Managed Trade, MITI, Mercantilism, Protection, Subsidy,

Industrial Revolution The emergence of the factory system of production, in which workers are brought together in one plant and supplied tools, machines and materials with which they work in return for wages. Narrowly speaking, the Industrial Revolution was spearheaded by the rapid changes in the manufacture of textiles, particularly in England, between about 1770 and 1830. More broadly, the term applies to continuing structural economic change in the world economy. The "domestic system" of production prevailed in the 16th and 17th centuries before the Industrial Revolution.
See also: Domestic System of Production, Production, Structural Change, Textiles,

Industrialized Countries Refer to: Developed Countries,

Infant Industry Argument The view that "temporary protection" for a new industry or firm in a particular country through tariff and non-tariff barriers to imports can help it to become established and eventually competitive in world markets. Historically, new industries that are soundly based and efficiently operated have experienced declining costs as output expands and production experience is acquired. However, industries that have been established and operated with heavy dependence on direct or indirect government subsidies have sometimes found it difficult to relinquish that support. The rationale underlying the Generalized System of Preferences is comparable to that of the infant industry argument.
See also: Competitive, Generalized System of Preferences, Protection, Subsidy,

Inflation A general increase in the prices of most goods and services within a market, resulting in diminishing purchasing power of a given nominal sum of the currency used in the market. Inflation results when demand increases more rapidly than supply, as when salaries and wages increase more rapidly than production. Since World War II, inflation has been a persistent phenomenon in most countries.
See also: Currency, Demand, Indirect Tax, Money, Price, Purchasing Power, Supply,

Informatics A term used to describe the complex of industries and products based on digital information-processing technologies. This includes computers, computer peripherals, computer software, data processing and most categories of microelectronic components.

Infrastructure The underlying capital of a society embodied in its roads and other transportation and communications systems, as well as its electric power, water supplies, sewage systems and other public services. Sometimes called social overhead capital, infrastructure may also include health, education and skills of a country's population.
See also: Capital, Economic Development, Welfare,

Inheritance Tax Refer to: Direct Tax,

Injury Refer to: Countervailing Duties, Dumping, Escape Clause, Market Disruption, Peril Point, Safeguards, U.S. International Trade Commission,

Input Dumping Refer to: Downstream Dumping,

Insurance An agreement or contract (commonly called a policy) between the insured, who pays a premium to the insurer, who in return promises to compensate the insured if he suffers specified

losses, as through fire, theft or automobile accident. The premiums are so calculated that the total amount paid by all insured parties will enable the insurer to pay claims of policy holders and administrative costs. In effect, insurance spreads risk so that an individual who suffers loss is compensated at the expense of all those who insure against it.
See also: Capital Market, Export Credit Insurance, Premium, Reinsurance, Risk, Services, Underwriter,

Intellectual Property Ownership conferring the right to possess, use or dispose of products created by human ingenuity, including patents, trademarks and copyrights.
See also: Copyright, Patent, Technology, Trademarks, Trade-Related Aspects of Intellectual Property Rights, in Counterfeit Goods and Services, Trafficking , Uruguay Round, World Intellectual Property Organization,

Interdependence Refer to: Structural Change,

Interest A sum paid for the use of borrowed capital, usually expressed in terms of a rate or percentage of the capital involved (the interest "rate"), which is normally higher when the risk (including the probability of inflation) is greater.
See also: Capital, Credit, Inflation, Loan, Profit, Risk,

Intermediate Goods Refer to: Capital Goods,

International Arrangement On Export Credits An agreement among 22 OECD governments that they will not lower interest rates for export credits below specified levels or offer most tied-aid credits without informing other OECD governments. The arrangement seeks to minimize subsidization of exports through official export credits offered at less than market rates of interest and to curb the use of tied-aid credits that distort trade patterns. It contains no enforcement provisions, but procedures encouraging transparency in official export credit and aid activities encourage compliance.
See also: Credit, Export Subsidies, Interest, Organization for Economic Cooperation and Development, Subsidy, Transparency,

International Bank For Reconstruction And Development Refer to: World Bank,

International Commodity Agreement (ICA) An international understanding, usually reflected in a legal instrument, relating to trade in a particular commodity, and based on terms negotiated and accepted by most of the countries that export and import commercially significant quantities of the commodity. Some commodity agreements such as those for coffee, cocoa, natural rubber and sugar have centered on economic provisions intended to stabilize the market price within a negotiated price range for the commodity through the use of buffer stocks or export quotas or both. Of these, only rubber currently has economic provisions as part of the agreement. Other commodity agreements (such as existing agreements for jute and jute products, olive oil and wheat) seek to promote cooperation among producers and consumers through improved consultations, exchange of information, research and development, and export promotion.
See also: Buffer Stocks, Commodity, Common Fund, Export Promotion, Export Quotas, Integrated Program for Commodities,

International Convention On The Simplification And Harmonization Of Customs Procedures Refer to: Kyoto Convention,

International Development Association (IDA) An affiliate of the World Bank, established in 1960, that extends concessional loans to the least developed countries and other relatively poor countries to finance long-term high-priority development projects. IDA resources are contributed by 33 donor countries. The World Bank would not be able to make loans to many of the poorest

countries, including most countries in Africa, without IDA resources.
See also: Least Developed Countries, Official Development Assistance, Soft Loan, World Bank,

International Emergency Economic Powers Act (IEEPA) U.S. legislation enacted in 1977 that extended emergency powers previously granted the U.S. president by the Trading with the Enemy Act of 1917 (TWEA). Specifically, the legislation enables the president, after declaring that a national emergency exists because of a threat from a source outside the United States, to investigate, regulate, compel or prohibit virtually any economic transaction involving property in which a foreign country or national has an interest. As of January 1992, sanctions administered by the Treasury Department were in force under TWEA against Cuba, Vietnam and North Korea, as well as certain controls on the involvement of U.S. persons in third-country strategic exports. IEEPA programs at the beginning of 1992 included Iraq, Libya and Haiti. Treasury also administered sanctions against Iran under IEEPA as well as under the International Security and Development Cooperation Act.

International Finance Corporation (IFC) An affiliate of the World Bank, established in 1956, to promote commercial enterprises in developing countries through loans and equity financing comparable to those extended by investment banks. It also facilitates the establishment of partnerships between private investors, wherever they may be located, and capital markets in the Third World. It does not require government guarantees.
See also: Capital Market, Market Economy, Private Sector, World Bank,

International Monetary Fund (IMF) An international financial institution proposed at the 1944 Bretton Woods Conference and established in 1946 that seeks to stabilize the international monetary system as a sound basis for the orderly expansion of international trade. Specifically, among other things, the Fund monitors exchange rate policies of member countries, lends them foreign exchange resources to support their adjustment policies when they experience balance of payments difficulties, and provides them financial assistance through a special "compensatory financing facility" when they experience temporary shortfalls in commodity export earnings.
See also: Adjustment: Balance of Payments Consultations, Bretton Woods Conference, Compensatory Finance, Conditionality, Convertibility, Exchange Rate, Special Drawing Rights,

International Trade Center UNCTAD/GATT (ITC) A quasi-autonomous, Geneva-based organization within the United Nations system (reporting to both GATT and UNCTAD) that provides a wide range of technical assistance to developing countries seeking to develop and promote their export potential. The ITC is the recognized U.N. Development Program executing agency in the field of trade promotion.
See also: Export Promotion, Agreement on Tariffs and Trade, United Nations Conference on Trade and Development, General , United Nations Development Program,

International Trade Commission (ITC) Refer to: U.S. International Trade Commission,

International Trade Organization (ITO) Refer to: General Agreement on Tariffs and Trade,

International Union For The Protection Of Industrial Property Refer to: World Intellectual Property Organization,

International Union For The Protection Of Literary And Artistic Works Refer to: World Intellectual Property Organization,

International Wheat Agreement Refer to: Kennedy Round,

Investment Performance Requirements Special conditions imposed on direct foreign investment by recipient governments, sometimes requiring commitments to export a certain percentage of

the output, to purchase given supplies locally, or to ensure the employment of a specified percentage of local labor and management.
See also: Industrial Policy,

Investor Refer to: Entrepreneur, Risk,

Invisible Trade Items such as freight, insurance and financial services that are included in a country's balance of payments accounts (in the "current" account), even though they are not recorded as physically visible exports and imports.
See also: Balance of Payments, Current Account, Services, Visible Trade,

IPC Refer to: Integrated Program for Commodities,

Iranian Transactions Refer to: International Emergency Economic Powers Act,

Island Developing Countries Refer to: Least Developed Countries,

ITC Refer to: International Trade Center UNCTAD/GATT, U.S. International Trade Commission,

ITO Refer to: General Agreement on Tariffs and Trade, Multilateral Trade Organization,

Joint Venture A form of business partnership involving joint management and the sharing of risks and profits as between enterprises based in different countries. If joint ownership of capital is involved the partnership is known as an equity joint venture.

Keiretsu Japanese keiretsu in the late 20th century are descendants of the pre-war zaibatsu, which were characterized by close, long-term business relationships between its members. Keiretsu firms are linked to one another through a network of formal and informal ties including cross shareholdings, time honored buyer-supplier arrangements, interlocking corporate directorates, interchange of personnel between member firms, and the sharing of information concerning product development and distribution. While keiretsu do have some positive aspects such as cost reduction and quality control, stemming from long-term relationships, their collusive and exclusionary nature act as an impediment to foreign market access. Keiretsu typically include a bank, trading company, manufacturing firms and often an insurance company.
See also: Codes of Conduct, Industry Policy, Managed Trade, Market Access, Restricted Business Practice,

Kennedy Round The popular name for the sixth and at that time the most ambitious "Round" of trade negotiations under the aegis of GATT. The Kennedy Round, which lasted from 1963 to 1967, yielded agreements reducing prevailing tariff levels maintained by developed countries on industrial products by about one-third, an "Anti-Dumping Code, "and a short-lived International Wheat Agreement which was intended to stabilize world wheat prices. (The Wheat Agreement replaced the latest in a series of International Wheat Agreements going back to the 1950s.)
See also: Anti-Dumping Code, Agreement on Tariffs and Trade, General , Round, Special and Differential Treatment, Tariff, Trade Expansion Act of 1962,

Key Currencies Refer to: Currency, Reserve Currency,

KYOTO Convention The objective of the "International Convention on the Simplification and Harmonization of Customs Procedures," also known as the Kyoto Convention, as reflected in its preamble, is the development of compatible national customs procedures in different countries as a means of encouraging and facilitating international trade.
See also: Customs, Harmonization, Harmonization,

Land-Locked Developing Countries Refer to: Least Developed Countries, Transit Zone,

Large Aircraft Sector Understanding (LASU) A 1985 agreement between the United States and the European Community providing for minimum terms and conditions for loans or loan guarantees for the support by government export-credit agencies of the export of aircraft of 70 seats or greater (or the equivalent in freight) and their engines and spare components. This agreement was later broadened to cover all size aircraft and supersedes previously existing "Standstill"and "Common Line" understandings covering government export-financing support for such articles. The understanding has since been incorporated as a sectoral annex into the "OECD Arrangement on Guidelines for Officially Supported Export Credits.
See also: Export Subsidies, Organization for Economic Cooperation and Development, Market Access,

LASU Refer to: Large Aircraft Sector Understanding,

LDCs Refer to: Developing Countries, Least Developed Countries,

Least Developed Countries (LLDCs or LDCs) Some 36 of the world's poorest countries, considered by the United Nations to be the "least developed" of the less developed countries. Most of them are small in terms of area and population, and some are land-locked or small island countries. They are generally characterized by low per capita incomes, literacy levels and medical standards; subsistence agriculture; and a lack of exploitable minerals and competitive industries. Many suffer from aridity, floods, hurricanes and excessive animal and plant pests, and most are situated in the zone 10 to 30 degrees north latitude. These countries have little prospect of rapid economic development in the foreseeable future and are likely to remain heavily dependent upon official development assistance for many years. Most are in Africa, but a few, such as Bangladesh, Afghanistan, Laos and Nepal, are in Asia. Haiti is the only country in the Western hemisphere classified by the United Nations as "least developed." The abbreviation "LDCs" has increasingly been used in recent years to refer to the least developed countries (although in the 1950s and 1960s the term" less developed countries" was more or less interchangeable with the term "developing countries").
See also: Developing Countries, Official Development Assistance, Substantial New Program of Action, Transit Zone,

Less Developed Countries (LDCs) Refer to: Developing Countries, Least Developed Countries,

Less Than Fair Value Refer to: Anti-Dumping Code, Dumping,

Level Of Trade Adjustment (LOT) Adjustment to U.S. sales price in an anti-dumping investigation that compensates for differences in the cost of selling to different commercial levels of trade.
See also: Dumping, United States Price,

Levy To assess or impose a tariff on imported merchandise (when used as a verb), or the charge on imports (when used as a noun).
See also: Imports, Tariff, Tax,

Liberal When referring to trade policy, "liberal" usually means relatively free of import controls or restraints and/or a preference for reducing existing barriers to trade, often contrasted with the protectionist preference for retaining or raising selected barriers to imports.
See also: Free Trade, Liberalization, Protectionism,

Liberalization Reductions in tariffs and other measures that restrict trade, unilaterally or multilaterally. Trade liberalization has been the objective of all "Rounds" of GATT trade negotiations.

See also: Codes of Conduct, Free Trade, General Agreement on Tariffs and Trade, Liberal, Round, Sensitive Products,

Licensing The requirement by a country of a formal application for a special permit, usually called a "license," as a prior condition for importing or exporting certain goods.
See also: Customs and Administrative Entry Procedures, Licensing Code, Non-Tariff Barriers, Prior Deposits, Quantitative Restrictions, Specific Limitations on Trade,

Licensing Code A Tokyo Round code aimed at simplifying import-licensing procedures and at ensuring their fair and equitable application. The code also seeks to improve the transparency of such proceedings by requiring the publication of relevant national laws and regulations. A Committee on Import Licensing, under the aegis of GATT, monitors adherence to the code.
See also: Codes of Conduct, Licensing, Non-Tariff Barriers, Tokyo Round, Trade Agreements Act of 1979, Transparency,

Linear Reduction Of Tariffs A reduction by a given percentage in all tariffs maintained by countries participating in a "Round" of trade negotiations, with or without "exceptions" for products deemed to be "sensitive." Sometimes called "horizontal reduction of tariffs," "across-the-board reduction of tariffs," or "equal percentage reduction of tariffs." The complexity and implicit limitations in negotiating tariff reductions on an item-by-item basis in the Dillon Round encouraged negotiators to try a "linear reduction" formula during the Kennedy Round. The U.S. Trade Expansion Act of 1962, while not specifying an across-the-board formula for the negotiations, authorized reductions of up to 50 percent on virtually all items in the U.S. tariff schedules, hence permitting a linear application.
See also: Dillon Round, Harmonization, Item-by-Item Negotiations, Kennedy Round, Sensitive Products, Tariff, Trade Expansion Act of 1962,

Liquid Hydrocarbons Refer to: Bulk Carrier,

Liquidation This is the point at which the U.S. Customs Services ascertainment of the rate of duty and amount of duty for items imported into the United States becomes final for most purposes.
See also: Tariff,

LLDCs Refer to: Least Developed Countries,

Loan The borrowing of a sum of money by a person, company, government or other organization.
See also: Interest, International Monetary Fund, Risk, Security, Soft Loan, Tied Loan, World Bank,

LOMÉ Convention An agreement--originally signed in 1975--through which the European Community provides financial and technical assistance to more than 50 Associated Countries of Africa, the Caribbean and the Pacific ("the ACP Countries"), as well as tariff preferences for many of their products in European markets. The ACP countries no longer grant reverse preferences, as they were required to under earlier Yaounde Conventions, as a condition for receiving EC preferences. The Lomé Convention also created a mechanism known as "STABEX," which was designed to stabilize the export earnings of individual "Associated Countries" from selected commodities. Compensatory payments from the European Community under STABEX are based on the amount by which a country's earnings from exports of specified commodities fall below designated levels. The Lomé Convention, which is renegotiated periodically, was last renegotiated in 1990.
See also: ACP Countries, Commodity, Compensatory Finance, European Community, Managed Trade, Reverse Preferences,

Long-Term Agreement On International Trade in Cotton Textiles (LTA) Refer to: Multi-Fiber

Arrangement Regarding International Trade in Textiles,

Loss Refer to: Profit, Risk,

LOT Refer to: Level of Trade Adjustment,

LTA Refer to: Multi-Fiber Arrangement Regarding International Trade in Textiles,

Machine Tools Refer to: Capital Goods,

Macroeconomics That part of economics that is primarily concerned with the study of relationships between broad economic aggregates, such as national income, savings, investment, consumption, employment, the money supply, the average price level, exports, imports and the balance of payments.
See also: Market Forces, Microeconomics,

Managed Trade Attempts by governments at the national or international level to influence or control exports and imports, based on the presumption that government perspectives are more likely to ensure "optimal" trade in some sense than would result from reliance on unmanaged market forces. "Managed trade" at the national level often reflects the political influence of protectionist elements in an economy. The term may also describe buffer stock and price stabilization arrangements, such as STABEX or the Integrated Program for Commodities.
See also: Industrial Policy, Integrated Program for Commodities, Lomé Convention, Market Forces, MITI, Protectionism,

Management The organization and coordination of an enterprise. The manager who conducts or supervises production for example, may be a paid expert in administration, as opposed to the entrepreneur who originally conceived the operation and took the risk in mounting it. In modern corporations, management and control tend to be separate from ownership, which is vested in the stockholders.
See also: Entrepreneur, Microeconomics, Production, Profit, Risk,

Man-Made Fibers Refer to: Multi-Fiber Arrangement Regarding International Trade in Textiles, Sensitive Products, Textiles,

Manufacturing Processes Refer to: Production, Property,

Margin Of Preference The difference between the duty payable under a given system of tariff preferences and the duty that would be assessed in the absence of preferences.
See also: Generalized System of Preferences, Preferences, Special and Differential Treatment, Tariff,

Market The area within which buyers and sellers interact to effect economic exchanges. The estimated or realized demand for a good or service may also be referred to as its "market."
See also: Demand, Distribution, Market Economy, Monopoly, Production, Purchasing Power, Supply, Trade Fair,

Market Access The ability of domestic providers of goods and services to penetrate a related market in a foreign country. The extent to which the foreign market is accessible generally depends upon the existence and extent of trade barriers.
See also: Market, Market Forces, Non-Market Economy, Offer List, Restrictive Business Practice, Special and Differential Treatment,

Market Disruption The situation that occurs when a surge of imports of a particular product

causes a precipitous decline in sales of similar domestically produced goods.
See also: Dumping, Escape Clause, Multi-Fiber Arrangement Regarding International Trade in Textiles, Orderly Marketing Agreements, Safeguards, Sensitive Products, U.S. International Trade in Commission,

Market Economy A national economy of a country that relies heavily upon market forces to determine levels of production, consumption, investment and savings without government intervention.
See also: Demand, Market Forces, Macroeconomics, Non-Market Economy, Price, Private Sector, Profit, Supply,

Market Forces Shifts in demand and supply that are reflected in changing relative prices, thus serving as indicators and guides for enterprises that make investment, purchase and sales decisions.
See also: Demand, Macroeconomics, Managed Trade, Market Access, Microeconomics, Non-Market Economy, Price, Private Sector, Supply,

Marshall Plan Refer to: European Recovery Program,

Medium Of Exchange Documentary instrument used in commercial transactions between buyers and sellers to measure the value of the goods exchanged. The value of such instruments is usually expressed in terms of a national currency, such as the U.S. dollar.
See also: Bill, Currency, Markets, Money,

Mercantilism A prominent economic philosophy in the 16th and 17th centuries that equated the accumulation and possession of gold and other international monetary assets, such as foreign currency reserves, with national wealth. Although this point of view is generally discredited among 20th-century economists and trade policy experts, some contemporary politicians still favor policies designed to create trade "surpluses," such as import substitution and tariff protection for domestic industries, as essential to national economic strength.
See also: Industrial Policy, Protectionism, Balance of Trade, Currency, Import Substitution,

Mercantilist A person who believes in or advocates mercantilism.
See also: Mercantilism,

Merchandise Exports And Imports Refer to: Balance of Trade, Current Account,

MFA Refer to: Multi-Fiber Arrangement Regarding International Trade in Textiles,

MFN Refer to: Most-Favored-Nation Treatment,

Microeconomics That part of economics that is primarily concerned with the study of individual decision makers, including consumers, entrepreneurs and firms, the way in which their decisions interrelate to determine relative prices of goods and factors of production, and the quantities of these that will be bought and sold.
See also: Consumers, Entrepreneurs, Macroeconomics, Management, Market Economy, Monopoly, Price, Private Sector,

MIGA Refer to: Multilateral Investment Guarantee Agency,

Minimum Valuation Customs valuation of certain low-cost items at a higher-than-actual value.
See also: Customs, Customs Valuation Code, Valuation,

MITI A frequently used acronym designating Japan's Ministry of Trade and Industry, which has

adopted, for some years, a comprehensive economic growth and development strategy, centering on export expansion.
See also: Export Promotion, Exports, Industrial Policy, Managed Trade,

Mixed Credits A financing package that involves official government credit to supplement normal commercial credit, thus enabling an exporter to deliver goods to a buyer in another country on credit terms comparable to those of his competitors.
See also: Competitive, Credit, Exports, International Arrangement on Export Credits,

Mixed Economies Refer to: State Trading Nations,

Mixed Tariff Refer to: Compound Tariff,

MNC Refer to: Multinational Corporation,

Monetary And Financial Conference Refer to: Bretton Woods Conference,

Money Any medium of exchange that is widely accepted in payment for goods and services or to settle debts. Money also serves as a standard of value for measuring the relative worth of different goods and services and as a means of storing wealth. The number of units of money required to buy a commodity is its price. Without money, trade would be reduced to barter. The "real" value of money declines during inflationary periods.
See also: Barter, Capital, Credit, Currency, Inflation, Medium of Exchange, Price, Purchasing Power, Value ,

Monopoly The condition that exists in a market when a single supplier controls the preponderant supply of a product to such an extent that it can set quantity and prices for maximum profitability with little or no regard for the pressures of demand and supply that operate in competitive economic markets. A high tariff or non-tariff barrier to imports can give a non-competitive producer a monopoly position for a particular product within a domestic market.
See also: Antitrust, Cartel, Competitive, Market, Microeconomics, Price, Protection, Supply,

Montreal Ministerial The mid-term review of progress in the Uruguay Round was held in Montreal, Canada, in December 1988. During the ministerial meeting, frameworks for completing the negotiations were agreed in 11 out of the 15 negotiating areas, with no agreement reached on frameworks for agriculture, intellectual property, textiles and safeguards.
See also: Montreal Protocol, Uruguay Round,

Montreal Protocol A multilateral agreement negotiated in 1988 to reduce and eventually eliminate the use of chlorofluorocarbons and halogens so as to prevent erosion of the ozone layer. The agreement is noteworthy for allowing the use of trade sanctions to enforce its provisions.
See also: Montreal Ministerial, Uruguay Round,

Most-Favored-Nation Treatment (MFN) The policy of non-discrimination in trade policy that provides to all trading partners the same customs and tariff treatment given to the so-called "most-favored-nation." This fundamental principle was a feature of U.S. trade policy as early as 1778. Since 1923 the United States has incorporated an "unconditional" most-favored-nation clause in its trade agreements, binding the contracting governments to confer upon each other all the most favorable trade concessions that either may grant to any other country subsequent to the signing of the agreement. The United States now applies this provision to its trade with all of its trading partners except for those specifically excluded by law. The MFN principle has also provided the foundation of the world trading system since the end of World War II. All Contracting Parties to GATT apply MFN treatment to one another under Article I of GATT.
See also: Column 1 Rates, Concession, Conditional Most-Favored-Nation Treatment, Customs,

Discrimination, Enabling Clause, General Agreement on Tariffs and Trade, Principal Suppliers, Reciprocity, Tariff,

MTN Refer to: Multilateral Trade Negotiations,

MTO Refer to: Multilateral Trade Organization,

Multi-Fiber Arrangement Regarding International Trade In Textiles (MFA) An internationally agreed derogation from GATT rules that allows an importing signatory country to apply quantitative restrictions on textile imports when it considers them necessary to prevent market disruption, even when such restrictions would otherwise be contrary to GATT rules. The objective of the MFA is to reconcile the interests of textiles-exporting and textiles-importing countries by permitting an orderly expansion of trade while avoiding market disruption. But the global system of bilateral textile and apparel quotas that comprise the MFA is scheduled to come to an end. Under the Uruguay Round agreement, countries agreed to eliminate the MFA quotas in phases to begin July 1, 1995 and to end July 1, 2005. At the end of the 10-year transition period rules on textile trade will be fully integrated into those of the World Trade Organization being set up under the Uruguay Round accord. All countries that are signatories to the Uruguay Round accord will be subject to the new textile agreement whether or not they were signatories to the MFA. MFA rules provide that quantitative restrictions should not reduce imports to levels below those attained during the preceding year, and should, if continued, permit trade to expand by specified percentages. Since an importing country may impose such quotas unilaterally to restrict rapidly rising textiles imports, most important textiles-exporting countries consider it advantageous to enter into bilateral agreements with the principal textiles-importing countries. The MFA went into effect on January 1, 1974, was renewed in December 1977, in December 1981, again in July 1986 and most recently in July 1991. The MFA succeeded the Long Term Agreement on International Trade in Cotton Textiles ("The LTA"), which had been in effect since 1962. Whereas the LTA applied only to cotton textiles, the MFA also applies to wool, man-made (synthetic) fiber, and silk blend and vegetable fiber textiles and apparel products.
See also: Bilateral Trade Agreement, General Agreement on Tariffs and Trade, Market Disruption, Quantitative Restrictions, Sensitive Products, Textiles,

Multilateral Having a number of participating "sides," or countries.
See also: Bilateral, Unilateral,

Multilateral Agreement An international compact involving three or more parties. For example, GATT has been, since its establishment in 1947, seeking to promote trade liberalization through multilateral negotiations.
See also: Codes of Conduct, General Agreement on Tariffs and Trade, Liberalization, Multilateral Trade Negotiations, Negotiations,

Multilateral Aid Development assistance given by donors to recipient countries through international institutions.
See also: Bilateral Aid, Official Development Assistance,

Multilateral Investment Guarantee Agency (MIGA) The Multilateral Investment Guarantee Agency began operations in April 1988. As part of the World Bank Group, MIGA was formed to encourage the flow of private foreign investment to its member developing countries by providing insurance against non-commercial risks, and by providing promotional and advisory services. MIGA's guarantee program protects investors against losses from currency transfer, expropriation, war, and civil disturbance, and investment-related breach of contract by host governments. MIGA works in close cooperation with the World Bank, the International Development Association, and the International Finance Corporation to promote sound investment policies, thereby assisting developing countries in creating attractive investment

environments for private foreign direct investment.
See also: International Development Association, International Finance Corporation, World Bank,

Multilateral Safeguard System Refer to: Safeguards,

Multilateral Trade Negotiations (MTN) Eight Rounds of "Multilateral Trade Negotiations" have been held under the auspices of GATT since 1947. Each Round represented a discrete and lengthy series of bargaining sessions among the participating Contracting Parties in search of mutually beneficial agreements aimed at the reduction of barriers to world trade. The agreements ultimately reached at the conclusion of each Round became new GATT commitments and thus amounted to important steps in the evolution of the world trading system. The acronym "MTN" most frequently refers to the Tokyo Round.
See also: Dillon Round, Kennedy Round, Multilateral Trade Organization, Negotiations; Reciprocity, Round, Tokyo Round, Uruguay Round,

Multilateral Trade Organization (MTO) Umbrella organization, replacing GATT, to oversee implementation of the Uruguay Round results. Also known at the World Trade Organization (WTO) or International Trade Organization (ITO).
See also: Multilateral Trade Negotiations, Uruguay Round, World Trade Organization,

Multinational Corporation (MNC) A large commercial organization with affiliates operating in a number of different countries. Sometimes referred to, especially in the United Nations, as a transnational corporation.
See also: Euro-dollars, Subsidiary,

Mutatis Mutandis Phrase signifying "the necessary changes having been made"; "substituting new terms."

Mutuality Of Benefits Refer to: Reciprocity,

NAFTA Refer to: North American Free Trade Agreement,

NAM Refer to: Non-Aligned Movement,

National Treatment A basic principle of international trade rules and policy. National treatment obligations generally prohibit discrimination on the basis of foreign nationality. GATT Article III, the central national treatment obligation in GATT, prohibits discrimination between imported and domestically produced goods with respect to internal taxation or other government regulation.
See also: Codes of Conduct, Restrictive Business Practices, Unfair Trade Practices, Codes of Conduct, Restrictive Business Practices, Unfair Trade Practices,

National Treatment A basic principle of international trade rules and policy. National treatment obligations generally prohibit discrimination on the basis of foreign nationality. GATT Article III, the central national treatment obligation in GATT, prohibits discrimination between imported and domestically produced goods with respect to internal taxation or other government regulation.
See also: Codes of Conduct, Restrictive Business Practices, Unfair Trade Practices, Codes of Conduct, Restrictive Business Practices, Unfair Trade Practices,

Negotiations Bargaining between and among representatives of governments seeking a mutually beneficial exchange of concessions.
See also: Concession, Multilateral Trade Negotiations, Offer List, Principal Supplier, Reciprocity, Request List, Round, United States Trade Representative,

Newly Industrializing Economies (NIEs) Relatively advanced developing countries whose

industrial production and exports have grown rapidly in recent years. Examples include Brazil, Hong Kong, Korea, Mexico, Singapore and Taiwan.
See also: Developing Countries, Graduation,

NIEs Refer to: Newly Industrializing Economies,

Nominal Tariff Rate The rate of duty charged on the gross value of a given product.
See also: Effective Tariff Rate, Tariff, Tariff Escalation,

Non-Aligned Movement (NAM) A loose coalition of developing countries that meets at the head of state level every few years in an attempt to coordinate positions on international political and economic issues. The movement traces its conceptual foundations to the Asian-African Conference at Bandung in 1955, under the inspiration of India (Nehru), Egypt (Nasser) and Yugoslavia (Tito). The first NAM Summit Conference took place in Belgrade in 1961; the second in Cairo in 1964; the third in Lusaka in 1970; the fourth in Algiers in 1973; the fifth in Colombo in 1976; the sixth in Havana in 1980; and the seventh in New Delhi in 1983. These countries now meet under the auspices of the Group of 77. Their last meeting took place in Tehran in November 1991. A goal of that meeting was to prepare a developing country position for the February 1992 UNCTAD VIII Conference.
See also: Group of 77,

Non-Discrimination Refer to: Discrimination, General Agreement on Tariffs and Trade, Most-Favored-Nation Treatment,

Non-Market Economy A national economy in which the government seeks to determine economic activity largely through a mechanism of central planning, as in the former Soviet Union, in contrast to a market economy which depends heavily upon market forces to allocate productive resources. In a "non-market" economy, production targets, prices, costs, investment allocations, raw materials, labor, international trade and most other economic aggregates are manipulated within a national economic plan drawn up by a central planning authority; hence, the public sector makes the major decisions affecting demand and supply within the national economy.
See also: Group D, Macroeconomics, Market Economy, Private Sector, Public Sector, State Trading Nations,

Non-Reciprocity Refer to: Framework Agreement, Reciprocity,

Non-Tariff Barriers (NTBs) Government measures other than tariffs that restrict imports. Such measures have become relatively more conspicuous impediments to trade as tariffs have been reduced during the period since World War II.
See also: Codes of Conduct, Concession, Consular Formalities and Documentation, Exchange Controls, Export Subsidies, Government Procurement Policies and Practices, Licensing, Non-Tariff Measures, Packaging, Labeling and Marking Regulations, Prior Deposits,

Non-Tariff Measures (NTMS) Government measures that may have a potential for restricting international trade even though they may not always do so, such as import monitoring systems and variable levies, as well as measures that are internationally perceived as trade restrictive, even though a trade-restricting intent or effect cannot objectively be ascribed to them.
See also: Non-Tariff Barriers, Variable Levy,

North Refer to: Developed Countries,

North American Free Trade Agreement (NAFTA) In June 1991 the United States, Canada and Mexico initiated negotiation of a comprehensive free trade agreement aimed at: eliminating over a mutually agreed upon time period all tariffs on trade between the three countries; reducing

impediments to trade in services; removing most restrictions on foreign investment among the signatory countries; ensuring adequate intellectual property protection. The negotiations were concluded in August 1992, and the draft text is structured along the lines of the U.S.-Canada Free Trade Agreement. The Clinton administration negotiated supplemental agreements on labor and environmental issues, and Congress approved the whole package of NAFTA agreements in November 1993. President Clinton signed the legislation into law in December. NAFTA went into effect January 1, 1994. It is being viewed as a testing ground for possible future agreements to be negotiated under the Enterprise for the Americas Initiative.
See also: Common External Tariff, Customs Union, Enterprise for the Americas Initiative, Free Trade Area Agreement, General Agreement of Tariffs and Trade, U.S.-Canada Free Trade Agreement, U.S.-Canada Trade Commission,

North-South Trade The exchange of goods and services between developed countries (the "North") and developing countries (the "South"). The Generalized System of Preferences negotiated at UNCTAD II and the Framework Agreement negotiated in the Tokyo Round were intended to stimulate additional North-South Trade.
See also: Developed Countries, Developing Countries, Framework Agreement, Generalized System of Preferences, International Trade Center UNCTAD/GATT, Reciprocity, Special and Differential Treatment, United Nations Conference on Trade and Development,

NTBs Refer to: Non-Tariff Barriers,

NTMs Refer to: Non-Tariff Measures,

Nullification (Of Trade Rights) Refer to: Consultations, Dispute Settlement,

ODA Refer to: Official Development Assistance,

OECD Refer to: Organization for Economic Cooperation and Development,

OECD Agreement On Export Credits Refer to: International Arrangement on Export Credits,

Offer List A selected list of measures through which a country participating in trade negotiations proposes to broaden access to its market in exchange for comparable concessions from its trading partners. A country's initial offer list during a given "Round" of negotiations represents its early response to the request lists submitted by its trading partners and may subsequently be lengthened or shortened, depending upon the responses of other countries to its own request lists. In addition to proposals for broadening market access through tariff reductions and expanded coverage under codes of conduct, offer lists may suggest exceptions to an agreed formula for tariff reductions on all other products.
See also: Codes of Conduct, Concession, Linear Reduction of Tariffs, Market Access, Negotiations, Principal Supplier, Request List, Round, Sensitive Products,

Official Development Assistance (ODA) Economic or technical assistance extended to developing countries by the governments of developed countries and international organizations, as contrasted with gifts, loans and investments financed by the private sector. Official development assistance is construed by the OECD Development Committee as including only "concessional" transfers to developing countries, meaning that all or part of each ODA transaction is a grant or is loaned at rate of interest and/or on repayment terms more beneficial to the recipient than market rates and terms.
See also: Additionality, Bilateral Aid, Development Assistance Committee, Economic Development, Interest, Least Developed Countries, Multilateral Aid, Soft Loan, Transfer Payments,

Offset Requirements Conditions imposed on certain large exporters in other countries by importing governments, usually to reduce cash outflows as by requiring the exporter to purchase goods or services produced in the importing country, establish manufacturing facilities in the country, or use locally produced components in manufacturing. Offset requirements are frequently associated with sales of military equipment.
See also: Countertrade,

OMAs Refer to: Orderly Marketing Agreements,

Omnibus Trade And Competitiveness Act Of 1988 Legislation passed by the U.S. Congress in August 1988 and signed into law on August 23, 1988, to enhance the competitiveness of American industry. Its major purposes were to: authorize the negotiation of reciprocal trade agreements; strengthen U.S. trade laws; improve development and management of U.S. trade strategy; and through these actions, improve standards of living in the world. The act made many changes in U.S. trade law, inter alia, significant changes to Section 301 and the adoption of Section 301 variants: "Super" 301 (§ 1302 of the act) provisions required, in 1989 and 1990, the U.S. trade representative (USTR) to identify priority practices (trade distorting practices whose elimination might substantially increase U.S. exports) and priority countries (countries with the highest trade barriers and best markets for U.S. Exports) and to initiate Section 301 investigations of such practices; "Special 301" (§ 1303 of the act), requires USTR to identify and self-initiate expedited Section 301 investigations of countries which deny adequate protection of intellectual property rights; "Telecommunications 301" (§ 1377 of the act) requires USTR to review, on an annual basis, trade agreements which involve telecommunications products or services to determine whether the foreign country is failing to comply with the agreement or is otherwise denying opportunities to U.S. Telecommunication products and services. In March 1994, President Clinton signed an executive order reinstituting the Super 301 provision; under this order USTR will identify in 1994 and 1995 priority foreign practices which may be actionable under Section 301.
See also: Concession, Export Subsidies, Intellectual Property, Patent, Section 301, Special 301, Technology, Trade Act of 1988, Transfer of Technology, Unfair Trade Practices,

One Hundred Thirteen (113) Committee A body of representatives from EC member states that assists the EC Commission in trade negotiations with third countries.
See also: European Community,

OPEC Refer to: Organization of Petroleum Exporting Countries,

OPIC Refer to: Overseas Private Investment Corporation,

Orderly Marketing Agreements (OMAs) International compacts negotiated between two or more governments, in which the trading partners agree to restrain the growth of trade in specified "sensitive" products, usually through the imposition of export quotas. Orderly marketing agreements are intended to ensure that future trade increases will not disrupt, threaten or impair competitive industries or their workers in importing countries.
See also: Export Quotas, Market Disruption, Sensitive Products, Voluntary Restraint Agreements,

Organization For Economic Cooperation And Development (OECD) An international agency based in Paris, through which some 24 developed countries (United States, Canada, Japan, Australia, New Zealand and countries of Western Europe) review international economic issues and coordinate their policies, looking toward the expansion of world trade and investment and the economic development of developing countries. The OECD succeeded the OEEC in 1961, after the post-World War II economic reconstruction of Europe had been largely accomplished.
See also: Developed Countries, Development Assistance Committee, Group B, International Arrangement on Export Credits, Organization for European Economic Cooperation ,

Organization For European Economic Cooperation (OEEC) An intergovernmental organization created in 1948 by 16 Western European countries to plan and implement the European Recovery Program, better known as the Marshall Plan, following the economic devastation left by World War II. The OEEC was superceded in 1961 by the OECD.
See also: European Recovery Program, Organization for Economic Cooperation and Development,

Organization Of Petroleum Exporting Countries (OPEC) A cartel comprising 13 leading oil-producing countries that seek to coordinate oil production and pricing policies.
See also: Cartel, Developing Countries,

Overseas Private Investment Corporation (OPIC) OPIC is a self-sustaining U.S. government agency whose purpose is to promote economic growth in developing countries by encouraging U.S. private investment in those nations through two principal programs: (1) financing investment projects through direct loans and/or loan guarantees and (2) insuring investment projects against a broad range of risks, such as expropriation. These programs are backed by the full faith and credit of the U.S. government.
See also: Additionality, Bilateral Aid, Developing Countries, Official Development Assistance, Soft Loan, Transfer Payments,

Packaging, Labeling And Marking Regulations The requirement or regulation, usually by the importing country, that imported goods be packaged, labeled or marked according to particular guidelines. Although ostensibly required to protect consumers, non-standard packaging, labeling and marking requirements frequently pose problems for exporters and may function as non-tariff barriers.
See also: Non-Tariff Barriers, Quarantine, Sanitary, Health Laws and Regulations, Standards,

Panel Of Experts An ad hoc group of experienced individuals with specialized skills established for specified purposes. Under GATT dispute settlement procedures, for example, panels composed of three to five trade policy experts may be designated to arbitrate disagreements over trade policy between governments with differing interpretations of their GATT obligations.
See also: Arbitration, Codes of Conduct, Dispute Settlement, General Agreement on Tariffs and Trade, Working Party,

Par Value The official fixed exchange rate between two currencies or between a currency and a specific weight of gold or a basket of currencies.
See also: Currency, Exchange Rate, International Monetary Fund,

Paris Club A popular designation for meetings between representatives of a developing country that wishes to renegotiate its "official" debt (normally excluding debts owed by and to the private sector without official guarantees) and representatives of the relevant creditor governments and international institutions. Such meetings normally take place at the initiative of a debtor country that wishes to consolidate all or part of its debt service payments falling due over a specified period. The meetings are traditionally chaired by a senior official of the French Treasury Department. Comparable meetings occasionally take place in London and in New York for countries that wish to renegotiate repayment terms for their debts to private banks. Such meetings are sometimes called "creditor clubs."

Paris Conference On The Least Developed Countries Refer to: Substantial New Program of Action,

Paris Union Refer to: World Intellectual Property Organization,

Part IV Of The GATT : Articles XXXVI, XXXVII, and XXXVIII of the GATT, added to the General Agreement in 1965, concerning the special needs of the developing countries (LDCs). Outlines principles and objectives for GATT treatment of LDCs, committing Contracting Parties to assist these countries through trade liberalization, and laying down the principle that developed countries should not expect LDCs, in the course of trade negotiations, to make contributions inconsistent with their individual needs.
See also: Framework Agreement, Enabling Clause,

Patent A patent is a 17-year grant by the government which covers any new, useful and non-obvious process, machine, manufacture or composition of matter or any new, useful and obvious improvements thereof. The grant is the right to exclude others from making, using or selling the invention for that period of time after which it passes into the public domain. See also Intellectual Property; Trade-Related Aspects of Intellectual Property Rights; Technology; Transfer of Technology; and World Intellectual Property Organization.

Peril Point A hypothetical limit beyond which a reduction in tariff protection would cause serious injury to a domestic industry. U.S. legislation in 1949 that extended the Trade Agreements Act of 1934 required the Tariff Commission to establish such "peril points" for U.S. industries. This requirement, which was a constraint on U.S. negotiating positions in early GATT Rounds, was eliminated by the Trade Expansion Act of 1962.
See also: Protection, Round, Safeguards, Trade Agreements Act of 1934, Trade Expansion Act of 1962, U.S. International Trade Commission,

Petition
See also: Countervailing Duties, Dumping, Escape Clause,

PL 480 Refer to: Public Law 480,

Plaza Accord An agreement in September 1985 by the G-5 (the United States, Japan, Germany, France and the United Kingdom) to take concrete actions aimed at reducing external imbalances and achieving exchange rates consistent with underlying economic fundamentals.
See also: Group of 7,

Port Of Entry Point at which individuals and imported goods enter a country and clear its national customs.
See also: Customs, Transit Zone,

Potential Uncollected Dumping Duty (PUDD) The aggregate amount of dumping for all U.S. sales of covered merchandise by a foreign manufacturer. In an initial anti-dumping investigation, this value is used to determine the prospective dumping margin. It is called potential uncollected dumping duty because it represents the amount of duty that the importer would owe if an annual review were conducted.
See also: Dumping, Omnibus Trade and Competitiveness Act of 1988, Tariff,

PPA Refer to: Protocol of Provisional Application,

Preferences Special advantages extended by importing countries to exports from particular trading partners, usually by admitting their goods at tariff rates below those imposed on imports from other supplying countries.
See also: Double-Column Tariff, Framework Agreement, Generalized System of Preferences, Global System of Trade Preferences, Lomé Convention, Margin of Preferences, Single-Column Tariff, Special and Differential Treatment, Tariff,

Premium A regular payment paid for an insurance policy that provides protection against a risk.

See also: Insurance,

Price The value of something expressed in terms of money, or the amount of money paid for it. Economists define the "equilibrium" price of goods and services in a competitive market economy as the level at which demand for them will match their supply.
See also: Demand, Equilibrium, Goods, Inflation, Market Economy, Market Forces, Microeconomics, Money, Monopoly, Services,

Price Elasticity Of Demand The percentage change in demand for a given product likely to result if its price changes by one percent. A slight lowering or raising of a tariff will have a larger effect on the volume of imports of a product with a high price elasticity of demand than the same tariff change will affect imports of a product with a low price elasticity of demand.
See also: Demand, Price, Purchasing Power,

Price Elasticity Of Supply The percentage change in supply for a given product likely to result if its price changes by one percent.
See also: Price, Supply,

Price Stabilization Refer to: Buffer Stocks, Managed Trade,

Primary Commodity A commodity in its raw or unprocessed state, such as iron ore. In contrast, pig iron is considered a semi-processed product, and a steel girder is a manufactured item.
See also: Commodity, Integrated Program for Commodities, Production, Tariff Escalation,

Principal Supplier The country that is the most important source of a particular product imported by another country. In GATT negotiations, a country offering to reduce its tariff or other barriers to imports of a particular item generally expects the principal supplier of that item to reduce restrictions on its imports of a product for which the first country is the principal supplier. Both countries then automatically grant the same concessions to all other countries to which they accord most-favored-nation treatment, including all Contracting Parties to GATT.
See also: Concession, General Agreement on Tariffs and Trade, Item-by-Item Negotiations, Most-Favored-Nation Treatment, Negotiations, Offer List, Round,

Prior Deposits Governments sometimes require that an importer deposit, in domestic or foreign currency, a specified sum, usually corresponding to a certain percentage of the value of the imported product. Such deposits are characteristically held without interest, sometimes for many months--from the time an order is placed until after the import transaction is completed--and hence represent a real cost. The purpose of prior deposits is usually to discourage imports, particularly for balance-of-payments reasons, and they generally are recognized as non-tariff barriers that impede trade. Prior deposits must usually be made at the time an import license is granted.
See also: Licensing, Non-Tariff Barriers,

Private Sector The part of a national economy comprised of privately owned enterprises and individuals and non-profit making organizations, as contrasted with the public sector, comprising government and government-controlled entities.
See also: Market Economy, Official Development Assistance, Price, Public Sector,

Process Patent A process patent is a process or method which consists of an act, operation or step or series thereof performed upon a specified subject matter to produce a physical result.
See also: Patent,

Procurement Refer to: Government Procurement Policies and Practices,

Producer Goods Refer to: Capital Goods,

Production The process of creating or changing the form of commodities, as through fabrication, manufacture, extraction, processing, curing or aging.
See also: Commodity, Consumption, Industrial Revolution, Management, Primary Commodity, Profit, Tariff Escalation, Technology, Welfare,

Profit The net earnings accruing from the successful production or sale of goods and services: that is, the residual remaining to the entrepreneur after all payments for capital (interest), land (rent), labor (including management costs, salaries and wages), raw materials, taxes and depreciation. If the business fares poorly, profits may be negative, in which case they become losses.
See also: Entrepreneur, Management; , Market, Production, Risk,

Progressive Tariff Refer to: Tariff Escalation,

Promissory Notes Refer to: Commercial Paper,

Property An asset whose ownership gives the right to present or future material benefits, as protected by law. The term property refers not only to the possession of material goods, such as land, buildings and production facilities, but also to less tangible assets, such as manufacturing processes, design and brand names.
See also: Copyright, Intellectual Property, Patent, Production, Security, Trademark, World Intellectual Property Organization,

Protection Government measures--including tariff and non-tariff barriers--that raise the cost of imported goods or otherwise restrict their entry into a market, and thus strengthen the competitive position of domestic goods.
See also: Competitive, Import Relief, Infant Industry Argument, Market, Monopoly, Non-Tariff Barriers, Peril Point, Protectionism, Quantitative Restrictions, Safeguards,

Protectionism The deliberate use or encouragement of restrictions on imports to enable relatively inefficient domestic producers to compete successfully with foreign producers.
See also: Competitive, Effective Tariff Rate, Imports, Infant Industry Argument, Liberal, Managed Trade, Mercantilism, Non-Tariff Barriers, Orderly Marketing Agreements, Protection,

Protocol Of Accession The legal document that records the obligations agreed to as a consequence of accession to an international accord or organization.
See also: Accession, Concession, State Trading Nations ,

Protocol Of Provisional Application (PPA) The agreement among the original GATT Contracting Parties to exempt from GATT provisions trade measures established by domestic legislation in force at the time of acceptance of the GATT. The protocol was intended to be temporary, pending implementation of the Havana Charter or definitive acceptance of GATT provisions by the Contracting Parties, but it has remained in effect, and countries that signed it in 1947 continue to invoke it to defend certain practices that are otherwise inconsistent with their GATT obligations. Countries that acceded to the GATT after 1947 have similar provisions incorporated in their protocols of accession.
See also: Accession, Contracting Party, Discrimination, General Agreement on Tariffs and Trade, Grandfather Clause, Protocol of Accession, Residual Restrictions,

Provisional Accession Refer to: Accession,

Public Law 480 (Agricultural Trade Development and Assistance Act of 1954) Provides for the

disposition of U.S. farm products outside the United States. Title I spells out conditions under which such products can be sold to developing countries for their own currencies and the purposes for which the proceeds of such sales can be used in the purchasing country. Title II authorizes the transfer of U.S. farm products to developing countries for economic development purposes. Title III permits the donation of surplus products through U.S. voluntary agencies that carry out relief operations in other countries. Title IV provides for agreements between the U.S. government and other governments and private organizations purchasing surplus U.S. farm products.
See also: Section 22, Surplus,

Public Sector The part of a national economy accounted for by government expenditures and state-owned or state-controlled enterprises.
See also: Non-Market Economy, Private Sector, State Trading Nations,

PUDD Refer to: Potential Uncollected Dumping Duty,

Punta Del Este Ministerial The Uruguay Round of Multilateral Trade Negotiations was launched in Punta del Este, Uruguay, in September 1986 at a ministerial meeting that produced the Punta del Este Declaration. The declaration included the objectives and agenda for the negotiations, and was the result of consultations that began in 1985.
See also: Uruguay Round,

Purchasing Power The ability of consumers to purchase goods and services, based on their possession of money and their recourse to credit. Aggregate purchasing power within a market or a national economy reflects total disposable income after taxes, and hence the level of employment.
See also: Credit, Demand, Inflation, Money, Price Elasticity of Demand,

Pure Risk Refer to: Risk,

QRs Refer to: Quantitative Restrictions,

Quantitative Restrictions (QRs) QUANTITATIVE RESTRICTIONS (QRs). Explicit limits, or quotas, on the physical amounts of particular commodities that can be imported or exported during a specified time period, usually measured by volume but sometimes by value. The quota may be applied on a "selective" basis, with varying limits set according to the country of origin, or on a global basis that only specifies the total limit and thus tends to benefit more efficient suppliers. Quotas are frequently administered through a system of licensing. GATT Article XI generally prohibits the use of quantitative restrictions, except under conditions specified by other GATT articles: Article XIX permits quotas to "safeguard" certain industries from damage by rapidly rising imports; Articles XII and XVIII provide that quotas may be imposed for balance of payments reasons under circumstances laid out in Article XV; Article XX permits special measures to apply to public health, gold stocks, items of archaeological or historic interest, and several other categories of goods; and Article XXI recognizes the overriding importance of national security. Article XIII provides that quantitative restrictions, whenever applied, should be non-discriminatory
See also: Balance of Payments Consultations, Discrimination, Export Quotas, Export Restraints, General Agreement on Tariffs and Trade, Licensing, Multi-Fiber Arrangement Regarding International Trade in Textiles, Residual Restrictions, Safeguards, Section 22,

Quarantine, Sanitary And Health Laws And Regulations Government measures to protect consumer, animal and plant health by regulating the use of dangerous preservatives and other additives in foods. The lack of internationally accepted standards makes it difficult to distinguish between legitimate health standards and protectionist measures. A Uruguay Round agreement

covering sanitary and phytosanitary standards will recognize norms set by specified international standard-setting bodies as the baseline standards for trade, ensure to the maximum extent possible that standards are scientifically justifiable, and for the first time, establish a meaningful dispute settlement procedure for health and sanitary issues.
See also: Customs and Administrative Entry Procedures, Discrimination, Packaging, Labeling and Marking Regulations, Standards, Uruguay Round,

Quid Pro Quo Refer to: Reciprocity,

Quotas Refer to: Quantitative Restrictions, Tariff Quota,

RBPs Refer to: Restrictive Business Practices,

Reciprocal Trade Agreements Act Of 1934 Refer to: Most-Favored-Nation Treatment, Trade Agreements Act of 1934,

Reciprocity The practice by which governments extend similar concessions to each other, as when one government lowers its tariffs or other barriers impeding its imports in exchange for equivalent concessions from a trading partner on barriers affecting its exports (a "balance of concessions"). Reciprocity has traditionally been a principal objective of negotiators in GATT "Rounds." Reciprocity is also defined as "mutuality of benefits," "quid pro quo" and "equivalence of advantages." GATT Part IV (especially GATT Article XXXVI) and the "Enabling Clause"of the Tokyo Round "Framework Agreement" exempt developing countries from the rigorous application of reciprocity in their negotiations with developed countries.
See also: Competitive, Concession, Efficiency, Enabling Clause, Framework Agreement, General Agreement on Tariffs and Trade, Most-Favored-Nation Treatment, Negotiations, Principal Supplier, Round,

Regressive Taxation Refer to: Indirect Tax,

Reinsurance The shifting by agreement (known in the insurance industry as a treaty) of part of the risk (or "exposure") of the original insurer (the ceding company) to another insurer (the reinsurer). Sometimes a reinsurer will, in turn, pass on part of its risk to another reinsurer through a process known as retrocession. International reinsurance is important to developed and developing countries alike.
See also: Insurance, Risk,

Relief Refer to: Escape Clause, Import Relief, Safeguards,

Reprisals Refer to: Retaliation,

Request List A list submitted by a country to a trading partner at an early stage of trade negotiations identifying the concessions it seeks through the negotiations.
See also: Concession, Negotiations, Offer List, Round,

Reserve Currency A national currency, such as the dollar or pound sterling, or international currency such as Special Drawing Rights, used by many countries to settle debit balances in their international accounts. Central banks generally hold a large portion of their monetary reserves in reserve currencies, which are sometimes called "key" currencies.
See also: Currency, Mercantilism, Special Drawing Rights,

Reserve Preferences Tariff advantages once offered by developing countries to imports from certain developed countries that granted them preferences in turn. Reverse preferences characterized trading arrangements between the European Community and some developing

countries (the "ACP" countries) prior to the advent of the Lomé Convention.
See also: ACP Countries, European Community, Generalized System of Preferences, Lomé Convention, Preferences,

Reserves Refer to: Mercantilism, Reserve Currencies,

Residual Restrictions Quantitative restrictions maintained by governments since they became Contracting Parties to GATT, despite the general GATT prohibition against such measures.
See also: Grandfather Clause, Protocol of Provisional Application, Quantitative Restrictions,

Restitutions Payments to agricultural exporters in the European Community under the Common Agricultural Policy to cover the difference between internal and world market prices.
See also: Common Agricultural Policy, Dual Pricing, European Community, Export Subsidies, Threshold Price, Variable Levy,

Restraints Refer to: Non-Tariff Barriers, Liberalization, Tariffs,

Restrictive Business Practices (RBPs) Acts or behavior of enterprises--whether private or government-controlled--that abuse a dominant economic position and limit access to markets or otherwise unduly restrain competition. Such practices include collusion to fix export or import prices, allocate markets or customers, practice discriminatory pricing, set prices at which export goods can be resold, or otherwise restrict imports and exports. A non-binding (or "voluntary") code of conduct negotiated in UNCTAD--formally called the "Set of Multilaterally Agreed Equitable Principles and Rules for the Control of Restrictive Business Practices"--lists business practices to be avoided and recommends steps that enterprises and governments should take to discourage such activity.
See also: Anti-Trust, Cartel, Market Access, Monopoly, Unfair Trade Practices,

Retaliation The suspension of concessions or other obligations under a trade agreement, or the imposition of other barriers to trade, by a government in response to the violation of a trade agreement or the imposition of other unfair trade barriers by another government. Section 301 of the Trade Act of 1974, as amended by sections 1301-1303 of the Omnibus Trade and Competitiveness Act of 1988, provides the domestic legal authority in the United States to impose retaliatory measures in response to trade agreement violations or other unjustifiable, unreasonable or discriminatory foreign trade practices that burden or restrict U.S. commerce. Such authority includes the authority to suspend trade agreement concessions; impose duties or other import restrictions; impose fees or restrictions on services; enter into agreements with the subject country to eliminate the offending practice or to provide compensatory benefits for the United States; and restrict service sector authorizations. The actions may be taken against all countries or solely against the subject country. Most actions may be taken against any goods or economic sectors, without regard to whether the goods or economic sectors were the subject of the investigation.
See also: Beggar-Thy-Neighbor Policy, Tariff Act of 1930,

Retrocession Refer to: Reinsurance,

Right Of Establishment A basic concept in bilateral investment treaties is that one party to the agreement will permit nationals and companies of the other party to establish (and maintain) investments on a non-discriminatory(national/most-favored-nation treatment) basis. A government will not place any special obstacles (e.g., a screening process, equity limitations) in the way of a foreign investor making an investment; that investor need comply only with the requirements placed on any other investor in that sector.
See also: Bilateral, Bilateral Investment Treaty, Multilateral,

Risk Speculative risk involves the possibility of profit or loss, depending upon the success or failure of the financial or commercial venture in question. Banks also accept risks when they make loans, which may either be repaid or defaulted. Capital investors are sometimes referred to as risk bearers; their investments may be considered "venture capital" if they appear to be subject to considerable risk, as in the case of new enterprises, or "security capital" if they appear to be subject to little risk. Pure risk is involved when there is no possibility of gain, but only the possibility of loss. Insurance is concerned with pure risks, not speculative risks.
See also: Credit, Entrepreneur, Insurance, Interest, Loan, Profit, Reinsurance,

Road Tax A tax imposed by a government on the operation of motor vehicles, usually based on weight or engine displacement. Some have the effect of discriminating in favor of one type of vehicle over another.
See also: Discrimination, Excise Tax, Non-Tariff Barriers, Tax,

Round A cycle of multilateral trade negotiations under the aegis of GATT, culminating in simultaneous trade agreements among participating countries to reduce tariff and non-tariff barriers to trade. Eight "Rounds" have been completed thus far: Geneva, 1947-48; Annecy, France, 1949; Torquay, England, 1950-51; Geneva, 1956; Geneva, 1960-62 (the Dillon Round); Geneva, 1963-67 (the Kennedy Round); Geneva, 1973-79 (the Tokyo Round); and Geneva, 1986-1993 (the "Uruguay Round").
See also: Dillon Round, General Agreement on Tariffs and Trade, Kennedy Round, Liberalization, Multilateral Trade Negotiations, Negotiations, Offer List, Peril Point, Reciprocity, Request List,

Safeguards Temporary and selective measures (such as increased tariffs, tariff quotas or quantitative restrictions) explicitly designed to slow imports in order to enable a particular industry to adjust to heightened competition from foreign suppliers. Safeguard actions are known in the United States as "escape clause" actions, and authority to take such actions is provided for in various U.S. laws. GATT Article XIX--entitled "Emergency Action on Imports of Particular Products"--recognizes a country's right to withdraw or modify concessions granted earlier, or to impose new restrictions, if a product is "being imported in such increased quantities...as to cause or threaten serious injury to domestic producers" and to maintain such restrictions "for such time as may be necessary to prevent or remedy such injury." Exporters have a complementary right under GATT not to be deprived arbitrarily of access to foreign markets. Under the Uruguay Round trade accord, GATT member countries strengthened safeguard rules by clarifying existing guidelines and tightening timetables. The duration of a safeguard measure has been limited (to a maximum of eight years), as has the degree of protection it provides. GATT members also agreed to prohibit "gray area measures" (such as voluntary export restraints, orderly marketing arrangements, and other informal trade-limiting agreements designed to curtail fairly traded imports), and to phase out all such pre-existing measures within four years of the July 1, 1995 entry into force of the new World Trade Organization. All countries do, however, receive one exception that it can keep in place until January 1, 2000. There are certain exceptions for developing countries. Safeguard measures can only be applied against a product originating in a developing country if the developing country's share of imports exceeds a certain percentage of the total imports to a country and the combined import share of developing countries is not more than a certain percentage of total imports. Also developing countries may apply a safeguard measure for up to 10 years--two years longer than that permitted to industrial countries.
See also: Adjustment, Codes of Conduct, Competitive, Concession, Escape Clause, Framework Agreement, General Agreement on Tariffs and Trade, Market Access, Protectionism, Quantitative Restrictions,

Sales Tax A tax levied on the exchange of goods and services at one or more stages in the process of distribution.
See also: Distribution, Indirect Tax, Value Added Tax,

Sanctions Refer to: Embargo,

Schedule Refer to: Concession, Demand, Supply, Tariff Schedules,

Schedule Of Concessions Refer to: Bound Rates, Concession, Tariff Schedules of the United States,

Schuman Plan Refer to: European Coal and Steel Community,

SDRs Refer to: Special Drawing Rights,

Section 201 Of The Trade Act Of 1974 Section 201 is the United States' implementation of Article XIX, the "escape clause," of the GATT. Under Section 201, the U.S. International Trade Commission (USITC) investigates whether an article is being imported into the United States in such increased quantities, absolute or relative to domestic production, as to be a substantial cause of serious injury, or threat thereof, to a domestic industry. The president has discretion to follow the USITC's recommendation on relief, which cannot exceed a total period of eight years, including extensions. Relief normally takes the form of increased duties or quantitative restrictions.
See also: Escape Clause, Safeguards, Trade Act of 1974,

Section 203 (Of The Trade Act Of 1974) Refer to: Escape Clause, Trade Act of 1974,

Section 22 (Of The Agricultural Adjustment Act Of 1933, As Amended) Authorizes the U.S. president to impose quantitative restrictions on imports of agricultural products when such imports appear likely to affect price support programs operated by the U.S. Department of Agriculture. The president has imposed such quotas on imports of wheat and flour, cotton, lint, peanuts, cheese, butter and other dairy products. In 1956 the Contracting Parties of GATT authorized a waiver of Article XI prohibitions against quantitative restrictions for U.S. actions under Section 22. Since that time, the United States has submitted an annual report to the Contracting Parties on all relevant actions and the reasons for them.
See also: Public Law 480, Quantitative Restrictions, Waiver,

Section 232 Investigations Under Section 232 of the Trade Expansion Act of 1962, as amended, the U.S. Department of Commerce's Bureau of Export Administration conducts investigations of the effect of imports on U.S. national security. Investigations may be initiated based on a request of an interested party, or may be self-initiated by the Commerce Department. Among the most important criteria considered are: requirements of the defense and essential civilian sectors; maximum domestic production capacity; quantity, quality and availability of imports; impact of foreign competition on the economic welfare of the essential domestic industry; other factors relevant to the unique circumstances of the specific case. The secretary of commerce has 270 days to present his/her findings and recommendations to the president. During this time, the Commerce Department may provide the public with an opportunity to comment and present information and advice relevant to the application, if appropriate. Upon receipt of the Commerce Department report, the president has 90 days to determine whether he agrees with the Commerce Department's findings, and to determine whether to use his/her statutory authority to "adjust imports" to remove any identified national security threat. Commerce has had authority for conducting Section 232 investigations since 1980.
See also: Codes of Conduct, Non-Tariff Barriers, Non-Tariff Measures, Quantitative Restrictions, Trade Expansion Act of 1962,

Section 301 Section 301 is the provision of the Trade Act of 1974, as amended, which gives the U.S. trade representative the authority to negotiate to eliminate a large range of foreign trade practices. The authority to take such action requires a finding that a foreign government has

denied U.S. rights under a trade agreement, or has taken action that is inconsistent with, or otherwise denies benefits to the United States under a trade agreement; or engaged in an act, policy or practice that is unjustifiable, unreasonable or discriminatory and that burdens or restricts U.S. commerce.
See also: Concession, Export Subsidies, Special 301, Super 301, Trade Act of 1974, Unfair Trade Practices,

Section 332 Of The Tariff Act Of 1930 Section 332 of the Tariff Act of 1930 provides the basic statutory authority for the U.S. International Trade Commission to conduct general fact-finding investigations and issue reports on any matter relating to trade. Such reports do not contain recommendations unless they have been specifically requested, and do not provide a legal basis for other trade actions by the president. Investigations conducted by the USITC under section 332 are instituted in response to a request from the Committee on Ways and Means of the U.S. House of Representatives, the Committee on Finance of the U.S. Senate, either branch of the Congress, the president, the U.S. trade representative under authority delegated by the president, or upon the Commission's own motion.
See also: Tariff Act of 1930,

Section 337 Section 337 of the Tariff Act of 1930 protects U.S. industries from imports which infringe valid patents, copyrights, trademarks and other intellectual property rights. Parties can obtain relief in the form of cease and desist and exclusion orders if they succeed in showing they are a "domestic industry" under the statute and that their intellectual property right is valid and infringed. Economic injury does not need to be demonstrated regarding patents and federally registered trademarks, copyrights and semiconductor mask works. For other forms of intellectual property, economic injury must be demonstrated. The president may approve, disapprove or fail to disapprove any U.S. International Trade Commission (USITC) order within a 60-day review period. The president may disapprove a USITC exclusion order for policy reasons, which include the effect of the order on the public health and welfare, competitive conditions in the U.S. economy, the production of like or directly competitive items in the United States, the effect of the order on U.S. consumers and the impact of an order on foreign relations.
See also: Copyright, Intellectual Property, Patents, Tariff Act of 1930, Trademark, Trade-Related Aspects of Intellectual Property,

Section 406 Refers to Section 406 of the Trade Act of 1974 which was established to provide a remedy against market disruption caused by imports into the United States from communist countries. The provisions of Section 406, as amended by the Omnibus Trade and Competitiveness Act of 1988, are similar to those under Sections 201-203 of the Trade Act of 1974. However, Section 406 provides a lower standard of injury causation and, unlike Section 201, the investigation can be brought against imports from a specific country rather than all imports of a specific product. Section 406 requires the U.S. International Trade Commission (USITC) to investigate complaints filed by domestic industries or workers claiming that imports from a communist country are causing market disruption with respect to a domestically produced article. If the USITC finds that market disruption exists, it must recommend to the president relief in the form of temporary import restrictions in the form of tariffs, quotas, or tariff quotas to prevent or remedy such market disruption.
See also: Import Relief, Protectionism, Safeguards, Trade Act of 1974, U.S. International Trade Commission,

Security A document giving title to property as collateral for a bank loan. Also saleable income yielding paper traded in a stock exchange, such as stocks and shares.
See also: Broker, Capital Market, Commercial Paper, Loan, Property, Spot Market,

Security Capital Refer to: Risk,

Selective Quotas Refer to: Quantitative Restrictions, Safeguards,

Self-Initiation The Office of the U.S. Trade Representative (USTR) may self-initiate a section 301 investigation or may do so in response to a petition from an interested person. The USTR retains discretion whether or not to initiate an investigation.
See also: Section 301,

Semiconductor Arrangement The U.S.-Japan Semiconductor Arrangement, which came into effect August 1, 1991, contains provisions to improve access to the Japanese market for foreign capital-affiliated semiconductor producers. It also provides for the expeditious processing by the U.S. government of anti-dumping complaints filed by domestic semiconductor producers. The arrangement, which replaced the 1986 Semiconductor Arrangement, is in force for five years.
See also: Bilateral Trade Agreement, Binding Concession, Trade Agreement,

Semi-Processed Product Refer to: Primary Commodity, Tariff Escalation,

Sensitive Products Domestically produced goods considered economically and politically important in a country whose competitive position would be threatened if protection against the imports of similar goods were reduced. The steel and textiles industries in many developed countries, for example, employ large numbers of workers, often in communities that cannot in the short term offer alternative employment. For these reasons, there has been strong opposition to the reduction of tariff and other trade-restricting measures affecting sensitive products.
See also: Adjustment, Competitive, Escape Clause, Generalized System of Preferences, Liberalization, Linear Reduction of Tariffs, Orderly Marketing Agreements, Protection, Textiles,

Services Economic activities--such as transportation, banking, insurance, tourism, telecommunications, advertising, the entertainment industry, data processing and consulting--that are normally consumed as they are produced, as contrasted with economic goods that are more tangible. Service industries, which are usually labor intensive, have become increasingly important in domestic and international trade since at least the 1920s. Services account for about two-thirds of the economic activity of the United States, and a rapidly increasing percentage of U.S. exports. Traditional GATT rules have not applied the same discipline to restrain the imposition of non-tariff barriers to trade in services that has been applied to international trade in goods. The establishment, and incorporation into GATT, of disciplines on trade in services was one of the major objectives of the Uruguay Round. The Uruguay Round agreement establishes a framework to permit freer trade in over 140 sectors including construction and tourism. It sets some basic rules including national treatment, transparency and recognition requirements for purposes of permitting foreign nationals to be professionally licensed or certified in another market. Negotiations aimed at agreement in some sectors including financial services and maritime services are continuing in 1996.
See also: GATT Ministerial Meeting of 1982, Goods, Insurance, Invisible Trade, Price, Structural Change, Structural Impediments Initiative, Uruguay Round, Utility,

Single-Column Tariff A tariff schedule listing only one duty rate for each imported product. The United States maintained a single-column tariff schedule until 1909, when special preferences were instituted for products imported from Cuba and the Philippines.
See also: Column 1 Rates, Column 2 Rates, Preferences, Tariff, Tariff Schedules of the United States,

Smoot-Hawley Tariff Act Of 1930 Refer to: Tariff Act of 1930,

Snapback Snapback is a return to earlier and usually higher tariff levels.
See also: Tariff Schedules, Tariff,

SNPA Refer to: Substantial New Program of Action,

Social Overhead Capital Refer to: Infrastructure,

Social Security Charges Refer to: Direct Tax,

Socialist Economies Refer to: State Trading Nations,

Soft Loan A credit providing for significantly easier repayment terms than credits that are normally obtainable from commercial banks. A soft loan frequently involves a grace period of several years and only a small servicing charge.
See also: Credit, Interest, International Development Association, Least Developed Countries, Loan, Official Development Assistance,

South Refer to: Developing Countries,

South-South Trade Trade between developing countries.
See also: Developing Countries, Economic Cooperation Among Developing Countries, Global System of Trade Preferences,

Special 301 Since May 1989 the U.S. trade representative (USTR) has implemented the so-called "special 301" intellectual property provision of the Omnibus Trade and Competitiveness Act of 1988. The special 301 authority is designed to formulate an overall strategy on intellectual property and market access, and to enhance the administration's ability to negotiate improvements in foreign intellectual property regimes through bilateral and/or multilateral initiatives. The statute requires the USTR to identify, on an annual basis, those foreign countries which deny adequate and effective protection of intellectual property rights or fair and equitable market access for Americans relying on intellectual property protection. Of those trading partners not making significant progress or entering into good faith negotiations, the countries that represent the most egregious cases may be identified as "priority foreign countries." Priority foreign countries are subject to investigation under section 301 conducted on an accelerated time frame.
See also: Concession, Intellectual Property, Omnibus Trade and Competitiveness Act of 1988, Section 301, Trade Act of 1988,

Special And Differential Treatment (S&D) The concept that exports of developing countries should be given preferential access to markets of developed countries, and that developing countries participating in trade negotiations need not fully reciprocate concessions they receive. This principle was first widely discussed during the Kennedy Round, leading to the adoption of Part IV of GATT, which obligated the developed countries to pursue trade policies that take into account the development needs of developing countries. The Tokyo Declaration subsequently proclaimed that exports of developing countries should receive particular benefits consistent with their trade, financial and development needs. Among proposals considered during the Tokyo Round negotiations for accomplishing this were: compensatory tariff reductions for exports of developing countries to offset any reductions in their margins of preference that might result from Tokyo Round tariff cuts; advance implementation of Tokyo Round tariff cuts affecting developing country exports; substantial reduction of elimination of tariff escalation; special provisions for developing country exports in any new codes of conduct covering non-tariff barriers; assurance that any new multilateral safeguard system would contain special provisions for developing country exports; and the principle that developed countries would expect less than full reciprocity for trade concessions granted to developing countries. The Framework Agreement concluded at the end of the Tokyo Round provides a legal basis for special and differential treatment in favor of exports from developing countries, and some of the codes of conduct negotiated in the Tokyo Round provided for such treatment. Under the Uruguay Round agreement, developing countries

are given much longer than developed countries for phasing in trade liberalization measures in several areas including agriculture, intellectual property and investment. The Uruguay Round also strengthened pre-existing GATT rules regarding dumping and subsidization, and developing countries were given a longer timetable for coming into compliance with these rules.
See also: Codes of Conduct, Concession, Framework Agreement, General Agreement on Tariffs and Trade, Generalized System of Preferences, Margin of Preferences, Market Access, North-South Trade, Preferences, Reciprocity,

Special Drawing Rights (SDRs) Created in 1969 by the International Monetary Fund (IMF) as a supplemental international monetary reserve asset, SDRs are available to governments through the IMF and may be used in transactions between the IMF and member governments. IMF member countries have agreed to regard SDRs as complementary to gold and reserve currencies in settling their international accounts. The unit value of an SDR reflects the foreign exchange value of a "basket" of currencies of several major trading countries (the U.S. dollar, the German mark, the French franc, the Japanese yen, and the British pound). The SDR has become the unit of account used by the IMF and several national currencies are pegged to it. Some commercial banks accept deposits denominated in SDRs.
See also: Currency, International Monetary Fund, Reserve Currency,

Special Representative For Trade Negotiations (STR) Refer to: United States Trade Representative,

Specific Duty Refer to: Specific Tariff,

Specific Limitations On Trade Government measures that restrict imports or exports of a product during a given period to an explicitly stated volume or value, usually by requiring a "license" or other government authorization for each export or import transaction.
See also: Boycott, Embargo, Exchange Controls, Export Quotas, Licensing, Non-Tariff Barriers, Quantitative Restrictions, Tariff Quota,

Specific Tariff A customs duty assessed as a stated monetary amount per unit of physical quantity, as so many cents a pound, bushel or yard, regardless of the value of the imported item.
See also: Ad Valorem Tariff, Tariff,

Speculative Risk Refer to: Risk,

Spot Market A market in which goods or securities are traded for immediate delivery. The spot price is therefore the price for immediate delivery.
See also: Forward Market, Market, Price, Security,

Stabex Refer to: Lomé Convention,

Standard Code Refer to: Standards,

Standards Technical specifications that lay down characteristics of a product such as size, quality, performance or safety. Standards may also cover terminology, testing methods, packaging, labeling or marking requirements. The Tokyo Round Agreement on Technical Barriers to Trade--usually known as the "Standards Code"--seeks to ensure that national standards are not used to impede trade.
See also: Codes of Conduct, Non-Tariff Barriers, Packaging, Labeling and Marking Regulations, Quarantine, Sanitary and Health Laws and Regulations, Trade Agreements Act of 1979,

State Trading Companies Government-owned or government-controlled enterprises that export and/or import goods and services. State trading companies exist in countries with "mixed

economies"--in which privately owned enterprises also play an important economic role--as well as in socialist countries.
See also: Public Sector, State Trading Nations, Unfair Trade Practices,

Steel Refer to: Sensitive Products, Trigger Price Mechanism,

Steel Voluntary Restraint Arrangements (VRAs) Formal agreements between the United States and the governments of 16 countries plus the EC. Although the structure of the arrangements varies, exports to the United States of both carbon and specialty steel products were restricted either to a specified quota or to a percentage of U.S. import penetration, based on quarterly estimates of U.S. domestic consumption. The VRA program was initiated for five years beginning October 1, 1984, and was subsequently extended in September 1989 for two-and-one-half more years. The last VRA program terminated March 31, 1992.
See also: Export Quotas, Export Restraints, General Agreement on Tariffs and Trade, International Commodity Agreement, Multilateral Agreement, Orderly Marketing Agreements, Sensitive Products,

Stockbroker Refer to: Broker,

Stockholm Convention Refer to: European Free Trade Association,

Stockpiles Refer to: Buffer Stocks, Strategic Stockpiles,

STR Refer to: United States Trade Representative,

Strategic Stockpiles Accumulated stocks of raw materials or other commodities deemed essential to national defense and maintained so that the country's actual or potential supply of the goods stocked will not fall below the quantity likely to be required for a given period of national emergency. The U.S. Strategic and Critical Stockpiling Act of 1946 authorizes the U.S. General Services Administration to maintain strategic stockpiles, and to expand or reduce them, according to changing estimates of defense needs, while making every effort to phase purchases or sales so as to have minimum effects on world prices. Buffer stocks, in contrast with strategic stockpiles, are intended to stabilize prices and thus protect exporters against economic losses they would face when prices decline precipitously.
See also: Buffer Stocks, Commodity,

Structural Change Secular trends in the principal elements of an economic system, including its patterns of production, consumption, trade and relative prices. Structural change can take place within national economies and is reflected in the ever wider and deeper linkages among them and the consequent increasing interdependence of the world economy. Expansion in the economy as a whole and temporary, cyclical shifts of its components, are not considered structural changes. Since the Industrial Revolution, structural change within most national economies has resulted principally from developments in comparative advantage associated with technological advance, improved infrastructure and changing consumer preference, factors that have characteristically reflected movement from subsistence to commercial agriculture, reduction in the percentage of the labor force engaged in agriculture, and increases in the relative significance of manufacturing (and, at a later stage, a further development toward service industries), changes in the relative economic importance of various industries, the rise and decline of specific economic activities in different countries and regions, and evolution in the composition of exports and imports.
See also: Adjustment, Comparative Advantage, Competitive, Economic Development, Industrial Revolution, Infrastructure, Progress, Secular Trend, Services, Technology,

Structural Impediments Initiative (SII) U.S.-Japan bilateral talks aimed at identifying and removing internal impediments that inhibit external account adjustment and market access.

See also: Bilateral Agreement, Market, Market Access, Market Forces, Restrictive Business Practices,

Subsidiary A company controlled by another company, usually through ownership of 50 to 100 percent of its shares or through other organizational or managerial arrangement.
See also: Multinational Corporation, Restrictive Business Practices, Unfair Trade Practices,

Subsidies Code Refer to: Countervailing Duties, Export Subsidies,

Subsidy An economic benefit granted by a government to producers of goods, often to strengthen their competitive position. The subsidy may be direct (a cash grant) or indirect (low-interest export credits guaranteed by a government agency, for example). Under the Uruguay Round accord, countries agreed to make trading rules concerning subsides more predictable by defining three classes of subsidies: prohibited, actionable and non-actionable. A country can retaliate against a subsidy that is prohibited; it can retaliate against a subsidy that is actionable if it can show injury to a domestic industry or harm to the benefits of a trade agreement. A country cannot retaliate against a non-actionable subsidy.
See also: Competitive, Export Subsidies, Industrial Policy, Infant Industry Argument, International Arrangement on Export Credits, Non-Tariff Barriers,

Substantial New Program Of Action (SNPA) A comprehensive statement of economic measures to be taken by the international community to enhance the outlook for economic development in the least developed countries, as agreed at an international conference held in Paris in August 1981.
See also: Least Developed Countries,

Super 301 Section 301 of the Trade Act of 1974, as added by section 1302 of the Omnibus Trade and Competitiveness Act of 1988, required the USTR in 1989 and 1990 to identify trade liberalization priorities and to initiate Section 301 investigations with respect to such priority practices in all countries where these liberalization priorities have not been met. This particular aspect of U.S. trade law expired in 1991. On March 3, 1994, President Clinton signed an executive order reinstituting the Super 301 trade law provision. Under this executive order, the U.S. trade representative will identify in 1994 and 1995 those "priority foreign country practices," the elimination of which have the greatest potential for the expansion of U.S. exports. After identification, the priority foreign country practices will become the subject of investigations under Section 301. The first step of that process is consultations with the foreign government in an effort to reach agreement on the elimination of the practices in question, or in appropriate cases, compensation for the damage done by the practices. If no agreement is reached, the investigation will continue. Where the foreign practices at issue constitute violations of trade agreements, such as the GATT, or the new WTO, the United States will take those practices to the dispute resolution process created in those agreements. At the end of the investigation, the trade representative will have to determine if the practices are actionable under Section 301 and, if so, what action should be taken in response to them.
See also: Liberalization, Omnibus Trade and Competitiveness Act of 1988, Section 301, Trade Act of 1974, Uruguay Round,

Supply The quantity of an economic good that sellers will make available at a given price at a certain time in a specific market. A supply schedule indicates the quantity of an economic good that might enter the market at all possible prices at a particular time. Supply in a market economy is principally determined by the response of many individual entrepreneurs and firms to their perceptions of opportunities for earning profits.
See also: Demand, Entrepreneur, Goods, Market, Market Economy, Microeconomics, Price Elasticity of Supply, Private Sector, Profit,

Supply Access Assurance that importing countries will have fair and equitable access at reasonable prices to supplies of raw materials and other essential imports. Such assurance might include explicit constraints against the use of the export embargo as an instrument of foreign policy. Requests for such assurance reflect the desire of countries to have a consistent supply of important raw materials at stable prices.
See also: Embargo, Market, Supply,

Supply Schedule Refer to: Supply,

Surplus The amount of a commodity that cannot be absorbed in a given market at the existing price.
See also: Market, Public Law 480,

Suspension Of Liquidation In the United States, the preliminary determination in an anti-dumping investigation (or final determination after a negative preliminary determination), if affirmative, shall provide for the suspension of liquidation of all entries of covered merchandise which are entered, or withdrawn from warehouse, for consumption on or after the date of publication of the notice in the Federal Register. Each district director of customs is directed to require a cash deposit, or the posting of a bond or other security, for each entry concerned equal to the amount by which the foreign market value exceeds the U.S. price.
See also: Anti-Dumping Code, Dumping, Foreign Market Value, Liquidation, United States Price,

Targeting A comprehensive mobilization of technology, capital and skilled labor involving direct or indirect government intervention in the marketplace in support of a specific industry. Tax benefits, government loans and government procurement policies which restrict foreign competition, as well as more subtle means of restricting competition and directing resources are but a few of the practices which support domestic industries targeted for growth. The end result is an allocation of resources to specifically defined priority sectors of industry.
See also: Government Procurement Policies and Practices, Market Access, Restrictive Business Practices, Unfair Trade Practice,

Tariff A duty (or tax) levied upon goods transported from one customs area to another either for protective or revenue purposes. Tariffs raise the prices of imported goods, thus making them generally less competitive within the market of the importing country unless the importing country does not produce the items so tariffed. After seven "Rounds" of GATT trade negotiations that focused heavily on tariff reductions, tariffs are less important measures of protection than they used to be. The term "tariff" often refers to a comprehensive list or "schedule"of merchandise with the rate of duty to be paid to the government for importing products listed, whereas the term "duty" applies only to the rate applicable to an individual tariff item.
See also: Ad Valorem Equivalent, Ad Valorem Tariff, Bound Rates, Column 1 Rates, Column 2 Rates, Competitive, Compound Tariff, Concession, Conventional Tariff, Customs Area,

Tariff Act Of 1930 Protectionist U.S. trade legislation that raised tariff rates on most articles imported by the United States, triggering comparable tariff increases by U.S. trading partners. The Tariff Act of 1930 is also known as the Smoot-Hawley Tariff, after the two legislators who sponsored it, and sometimes as the Grundy Tariff, after Joseph Grundy, president of the Pennsylvania Manufacturers Association, who was the chief lobbyist for it.
See also: Beggar-Thy-Neighbor Policy, Column 2 Rates, Countervailing Duties, Imports, Protectionism, Reciprocity, Retaliation, Tariff, Trade Agreements Act of 1934,

Tariff Commission Refer to: U.S. International Trade Commission,

Tariff Escalation A situation in which tariffs on raw materials are nonexistent or relatively low, tariffs on semi-processed goods are moderate, and tariffs on manufactured goods are relatively

high. Such "escalation"--which exists in the tariff schedules of many developed countries-- amounts to greater protection of the manufacturing processes involved than is implied by the actual tariff rate and may therefore have the effect of discouraging the development of production facilities in developing countries.
See also: Effective Tariff Rate, Primary Commodity, Production, Protection, Tariff, Tariff Schedules,

Tariff Extirieur Commun
See also: Common External Tariff,

Tariff Harmonization
See also: Harmonization,

Tariff Quota Application of a reduced or zero duty rate for a specified quantity of imported goods, or for goods imported during a given period.
See also: Specific Limitations on Trade, Tariff,

Tariff Schedules Comprehensive lists of the tariffs a country applies to imported goods.
See also: Single-Column Tariff, Tariff,

Tariff Schedules Of The United States (TSUS) Refer to: Bound Rates, Customs, Harmonized Tariff Schedule of the United States, Tariff,

Tax A payment exacted on persons, corporations and other economic entities by a government to help pay for government operations or to discourage the consumption of the goods or services taxed by raising their cost. Taxes are distinguished by their compulsory character and by the lack of correlation between the amount paid and the value of the public services financed by the taxes to the taxpayers.
See also: Border Tax Adjustments, Direct Tax, Excise Tax, Indirect Tax, Road Tax, Sales Tax, Tariff, Value Added Tax,

Tax Incentives Refer to: Industrial Policy,

TEC Refer to: Common External Tariff,

Technical Barriers To Trade Refer to: Non-Tariff Barriers, Quarantine, Sanitary, Health Laws and Regulations, Standards,

Technical Regulations Regulations which lay down characteristics for products or related processes and production methods, including applicable administrative provisions, with which compliance is mandatory. It may also include or deal exclusively with terminology, symbols, packaging, marking or labeling requirements as they apply to a product, processor production method. The GATT Agreement on Technical Barriers to Trade obliges its signatories to accord national treatment to other signatories in the administration of its technical regulations, and to not apply technical regulations to create unnecessary obstacles to international trade, among other things.
See also: General Agreement on Tariffs and Trade,

Technological Development The acquisition by a country's nationals of the knowledge, skills and organizational ability that enable them to produce goods and services more efficiently than they were able to prior to such acquisition.
See also: Technology,

Technology Knowledge of the means and methods of producing goods and services, or the

application of science to production or distribution, resulting in the creation of new products, new manufacturing processes or more efficient methods of distribution.
See also: Adjustment, Developing Countries, Distribution, Patent, Production, Structural Change, Trademark, Transfer of Technology, World Intellectual Property Organization,

Terms Of Trade The ratio of prices (unit values) of a country's exports to the prices (unit values) of its imports. Some economists have discerned an overall deteriorating trend in this ratio for developing countries as a whole. Other economists maintain that whereas the terms of trade may have become less favorable for certain countries during certain periods--and even for all developing countries during some periods--the same terms of trade have improved for other developing countries in the same periods and perhaps for most developing countries during other periods.
See also: Developing Countries, Export Prices, Secular Trend, Unit Value,

Textiles The Multi-Fiber Arrangement Regarding International Trade in Textiles (MFA) defines textiles as yarns, piece-goods, made-up articles, garments, and other products made of cotton, wool, man-made fibers, or blends thereof, in which any or all of those fibers in combination represent either the chief value of the fibers or 50 percent or more by weight (or 17 percent or more by weight for wool) of the product. Historically, the production of textiles has required more unskilled labor and less sophisticated (and hence cheaper) capital goods and technology than other manufacturing industries. The textiles industry has thus often been among the first industries to operate efficiently in many developing countries. The structure of the industry has changed in recent years as textiles manufacturers in developed countries and the newly industrializing countries have increasingly adopted more capital-intensive mass production methods, especially for the latest synthetic fibers and complex knit cloths. Under the Uruguay Round agreement, GATT members agreed to eliminate the MFA's global system of bilateral textile and apparel quotas by the year 2005.
See also: Capital Goods, Efficiency, Industrial Revolution, Multi-Fiber Arrangement Regarding International Trade in Textiles, Sensitive Products, Technology,

Third-Country Dumping A situation in which the exports of a product from the first country are being injured or threatened with injury as a result of exports of the same product from a second country into a third country at less than fair value. The Omnibus Trade and Competitiveness Act of 1988 established procedures for U.S. industries to petition the Office of the U.S. Trade Representative (USTR) to request a foreign government which is a signatory to the GATT Anti-Dumping Code to initiate an anti-dumping (AD) investigation on behalf of a U.S. industry that claims it is being injured by dumping in that country's market.
See also: Anti-Dumping, Dumping, Omnibus Trade and Competitiveness Act of 1988, U.S. Trade Representative, Market Disruption,

Threshold Price A minimum price. In the case of the European Community, the price for grains and other agricultural products under which the Common Agricultural Policy of the European Community operates. The threshold price is fixed at a level that will bring the selling price of grains up to the existing price level in the marketing region within the European Community where supplies are lowest.
See also: Common Agricultural Policy, European Community, Price, Restitutions, Variable Levy,

Tied Loan A loan made by a government agency that requires a foreign borrower to spend the proceeds in the lender's country or to buy the lender's products.
See also: Countertrade, Loan,

TNC Refer to: Multinational Corporation, Final Act,

Tokyo Declaration Statement signed in September 1973 by ministers of 105 countries that

formally initiated the Tokyo Round of Multilateral Trade Negotiations. The declaration stressed the intent of the participants to give special priority to the trade interests of developing countries throughout the negotiations.
See also: Framework Agreement, Special and Differential Treatment, Tokyo Round,

Tokyo Round The Tokyo Round of Multilateral Trade Negotiations, formally initiated by the 1973 Tokyo Declaration, was the most comprehensive effort up to that time to eliminate, reduce or control non-tariff barriers that restrict non-agricultural trade, and was especially notable for having negotiated several codes of conduct designed to curtail the use of non-tariff barriers as instruments of protection. More countries participated in these negotiations than in any previous Round, including more than 20 developing countries that were not GATT members and several countries of Eastern Europe. The Tokyo Round was carried out in Geneva and concluded there in 1979.
See also: Anti-Dumping Code, Case Law, Codes of Conduct, Customs Valuation Code, Dispute Settlement, Enabling Clause, Framework Agreement, Government Procurement Policies and Practices, Multilateral Trade Negotiations, Non-Tariff Barriers,

Tourism Refer to: Services,

TPC Refer to: Trade Policy Committee,

TPM Refer to: Trigger Price Mechanism,

TPRM Refer to: Trade Policy Review Mechanism,

Trade Act Of 1974 Legislation enacted by the U.S. Congress in late 1974 and signed into law on January 3, 1975, granting the U.S. president broad authority to enter into international agreements to reduce import barriers. The act states that its major purposes are: to stimulate U.S. economic growth and to maintain and enlarge foreign markets for the products of U.S. agriculture, industry, mining and commerce; to strengthen economic relations with other countries through open and non-discriminatory trading practices; to protect American industry and workers against unfair or injurious import competition; and to provide "adjustment assistance" to industries, workers and communities injured or threatened by increased imports. The act also grants the president authority to extend tariff preferences to certain imports from developing countries and set conditions under which most-favored-nation treatment can be extended to non-market economy countries that previously have not received MFN treatment from the United States.
See also: Adjustment Assistance, Countervailing Duties, Dumping, Clause, Generalized System of Preferences, Most-Favored-Nation Treatment, Safeguards, Section 301, Tokyo Round, U.S. International Trade Commission,

Trade Act Of 1988
See also: Omnibus Trade and Competitiveness Act of 1988,

Trade Agreement A bilateral or multilateral treaty or other enforceable compact committing two or more nations to specified terms of commerce, usually involving mutually beneficial concessions.
See also: Binding, Concession, General Agreement on Tariffs and Trade, Round,

Trade Agreements Act Of 1934 Legislation that amended the Tariff Act of 1930 (Smoot-Hawley Tariff Act), providing authority for the United States to negotiate agreements with other countries for reciprocally beneficial tariff reductions. The resulting agreements were then applied to other countries through most-favored-nation clauses. The original 1934 legislation, as extended by several further acts of the U.S. Congress, provided authority for U.S. participation in the first five "Rounds" of GATT trade negotiations, from 1947 through the Dillon Round. It was superseded by

the Trade Expansion Act of 1962.
See also: Bilateral Trade Agreement, Dillon Round, Negotiations, Peril Point, Reciprocity, Round, Tariff Act of 1930, Trade Agreement, Trade Expansion Act of 1962,

Trade Agreements Act Of 1979 Legislation authorizing the United States to implement trade agreements dealing with non-tariff barriers negotiated during the Tokyo Round, including agreements that required changes in existing U.S. laws, and certain concessions that had not been explicitly authorized by the Trade Act of 1974. Specifically, the Trade Agreements Act of 1979 incorporated into U.S. law the Tokyo Round agreements on dumping, customs valuation, import licensing procedures, government procurement practices, product standards, civil aircraft, meat and dairy products, and liquor duties. In addition, it extended the president's authority to negotiate trade agreements with foreign countries to reduce or eliminate non-tariff barriers to trade.
See also: Anti-Dumping Code, Countervailing Duties, Customs Valuation Code, Dumping, Government Procurement Policies and Practices , Licensing Code, Non-Tariff Barriers, Standards, Tokyo Round, Trade Act of 1974,

Trade And Development Refer to: United Nations Conference on Trade and Development,

Trade Creation Refer to: Trade Diversion,

Trade Diversion A shift in the pattern of origin of a country's imports resulting from changes in trade policies or practices, which may or may not involve change in the overall volume or composition of the imports involved. Trade creation results when increased economic activity generates a larger total demand for imports. The establishment of a customs union will cause participating countries to import goods from other countries in the union in place of traditional imports from countries outside the union, but at the same time, greater economic efficiency may increase the total level of imports into the countries comprising the union. Trade theorists say the customs union will be beneficial to outside suppliers as well as participating countries if the "trade creation" resulting from the customs union exceeds the "trade diversion," because this would entail a more efficient allocation of productive resources.
See also: Customs Union, Demand, Efficiency, Imports, Structural Change, Welfare,

Trade Expansion Act of 1962 The legislative authority for U.S. participation in the Kennedy Round of Multilateral Trade Negotiations. The legislation itself heavily influenced the content and procedures of the Kennedy Round, especially by granting the U.S. president general authority to negotiate--on a reciprocal basis--reductions of up to 50 percent in U.S. tariffs. (This authority expired June 30, 1967, thus predetermining the concluding date of the Kennedy Round.) U.S. duties below five percent ad valorem, duties on certain agricultural commodities, and duties on tropical products exported by developing countries could be reduced to zero under the act. The 1962 legislation explicitly eliminated the "Peril Point" provision that had limited U.S. negotiating positions in earlier GATT Rounds, and instead called on the Tariff Commission and other agencies of the U.S. government to provide the president and his negotiators with information regarding the probable economic effects of specific tariff concessions. This act superseded the Trade Agreements Act of 1934, as amended. Some parts of the Trade Expansion Act were subsequently amended by the Trade Agreements Act of 1979.
See also: Kennedy Round, Linear Reduction of Tariffs, Trade Agreements Act of 1934, United States Trade Representative,

Trade Fair A market or trade exhibition, usually arranged under public or semi-public auspices, at which manufacturers and traders display their products to stimulate sales. Trade fairs were particularly popular in Europe during the Middle Ages, when they provided important large-scale markets. Since World War II general trade fairs have served chiefly as international exhibitions of wares rather than as markets. Specialized trade fairs have played an important and increasing

role in recent years as meeting places for buyers and sellers of specialized merchandise.
See also: Demand, Distribution, Export Promotion, Market, Supply,

Trade Mission Experts and/or businessmen sent by a government or by commercial interests in one country to encourage exports to the market of another country.
See also: Distribution, Export Promotion, Exports, Market,

Trade Negotiations Refer to: Negotiation, Round, United States Trade Representative,

Trade Policy Committee (TPC) A senior inter-agency committee of the U.S. government, chaired by the U.S. trade representative, that provides broad guidance to the president on trade policy issues. Members include the secretaries of state, treasury, commerce, agriculture and labor.
See also: United States Trade Representative,

Trade Policy Review Mechanism (TPRM) Consultations established provisionally at the Mid-term Review of the Uruguay Round providing for periodic review of each GATT member's trade policy regime. The country under review and the GATT Secretariat produce documents describing the trade policy regime of the country, and all interested Contracting Parties participate in a special meeting of the GATT Council where these documents are reviewed. The United States, European Community, Japan and Canada are reviewed every two years, with other Contracting Party reviews conducted on a four-or six-year cycle. The TPRM was confirmed at the close of the Uruguay Round.
See also: Montreal Ministerial, Uruguay Round,

Trademark A mark or symbol secured by legal registration used by a manufacturer or trader to distinguish his goods from competing goods.
See also: Commercial Counterfeiting, Intellectual Property, Trade-Related Aspects of Intellectual Property Rights, Technology,

Trade-Related Aspects Of Intellectual Property Rights (TRIPS) Government regulations or administrative procedures--or the lack thereof--which diminish or deny intellectual property protection. Under the Uruguay Round accord of December 1993, GATT member countries agreed to a comprehensive set of international rules and stronger measures at international borders to stop trade in goods that infringe on intellectual property rights. Under the TRIPS agreement, nations are obliged to rewrite national laws to make them conform to internationally agreed norms for the protection of patents, trademarks, copyrights, industrial designs, trade secrets, integrated circuits (semiconductor chip mask works), and geographical indications. It also broadens the areas of protection to include technological areas--such as pharmaceutical products, computer software, and inventions and works arising from new technologies--that are not currently protected in many countries. Industrialized countries are given one year for implementation from the entry into force of the agreement on July 1, 1995. Developing countries and those shifting from centrally planned economies to market economies are given an additional four years for implementation, except in the pharmaceutical and agricultural products sectors where they are given an additional nine years (for a total of 10 years from the entry into force of the agreement). Least-developed countries will have until 2006 to comply. The TRIPS accord includes enforcement provisions which provide for the use of improved international dispute settlement procedures under the WTO for disputes between countries. The accord also permits cross-sectoral retaliation for a violation of TRIPS obligations; if a country fails to protect patents, for example, it could face retaliation in an unrelated sector.
See also: Intellectual Property, Uruguay Round,

Trade-Related Investment Measures (TRIMS) Restrictions on direct investment that have the effect of distorting trade and investment (e.g., performance and local content requirements). Under the Uruguay Round accord of December 1993, GATT member countries agreed to

eliminate investment measures that limit or force certain types of investments, and to offer "national treatment" to foreign investors and to eliminate quotas and other restraints. The accord, once enacted on July 1, 1995, will restrict the use of three TRIMS requirements: local content requirements (specifying that some minimum level of local resources be used in operations at foreign-owned plants), trade balancing requirements (specifying that an investor not import more than is exported, or some proportion of exports, or that a minimum trade surplus be maintained) and foreign exchange balancing requirements (limiting the importation of products used in local production by restricting a firm's access to foreign exchange to an amount related to its exchange inflows). Under the accord, once enacted, developed countries have two years in which to eliminate the affected TRIMS, developing countries have five years, and least developed countries have seven years. During the transition, countries can impose temporary TRIMS on new investors so as not to disadvantage existing investments that would be subject to the TRIMS until the transition period is over.
See also: Investment Performance Requirements, Restrictive Business Practices, Uruguay Round,

Trading With The Enemy Act Refer to: International Emergency Economic Powers Act,

Trafficking In Counterfeit Goods And Services Intentionally dealing or attempting to deal with goods or services in connection with which one knowingly uses a mark that is identical with or substantially indistinguishable from a mark registered for those goods or services, the use of which is likely to cause confusion, to cause mistake or to deceive the consumer. Counterfeit trademark goods are generally regarded as any goods, including packaging, bearing without authorization a trademark which is identical to the trademark validly registered in respect of such goods, or which cannot be distinguished in its essential aspects from such a trademark, and which thereby infringes the rights of the owner of a trademark in question under the law of the country of importation. Under the Uruguay Round accord of December 1993, GATT member countries agreed to a comprehensive set of international rules and stronger measures at international borders to stop trade in counterfeit goods and services. The negotiation of the agreement on TRIPS, trade-related aspects of intellectual property rights, was a priority U.S. objective in the Uruguay Round negotiations.
See also: Commercial Counterfeiting, Copyright, Intellectual Property, Multilateral Trade Agreement, Patent, Trademark, Trade-Related Aspects of Intellectual Property Rights, Uruguay Round,

Tranparency Visibility and clarity of laws and regulations. Some of the codes of conduct negotiated during the Tokyo Round sought to increase the transparency of non-tariff barriers that impede trade.
See also: Codes of Conduct, Government Procurement Policies and Practices, International Arrangement on Export Credits, Non-Tariff Barriers,

Transaction Value Refer to: Customs Valuation Code, Valuation ,

Transfer Of Technology The movement of modern or scientific methods of production or distribution from one enterprise, institution or country to another, as through foreign investment, international trade, licensing of patent rights, technical assistance or training.
See also: Distribution, Production, Property, Structural Change, Technology,

Transfer Payments Within a national economy, payments made by the government or the wealthier sectors of a population to the poorer people in the country, as through Social Security payments, unemployment benefits and widows' pensions. Such payments are not made in return for goods or services but to redistribute income. International transfer payments include grant aid by governments to developing countries and programs and activities of private voluntary agencies based in one country that bring financial benefits to people in another country, and are

considered part of the current account in the balance of payments.
See also: Additionality, Current Account, Direct Tax, Official Development Assistance ,

Transit Zone The area surrounding a port of entry in a coastal country that serves as a storage and distribution center for the convenience of a neighboring country--a land-locked country, for example--lacking adequate port facilities or access to the sea. A transit zone is administered so that goods in transit to and from the neighboring country are not subject to the customs duties, import controls or many of the entry and exit formalities of the host country. A transit zone is a more limited facility than either a free trade zone or free port.
See also: Customs, Free Zone, Port of Entry,

Transnational Corporation Refer to: Multinational Corporation,

Transportation Refer to: Services,

Treaty Of Rome Refer to: European Community,

Trigger Price Mechanism (TPM) A U.S. system for monitoring imported steel to identify imports that are possibly being "dumped" in the United States or subsidized by the governments of exporting countries. The minimum price under this system is based on the estimated landed cost at the U.S. port of entry of steel produced by the world's most efficient producers. Imported steel entering the United States below that price may "trigger" formal anti-dumping investigations by the U.S. Department of Commerce and the U.S. International Trade Commission. The TPM was in effect between early 1978 and March 1980. It was reinstated in October 1980 and suspended in January 1982. Between April 1982 and June 1988 TPM was used for imports of stainless steel round wire only.
See also: Dumping, Export Subsidies, Sensitive Products, Subsidy, U.S. International Trade Commission,

TRIMS Refer to: Trade-Related Investment Measures,

TRIPS Refer to: Trade-Related Aspects of Intellectual Property Rights,

Tropical Products Traditionally, agricultural goods of export interest to developing countries in the tropical zones of Africa, Latin America and East Asia (e.g., coffee, tea, spices, natural rubber, palm oil, bananas, and tropical hardwoods.
See also: Commodity,

TSUS Refer to: Harmonized Tariff Schedule of the United States ,

Turnkey Contract A compact under which the contractor assumes responsibility to the client for constructing productive installations and ensuring that they operate effectively before turning them over to the client. By centering responsibility for the contributions of all participants in the project in his own hands, the contractor is often able to arrange more favorable financing terms than the client could. The responsibility of the contractor ends when he hands the completed installation over to the client.
See also: Countertrade,

TVA Refer to: Value Added Tax,

TWEA
See also: International Emergency Economic Powers Act,

U.S. International Trade Commission (USITC) Formerly the U.S. Tariff Commission, created in

1916 by an act of Congress. Its mandate was broadened and its name changed by the Trade Act of 1974. The USITC is an independent fact-finding agency of the U.S. government, reporting to Congress, that studies the effects of tariffs and other restraints to trade on the U.S. economy. It conducts public hearings to assist in determining whether particular U.S. industries are injured or threatened with injury by dumping, export subsidies in other countries or rapidly rising imports. It also studies the probable economic impact on specific U.S. industries of proposed reductions in U.S. tariffs and non-tariff barriers to imports. Its six commissioners are appointed by the president, with the advice and consent of the U.S. Senate, for nine-year terms.
See also: Countervailing Duties, Dumping, Escape Clause, Export Subsidies, Imports, Peril Point, Tariff, Trade Act of 1974,

U.S. Revenue Act Of 1971 Refer to: Domestic International Sales Corporation,

U.S. Strategic And Critical Stockpiling Act Of 1946 Refer to: Strategic Stockpiles,

U.S. Tariff Commission Refer to: U.S. International Trade Commission,

U.S. Trade Policy Committee Refer to: Trade Policy Committee,

U.S.-CANADA Free Trade Agreement (FTA or CFTA) A free trade agreement implemented on January 1, 1989, between the United States and Canada following approval and implementation of its terms by the Congress in 1988. The United States and Canada decided to suspend the FTA upon NAFTA's entry into force, January 1, 1994. The agreement provided for the elimination of tariffs on all U.S.-Canada trade by 1998. The agreement also provided improved access with respect to government procurement and a code of principles on services trade, including national treatment, the right to sell across borders, the right of establishment and transparency in regulations. Additional commitments were made in the areas of telecommunications, tourism, financial services and architectural services. Provisions in this comprehensive free trade agreement dealt with foreign investment regulation, bilateral energy trade and access to energy supplies, border crossing procedures for certain professional and technical personnel, agriculture and dispute settlement. The FTA was the world's largest and most comprehensive bilateral free trade agreement until NAFTA entered into force.
See also: Bilateral Trade Agreement, Common External Tariff, Customs Union, General Agreement on Tariffs and Trade, North American Free Trade Agreement, U.S.-Canada Trade Commission,

U.S.-Canada Trade Commission Created under Chapter 18 of the U.S.-Canada Free Trade Agreement to consult on all matters affecting the implementation and operation of the FTA.
See also: North American Free Trade Agreement, U.S.-Canada Free Trade Agreement,

U.S.-Israel Free Trade Area Agreement The first free trade agreement entered into by the United States took effect on September 1, 1985. The agreement called for the staged elimination of tariffs between the two countries over a 10-year period. All tariffs will be eliminated by January 1, 1995. The agreement also established a Joint Commission to supervise the agreement and to periodically review the bilateral relationship.
See also: Bilateral Trade Agreement, Binding Concession, Consultation, Tariff, Trade Agreement,

Unconditional Most-Favored-Nation Treatment Refer to: Conditional Most-Favored-Nation Treatment, Most-Favored-Nation Treatment,

UNCTAD Refer to: United Nations Conference on Trade and Development,

UNCTAD/GATT International Trade Center (ITC)
See also: International Trade Center UNCTAD/GATT,

Understanding On Notification, Consultation, Dispute Settlement And Surveillance Refer to: Dispute Settlement, Framework Agreement,

Underwriter As used in the insurance industry, an insurance company, investment banker or other financial agent that accepts the risk of insuring specified goods, especially in shipping.
See also: Capital Market, Insurance, Risk,

UNDP Refer to: United Nations Development Program,

Unfair Trade Practices Unusual government support to firms--such as export subsidies, or certain anti-competitive practices by firms themselves, such as dumping, boycotts or discriminatory shipping arrangements--that result in competitive advantages for those firms in international trade.
See also: Boycott, Dumping, Export Subsidies, Restrictive Business Practices, Section 301, Trade Act of 1974,

Unilateral An action taken by a single country, on its own initiative, and not in any way dependent upon, or conditional upon, actions of any other country or countries.
See also: Bilateral, Multilateral,

Unit Value The quotient showing the total value of a particular trade flow during a specified period divided by its volume. Unit values are often reflected in international trade statistics instead of prices.
See also: Secular Trend, Terms of Trade,

United Nations Conference On The Least Developed Countries Refer to: Substantial New Program of Action,

United Nations Conference On Trade And Development (UNCTAD) A subsidiary organ of the United Nations General Assembly that seeks to focus international attention on economic measures that might accelerate Third World development. The first conference, UNCTAD-I, was convened in Geneva in 1964, and sessions were held quadrennially up to 1976: UNCTAD-II, New Delhi, 1968; UNCTAD-III, Santiago, 1972; and UNCTAD-IV, Nairobi, 1976. UNCTAD-V met in Manila in 1979, UNCTAD-VI in Belgrade in 1983, UNCTAD-VII in Geneva in 1987, and UNCTAD VIII in Cartagena, Colombia in 1992. The UNCTAD Trade and Development Board, which exercises the powers of the conference between its sessions, meets twice a year; and the main UNCTAD committees--which include those concerned with commodities, shipping, manufactures, invisibles and financing related to trade, and the transfer of technology--meet several times between sessions of the conference. Negotiations in UNCTAD take place principally between "Group B" (developed countries) and the "Group of 77" (developing countries) which separately determine their own positions through intra-group discussions prior to the negotiations. UNCTAD is supported by a permanent secretariat based in Geneva. UNCTAD has been an executing agency for UNDP technical assistance projects since 1968, and now administers such projects as ports management, regional economic integration, the transfer of technology, the improvement of customs procedures and other fields related to its programs and activities.
See also: Common Fund, Economic Cooperation Among Developing Countries, Generalized System of Preferences, Group B, Group D, Group of 77, Integrated Program for Commodities, International Trade Center UNCTAD/GATT, Restrictive Business Practices, United Nations Development Program,

United Nations Development Program (UNDP) The arm of the United Nations that provides financial resources to support technical assistance activities designed to stimulate economic development in developing countries, normally through such specialized agencies of the United

Nations system as the World Health Organization, International Labor Organization, and Food and Agriculture Organization, which serve as "executing agencies" for UNDP.

United Nations Monetary And Financial COnference Refer to: Bretton Woods Conference,

United States Price (USP) The price compared to foreign market value to determine whether imported merchandise is sold at less than fair value. The U.S. price is either the purchase price or the exporter's sales price.
See also: Level of Trade Adjustments,

United States Trade Representative (USTR) A Cabinet-level official with the rank of ambassador who is the principal adviser to the U.S. president on international trade policy. The U.S. trade representative is concerned with the formulation of U.S. trade policy, the expansion of U.S. exports, U.S. participation in GATT, commodity issues, East-West and North-South trade, and direct investment related to trade. As chairman of the U.S. Trade Policy Committee, he/she is also the primary official responsible for U.S. participation in all international trade negotiations. Prior to the Trade Agreements Act of 1979, which created the Office of the U.S. Trade Representative, the comparable official was known as the president's special representative for trade negotiations (STR), a position first established by the Trade Expansion Act of 1962.
See also: General Agreement on Tariffs and Trade, Negotiations, Trade Agreements Act of 1979, Trade Expansion Act of 1962, Trade Policy Committee,

Universal Copyright Convention Refer to: Bern Convention,

Upstream Subsidies Subsidies provided to a manufacturer's supplier of inputs for a product. To be included in the calculation of the countervailing duty, the upstream subsidy must provide a "competitive benefit", or be passed through, to the downstream producer of the product under investigation and must have a significant effect on the cost of manufacturing the product under investigation. Petitioners must submit substantial argumentation and evidence before an upstream subsidy investigation is started.
See also: Countervailing Duties, Code, Subsidies , Subsidy,

UR Refer to: Uruguay Round,

Uruguay Round The Uruguay Round, concluded in Geneva in December 1993, was the latest series of multilateral trade negotiations aimed at revising, updating and expanding the coverage of the GATT. The Round was formally launched in September 1986 at the GATT Ministerial in Punta del Este, Uruguay. The negotiations focused on the elimination of tariff and non-tariff barriers to trade and on the development of clear, enforceable international trading rules. The provisions of the Uruguay Round agreement accorded more time to developing countries than industrialized countries for coming into compliance; least developed countries sometimes were accorded even more time or exempted altogether. The following are highlights of the agreement. Tariffs: GATT member countries agreed to cut their import tariffs by a 36-percent average. Textiles: Countries agreed to end the 20-year-old system of import quotas on textiles and apparel by 2005; quotas will be converted into tariffs, which will be reduced over time. Agriculture: Countries agreed to scale back direct export subsidies by 36 percent below rates in place between 1986 and 1990, by 2001, and to reduce the quantity of subsidized commodities exported. They also agreed to convert quotas, import licenses and other import limits into tariffs that would be gradually reduced. Services: Countries agreed to create basic rules so that services providers are afforded the same treatment overseas as in their home markets. Negotiations in some services sectors will continue into 1996. Intellectual Property: Countries agreed to protect and enforce patents, trademarks and copyrights, and to limit the trade of counterfeited creative works and inventions. Investments: Countries agreed to eliminate investment measures that limit or force certain types of investments, to offer "national treatment"

to foreign investors and to eliminate quotas and other restraints. Subsidies: Countries agreed to make rules concerning the trade-legality of subsidies more predictable by defining three classes: prohibited, actionable and non-actionable subsidies. Dumping: Countries agreed to create more detailed rules governing the ability to GATT members to take action against the imports of a product sold at an unfairly discounted export price. Safeguards: Countries agreed to strengthen rules concerning temporary import limits applied to protect domestic industries from surges of fairly traded imports (i.e., safeguards). Members agreed not to maintain safeguard protections for more than eight years, and to prohibit "gray area measures"--voluntary export restraints and other informal agreements to curtail fairly traded imports. Institutional Structure: Members agreed to create a World Trade Organization, a permanent organization, that would replace the GATT (which was meant to be a temporary structure) with a stronger institution. Dispute Resolution: Members agreed to strengthen GATT's dispute resolution rules by allowing countries only to block findings by GATT expert panels if all members oppose the finding.
See also: Brussels Ministerial, Cairns Group, Dispute Settlement, Dumping, Final Act, General Agreement on Tariffs and Trade, Montreal Ministerial, Multi-Fiber Arrangement Regarding International Trade in Textiles, Multilateral Trade Negotiations, Multilateral Trade Organization,

USITC Refer to: U.S. International Trade Commission,

USP Refer to: United States Price,

USTR Refer to: United States Trade Representative,

Utility The ability of goods and services to satisfy human wants or desires. Since utility involves subjective appraisal and depends upon the personal tastes of the consumer, it cannot be measured by any standard yardstick
See also: Consumption, Demand, Goods, Price, Services, Value,

Valuation The appraisal of the worth of imported goods by customs officials for the purpose of determining the amount of duty payable in the importing country. The GATT Customs Valuation Code obligates governments that sign it to use the "transaction value" of imported goods--or the price actually paid or payable for them-- as the principal basis for valuing the goods for customs purposes.
See also: Customs, Customs Classification, Customs Valuation Code, Minimum Valuation, Tariff, Tariff Schedules, Tokyo Round,

Value The intrinsic worth of specific goods or services, generally identifiable as the amount of money they can be exchanged for at any given time.
See also: Money, Price, Utility,

Value Added Tax (VAT) An indirect tax on consumption that is levied at each discrete point in the chain of production and distribution, from the raw material stage to final consumption. Each processor or merchant pays a tax proportional to the amount by which he increases the value of the goods he purchases for resale after making his own contribution. The value added tax is imposed throughout the European Community and EFTA countries and many other trading nations but not the United States.
See also: Border Tax Adjustments, Consumption, Distribution, Harmonization, Indirect Tax, Sales Tax, Tax, Value,

Variable Levy A duty that increases or decreases as domestic or world prices fluctuate, to ensure that the price of the imported product after payment of duty will equal a predetermined "gate" price.
See also: C and F, Common Agricultural Policy, European Community, Restitutions, Threshold Price,

VAT Refer to: Value Added Tax,

Venture Capital Refer to: Risk,

Visible Trade Imports, exports and re-exports of merchandise.
See also: Balance of Payments, Goods, Invisible Trade, Trade,

Voluntary Restraint Agreements (VRAs) Arrangements through which exporters voluntarily restrain certain exports, usually through export quotas, to avoid economic dislocation in an importing country, and to avert the possible imposition of mandatory import restrictions. Such arrangements do not normally entail "compensation" for the exporting country.
See also: Compensation, Export Quotas, Export Restraints, Orderly Marketing Agreements,

VRA Refer to: Steel Voluntary Restraint Arrangements,

Waiver A formal exemption of a right or claim. A waiver in GATT is a formal agreement of the Contracting Parties to relinquish or forego legal rights, or to suspend the application of specific GATT provisions.
See also: General Agreement on Tariffs and Trade, Section 22,

Wealth Capital, money, property, possessions, evidence of ownership, access to benefits, or anything else that has material value.
See also: Capital, Money, Property, Value,

Wealth Tax Refer to: Direct Tax,

Webb-Pomerene Act U.S. legislation enacted in 1918 that exempts associations of U.S. firms engaged in export trade from U.S. antitrust laws, so long as they do not restrain any U.S. competitor of the association.
See also: Antitrust, Export Trading Company,

Welfare State or degree of economic well-being. According to classical economists, advances in the overall welfare of a country are the proper objective of economic and trade policy. The term is associated with the work of Arthur Cecil Pigou, a British economist who conceived of the costs of production as including social costs.
See also: Comparative Advantage, Economic Development, Efficiency, Imports, Infrastructure, Production, Progress, Structural Change , Trade Diversion,

West Refer to: East-West Trade,

Williams Commission A prestigious panel appointed by President Richard Nixon in 1970 to explore U.S. trade policy interests. The commission's basic 1971 recommendation--that the U.S. government should initiate a major Round of trade negotiations--ultimately led to the Trade Act of 1974 and the Tokyo Round of Trade Negotiations.
See also: Tokyo Round, Trade Act of 1974,

Williamsburg Summit A meeting in May 1983 of the heads of state of seven major developed countries at Williamsburg, Virginia (U.S.A.), which concluded, inter alia, that international consultations should be initiated, looking toward a new GATT Round of trade negotiations and on conditions for improving the international monetary system.
See also: General Agreement on Tariffs and Trade, Liberalization, Round,

WIPO Refer to: World Intellectual Property Organization,

Woolen Textiles
See also: Multi-Fiber Arrangement Regarding International Trade in Textiles , Sensitive Products, Textiles,

Workers' Rights The 1974 Trade Act, as amended by the 1988 Trade Act, specifies acts, policies and practices of a foreign government that may be considered unreasonable. These practices may include, inter alia, denial of certain workers' rights. These practices can be actionable under Section 301 if they also burden or restrict U.S. commerce.
See also: Trade Act of 1974, Trade Act of 1988, Section 301,

Working Party A specialized intergovernmental body established by a higher body to study a particular set of issues and report its findings, and often recommendations, to the higher body. In GATT, for example, a Working Party maybe designated by the Contracting Parties to consider a specialized trade policy problem, such as the formation of a customs union. Its recommendations may include suggestions regarding actions that specific Contracting Parties might take. Such Working Parties are customarily open to all countries that wish to participate.
See also: Contracting Party, Dispute Settlement, General Agreement on Tariffs and Trade, Panel of Experts,

World Bank The International Bank for Reconstruction and Development (IBRD), commonly referred to as the World Bank, is an intergovernmental financial institution located in Washington, D.C. Its objectives are to help raise productivity and incomes and reduce poverty in developing countries. It was established in December 1945 on the basis of a plan developed at the Bretton Woods Conference of 1944. The World Bank loans financial resources to creditworthy developing countries. It raises most of its funds by selling bonds in the world's major capital markets. Its bonds have, over the years, earned a quality rating enjoyed only by sound governments and leading corporations. Projects supported by the World Bank normally receive high priority within recipient governments and are usually well planned and supervised. The World Bank earns a profit, which is plowed back into its capital.
See also: Bretton Woods Conference, Capital Market, Developing Countries, International Development Association, International Finance Corporation, Loan,

World Intellectual Property Organization (WIPO) A specialized agency of the United Nations system that seeks to promote international cooperation in the protection of intellectual property. WIPO administers the International Union for the Protection of Industrial Property (the "Paris Union"), which was founded in 1883 to reduce discrimination in national patent practices, the International Union for the Protection of Literary and Artistic Works (the "Bern Union"), which was founded in 1886 to provide analogous functions with respect to copyrights, and other treaties, conventions and agreements concerned with intellectual property.
See also: Copyright, Intellectual Property, Patent, Technology,

World Trade Organization (WTO) As part of the Uruguay Round agreement, GATT Contracting Parties agreed to create a new, permanent umbrella organization to replace GATT: the World Trade Organization. The WTO will facilitate the implementation and administration of the Uruguay Round accord. Like the GATT, it will provide a forum for multilateral trade negotiations; conduct reviews of member country trade policies; and cooperate with the World Bank and the International Monetary Fund in an attempt to achieve greater coherence in global economic policymaking. However, the WTO departs from the GATT model in several ways that will narrow the scope for unilateral action. First, the range of trade issues that the WTO will address has been significantly expanded. Second, the WTO has a much stronger dispute settlement procedure. Third, it provides a permanence that GATT (which was planned as a temporary structure) did not supply. Finally, countries will no longer be able to sign individual codes of conduct in various areas, as was the case in the Tokyo Round accord (1979). Instead, nations

that join the WTO must agree to accept automatically all the Uruguay Round accords without exception. Like the GATT, the WTO will have a secretariat headed by a director-general. It will meet in ministerial session at least once every two years. Between these sessions, the WTO will have a General Council composed of representatives of all WTO members that will generally meet once monthly. The General Council will oversee the running of the dispute settlement body and the trade policy review mechanism, under which the trade policies of individual WTO members will be examined periodically. Under the General Council will be several subsidiary bodies, including a Council on Trade in Goods, a Council on Trade-Related Intellectual Property Rights, and a Council for Trade in Services.
See also: Codes of Conduct, Multilateral Trade Negotiations and Uruguay Round,

WTO
See also: World Trade Organization, Multilateral Trade Organization,

Yaoundé Convention Refer to: Lomé Convention,

Yarns Refer to: Multi-Fiber Arrangement Regarding International Trade in Textiles, Sensitive Products, Textiles,